Landscape and Garden Design Sketchbooks

Tim Richardson

Landscape and Garden Design Sketchbooks

pp. 2–3: Piet Oudolf, Il Giardino delle Vergini, Venice Biennale, 2010
right: Edward Hutchison, Eden Project, Cornwall, UK
overleaf: Proap, L'And Vineyards Masterplan, Montemor-O-Novo, Portugal, 2006

On the cover: *Front, clockwise from top left* Works and sketches by Helle Nebelong, Raymond Jungles, Gustafson Porter, Péna & Peña, Piet Oudolf, Taylor Cullity Lethlean, Cao | Perrot; *Back, clockwise from top left* Péna & Peña, Gustafson Porter, Estudio OCA

First published in the United Kingdom in 2015 by Thames & Hudson Ltd, 181A High Holborn, London WC1V 7QX

Landscape and Garden Design Sketchbooks
© 2015 Tim Richardson

Designed by This-Side

All Rights Reserved. No part of this publication may be reproduced or transmitted in any form or by any means, electronic or mechanical, including photocopy, recording or any other information storage and retrieval system, without prior permission in writing from the publisher.

British Library Cataloguing-in-Publication Data
A catalogue record for this book is available from the British Library

ISBN 978-0-500-51804-5

Printed and bound in China by C&C Offset Printing Co Ltd

To find out about all our publications, please visit www.thamesandhudson.com. There you can subscribe to our e-newsletter, browse or download our current catalogue, and buy any titles that are in print.

Introduction	6
Atelier Dreiseitl Überlingen, Germany	8
Balmori New York, USA	14
I & J Bannerman Cornwall, UK	20
BCA Landscape Liverpool, UK	26
Prabhakar B. Bhagwat Mumbai, India	34
Cao | Perrot Los Angeles, USA / Paris, France	46
Fernando Caruncho Madrid, Spain	54
Claude Cormier Montreal, Canada	58
Paul de Kort De Meern, Netherlands	64
Doxiadis+ Athens, Greece	70
Estudio OCA Barcelona, Spain	76
Monika Gora Malmö, Sweden	86

GreenInc	92
Randburg, South Africa	
Gross Max	104
Edinburgh, UK	
Gustafson Porter	110
London, UK	
Hassell	122
Melbourne, Australia	
Hocker Design	126
Dallas, USA	
Edward Hutchison	134
London, UK	
Raymond Jungles	146
Miami, USA	
Mikyoung Kim	158
Boston, USA	
Cristina Le Mehauté	168
Buenos Aires, Argentina	
Ken McCown	174
Las Vegas, USA	
Helle Nebelong	184
Copenhagen, Denmark	
Piet Oudolf	194
Hummelo, Netherlands	
Péna & Peña	206
Paris, France	

Pola	216
Milan, Italy	
Patrizia Pozzi	222
Milan, Italy	
Sarah Price	230
Monmouthshire, UK	
Proap	240
Lisbon, Portugal	
Daniel Roehr	248
Vancouver, Canada	
SLA	258
Copenhagen, Denmark	
Ken Smith	264
New York, USA	
Tom Stuart-Smith	268
London, UK	
Taylor Cullity Lethlean	282
Victoria, Australia	
Mario Terzic	290
Vienna, Austria	
Cleve West	298
Surrey, UK	
ZUS	312
Rotterdam, Netherlands	

Directory	316
Picture credits / acknowledgments	318

Introduction

TIM RICHARDSON

At a conference on landscape design in Germany in 2014, the keynote speech was given by the head of one of the leading university design departments in the US. The theme was computer-aided design, specifically the development of 'fly-through' technology with the ability to produce sections, or slices, through any given design. The program – undeniably useful – was enthusiastically demonstrated as a breakthrough. It was then described as the most important innovation relating to design since the discovery of perspective in the Renaissance. This statement was not intended as a joke.

The idea of a computer program setting the agenda in the field of landscape design is indicative of just how pervasive computer-based approaches to design have become (despite the fact that it so often leads to blandly homogenized work). This book is in part a riposte to the idea, not so much a blow for the 'good old-fashioned values on which we used to rely', but a reassertion of the dynamic creative value of hand-drawing in the design process. Landscapes are not objects but complex sites amounting to 'places' that cannot be described by plan, section and elevation alone.

But the thrust of this book is not 'anti-computer'. The point being made is that computer-aided design on the one hand, and handmade drawing or modelling on the other, are different 'tools' with complementary strengths and weaknesses. It is perfectly possible to integrate computer technology into a handmade aesthetic – witness the many examples of drawings melded with Photoshop. All design offices use computers; problems only arise when technology is allowed to dictate design.

The rise of computer-aided design has been helpful in that it has concentrated minds on the value of hand-drawing, which can now be appreciated afresh for its power as an aid to design, as an intimate reflection of the imagination and as a highly effective presentation and communication tool.

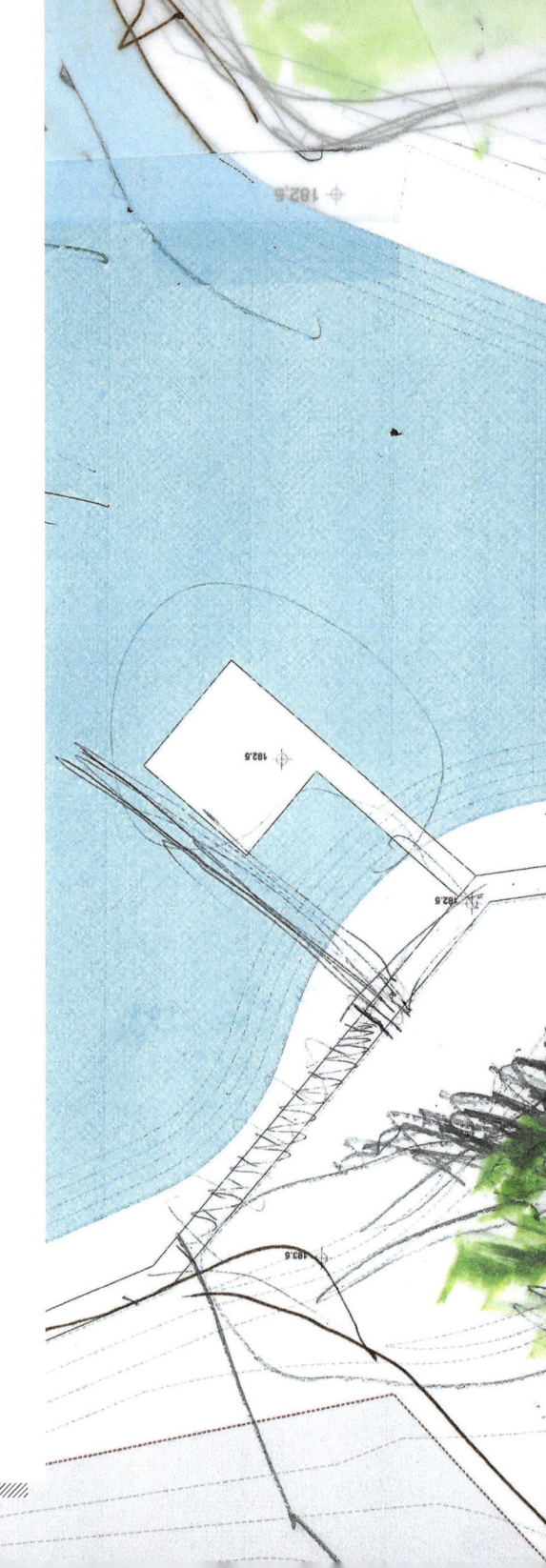

Atelier Dreiseitl
Überlingen, Germany

The company, founded in 1980, is known internationally for its specialism with water. Working in three dimensions – the development of spatial understanding by means of the creation of physical models – has always been a key method of both communication and design development.

Atelier Dreiseitl state: 'The way we create spaces that speak to people intellectually, emotionally and physically is not just about understanding space virtually and intellectually. It is also achieved by means of physical model-building.

'The act of place-making and the experience of being embedded in space is not a solely intellectual one, since spatial experience affects most of our senses. Volumes, shapes and forms will all affect our spatial perception. With these parameters in mind, we create physical models in order to have direct experience of the spaces we are proposing and to understand the effects of our architectural and landscape elements.

'Drawing is the primary way of representing space, while also revealing one's personal understanding of it. Our projects all have an individual and emotional layer, and it is easier to express this layer through hand-drawings. It is not possible to represent everything that one sees, so the intellectual process of abstracting what is important and what is not is a crucial skill to develop over time.'

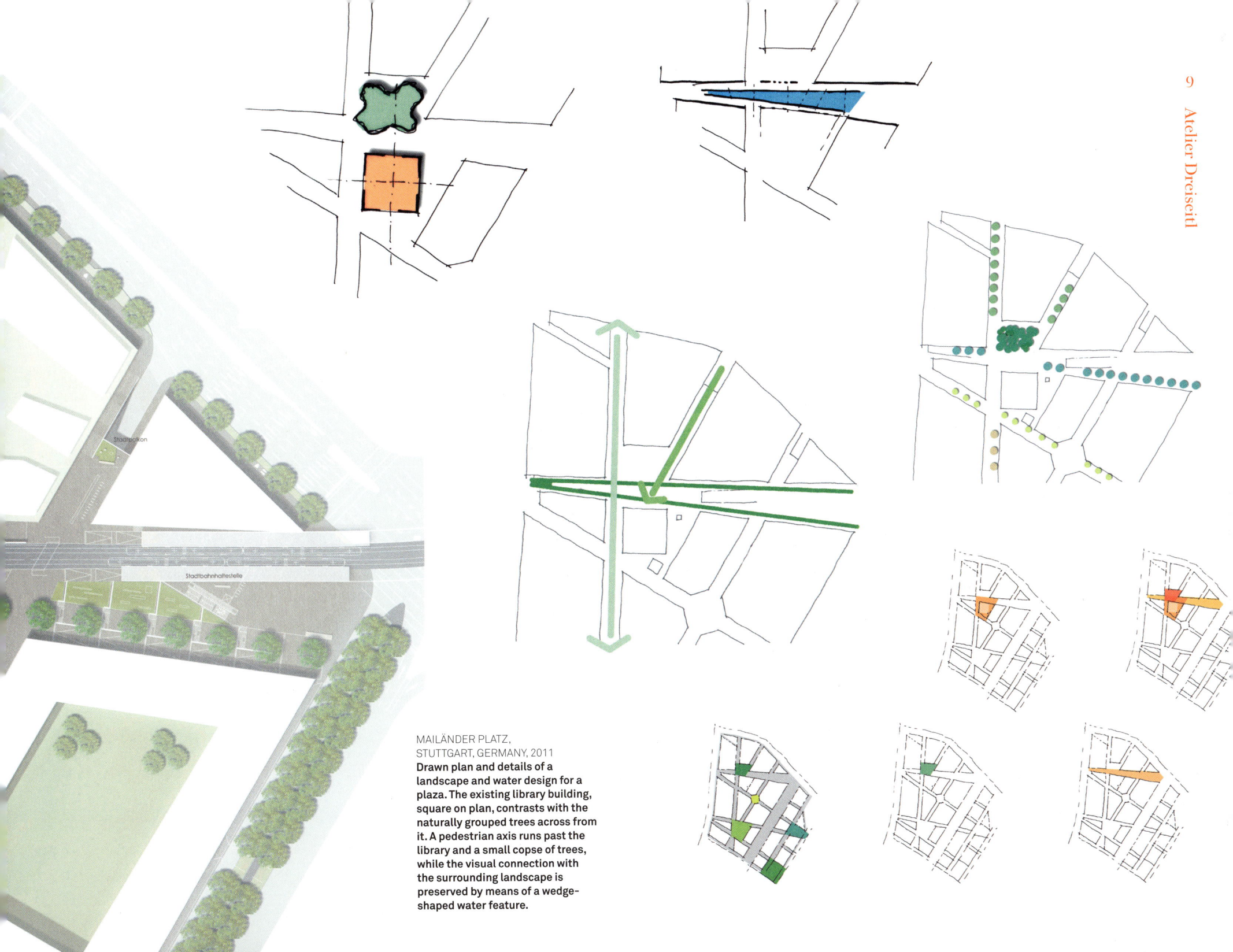

MAILÄNDER PLATZ,
STUTTGART, GERMANY, 2011
Drawn plan and details of a landscape and water design for a plaza. The existing library building, square on plan, contrasts with the naturally grouped trees across from it. A pedestrian axis runs past the library and a small copse of trees, while the visual connection with the surrounding landscape is preserved by means of a wedge-shaped water feature.

ZOLLHALLENPLATZ,
FREIBURG, GERMANY, 2011
Preparatory coloured hand-sketches, in which the design plays with the historic past of the site: an ex-railyard. Old railway tracks are inlaid into the paving, while the benches recall buffers. A bright grove of cherry trees provides shade and filtrated planters with perennials and ornamental grasses create an attractive softness.

TANNER SPRINGS PARK,
PORTLAND, OREGON, USA, 2010
The design concept for this park was based on the idea of the geological layers of the city that existed before human intervention. Three layers were identified: the pre-existing natural wetland, at the right of the sketch; the industrial history of the city, in the centre, expressed through an 'art wall' made from old railway tracks; and, lastly, the current mixed-use urban layer, seen on the left.

SULMPARK NECKARSULM,
DENMARK
Based on the concept of re-establishing the River Sulm in the heart of the town, this project was developed from the start with sketches and 3D models. Modelling was used because it was the best way of expressing and developing intuitively natural forms.

Atelier Dreiseitl

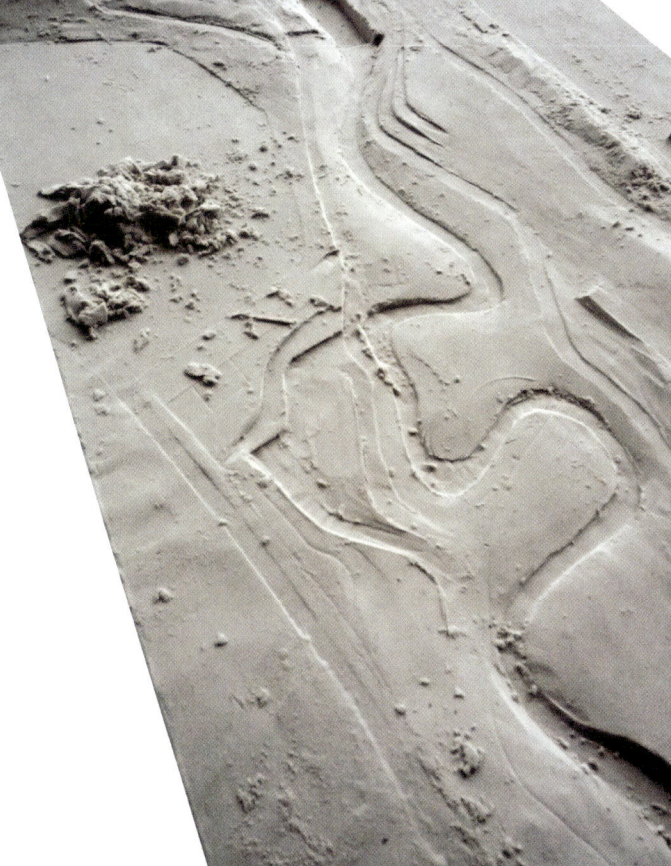

Balmori
New York, USA

For Diana Balmori, a return to drawing would mark the return of landscape architecture as an artistic discipline, as opposed to an adjunct to sustainability or a problem-solving, process-based service industry. Drawing is actively encouraged among her staff, including interns, who come via architecture courses as well as landscape backgrounds. For Balmori, it is only through drawing or painting that landscape can be authentically expressed, since model-making is by necessity object-based.

Diana Balmori writes: 'In our office, drawing is a conscious activity, discussed and presented on a bi-weekly basis. Why pay attention to drawing, when the work of creating a physical landscape occurs out on a site? Because to get to that point, landscape needs to project an image of what it is, and of its artistic value. And it needs to be able to convince a client of its value as a place.

'Landscape was a powerful art that emerged from painting in the seventeenth century, and was considered a sister to the other arts until the late nineteenth century. The aim of our emphasis on drawing is to allow landscape to regain its status as a major art form, reinventing itself as a completely new discipline, with little or no connection with its twentieth-century past.

'In the work of our office, the role of landscape is to change the relationship of humans to nature – to trees, the earth, rivers and oceans, as well as to other sentient beings. It is through drawing a design that we seek to develop an artistic language that speaks of such an aim for landscape. By representing design artistically, we will be able to show what landscape can achieve, and how it can achieve it.'

PRIVATE RESIDENCE, GREENWICH, CONNECTICUT, USA, 2014
The separation of trees, plants, walls and house into different planes creates a third dimension (above). Interruptions in the surface of the drawing – dots, vertical lines – give depth (opposite), much as perspective was brought into seventeenth-century landscape painting for that purpose.

HERMAS DEVELOPMENT,
DOHA, QATAR, 2014
The image widens in the peripheral vision (below). How far can you break apart an image and yet keep it spatially coherent? (right). Plan and elevation are combined to render the courtyard (opposite, left). Visualization of tree plantings, palms and acacias (opposite, above right). An extruded dot matrix blurs the sharp contours of objects in the peripheral vision (opposite, below right).

CUIDAD EMPRESARIAL SARMIENTO ANGULO, BOGOTÁ, COLOMBIA, 2014
On p. 18: Breaking into the continuous plane of an image to emphasize space over the objects in it (left and above right). Topographical study of landforms (below right).

ARC WILDLIFE CROSSING, COLORADO, USA, 2011
On p. 19: Three-dimensional stereoscopic visualization of a proposed wildlife crossing in wood, with red (left-eye) and cyan (right-eye) filters.

I & J Bannerman
Cornwall, UK

The quirkiness and 'English eccentricity' of Isabel and Julian Bannerman's work has led to them being consistently underestimated as landscape designers by those in the mainstream. They made their name as makers of grottoes, pavilions and other 'follies', but they have also undertaken large-scale landscape design work. Both designers have an art background, an emphasis that is to the fore in their evocative yet accurate drawings and sketches.

Isabel Bannerman writes: 'We make a lot of strange buildings, which we have made models of from popcorn, cork, clay, marzipan ... Drawing and model-making can be an important part of our work, and often it helps clients understand a project in three dimensions. Finding time to do drawings is difficult, and only occasionally do we make a collage or even pen-and-ink sketches. Neither of us are great draughtsmen, which is a handicap, but we do use drawing and doodling in a vigorous and instructive way. It helps with the process.

'Sometimes we have worked like those people in *Close Encounters of the Third Kind*, who have to mould and scrape a vision out of mud. Often Julian draws on the pavement or tarmac or gravel with chalk or slate, and he uses the "drawing on the back of a fag [cigarette] packet" method at all times. We find that everything can be devised on the back of a fag packet. Colour is always tricky and we use it very rarely.

'Drawings are, on the whole, tools. They might contain the soul of a project, but they are not pivotal to the process. Drawing can help – it is a great act of observation, and observation is crucial – but a beautiful drawing does not guarantee a successful design. It can be very deceptive. Being able to draw conventionally, therefore, is not an essential requirement in making good design. Russell Page, for example, was a very inferior draughtsman but a brilliant landscape designer.'

THE COLLECTOR EARL'S GARDEN, ARUNDEL, SUSSEX, UK, 2006–10
The design for Oberon's Palace (left) was taken directly from a drawing for a court masque by Inigo Jones in 1611. The design of the structure, realized in green oak and set on a rocky outcrop, was deliberately simplified and exaggerated. Gouache and coloured pencils were used to create the drawing of the Arundel House doorway (below), and associated planting of echiums, canna lilies and palm trees. The Antler Temple (right) has antlers in the tympanum and as accretions, all of which are now 'gilded' by nature with chrome-yellow lichen growth. This structure is a simple oak box about 5m² (538 sq ft), lined with moss and fir cones.

**CASTLE OF MEY,
CAITHNESS, UK, 2004**
A drawing made for the Prince of Wales of an oak bench (opposite, above left); the estate was left in trust by Queen Elizabeth the Queen Mother, hence the initials. A rustic corner pavilion with viewing platform (opposite, below left) and a proposed border in elevation (below).

**DUMFRIES HOUSE,
CUMNOCK, UK, 2010**
Aerial view of a proposed woodland garden with obelisks and a bridge in green oak (left). Evidence of a vestigial avenue of lime trees perpendicular to the house guided the decision to have an axis connecting the stables – now a visitor centre – to the main building via a garden with bridges over the stream.

**TEMPLE OF BRITISH WORTHIES,
HIGHGROVE, GLOUCESTERSHIRE,
UK, 2000**
The Temple of British Worthies (right) – in fact, poets – was intended for Highgrove, the home of the Prince of Wales. It was to be executed in green oak and centred on a bronze plaque dedicated to Ted Hughes, with turned acorn urns adorning the central pyramid and a series of vermiculated oak monoliths, embellished with inscriptions against a backdrop of roots and ferns. Ultimately, only the central monument was made.

SEEND MANOR,
WILTSHIRE, UK, 1997–2007
The groundplan for this walled garden is deceptively formal, with each section enclosed by yew hedges. The owner had spent his life abroad, and wanted this to be reflected in four distinct areas of the garden. 'Italy' (right) was highly formalized, with a narrow swimming pool and a Florentine loggia rescued from an early nineteenth-century house being demolished in Bristol. It was enclosed in yew with lollipop holm oaks and box parterres with terracotta pots filled with agapanthus, and a vine-clad pergola. The huts in 'Africa' (below) are based on the granary buildings typically seen in Mali, while 'Egypt' (bottom) was inspired by French Napoleonic wallpaper, all obelisks and sphinxes with palm trees and a formal tank of water.

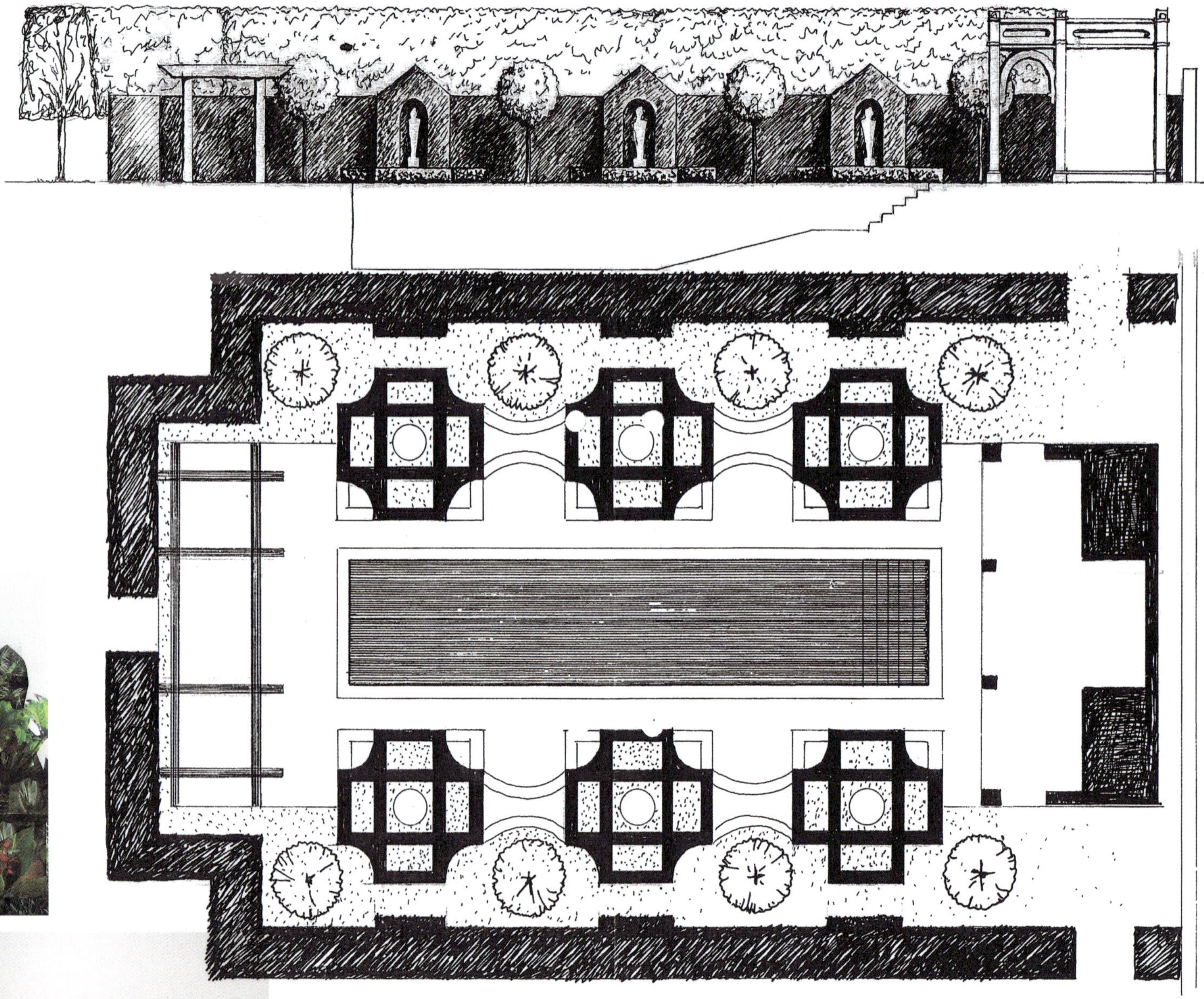

WOOLBEDING GARDENS, SUSSEX, UK, 2007
This pen and ink drawing illustrates a proposed dramatic cut beneath Philip Jebb's Gothic Pavilion, already in situ on a broad grass bank but disconnected from the lake below. The proposal was to extend the lake right up to the pavilion, creating an exciting circuit around and through the building and a crashing 5m (16 ft)- high cascade of water from the River Rother. On the left is a very sketchy river god in his monolithic cave of local Fittleworth ragstone. He was made from carved limestone with a cloak of oyster shells in collaboration with Tom Verity. The background woodland is dark and coniferous in the manner of Caspar David Friedrich, while the foreground comprises king ferns (*Ptisana salicina*).

BCA Landscape
Liverpool, UK

A strong graphic style distinguishes the work of this firm – not just during the design process, but also as a constituent part of the finished product, which comprises the landscape design, itself supported by a suite of printed materials. These may be graphic, informative or both – a reflection of BCA's emphasis on intimate collaboration with local communities, user groups and the 'client' in the widest sense of the word. In many cases, the company presents books, posters, postcards and other printed matter as part of the overall design concept. Strident use of text (including poetry) is a typical strategy, both in the printed works themselves and as inscribed stone or metalwork, which frequently become elements of the landscape design.

Andy Thomson writes: 'For me, drawing, just like designing, is a process of discovery, of testing things out, of trying to transfer a half-developed picture from your mind to the visible world. I don't know why, but people now seem to trust computer-generated imagery more than hand-drawn sketches, which is strange, as both are works of fiction.

'Doodling can be a free and intuitive process that unlocks the restrictions of scale and the exactitude of computers. Words are powerful and, put in a certain order, can be beautiful. But writing and verbalizing ideas for me feels like hard work, whereas sketching and drawing flows easily. It is exciting and enjoyable.

'Sketching and painting with watercolours help to create a feeling of impermanence, transition and movement, since life and landscapes are never still. This helps to bring us closer to a messier and more interesting reality. All designs are in a constant state of flux – in your mind, on the page, on site and into the future. We just like to fool ourselves and imagine that things are more certain and fixed than they actually are.'

PEN SKETCHES FOR TWO DESIGN COMPETITIONS
Andy Thomson notes: 'I tend to freehand sketch, but sometimes with a print of a very basic wire-frame backdrop from SketchUp sitting next to me, to help get existing backdrops and new buildings in roughly the right place and to scale.'

BCA Landscape

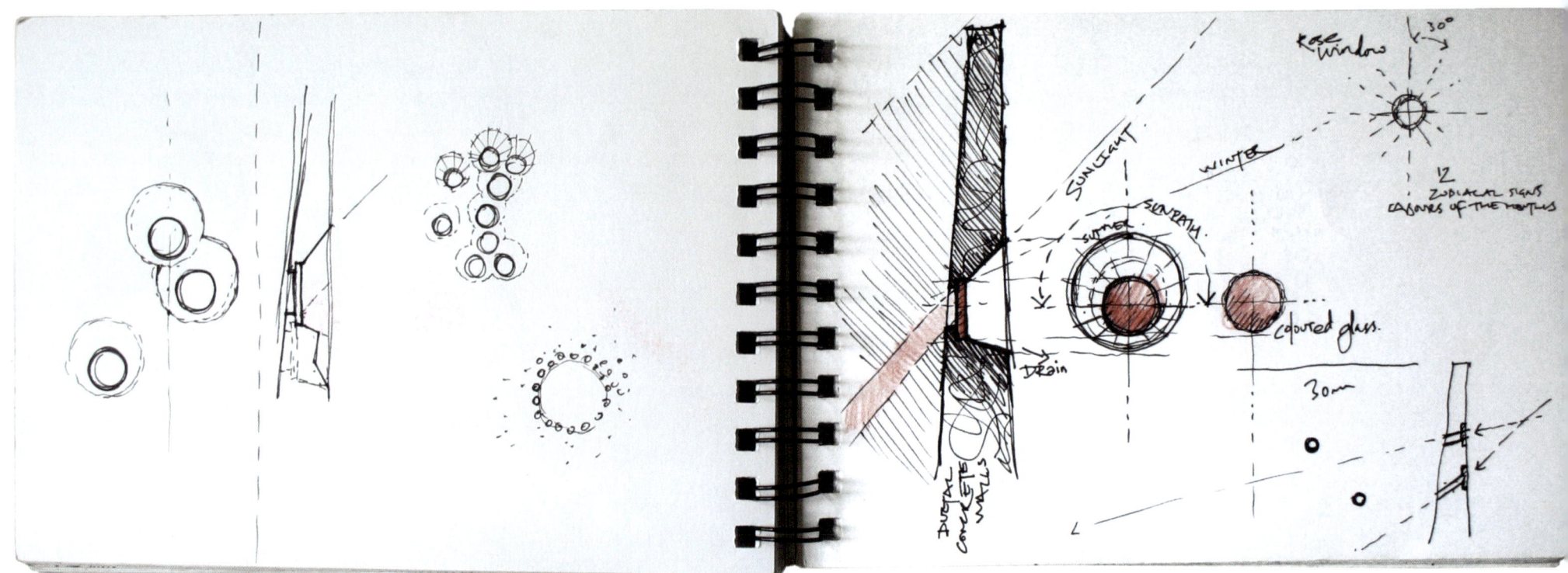

VARIOUS SKETCHES
Watercolours add an additional layer of fluidity and movement to these pen sketches made for design competitions (this page and opposite, above).

BISHOP'S PALACE,
WELLS, SOMERSET, UK, 2015
Exploratory designs for a series of stained-glass window slots within a ductal concrete room, set in a wooded glade (opposite, below). Thumbnail sketches from different viewpoints and angles can be a quick way to explore detail options from all sides, without the need for time-consuming 3D computer work.

ONE THE ELEPHANT, LONDON, UK, 2012
Sketchbook studies testing possible detail combinations of paving, planting and seating for a project in the Elephant and Castle neighbourhood of South London (right, above).

HOUSING SCHEME, BRADFORD, YORKSHIRE, UK, 2005
Exploratory sketch for a large courtyard in the centre of a new housing scheme – a conversion of mill buildings in Bradford (right, below). Following a period of historical research, these freestyle doodles were inspired by a loose narrative of fabrics, textures and materials from the local textile industry.

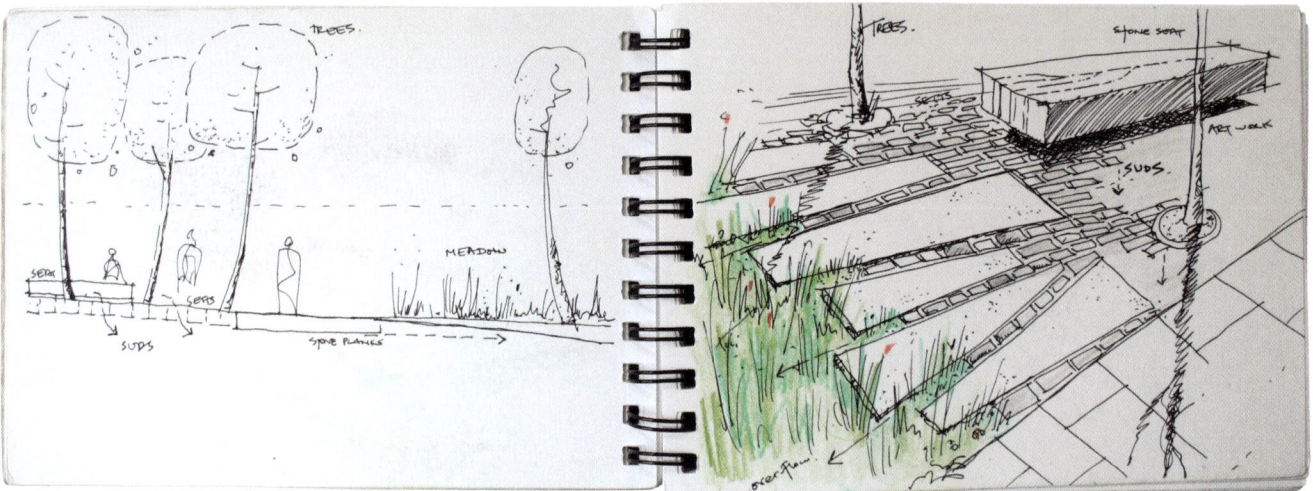

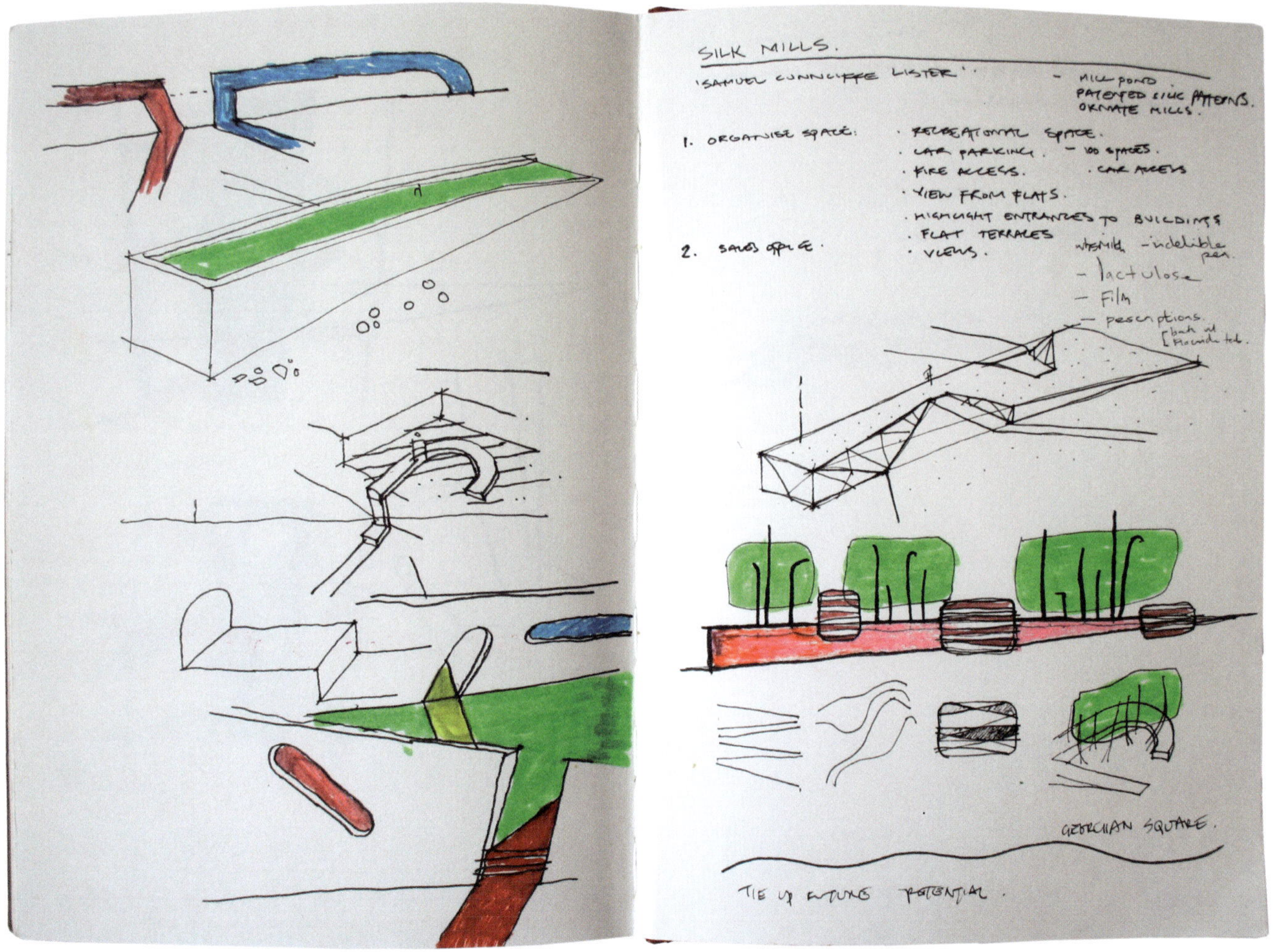

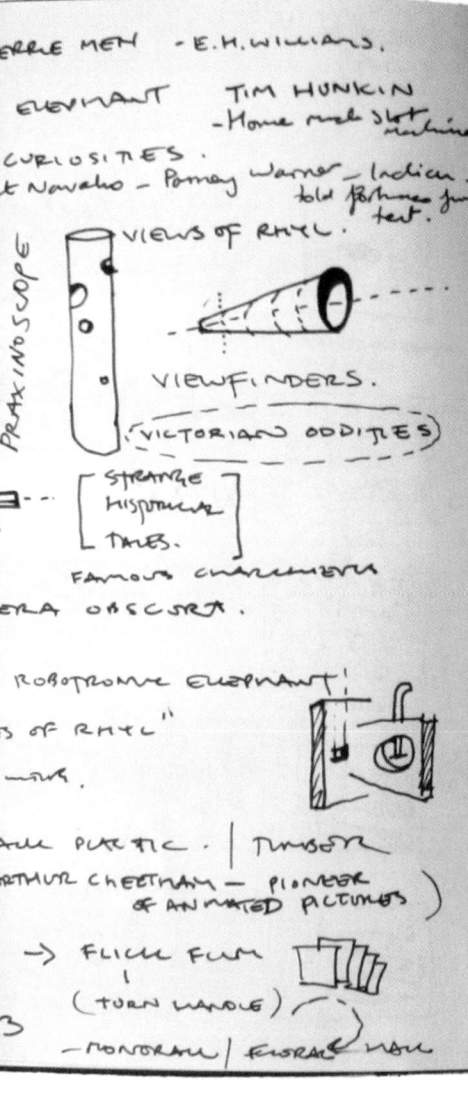
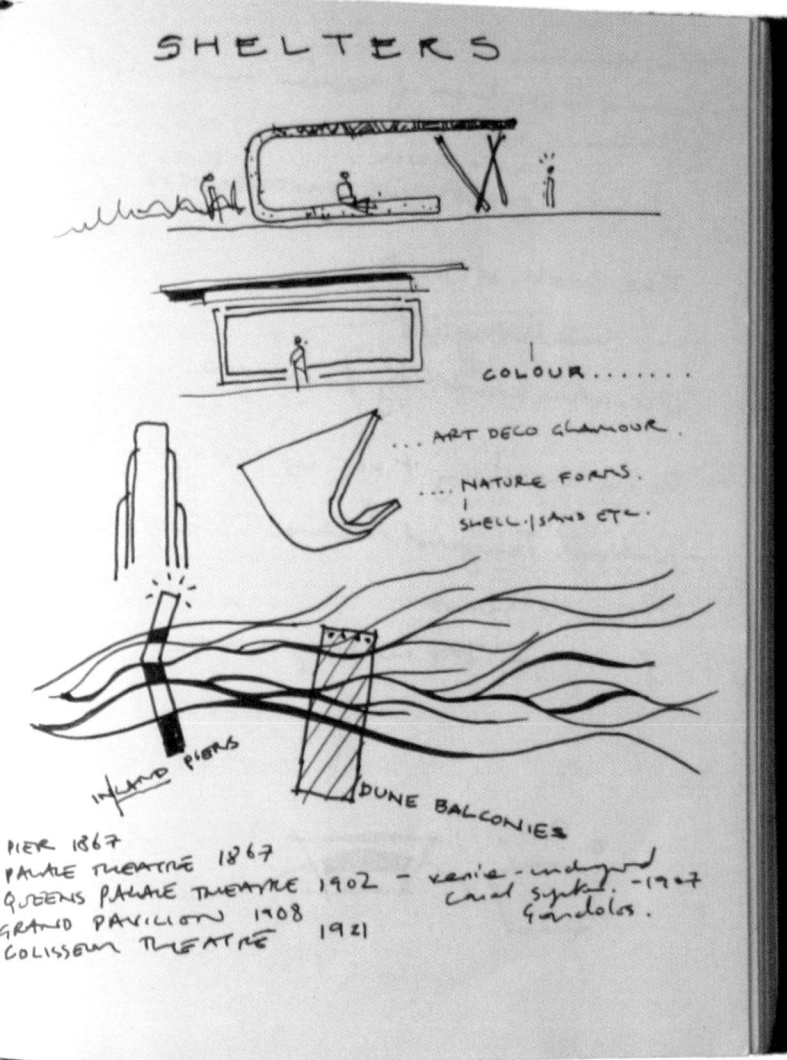

**DRIFT PARK,
RHYL, UK, 2005–7**
These ideas (left) began as written notes and soon mutated into doodles, testing thoughts and potential narrative threads.

**ANGEL FIELD,
LIVERPOOL, UK, 2010**
Early exploratory sketch in plan and detail for a garden at Liverpool Hope University (below).

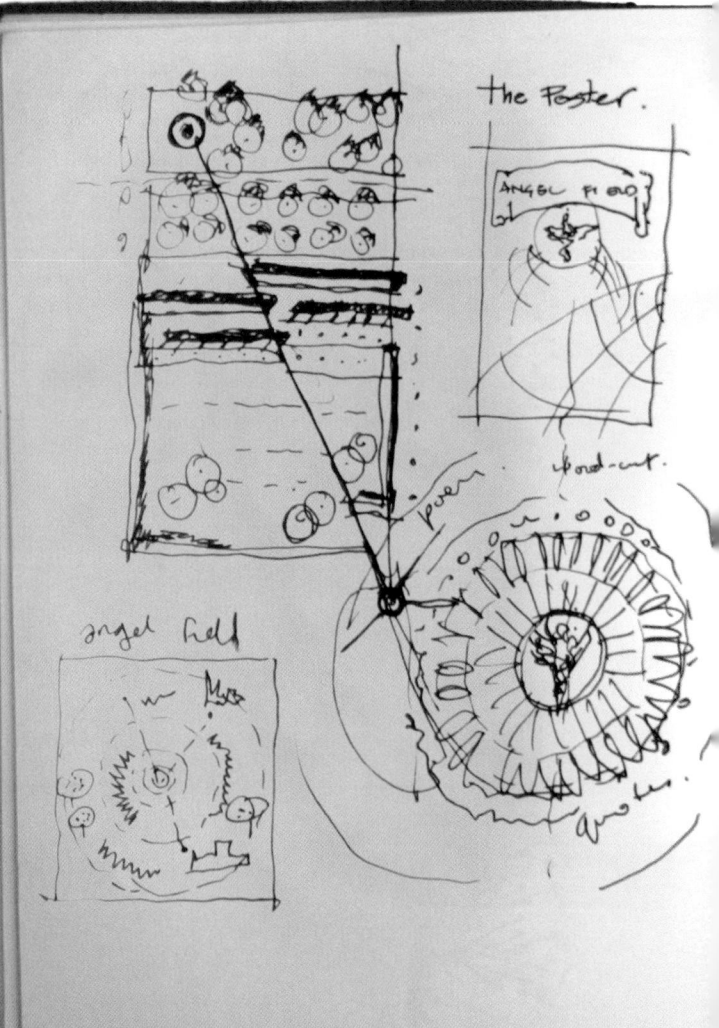

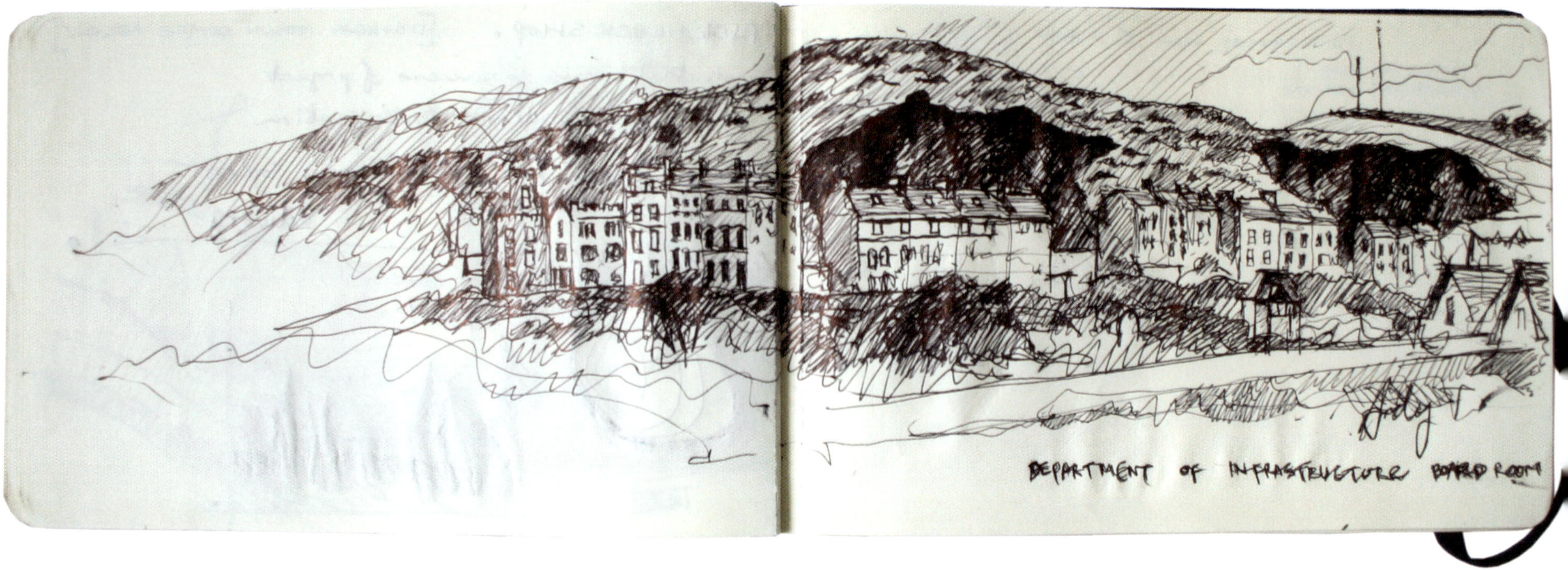
DEPARTMENT OF INFRASTRUCTURE BOARD ROOM

elephant + castle

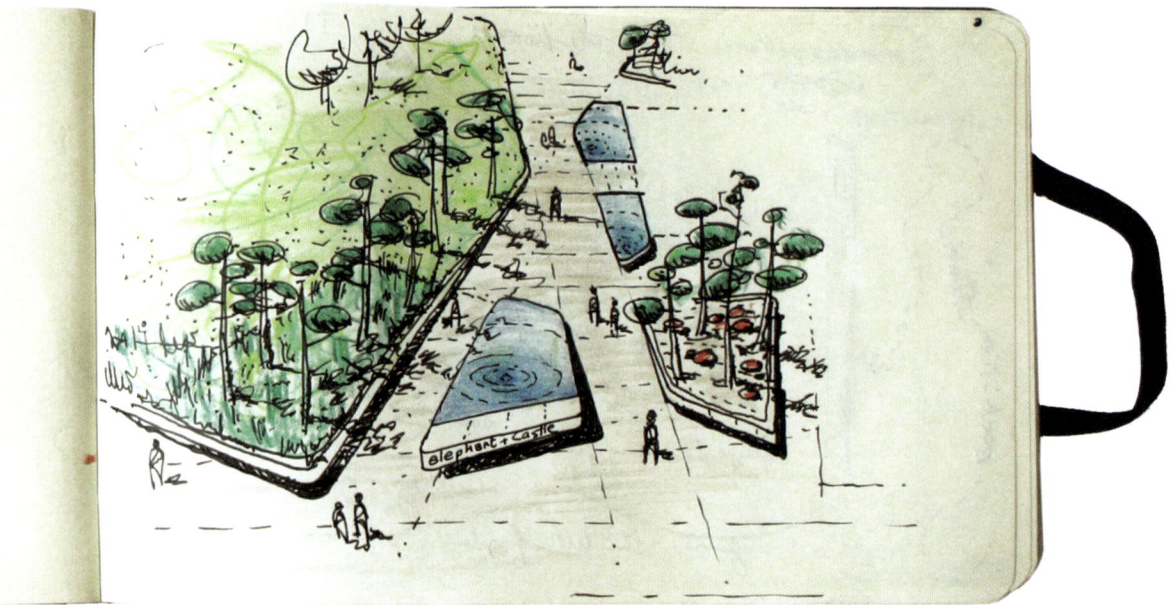

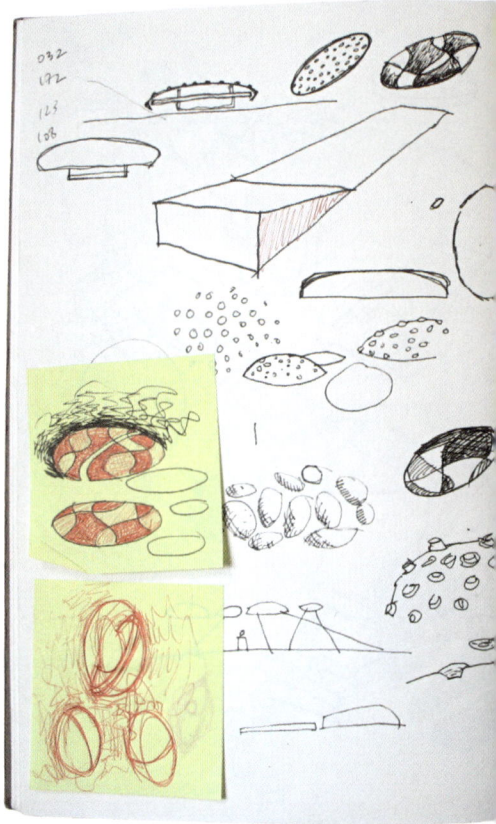

DEPARTMENT OF INFRASTRUCTURE,
DOUGLAS, ISLE OF MAN, UK, 2013
A meeting room with a view on the Isle of Man (opposite, above). Sketching can help to define the detail in the existing landscape, as well as within design work in development.

ONE THE ELEPHANT,
LONDON, UK, 2012
Sketchbook studies in pen and crayon, testing ideas for a project in Elephant and Castle (opposite, below).

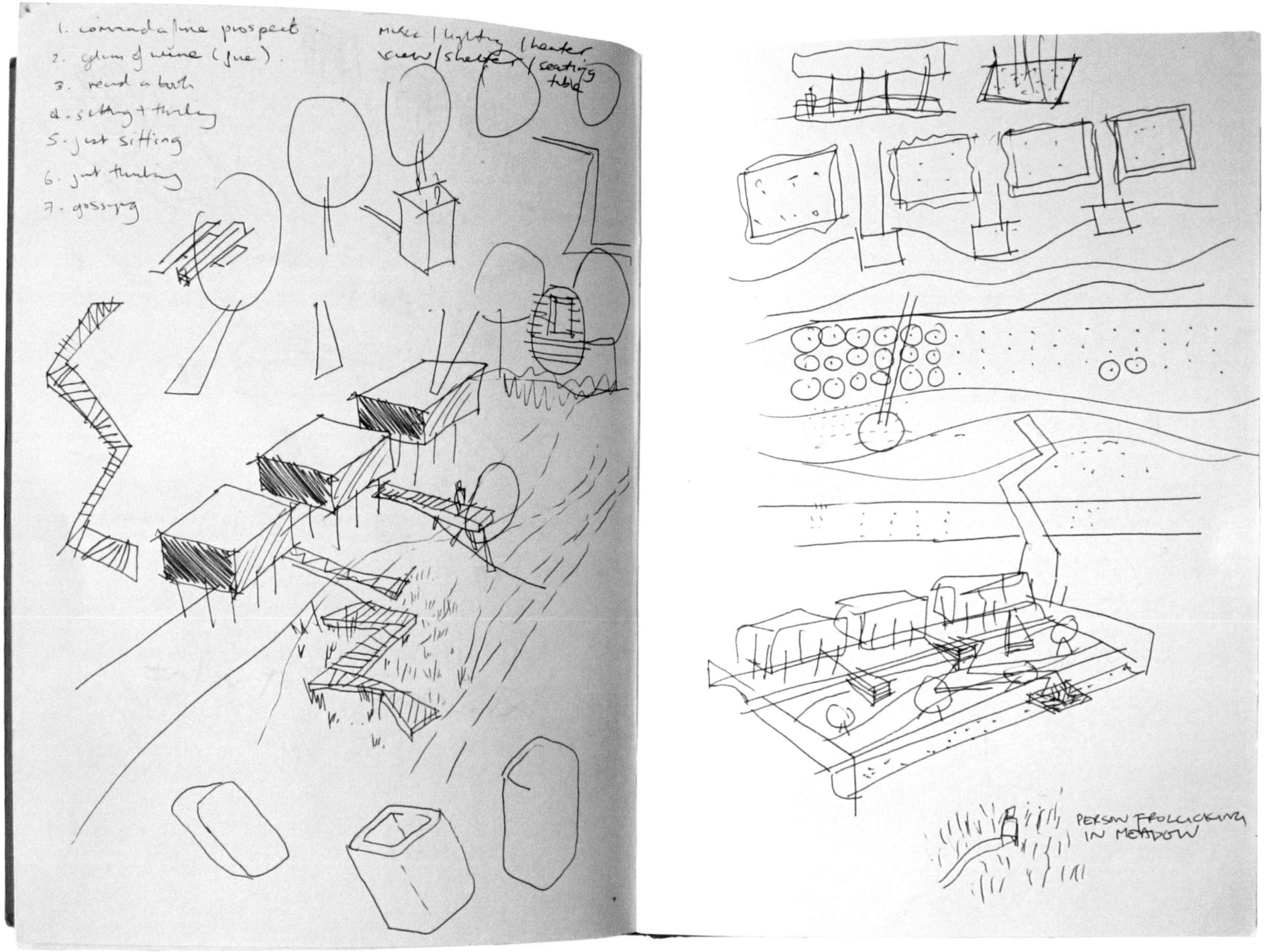

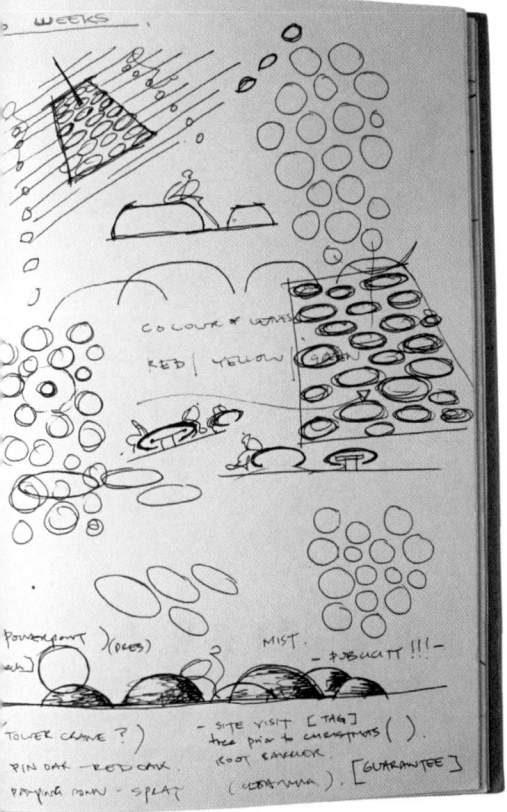

HOUSING SCHEME, BRADFORD,
YORKSHIRE, UK, 2005
Early sketchbook studies for a courtyard in the centre of a new housing scheme in Bradford (above).

STUDY FOR SEATING
Speculative, non-project-specific sketchbook study in pen and pencil for a 'field of seats' (left).

Prabhakar B. Bhagwat
Mumbai, India

Large-scale, intricate yet always somehow intimate, the landscape designs of Prabhakar B. Bhagwat and the company Landscape India – now led by his son, Aniket Bhagwat – are always conceived and understood in the first instance on an artistic level. Issues related to topography and climate are not considered as problems to be solved, but rather as the framework in which artistic activity will ensue.

Aniket Bhagwat writes: 'At our studios, most of us sketch. We use it as a language, at all stages of the project – from doodles laden with the kernel of early thought to refined sketches that articulate and prioritize the reading of the space or as a means of communicating with clients. I don't believe that it's a tool that needs to be compared with computer drawings, as is often imagined. They serve different purposes; an office that chooses one over the other loses valuable ways of developing their designs or communicating them. We have three full-time computer visualizers in the studio and a full-time model maker. And then, of the forty-odd people in our company, at least thirty sketch all of the time, though many of them are equally adept in other technologies.

'Typically, the design process starts with a sketch, which is discussed, refined and then sketched again. When we are broadly satisfied with the structure of the proposed space, it is then drafted on the computer. Using that as a base, it is sketched again, this time with more refinement and details, more nuances. Then it is drafted again. Parts of the design are enlarged, and sketched again – not just in plan form, but in three dimensions. It is evaluated, and sometimes small models are made of elements of the design. It is then redrawn on the computer, broken down into its elements and those elements reassembled to create the complete design.'

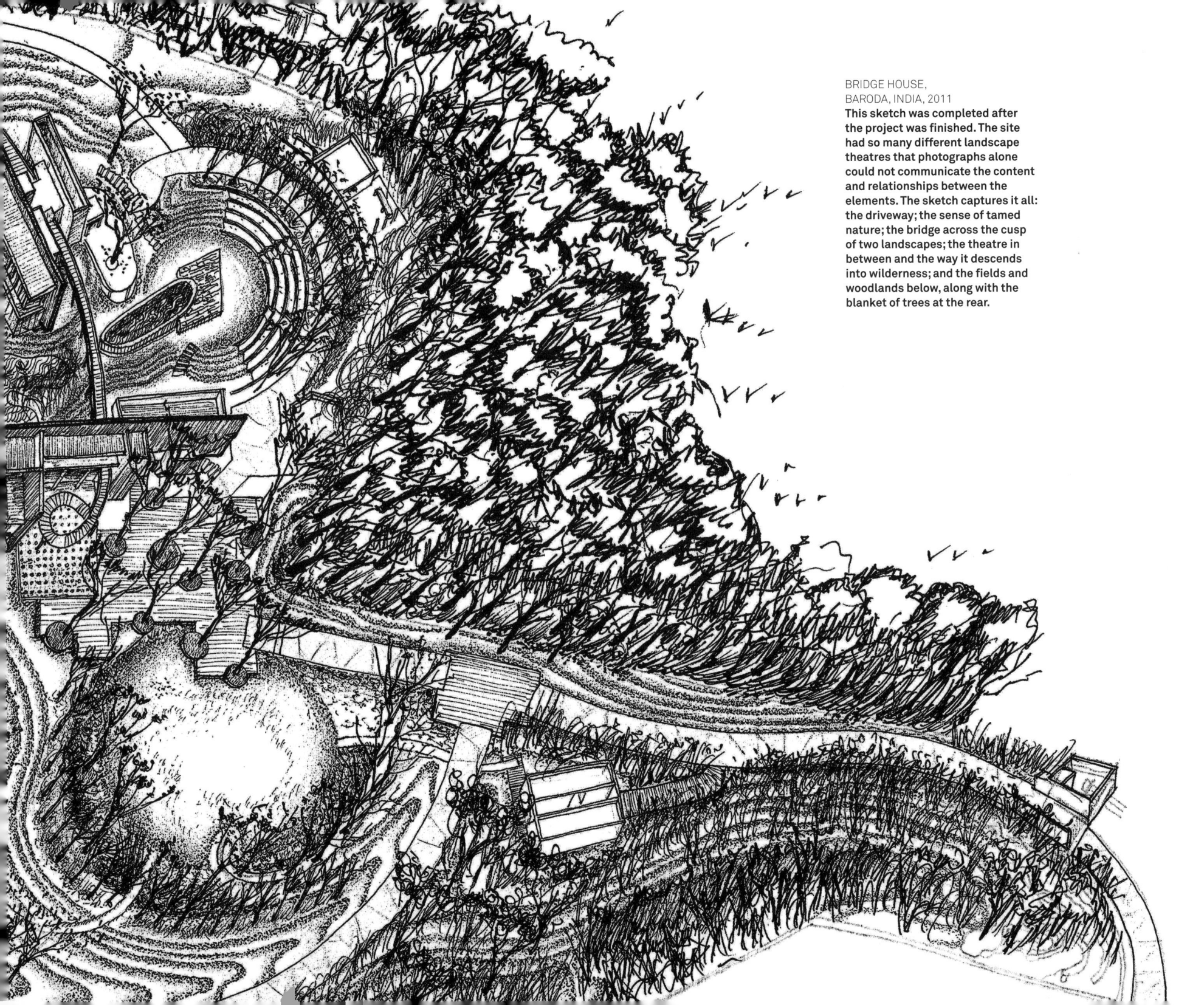

BRIDGE HOUSE,
BARODA, INDIA, 2011
This sketch was completed after the project was finished. The site had so many different landscape theatres that photographs alone could not communicate the content and relationships between the elements. The sketch captures it all: the driveway; the sense of tamed nature; the bridge across the cusp of two landscapes; the theatre in between and the way it descends into wilderness; and the fields and woodlands below, along with the blanket of trees at the rear.

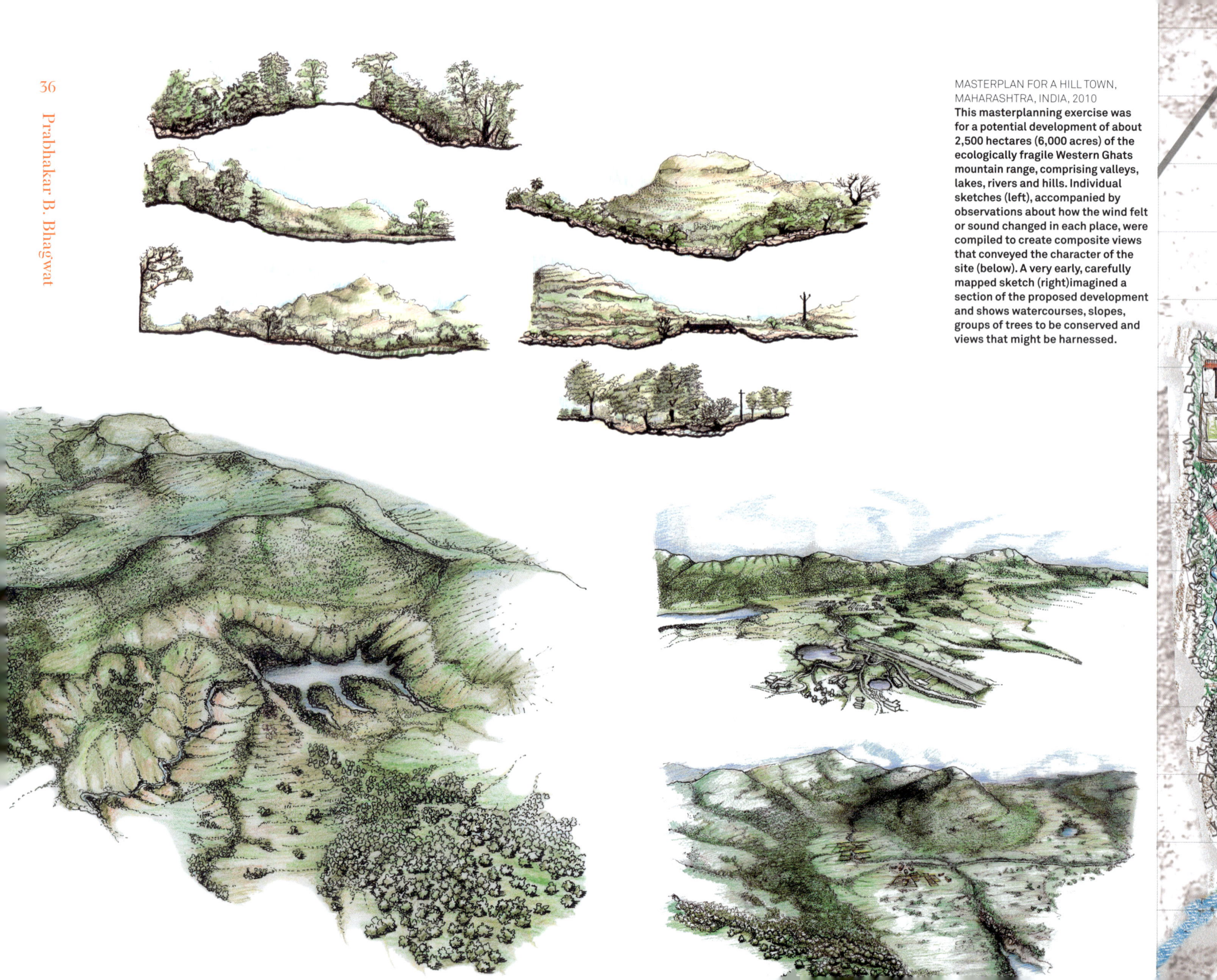

MASTERPLAN FOR A HILL TOWN, MAHARASHTRA, INDIA, 2010

This masterplanning exercise was for a potential development of about 2,500 hectares (6,000 acres) of the ecologically fragile Western Ghats mountain range, comprising valleys, lakes, rivers and hills. Individual sketches (left), accompanied by observations about how the wind felt or sound changed in each place, were compiled to create composite views that conveyed the character of the site (below). A very early, carefully mapped sketch (right) imagined a section of the proposed development and shows watercourses, slopes, groups of trees to be conserved and views that might be harnessed.

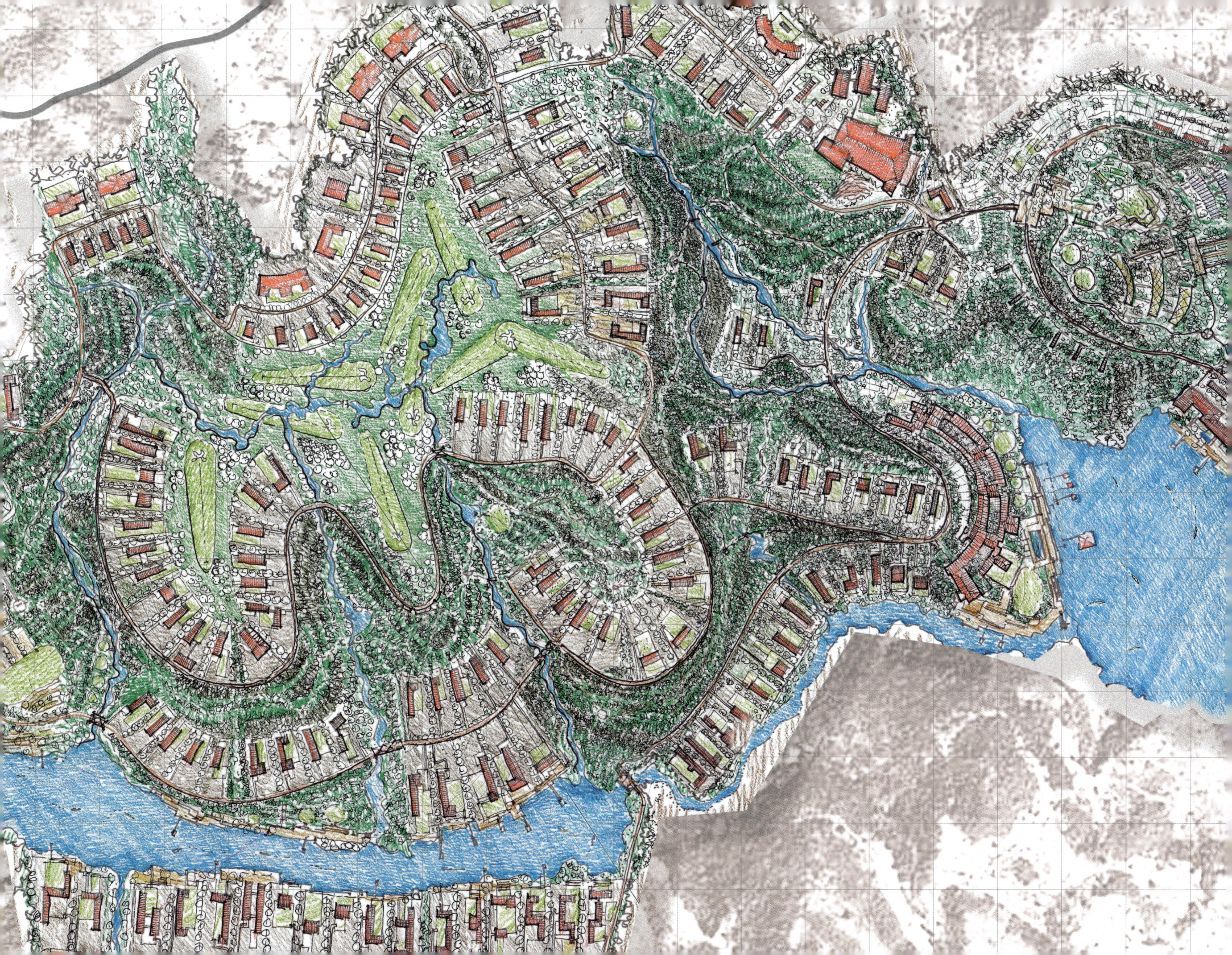

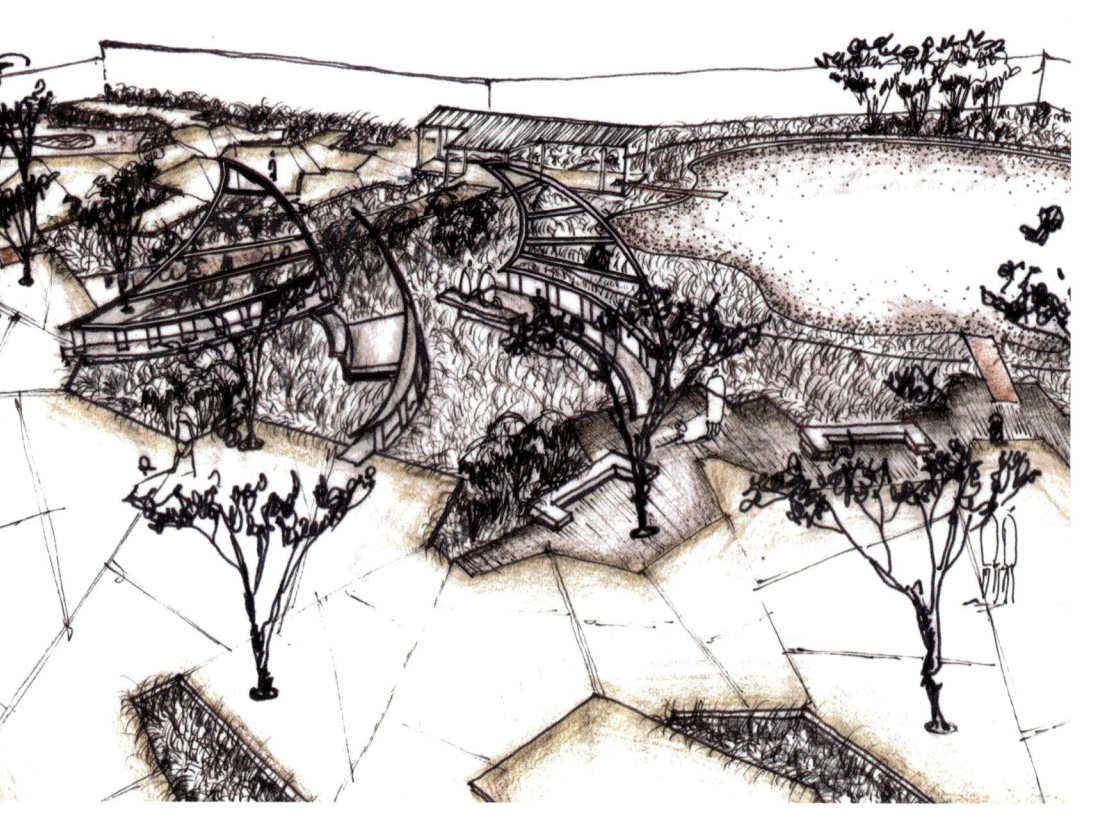

CASA RIO HOUSING DEVELOPMENT, MUMBAI, INDIA, 2010
These sketches reflect early ideas for a landscape plaza near edge of a large new housing development, spread over 80 hectares (200 acres) in Mumbai. The site overlooks a small river and the mountains beyond. The sketches reflect the fractal plates of rock present on the site, and the way basalt expresses itself when exposed. One of the sketches (left) includes boats moored in the landscape, a reference to the drying of the waters in our rivers.

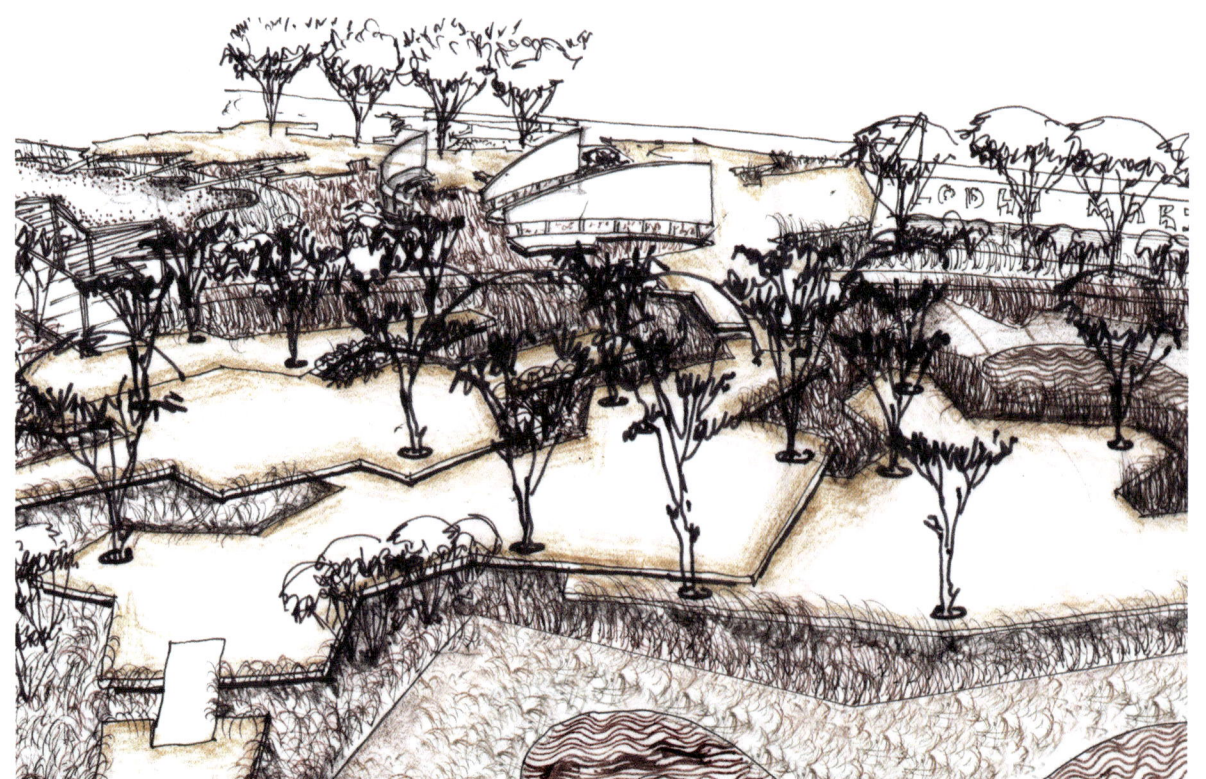

39 Prabhakar B. Bhagwat

CASA RIO HOUSING DEVELOPMENT,
MUMBAI, INDIA, 2010

These initial drawings were used as a way of evaluating and expressing the firm's commitment to making an extremely high density of building blocks recede when experienced on the ground, and to communicate a sense of the wild. Now that the project is nearing completion, the company believes the design is consistent with the vision expressed in these first drawings.

41 Prabhakar B. Bhagwat

Prabhakar B. Bhagwat

NASMED, AHMEDABAD, INDIA, 2010

This series of sketches maps the evolution of a section of agricultural land. From left to right, the first sketch shows thickets, trees and small farms, while in the second the woodland is more clearly expressed, thickets reinforced, topography defined and ponds marked. In the third sketch, human habitations have been added in a natural process of site-selection. The final sketch shows the roads and pathways that connect them. The team felt this was an interesting way of looking at site-planning as an articulation of the existing features of a site.

Prabhakar B. Bhagwat

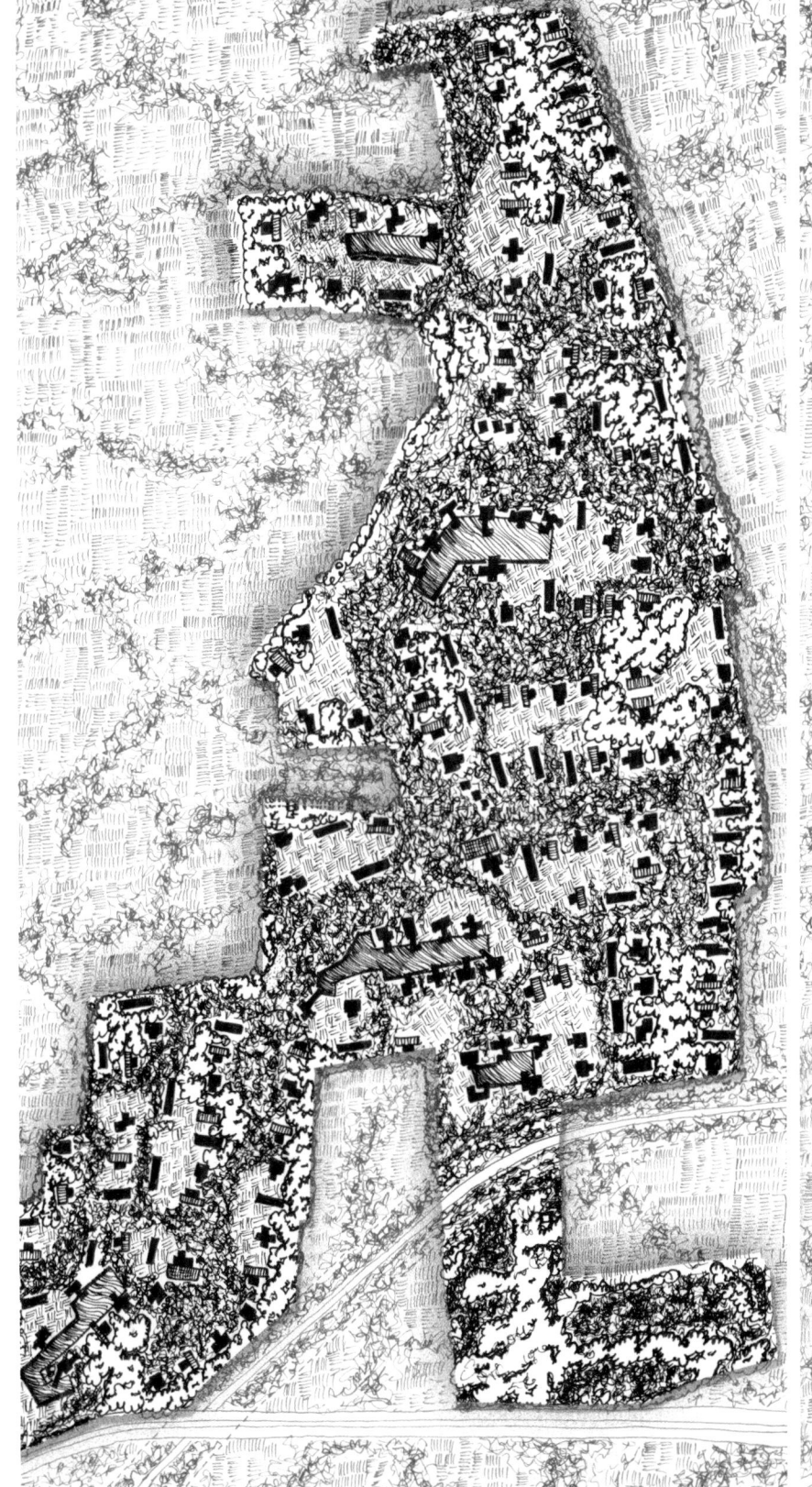

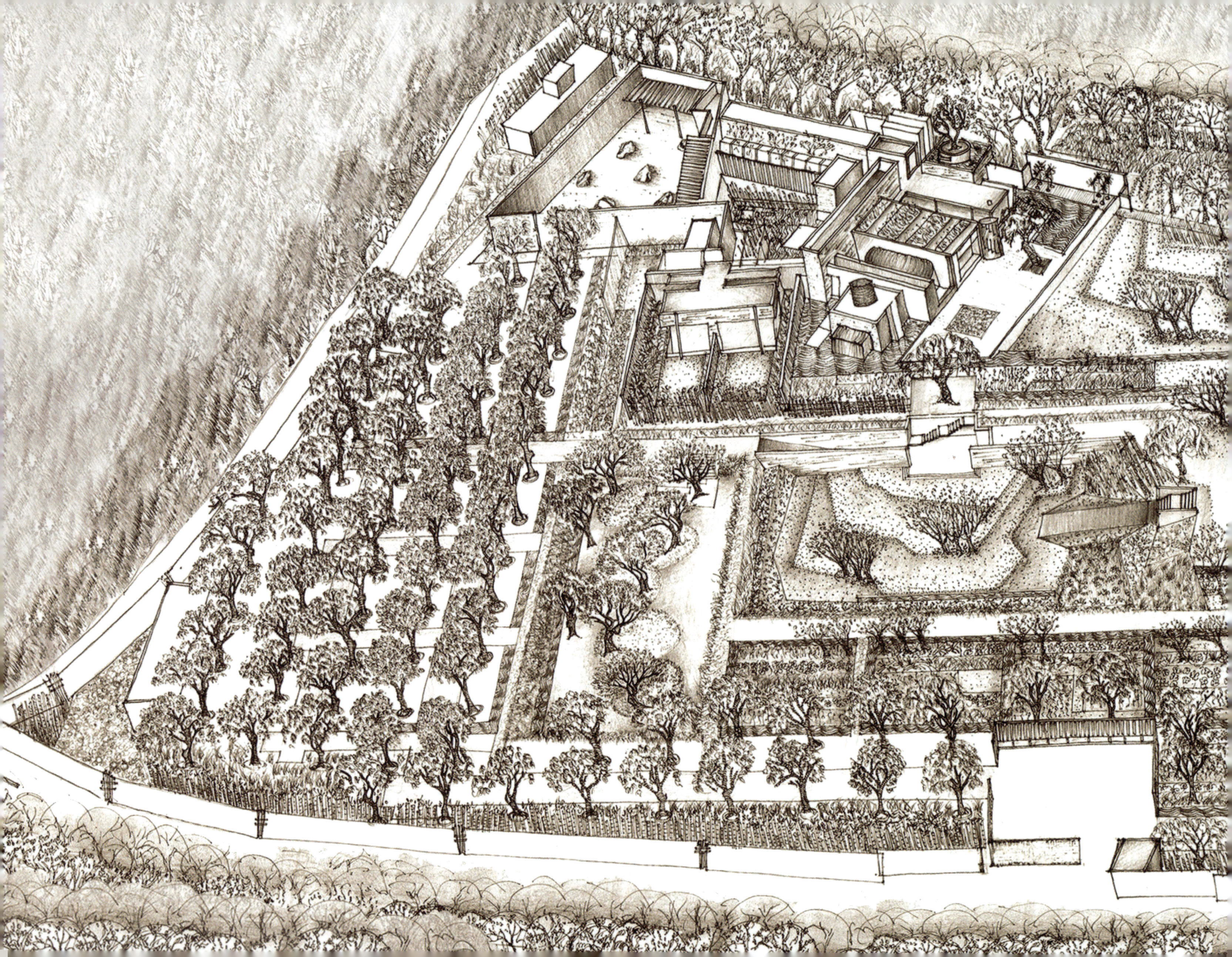

KRISHORE MARIWALA,
ALIBAUG, INDIA, 2004

The first visualization of a landscape design for a private house in Alibaug, near Mumbai (left). It shows the way the shape of the land echoes the voluptuous form of the roof, the dark gravel court with a lone tree, the agriculture that mediates the existing orchard, and the water and its geometry. The drawing was so strong with regard to mood, and so clear in terms of space-making, that there was no reason to revisit it. This is more or less how the landscape was executed.

PRIVATE HOUSE AND GARDEN,
AHMEDABAD, INDIA, 2006

As photographs do not adequately show the relationship between the different elements, this drawing (opposite) was made after the project was completed. An angle of elevation was chosen for this perspective view to illustrate all of these connections. A densely shaded driveway leads to a stark, sun-bathed court, enclosed by a wall. There is a shaded walk to the house, and a cool, dark courtyard. The landscape is terraced in spiral form, defined by trees, with a different geometry for the water channels that cross it. The sketch shows the small, private garden courts in some detail, and specific trees near the pool.

Prabhakar B. Bhagwat

Cao | Perrot

Los Angeles, USA / Paris, France

The joyous simplicity – allied with originality – of the work of Andy Cao and Xavier Perrot is initially expressed by means of drawings and computer-aided photomontages with an authentically handmade feel. For Cao and Perrot, these images are a way of capturing the essence of the piece in one gulp – something of the beguiling, almost childlike romance that distinguishes their work. By focusing entirely on one simple move in these preparatory studies, they are able to communicate with disarming precision the atmosphere that will be created by the piece, an aura that often remains with those who subsequently experience it in the mind. Since many of these pieces are temporary installations – or 'slow-temporary': they might last up to five years – these images also document and archive the piece, capturing aspects that photography cannot hope to preserve.

Andy Cao and Xavier Perrot write: 'We are drawn to the handmade, to crafting by intuition. We find beauty in imperfection. Our environments are formless, shapeless. They have a story, but no meaning. We usually shape an image in our heads before we draw, rather than working out an idea using kilometres of trace paper. We mostly use hand-drawings and photomontage in 2D and clay models in 3D, all made in-house.

'Our drawings and renderings are intended to convey the moods and atmospheres of our projects, rather than trying to simulate the reality, as a video-game designer might. We find the concept of "low-tech" quite refreshing nowadays. Behind a sketch, there is often a specific location proposed. We "fabricate" images by means of photomontages, which help a client to visualize the project in its context, and to give a feel for the materials and atmosphere. But our clients often appreciate the simplest of sketches, and these can be equally efficient at communicating our ideas.'

COMPETITION FOR AN ANIMAL SHELTER, DENVER, COLORADO, USA, 2011
This photomontage for a public art competition shows two variations of the artwork (daytime and nighttime), which was to consist of mother-of-pearl shells on a deconstructed chain-link fence.

48 | Cao | Perrot

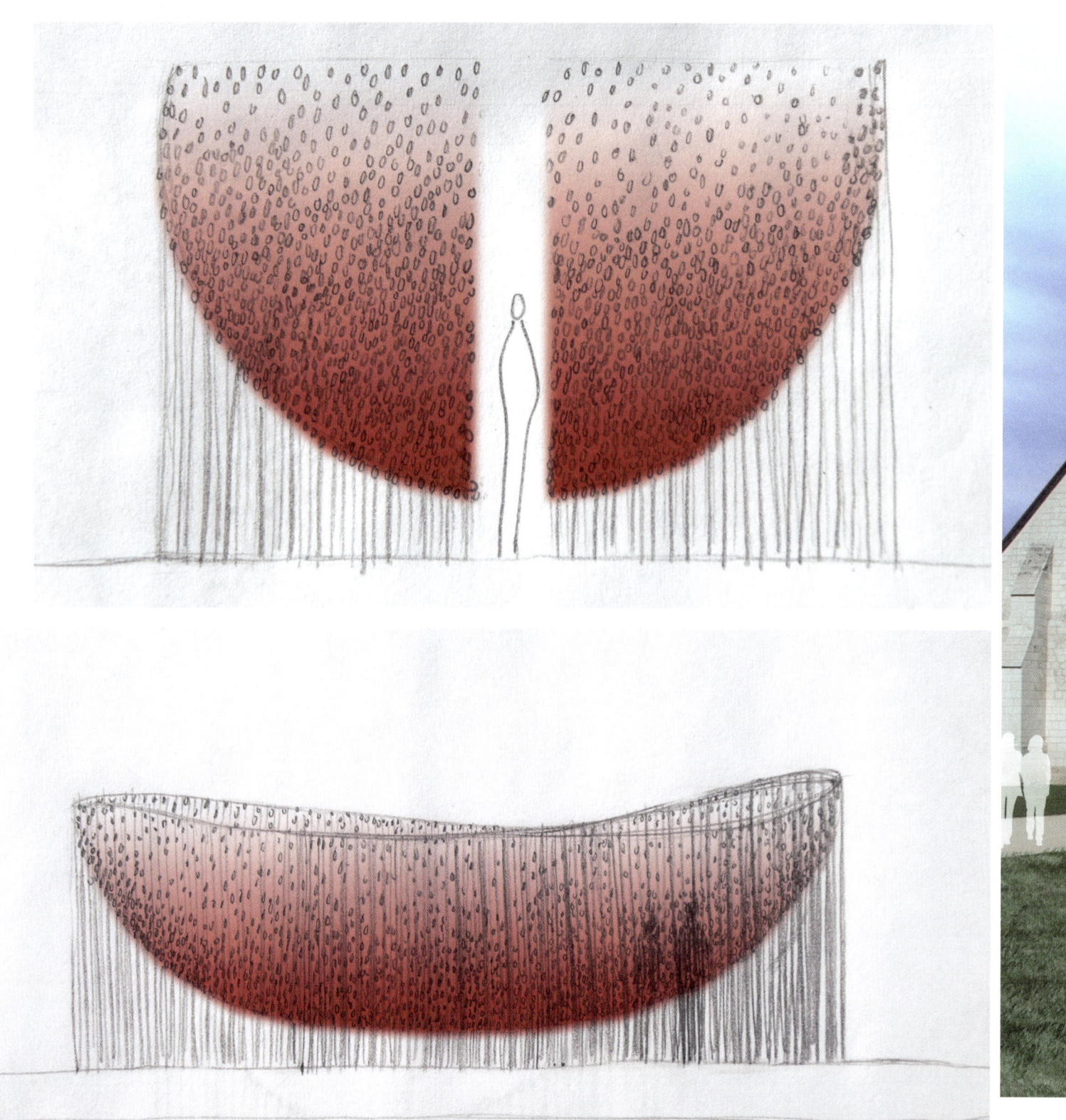

RED BOWL INSTALLATION, BEAUVAIS, FRANCE, 2012
This photomontage shows the installation at the Maladrerie St-Lazare, composed of 5,000 red Bohemian glass balls suspended on spring steel rods. A burnt-wood pathway around the water surface was covered with duckweed. Hand-drawn sketches with Photoshop (opposite) of the same project.

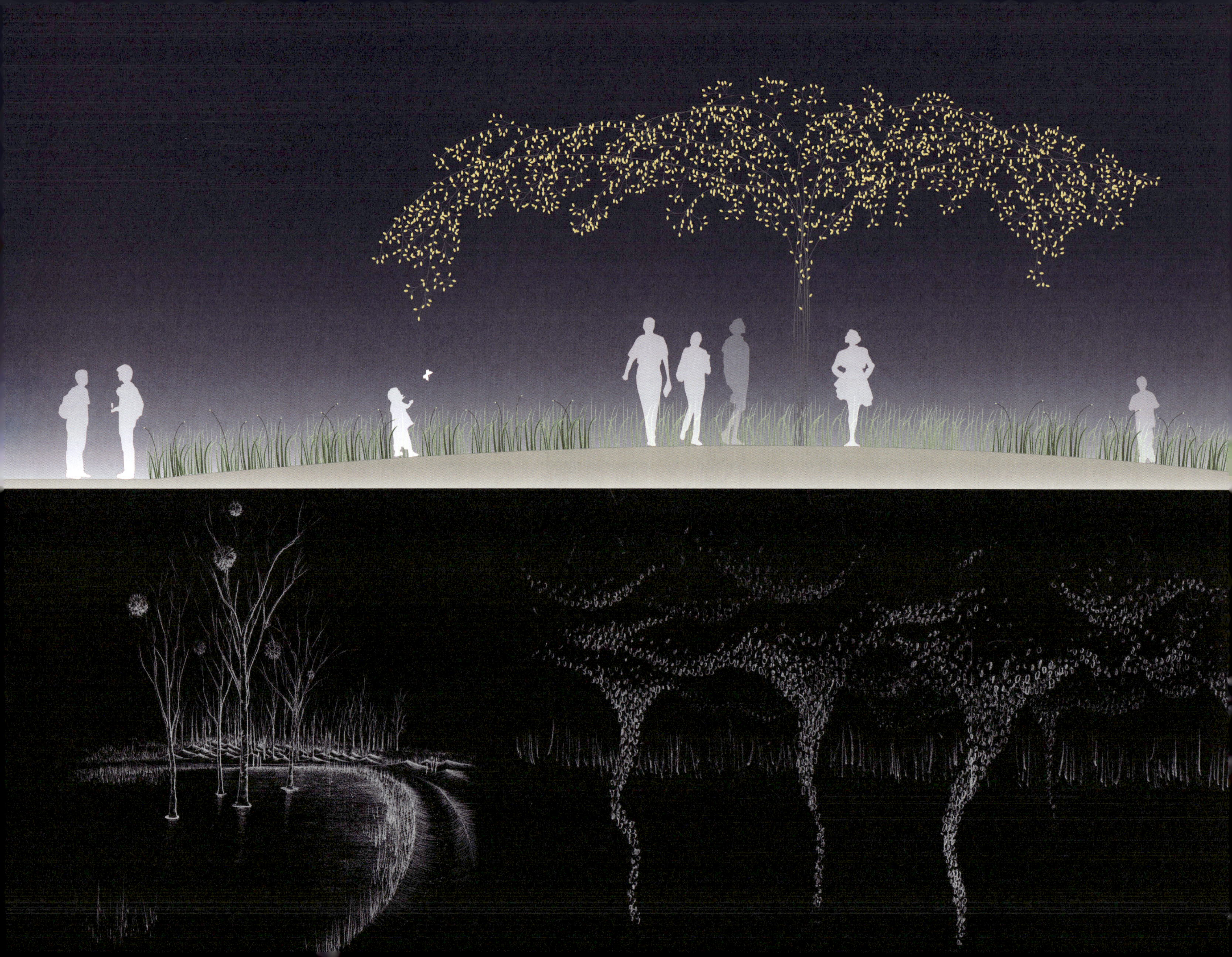

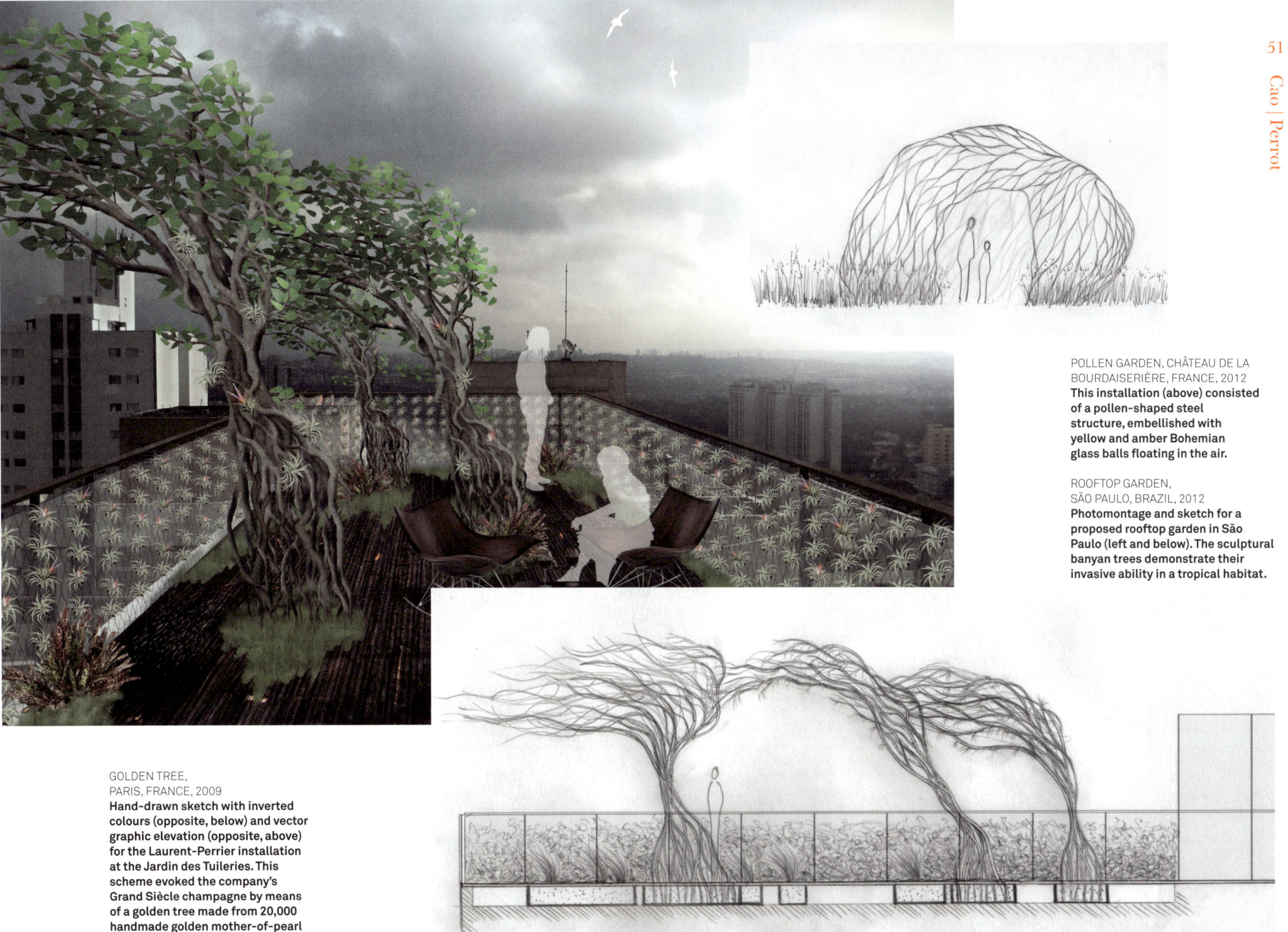

POLLEN GARDEN, CHÂTEAU DE LA
BOURDAISERIÈRE, FRANCE, 2012
This installation (above) consisted of a pollen-shaped steel structure, embellished with yellow and amber Bohemian glass balls floating in the air.

ROOFTOP GARDEN,
SÃO PAULO, BRAZIL, 2012
Photomontage and sketch for a proposed rooftop garden in São Paulo (left and below). The sculptural banyan trees demonstrate their invasive ability in a tropical habitat.

GOLDEN TREE,
PARIS, FRANCE, 2009
Hand-drawn sketch with inverted colours (opposite, below) and vector graphic elevation (opposite, above) for the Laurent-Perrier installation at the Jardin des Tuileries. This scheme evoked the company's Grand Siècle champagne by means of a golden tree made from 20,000 handmade golden mother-of-pearl 'leaves' and a steel trunk.

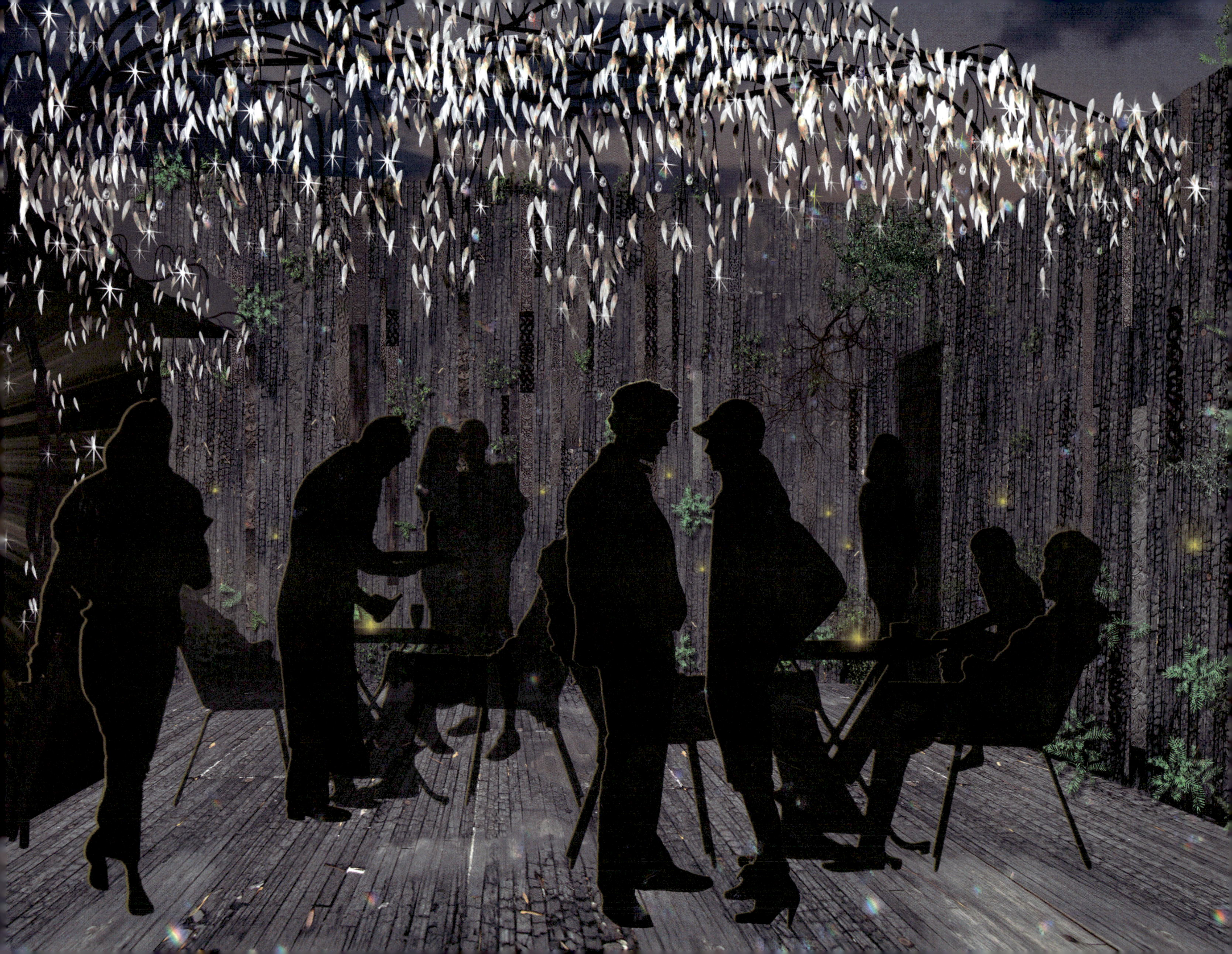

Q BAR, HOI AN, VIETNAM, 2011
Photomontage of an ethereal outdoor room (left), inspired by the subtropical vegetation and aspects of local craftsmanship.

BAI YUN GARDEN, CORNERSTONE, SONOMA, CALIFORNIA, USA, 2011
Photomontage of an installation (below) that revisited the earlier Lullaby Garden. It was made from existing landforms with the addition of a wire-mesh cloud with crystals and cactus.

Fernando Caruncho

Madrid, Spain

One of the true visionaries of the landscape scene, Caruncho does not need to employ spurious critical and technical jargon to create a false impression of depth, profundity and intellectual awareness. His training in philosophy, coupled with his unwavering belief in and understanding of the nuances of his own artistic development and practice, create a truly original sensibility. This is reflected in his drawings, which are not made for public consumption but reflect instinctive processes that are effectively a nexus of the disciplines of art and design, and a place where such distinctions are unselfconsciously blurred.

Fernando Caruncho writes: 'Drawing is essential to landscape description. It is primordial and original. My starting point when designing is a series of sketches that represent the conceptual vision of the project in a very abstract way. The reason I use scale models is to place ideas on the ground as a way of adjusting the mechanism of that idea to the terrain. For me, there is no better medium than this, because it allows you to see the different phases of the idea and to develop it at your own scale and with your own perspective. It is quite different to working on a computer, which feels more mathematical and less human.

'Drawing is the simplest tool. Ideas travel immediately and unhindered from the mind to the hand. It is like automatic writing, like the first babblings of a baby. I let my hand express what my mind does not see. By means of drawing, you can progress directly from intuition to the first realization of your ideas. A sketch is the most substantial representation of the first and most direct concept of a project idea – the most pure, abstract and authentic.'

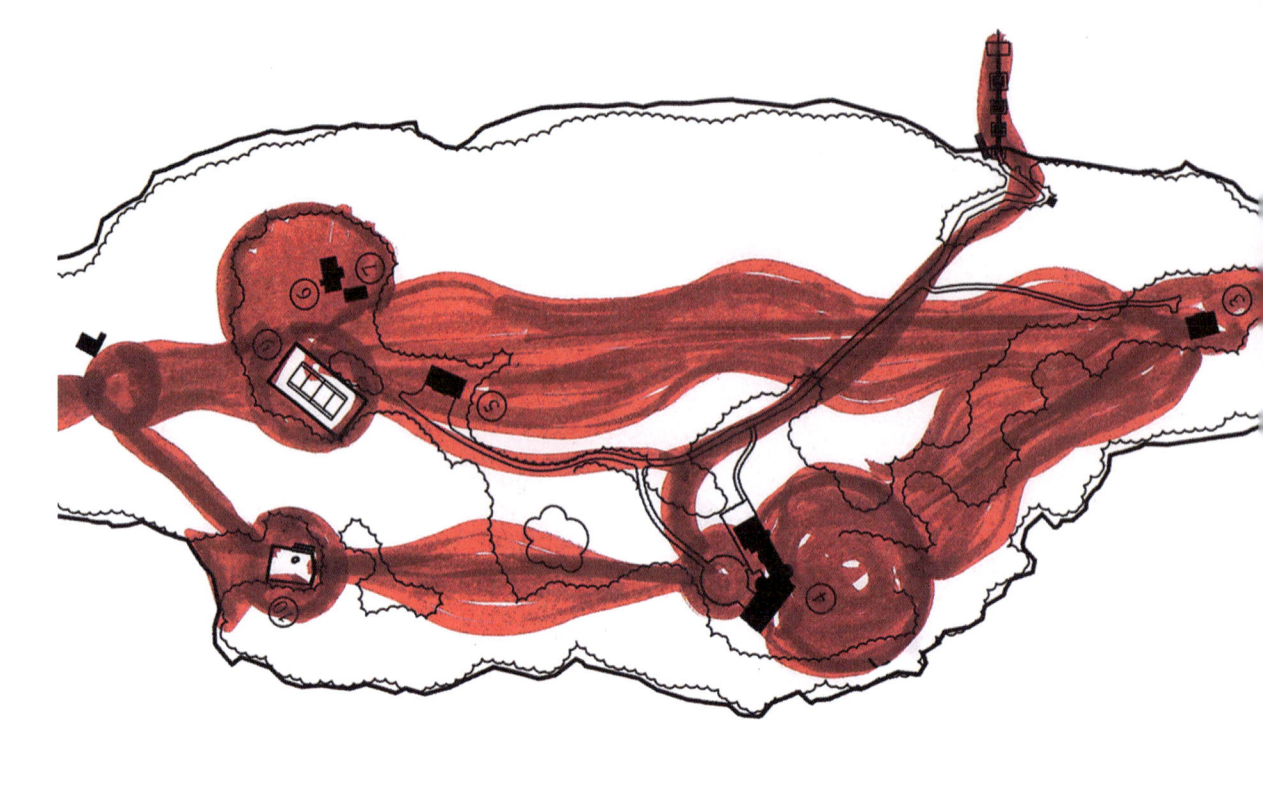

PAVILLION BALDESBERGER,
LUGANO, SWITZERLAND, 2010
For this project, the designer was asked to create a masterplan for both house and garden. This sketch, drawn with Flo-Master pens, represents the way the space was apportioned to find connections between house and landscape and a 'middle way' of expressing a single overarching idea for the project.

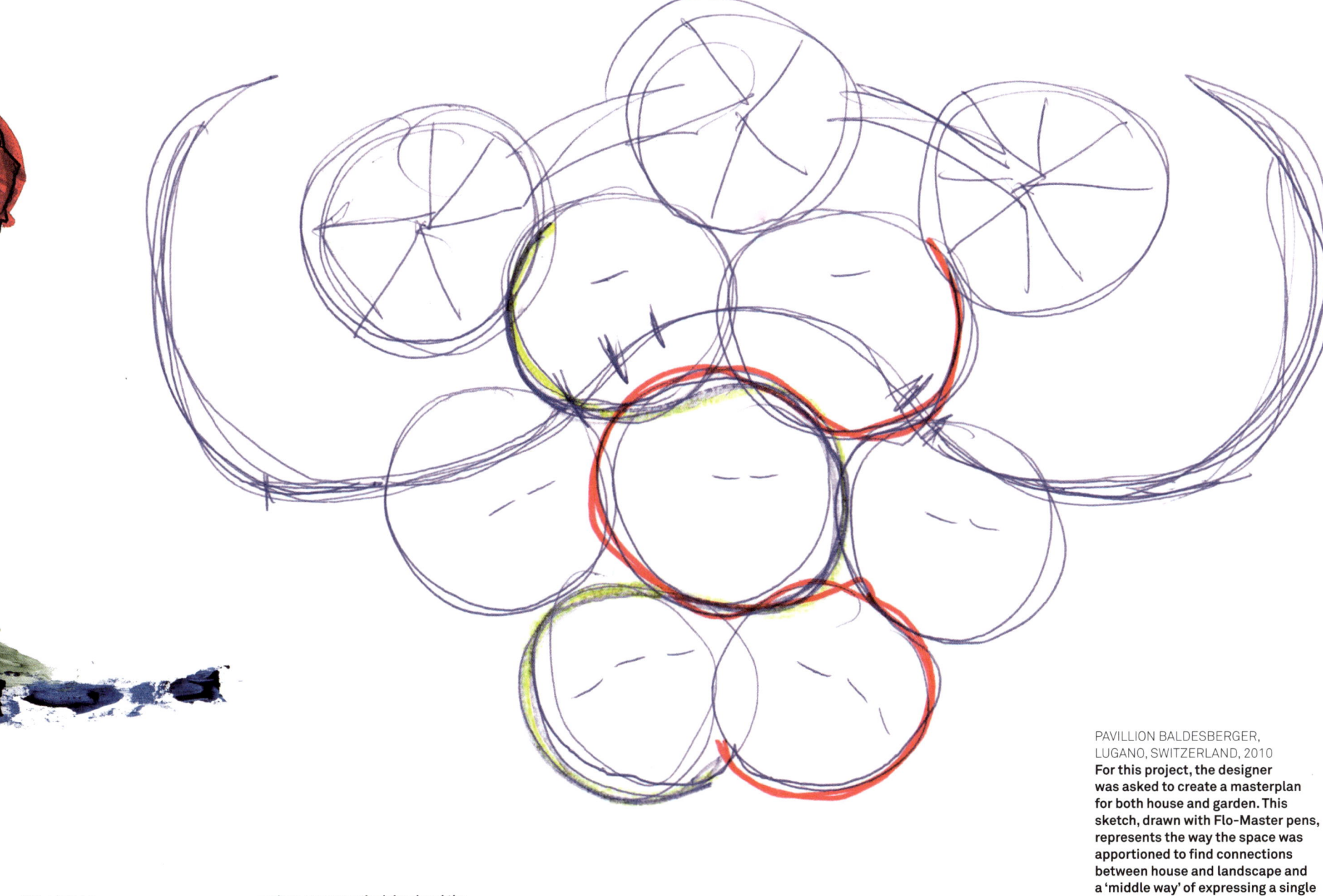

ISOLA BELLA,
MAINE, USA, 2013
This pair of sketches (left) express complementary ideas for a landscape design on an island in Maine. The Flo-Master pen drawing at the top, titled *The Swimmer*, illustrates the internal connections between various areas on the island and the way different spaces open up to create new perspectives. The acrylic sketch below shows the island as a green mass above the intense blue of the ocean. These drawings are not explicatory tools for clients: they are the private thoughts of the designer.

JARDINES DE PEREDA, SANTANDER, SPAIN, 2015
The objective was simple: to connect the geometry of the garden with that of the adjacent Botín Centre, designed by Renzo Piano, and the setting of the bay (below). The idea was that the blue of the ground plane would appear to merge with the sea beyond, while reflecting the brilliant mother-of-pearl of the building, like a seashell set in a garden facing the water.

DESIGN FOR A HOUSE AND GARDEN, AUCKLAND, NEW ZEALAND, 2005
The major elements of this sketch (right) are the bay setting of the house and garden, and a volcanic island, which serves as an eye-catcher. As a means of viewing this land- and seascape, a pavilion was constructed in front of a crescent-shaped pool, on top of a little mound of vegetation. From here, the strongly geometric character of the landscape could be appreciated.

CAPRICHOSA,
SEVILLE, SPAIN, 2002
The agricultural gardens of the ancient world of Islamic Spain had a strongly orthogonal expression, reflected in this Flo-Master pen sketch for a garden in Seville (below).

COTONER GARDEN,
MALLORCA, SPAIN, 1991
In this acryllic sketch (right), each square in the grid contains a different group of plants – palms, olives – which open an arrow-like perspective towards a crescent of cypress trees. At the centre is a pond, with the whole wrapped in an ellipse of wheat.

Fernando Caruncho

Claude Cormier

Montreal, Canada

The conceptual work of this well-established but still-behaving-badly practice is characterized formally by the gutsy use of colour, pattern and texture, and imaginatively by humour and an irreverent attitude to history – qualities that are expressed in the company's preparatory and presentation drawings. It is not surprising that the concept of 'play' is an important component of the working method, although it does not undercut the overall seriousness of the endeavour.

Claude Cormier writes: 'The design process is eminently non-linear, and that immediacy is made possible through the use of hand-drawing, which is of the highest importance in the firm's methodology. More than anything, drawing requires intention: the act becomes a means of crystallizing the intent. Being unadulterated by technological interference and by the "noise" of technical prerequisites, it allows us to address what truly drives the project, and to "play" with it freely.

'But drawing does not constitute an absolute result. A sketch plays a role similar to that of a sentence in a conversation – it is food for thought and exchange. It allows for open-ended discussions. In that sense, drawing can be understood as the polar opposite of a PowerPoint or other presentation, where the audience is placed in front of a fait accompli that unfolds before their eyes, and where they are politely but firmly instructed to wait until the presentation is over before they can offer any opinion.

'The inherent risk of this mode of presentation is that it is draped in an aura of accomplishment – it invites criticism of the minutest details, or mesmerizes the audience with the less important elements of the proposal. A sketch, on the other hand, generally omits superfluous detail and sets the parameters for a discussion about the underlying motivations behind a proposed project – its soul, one might say.'

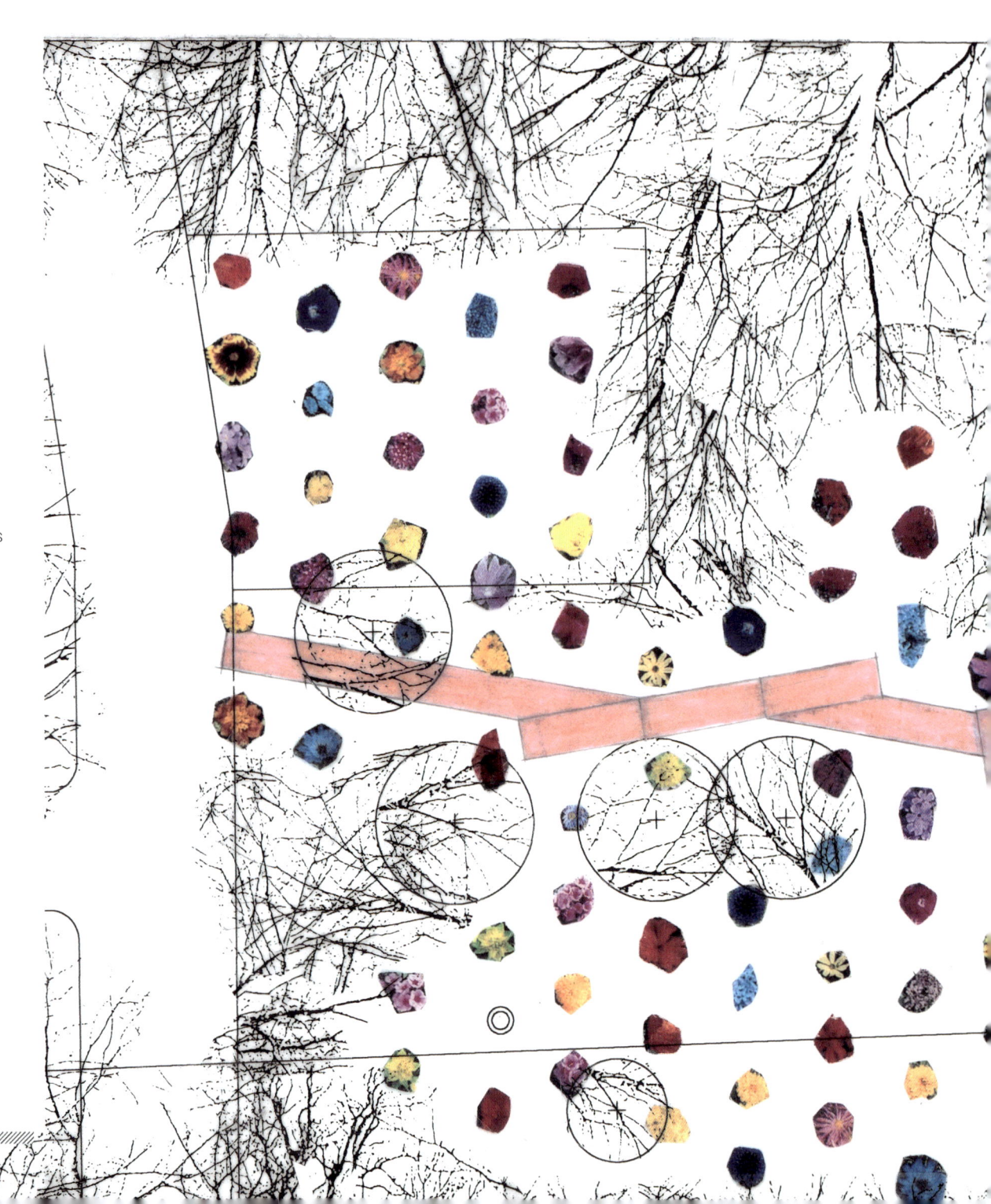

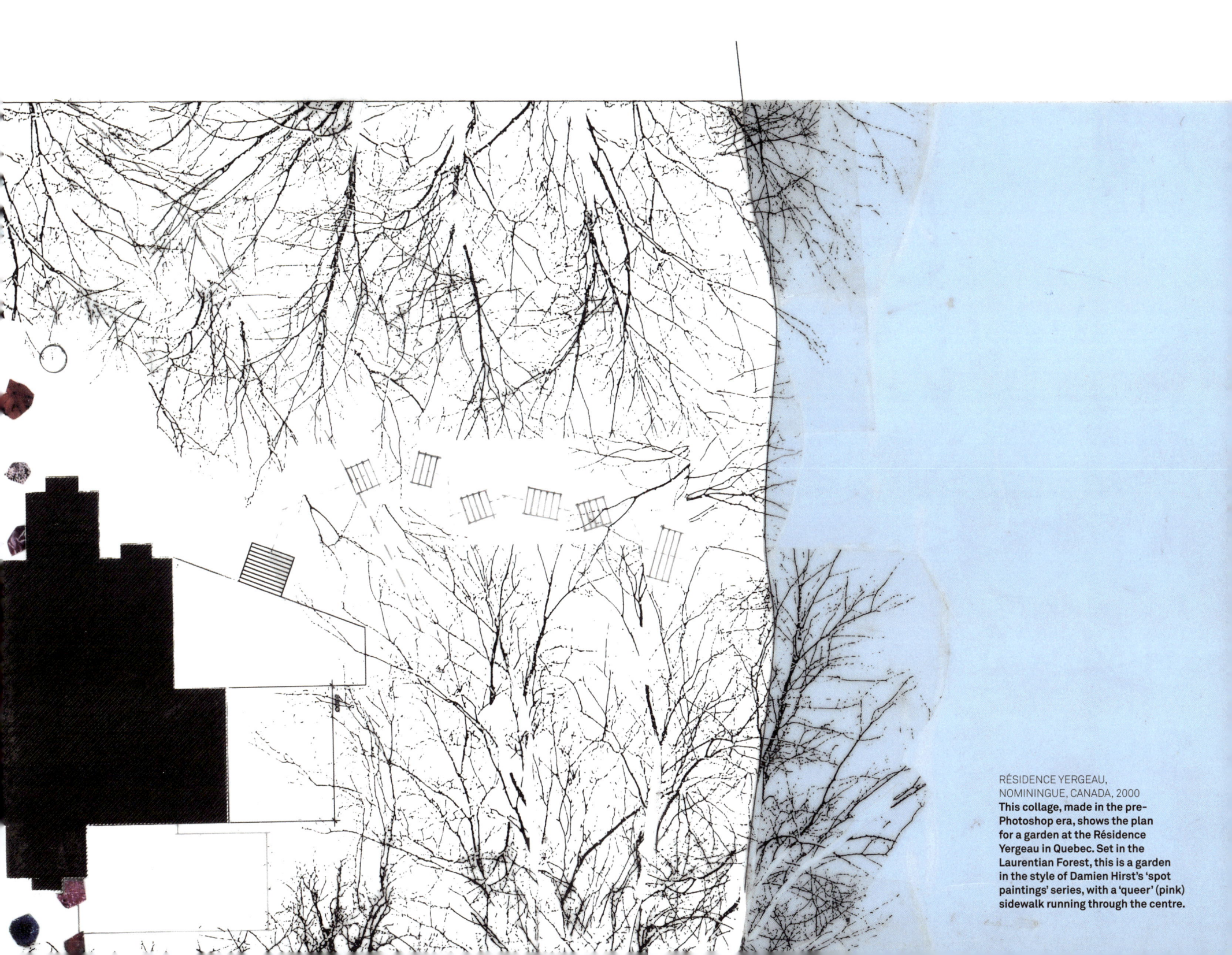

RÉSIDENCE YERGEAU, NOMININGUE, CANADA, 2000
This collage, made in the pre-Photoshop era, shows the plan for a garden at the Résidence Yergeau in Quebec. Set in the Laurentian Forest, this is a garden in the style of Damien Hirst's 'spot paintings' series, with a 'queer' (pink) sidewalk running through the centre.

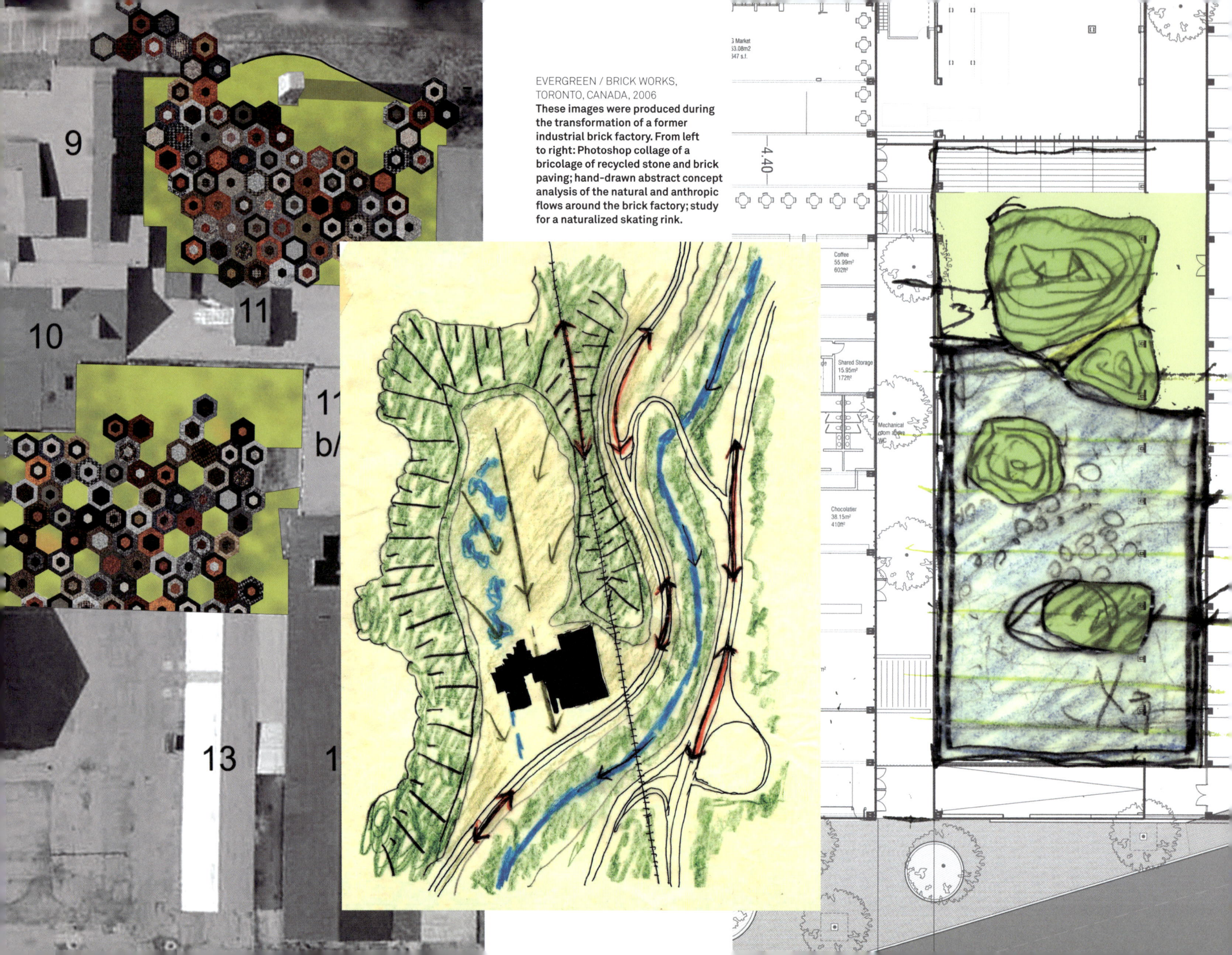

EVERGREEN / BRICK WORKS,
TORONTO, CANADA, 2006
These images were produced during the transformation of a former industrial brick factory. From left to right: Photoshop collage of a bricolage of recycled stone and brick paving; hand-drawn abstract concept analysis of the natural and anthropic flows around the brick factory; study for a naturalized skating rink.

HTO PARK AND URBAN BEACH,
TORONTO, CANADA, 2002
These sketches show the individual conceptual layers that create the transition from city to lake along the urban waterfront.

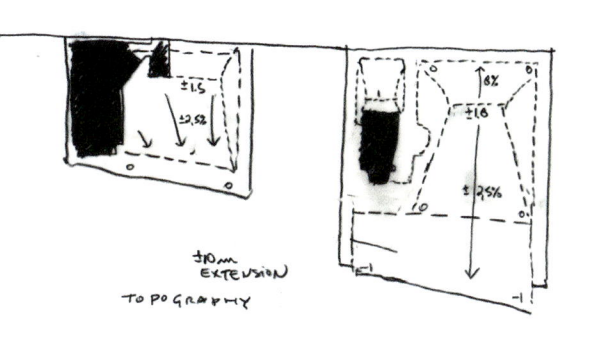

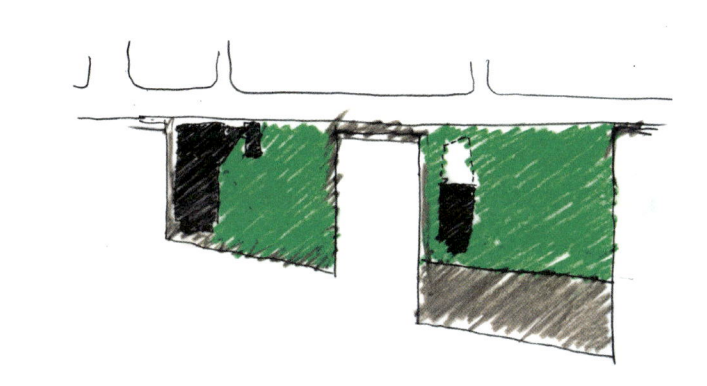

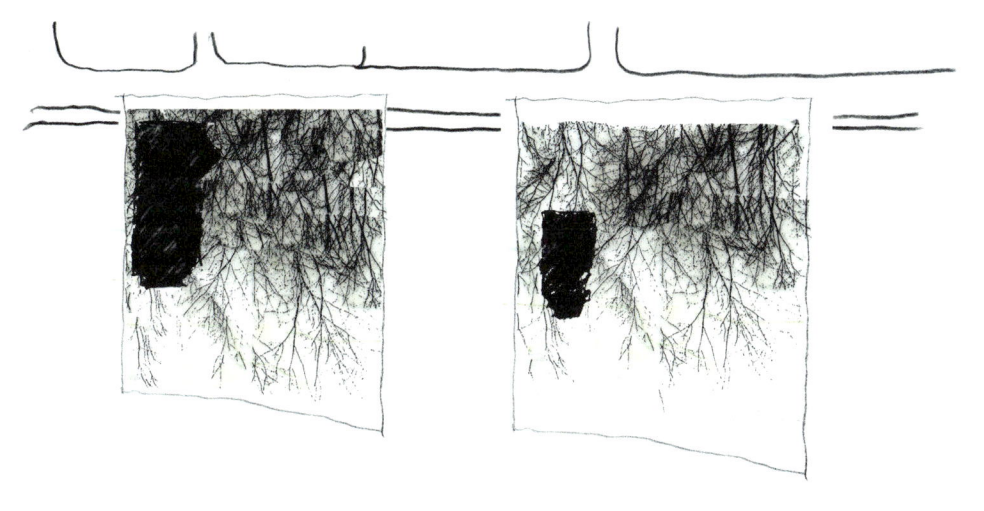

TOPOGRAPHY

GREEN

DUNES

WATER MARKS

PHILLIPS SQUARE,
MONTREAL, CANADA, 1997
Fabric samples in various iterations of Prince of Wales Check (below) were used to create a collage of the proposed redesign of Phillips Square (right). The 'weave' of black and white pavers transposed onto the ground plane is a nod to the monument to Edward VII in the square, and an acknowledgment of his tastes in fashion.

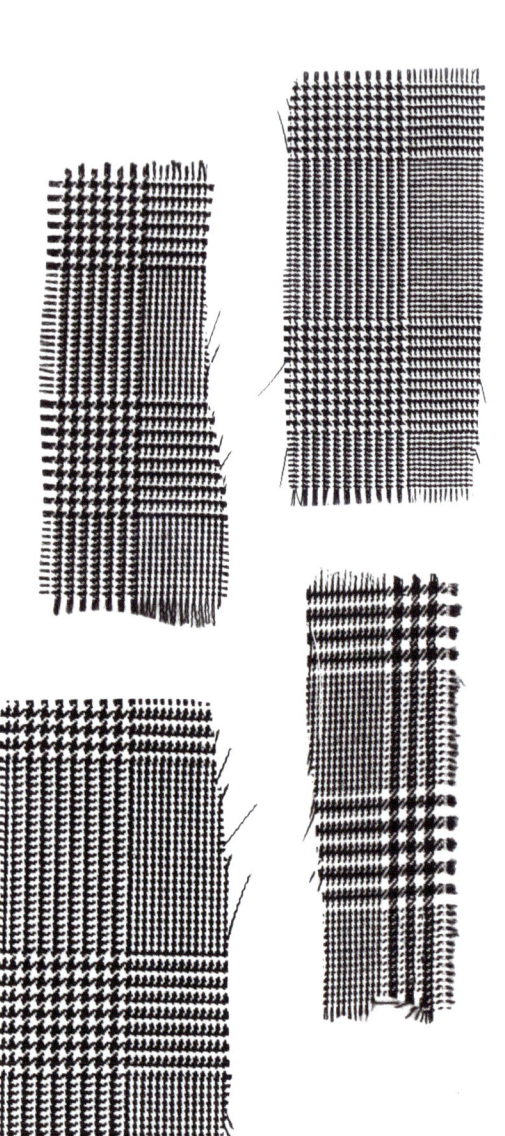

GARRISON POINT,
TORONTO, CANADA, 2012
This collage captures the design intention: an Olympic-sized swimming pool with an urban-skyline infinity edge within a new 3.5-hectare (14-acre) park in downtown Toronto. The collage consists of photography of the city skyline set over David Hockney's *Paper Pool 25*.

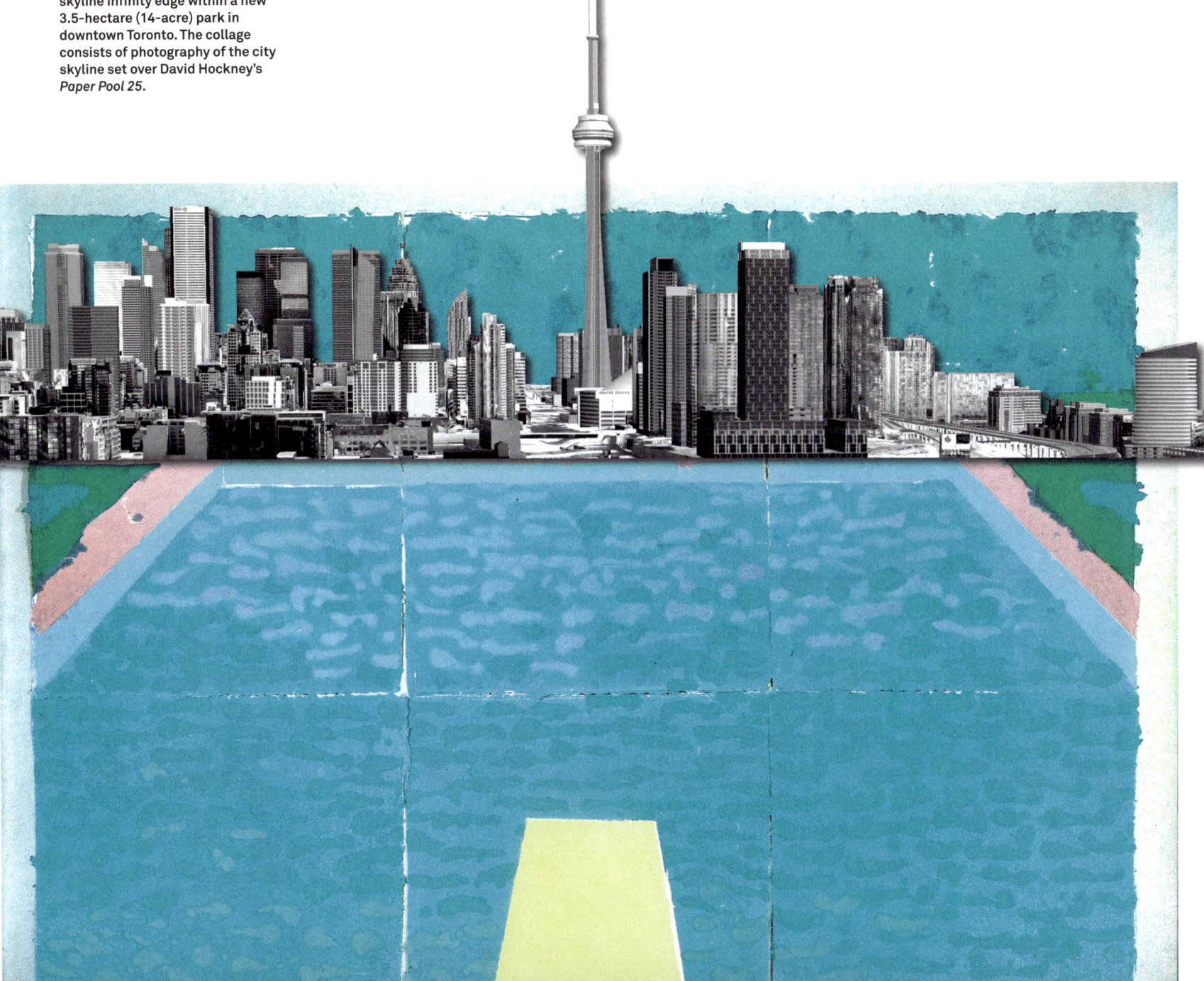

Paul de Kort

De Meern, Netherlands

It is relatively unusual for landscape designers to work with visual artists, but Paul de Kort has struck up a good working relationship with Parklaan Landscape Architects and several other companies. The clarity of intention signalled by the working drawings illustrated here is something that remains at the heart of a project from start to finish, not least because the artist is present as an advocate of this element of a design, which might otherwise easily be altered or reduced.

Paul de Kort writes: 'The sketches and visualizations shown in these pages span a period of more than two decades. It was during this period that computers and digital-drawing programs were introduced into the field of design. The drawings for Mandercirkels [right] explore whether my interventions would work on the scale of the site, inspiring a series of elaborate drawings that helped persuade my client to realize my ideas. The visualizations turned out to be extremely helpful during the process of trying to inspire potential sponsors.

'When I made some rough sketches for the Open (Polder) project in 2006 [overleaf], the computer had already taken up an important space in my design practice. But in that early phase, when developing ideas exist only in my head, I like to explore them with just a pencil or pen on any scrap of paper that happens to be at hand. Afterwards I cherish these early studies as the first steps of what, sometimes years later, becomes a beautiful and complete work of art.

'This is also true of some of the sketches for Thesaurus Fectio [pp. 68-9], a collaboration with Parklaan. In these and other visualizations, hand-drawn sketches and photographs were put together in Photoshop to create a single coherent image. For a design team, visualizations are also a way of seeing if everyone is "on the same page". It is also a good way of improving the developing design.'

Paul de Kort

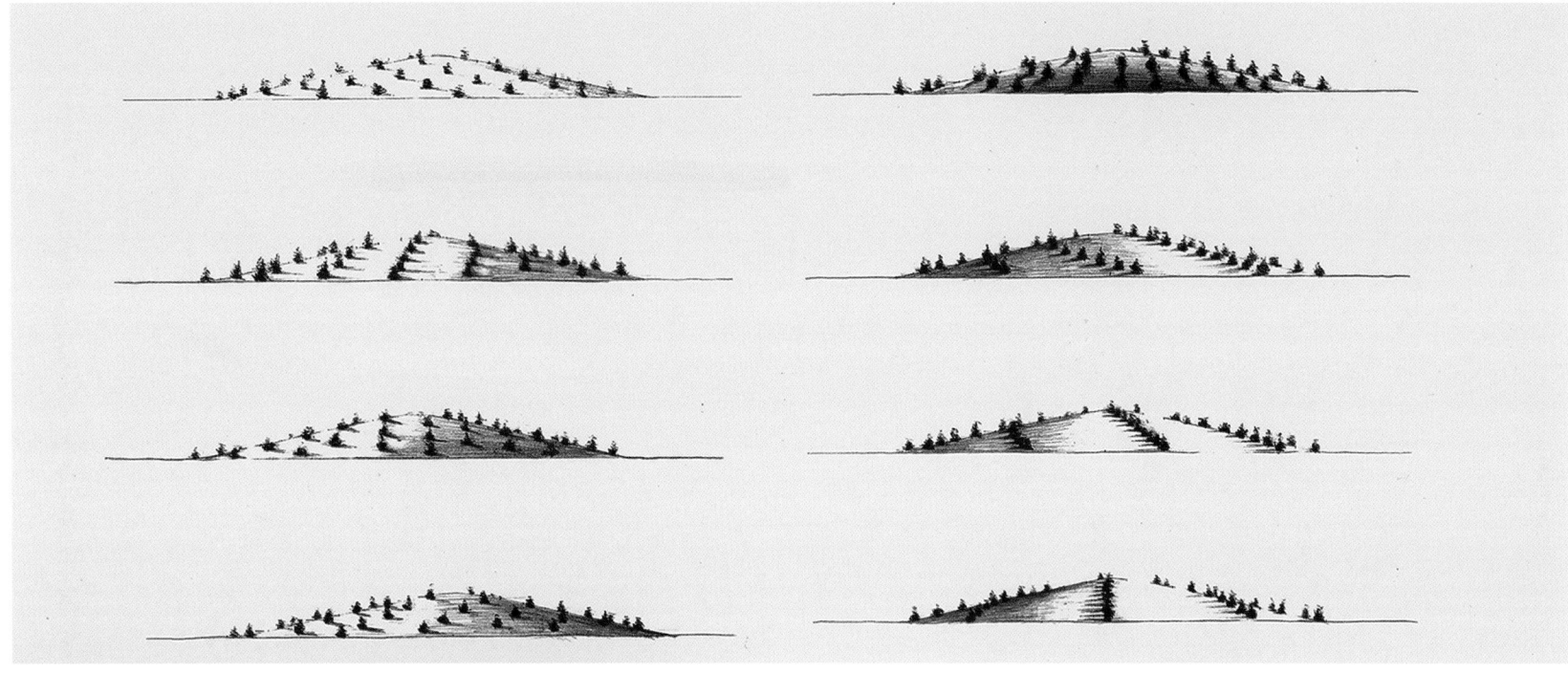

MANDERCIRKELS,
TWENTE, NETHERLANDS, 1999
Studies in graphite on paper, made in 1994–5 for the preparation and presentation of a landscape-art project in Twente, near the village of Mander. These early designs are strikingly similar to aerial photos taken after the project was completed in 1999.

Paul de Kort

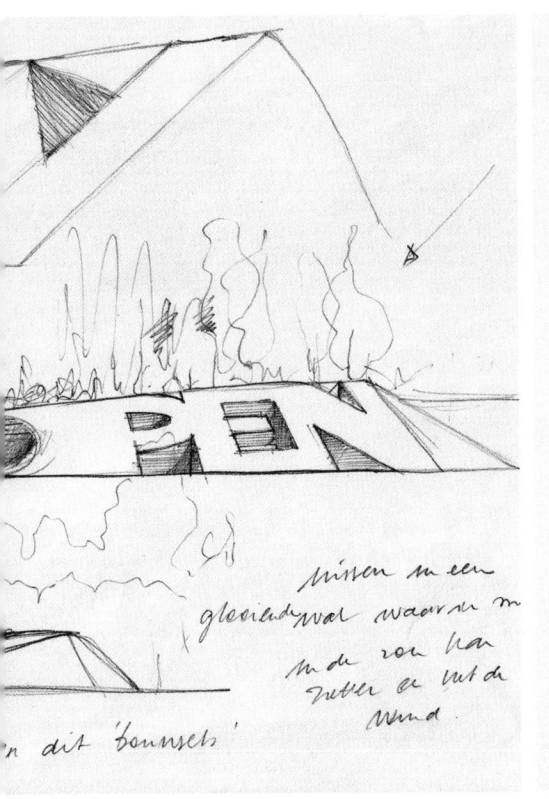

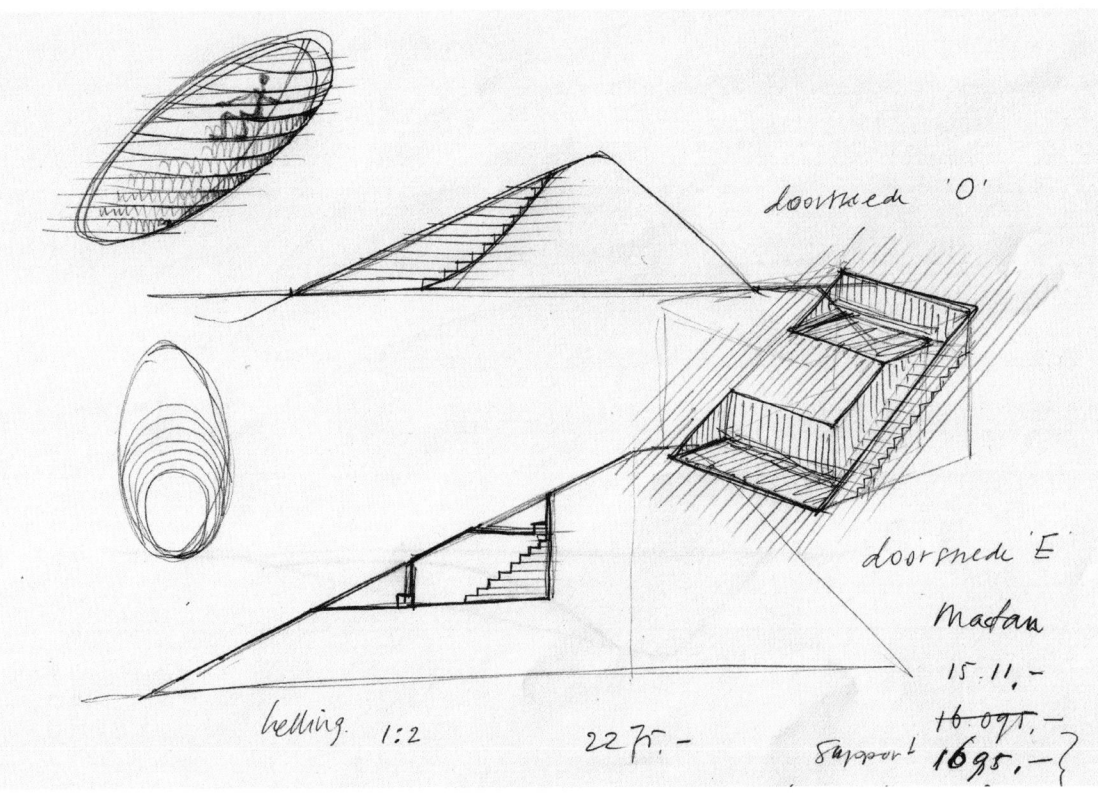

OPEN (POLDER),
NIJMEGEN, NETHERLANDS, 2011
Sketches and visualizations for the exploration and presentation of ideas related to a landscape-art project in the Ooijpolder, near Nijmegen. They were executed in pencil and graphite on paper, and mixed media including Photoshop.

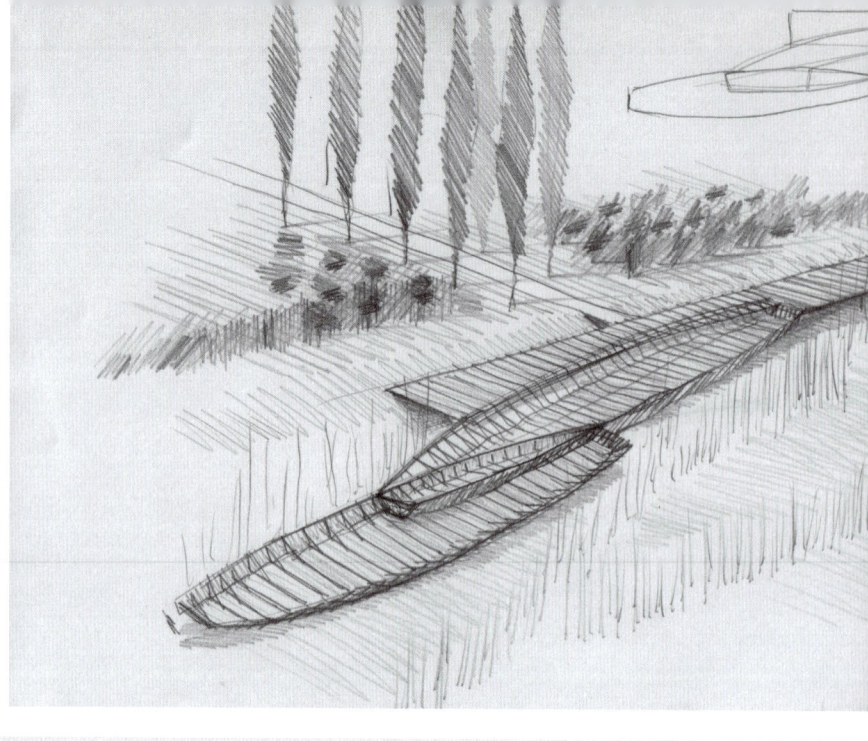

THESAURUS FECTIO,
UTRECHT, NETHERLANDS, 2015
Visualizations of the Roman Castellum Fectio, an archaeological site southeast of Utrecht. These sketches were made for the presentation of the project, which was realized in collaboration with Parklaan Landscape Architects.

69 Paul de Kort

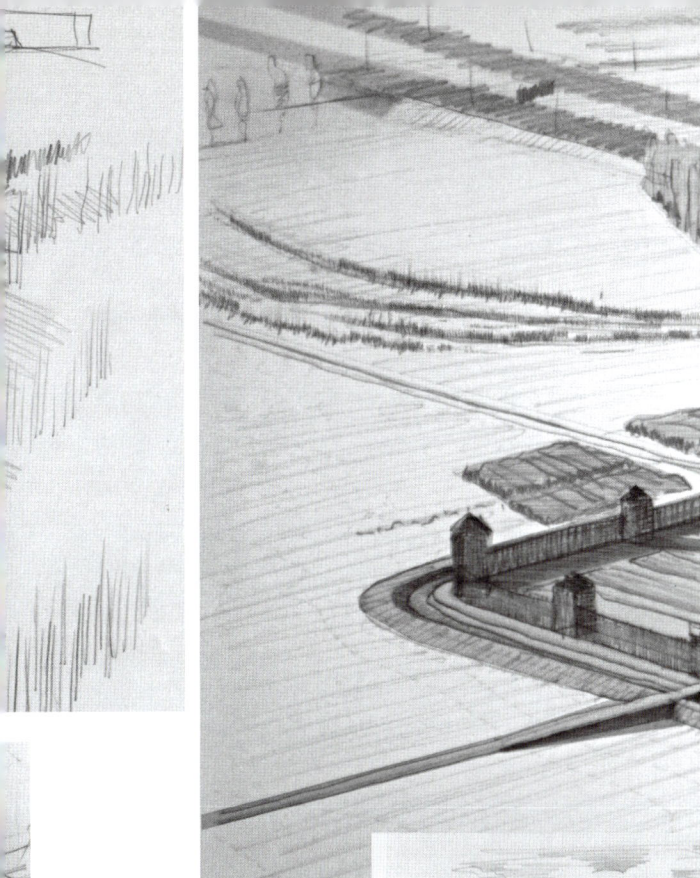

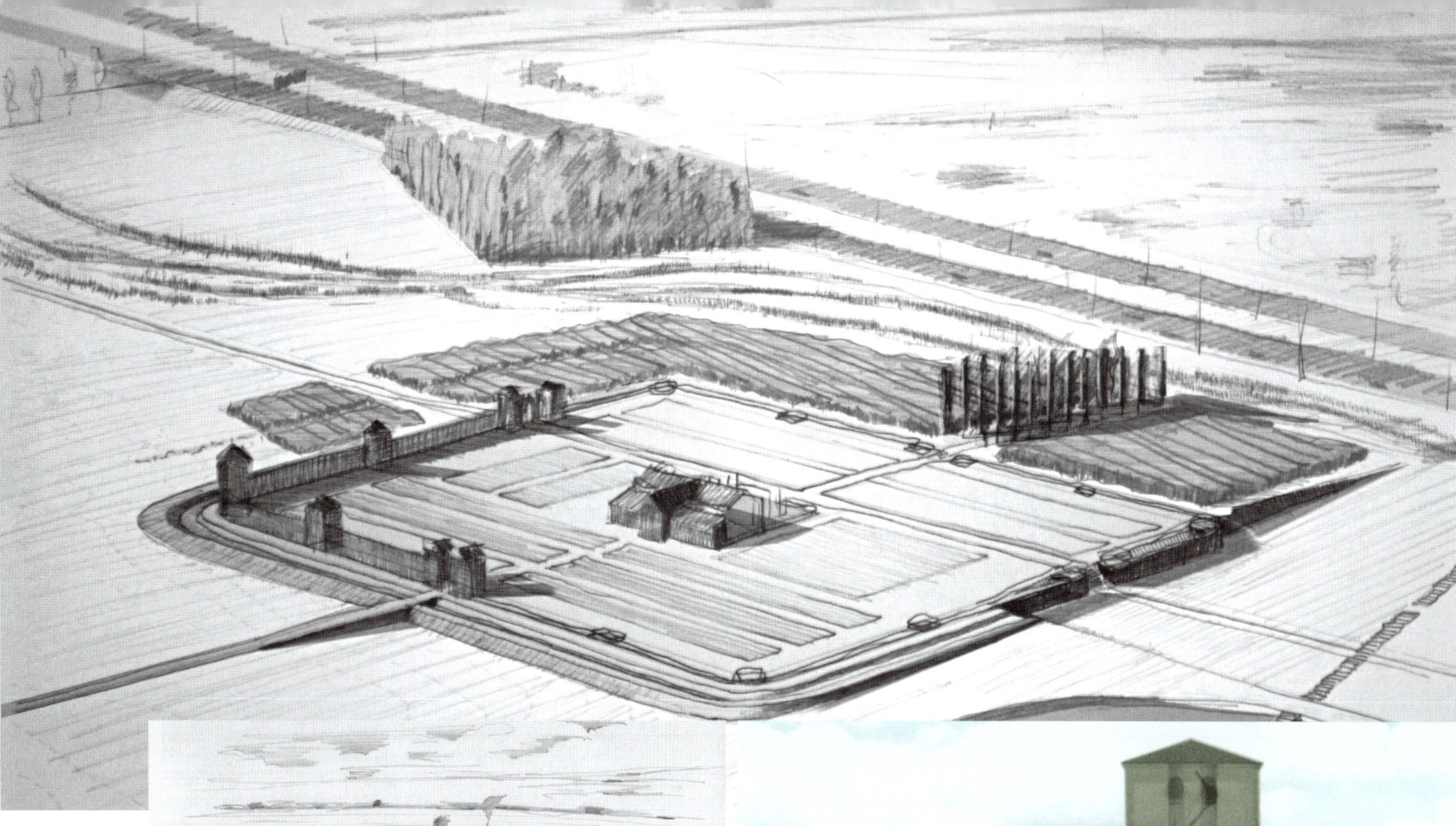

Doxiadis+
Athens, Greece

Thomas Doxiadis says he studied architecture 'at the cusp'. When he entered the Graduate School of Design at Harvard University in 1993, the great majority of students were drawing by hand. When he graduated five years later, almost everyone was working on their projects digitally. When teaching at the university during 2003–7, he saw that some students were content to forego hand-sketching altogether. And he says that for a long period through the 1990s and 2000s, clients seemed most impressed with photorealistic images. But now, he says, the tide is starting to turn …

Thomas Doxiadis writes: 'The sketch is a way of thinking. It allows us to communicate with ourselves, with each other and ultimately with the client. Sketching allows the distillation not only of a project's essence, but also of its dynamic character. We use sketches to explore and communicate how things will change over time. After consuming the data and requirements of a project and allowing for the necessary mental fermentation, we develop an attitude that will then inform the whole design. We do so collaboratively. We do not see creativity as the pursuit of the lone artist.

'Sketching is a multi-faceted medium. A hand-drawing or a rough model can be a "sketch" of sorts. More and more, we are finding that we can sketch by hand directly onto digital media such as tablets, so we are becoming less concerned with whether the image is analogue or digital, and more concerned with whether or not it captures the form and, more importantly, the spirit of what we are trying to achieve. Different members of our team have different modes of visual expression. After some soul-searching, we decided to let each one of us explore his or her own mode of expression freely, rather than establish a standard corporate style.'

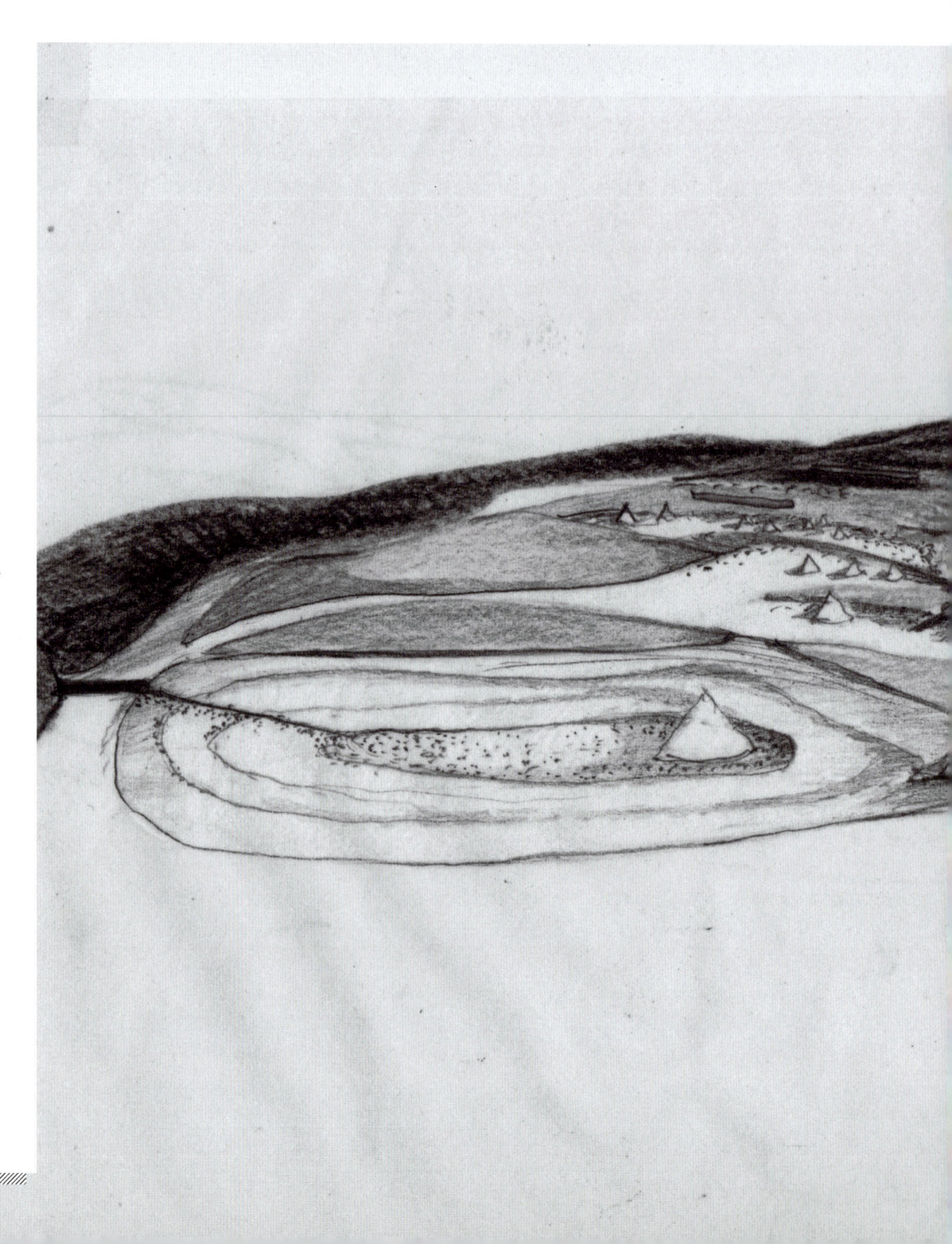

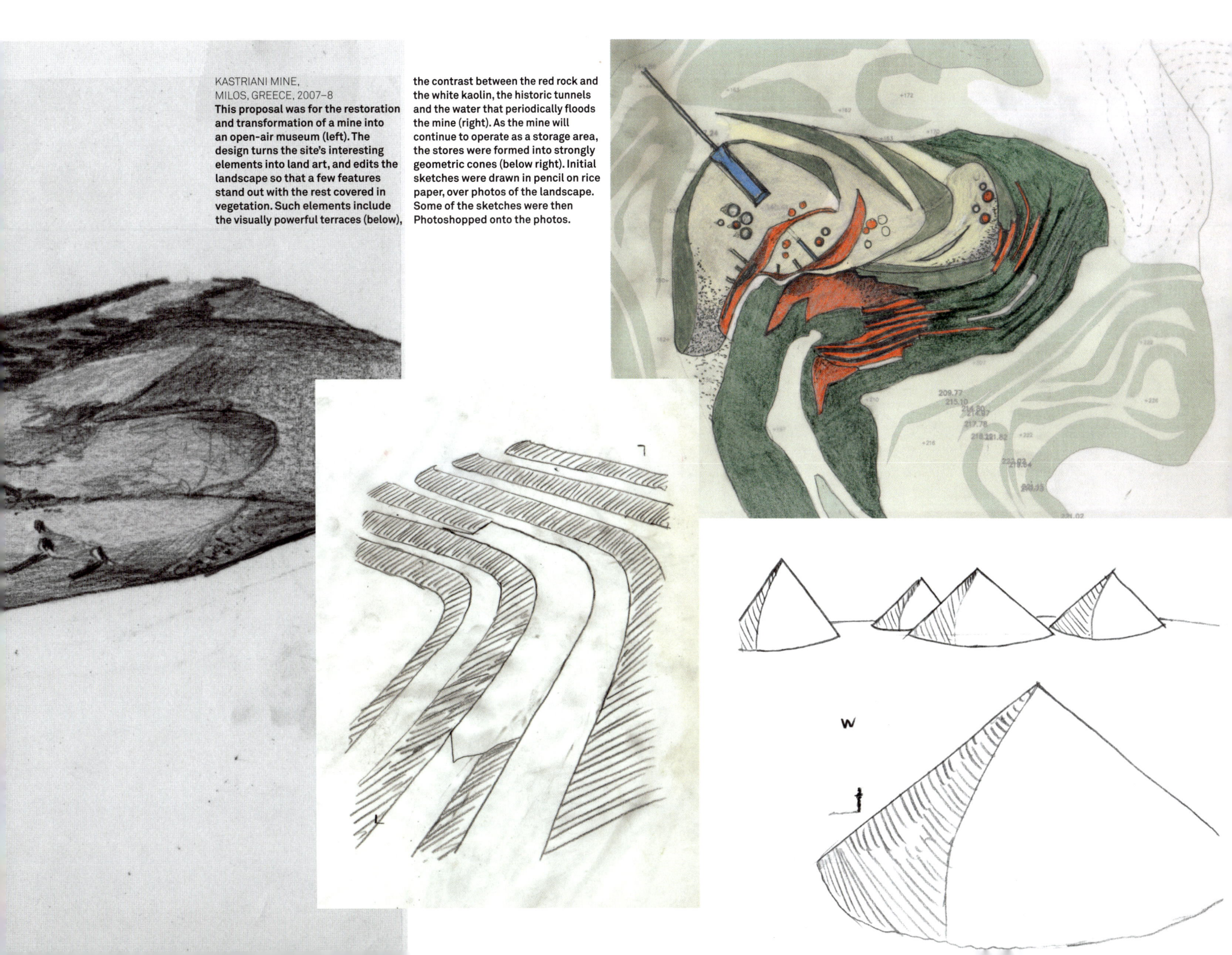

KASTRIANI MINE,
MILOS, GREECE, 2007–8
This proposal was for the restoration and transformation of a mine into an open-air museum (left). The design turns the site's interesting elements into land art, and edits the landscape so that a few features stand out with the rest covered in vegetation. Such elements include the visually powerful terraces (below), the contrast between the red rock and the white kaolin, the historic tunnels and the water that periodically floods the mine (right). As the mine will continue to operate as a storage area, the stores were formed into strongly geometric cones (below right). Initial sketches were drawn in pencil on rice paper, over photos of the landscape. Some of the sketches were then Photoshopped onto the photos.

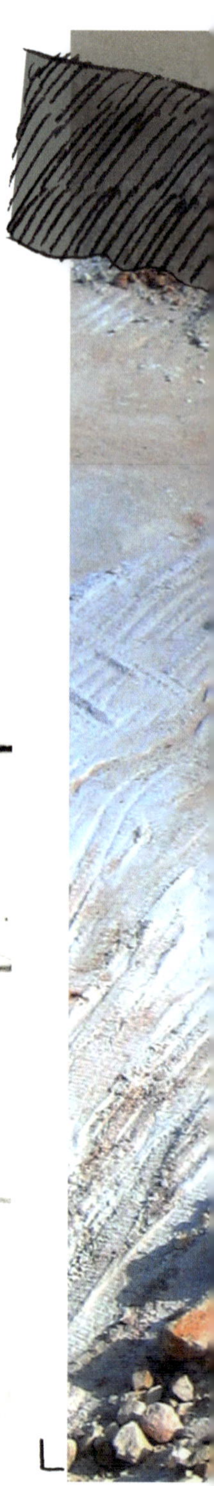

KASTRIANI MINE,
MILOS, GREECE, 2007–8
The 'edited' terraces, with a line of red earth left visible through the vegetation (above left). This sketch (above right) captures the atmosphere of the hand-hewn galleries as entrances to the 'underworld', or to what is unreachable. The cutting that connects the water in the mine to the stream beyond (right). Proposal for the edited landscape, with boulders strewn as if thrown by a Cyclops (opposite, left). Sketch illustrating the flooded mine in winter (opposite, above right). The mounds of kaolin (opposite, below right).

73 Doxiadis+

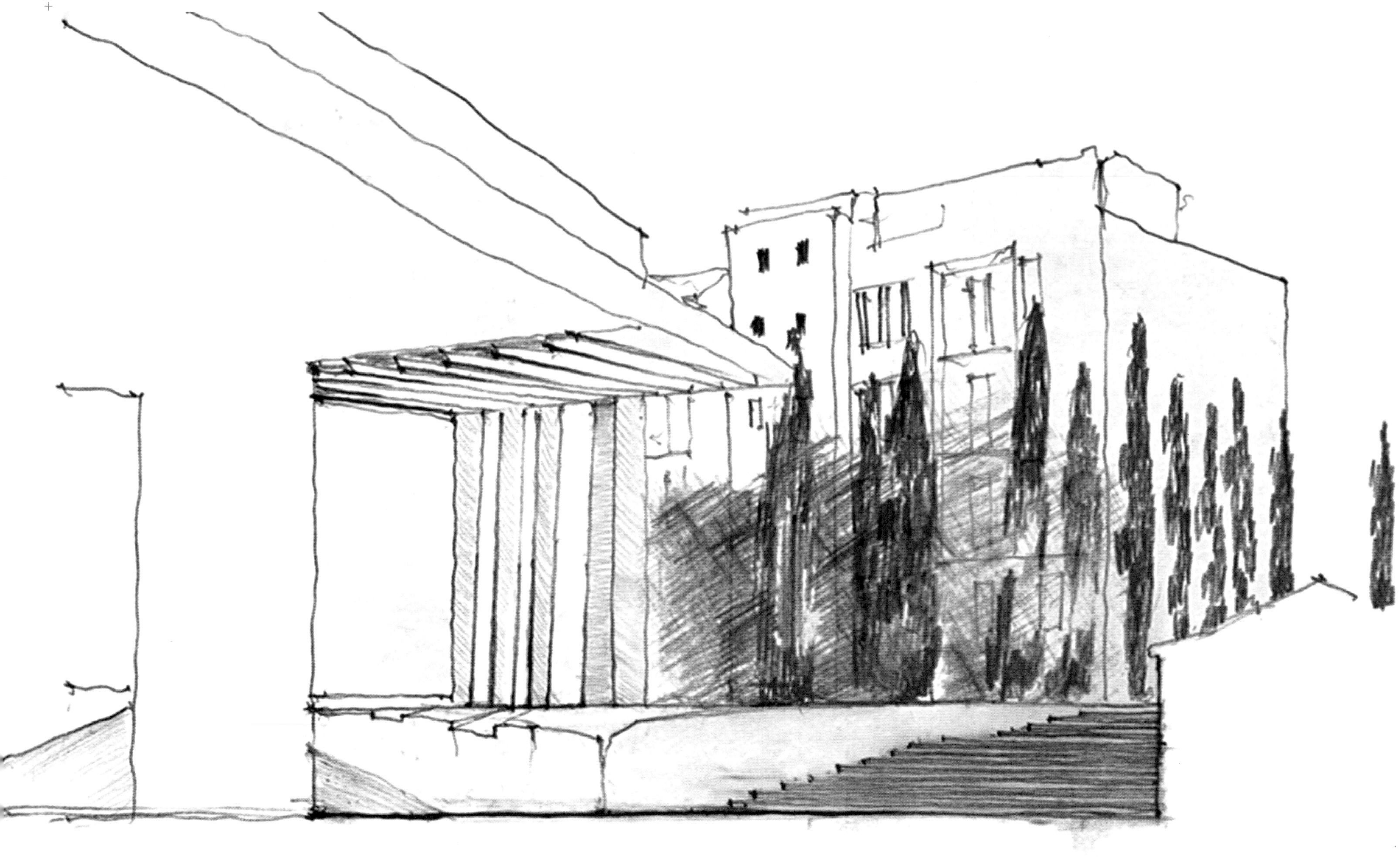

THE ROCK,
ATHENS, GREECE, 2008

Sketches for the winning entry in a competition for the design of the urban landscape at the New Acropolis Museum. The team decided that the existing buildings at the site should not be hidden from view but integrated into a new unity of rocky substrate, buildings, museum and urban space. The medium of pencil on paper was used to abstract and unify the disparate elements of the space and to show that the simple devices of a worn stone platform and a grove of cypress trees can resolve the difficult relationships between existing and new buildings.

Estudio OCA
Barcelona, Spain

The sketches on these pages reveal the rough, if not messy, beginnings of some highly refined projects. One of the paradoxes of drawing is that imagery that lacks the clarity and precision of computerized design contains within it a far clearer and more precise expression of the central move or theme of a nascent design, whether a formal aspect, such as the shape of a park, or an intellectual, aesthetic or emotional idea that will come to inform every aspect of the design as it evolves. Precision is not just about straight lines, as these sketches show.

Estudio OCA states: 'Sketching provides an immediacy for studies used throughout the entire design process. It allows for open experimentation, working through ideas – both good and bad – and then editing these down into a cohesive form. As this iterative process unfolds, relationships begin to appear, leaving a tracing of the formal history of this exploration. This history represents not just formal and spatial intent: representations of ephemerality and movement begin to appear within the lines, connections, erasures and stacking of drawings.

'Our process begins with conceptual sketches, typically pencil on trace paper, which begin to develop loosely into coherent forms. At a certain point, CAD [computer-aided design] drawings and digital and physical models evolve concurrently, with studies moving between printing, sketching, scanning and refining. This immediacy allows us to sort through potential options at a speed unachievable with current digital solutions. We try to utilize fully the potential of both physical and digital media. As the project moves on, we continue hand-sketching details, studying them to see how they fit within the larger context. These drawings morph into dimensioned computer drawings, which then get printed and overlaid repeatedly.'

77 Estudio OCA

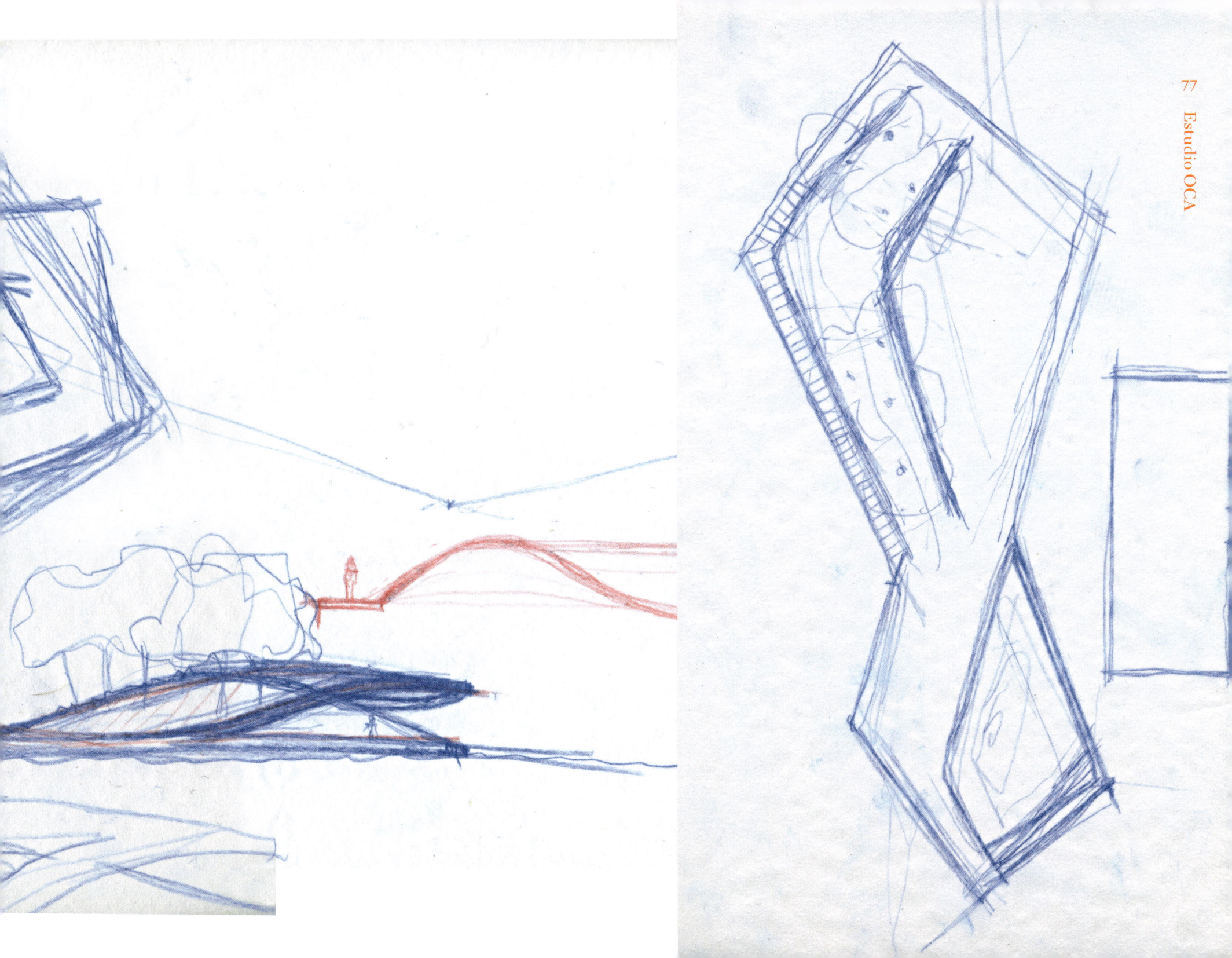

78 Estudio OCA

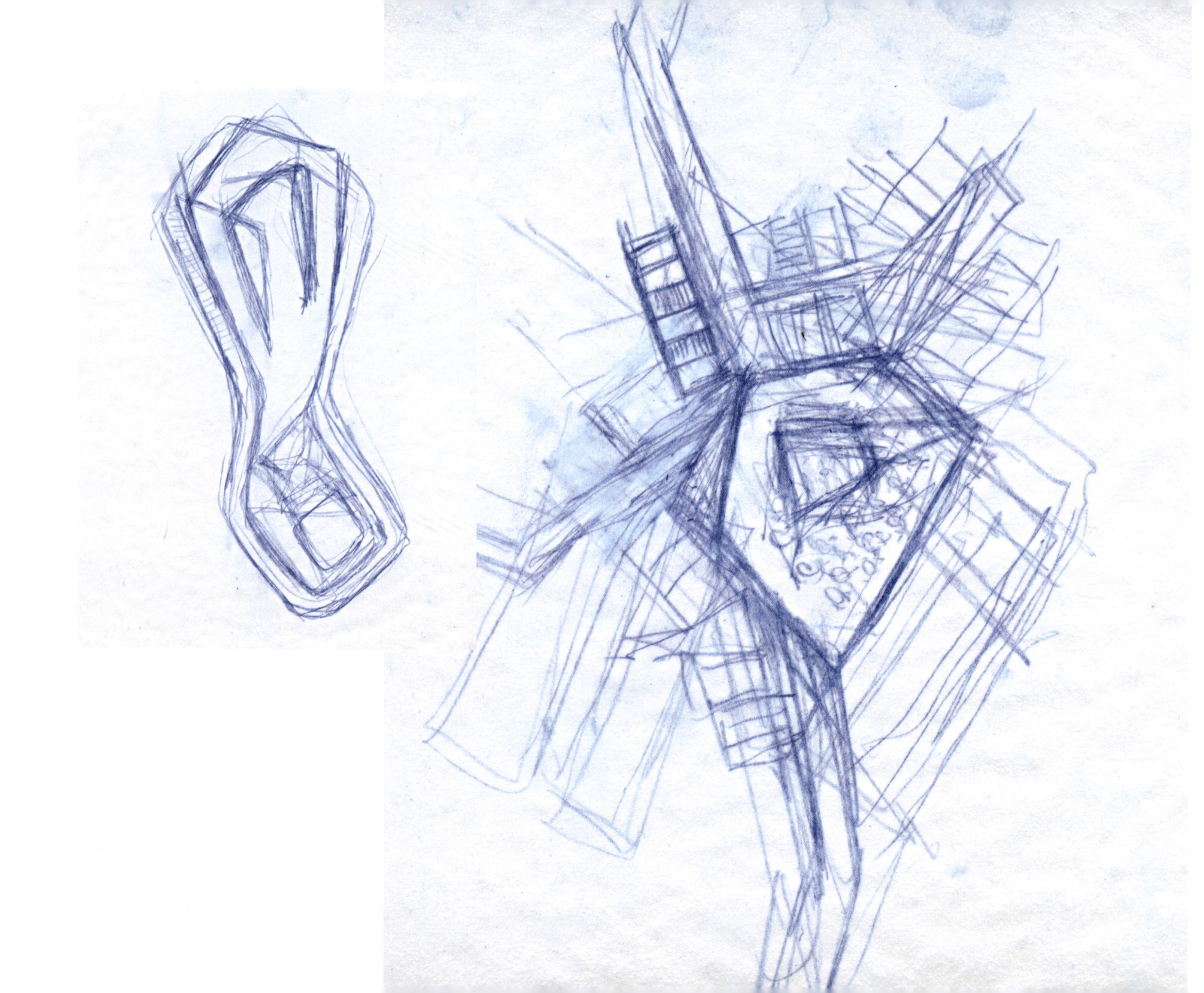

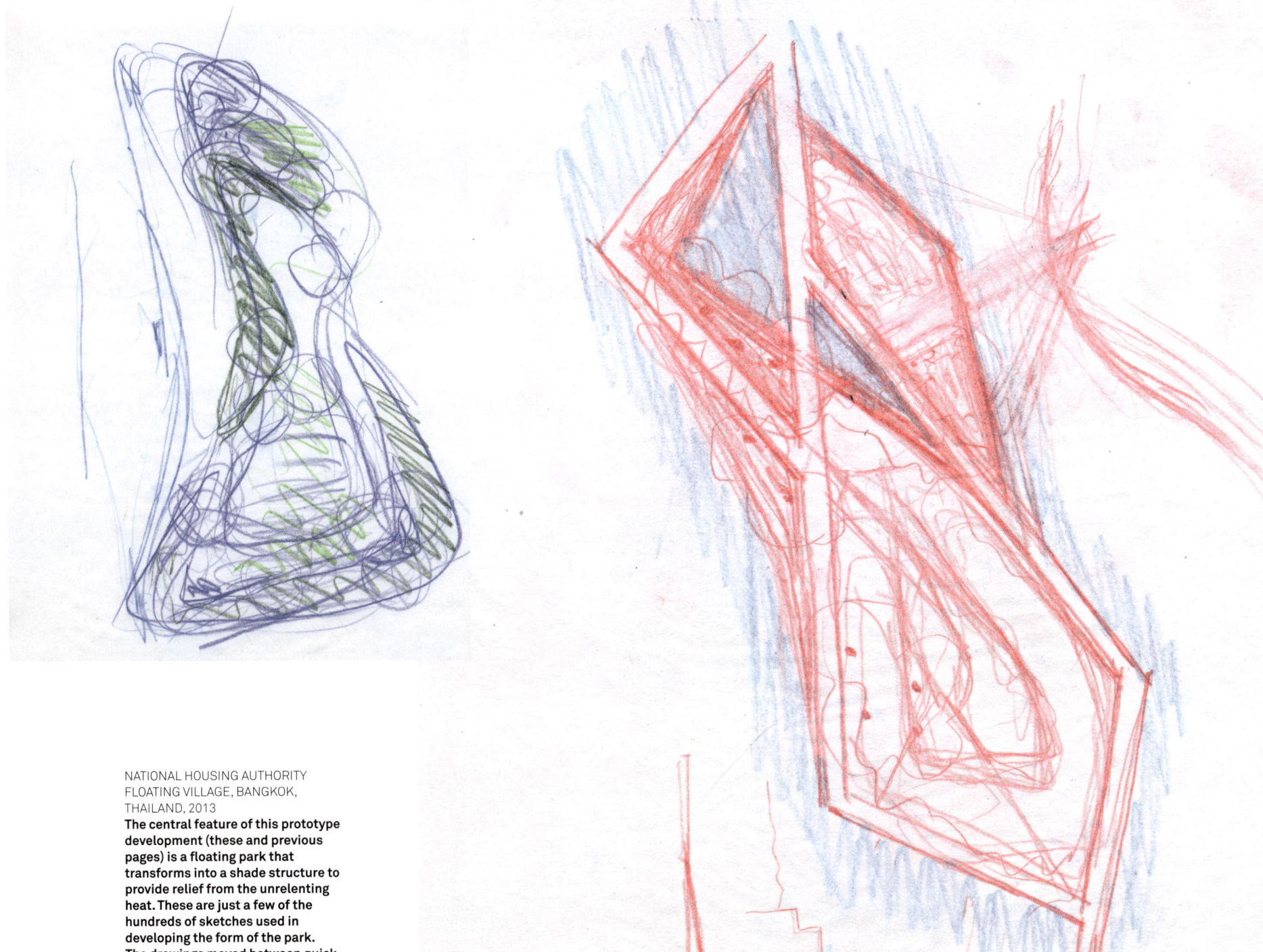

NATIONAL HOUSING AUTHORITY
FLOATING VILLAGE, BANGKOK,
THAILAND, 2013

The central feature of this prototype development (these and previous pages) is a floating park that transforms into a shade structure to provide relief from the unrelenting heat. These are just a few of the hundreds of sketches used in developing the form of the park. The drawings moved between quick sketches, accurate CAD drawings and digital-model studies, all working concurrently to explore optimum forms.

DRAVA RIVER,
MARIBOR, SLOVENIA, 2012

This project was developed by the firm's three offices in three different countries, so the ability to communicate clearly the design intent was critical. As the project aimed to form a cohesive waterfront landscape with little impact, these drawings were more deliberate and careful in their representation of contextual relationships. To maintain this accuracy, dimensional CAD drawings were developed and used as a base for the hand-drawings. The images were only circulated internally; digital models were then developed that were based on approved sketches.

• VIEWING PLATFORM – VIEW TO S

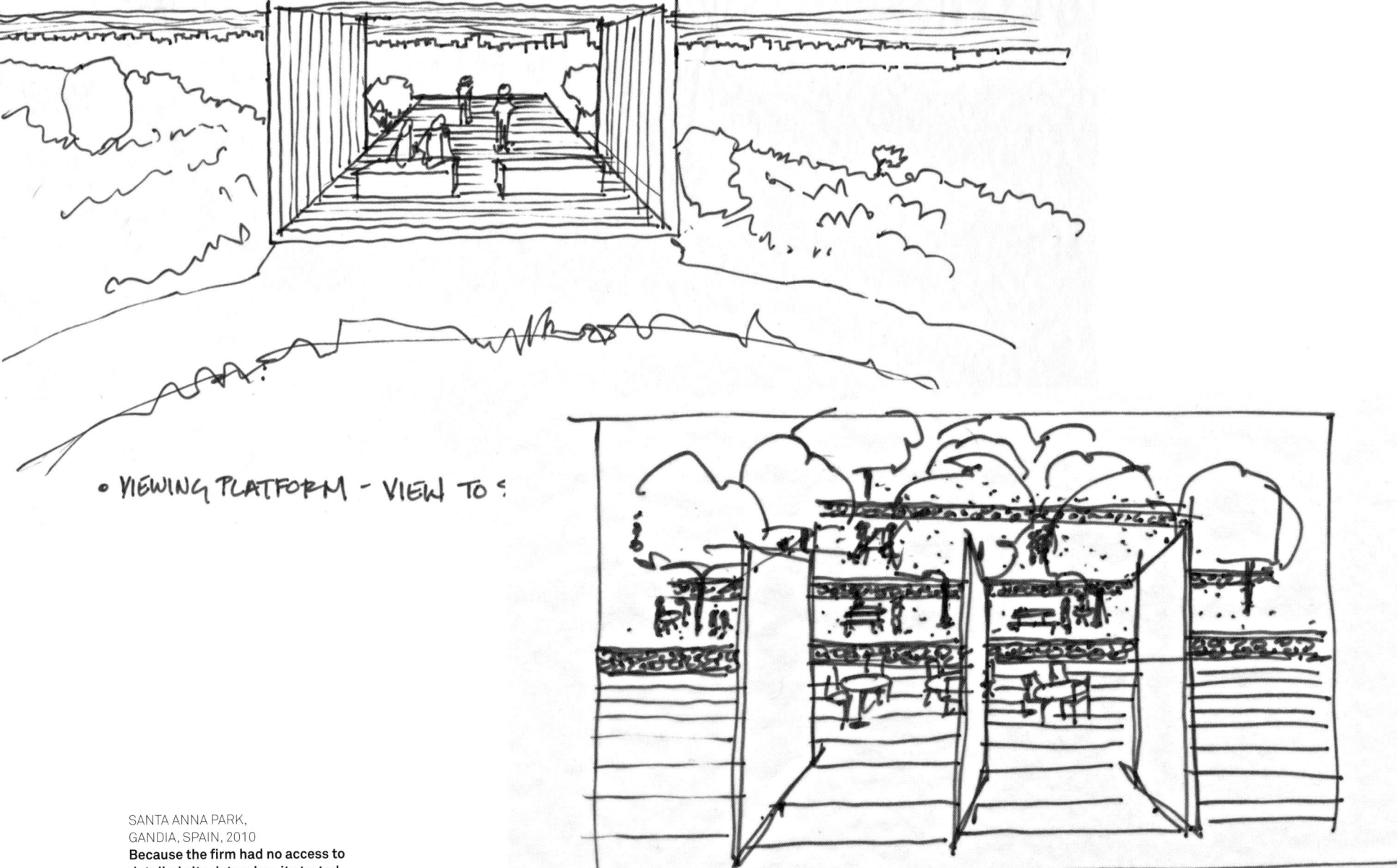

SANTA ANNA PARK,
GANDIA, SPAIN, 2010
Because the firm had no access to detailed site data when it started work on the design, a series of sketches was developed to represent the various possibilities of exploiting the existing landscape to provide a heightened experience of the environment. These vignettes were developed with pen on trace paper, then finalized as more detailed computer models.

• VIEW FROM RESTAURANT TO DINING TERRACE AND ORCHARD

Estudio OCA

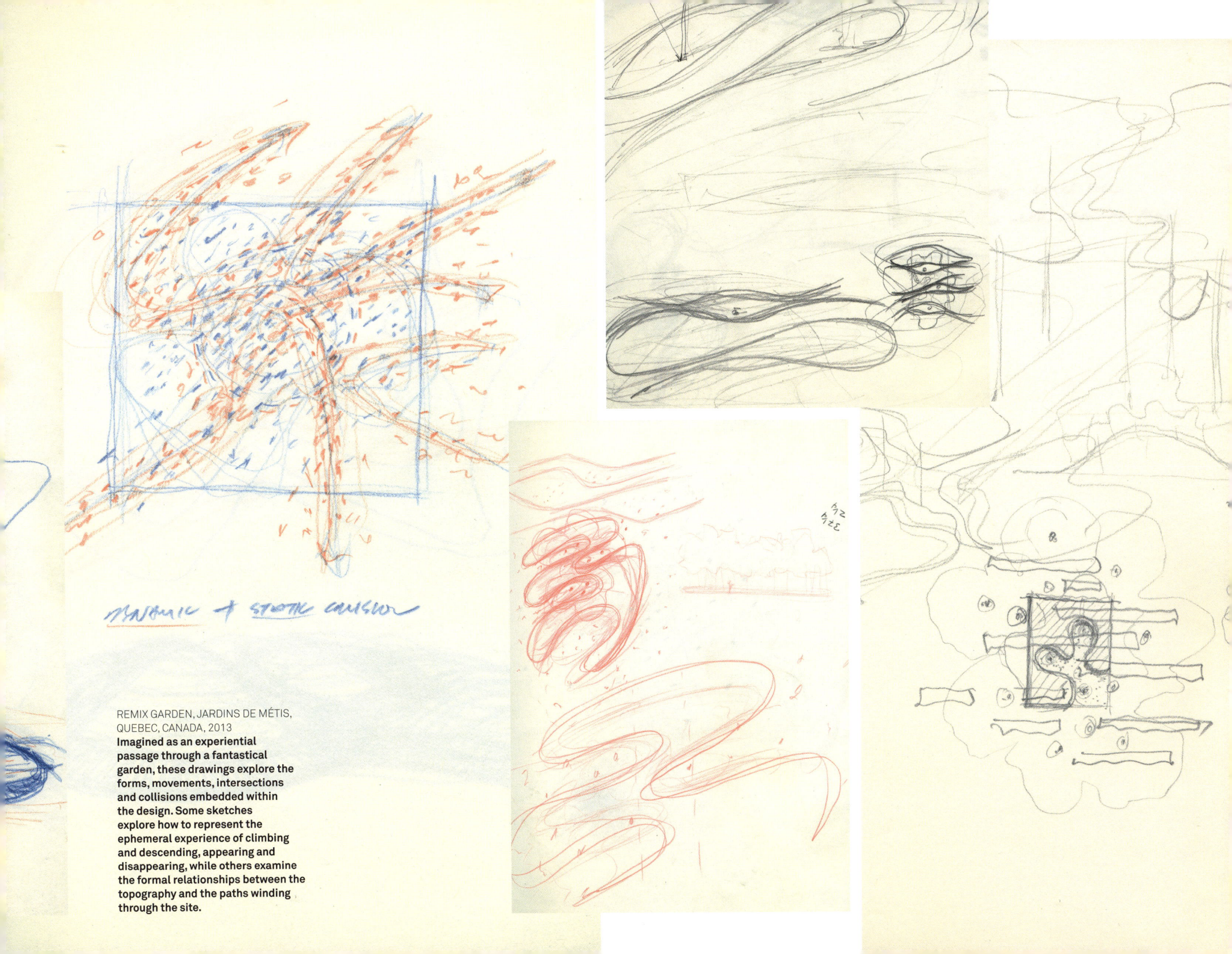

REMIX GARDEN, JARDINS DE MÉTIS, QUEBEC, CANADA, 2013
Imagined as an experiential passage through a fantastical garden, these drawings explore the forms, movements, intersections and collisions embedded within the design. Some sketches explore how to represent the ephemeral experience of climbing and descending, appearing and disappearing, while others examine the formal relationships between the topography and the paths winding through the site.

JINZHOU WORLD LANDSCAPE
ART EXPOSITION, CHINA, 2009
The drawings for this project consist of pencil sketches on trace paper (this page) and pen-on-paper drawings (opposite). The latter explore the idea of the spaces between the landforms and the rhythms created by modulating the vertical dimension, while maintaining horizontal dimensions. The pencil sketches represent a more developed plan, showing the overall layout and the relationships between colour and form. These final drawings were created before a dimensional CAD plan and digital model were developed.

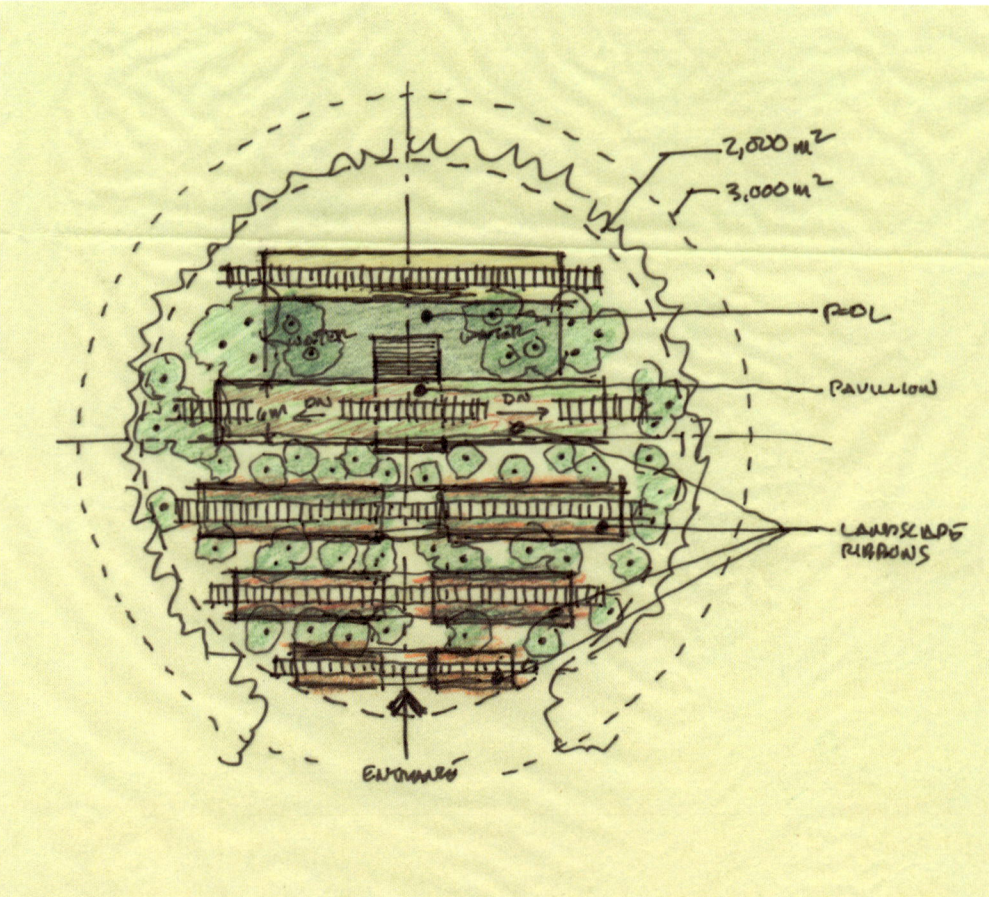

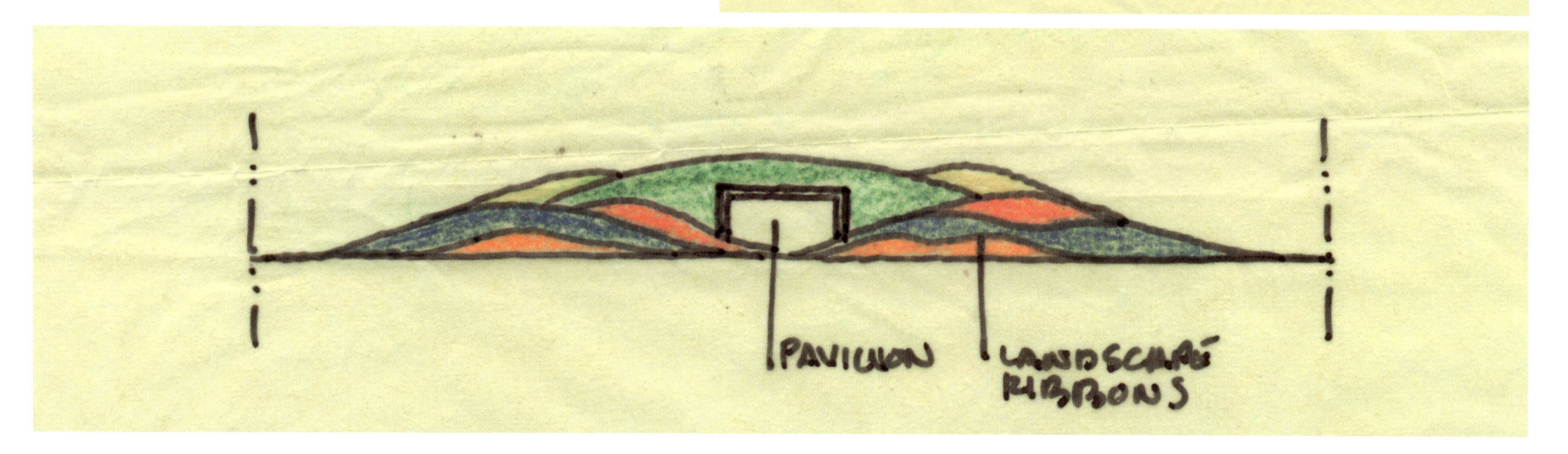

WAVE GARDEN

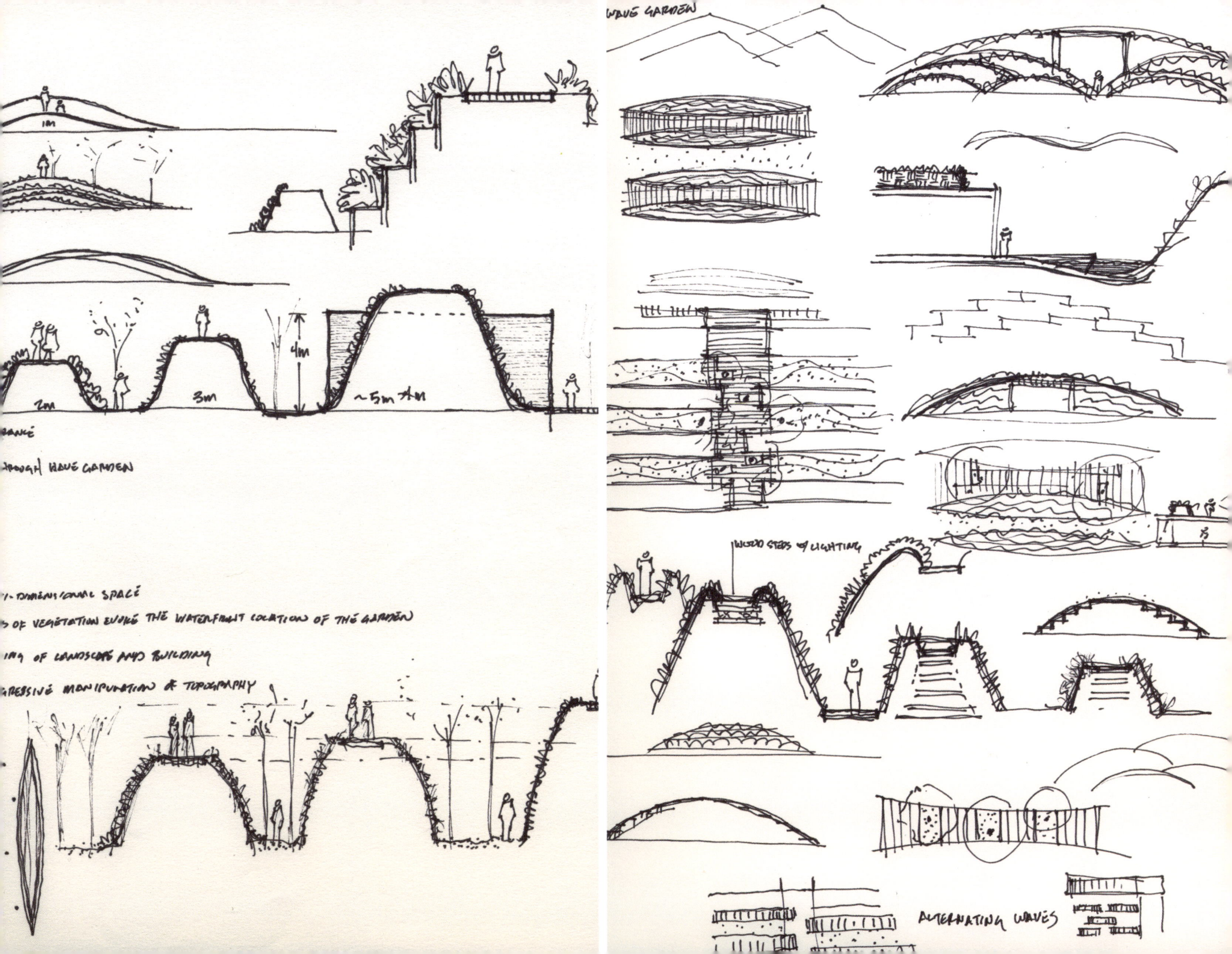

ALTERNATING WAVES

Monika Gora

Malmö, Sweden

It is never quite clear whether Monika Gora is an artist or a landscape designer – which is one of her greatest strengths. Her working method is certainly based more on ideas than on the traditional preoccupations of spatial design. For Gora, if the idea is strong enough, everything else will follow.

Monika Gora writes: 'Drawings are simplifications of reality. That is one purpose of drawing. Sketching is drawing thoughts – a way to think, search and explore ideas. Sketches are, like any other drawing or picture, representations of a reality. These images are filtered through the mind of the artist or architect and reveal different aspects of the whole truth. I always start with sketching on what is at hand: a napkin, a ticket, a newspaper. Later, I will often make three-dimensional models in paper or plasticine; these models can be scanned and worked up further on the computer.

'The problem with computer renderings is that they do not allow for the concept of time within their imagery: what is deleted leaves no trace. It's different when drawing or sketching by hand. There needs to be a balance, and an awareness about how various media are used, as well as when and for what. To create is to leave your own personal mark on the world. The sketch awakens and opens the mind to be free of interpretation. A drawing stimulates the imagination. To sketch is to search, exploring what is or what the future will be. Each sketch is a beginning, and everyone sketching is a beginner. We sketch both what is and what isn't.

'The aspect of "truth" or "reality" is interesting. What is the real tree – or the experience of it, which is different for everyone? Is it the sketch that captures its soul, the photograph of its broken branches or the way it looks in full bloom and in perfect shape? Sometimes memories feel more real than reality itself.'

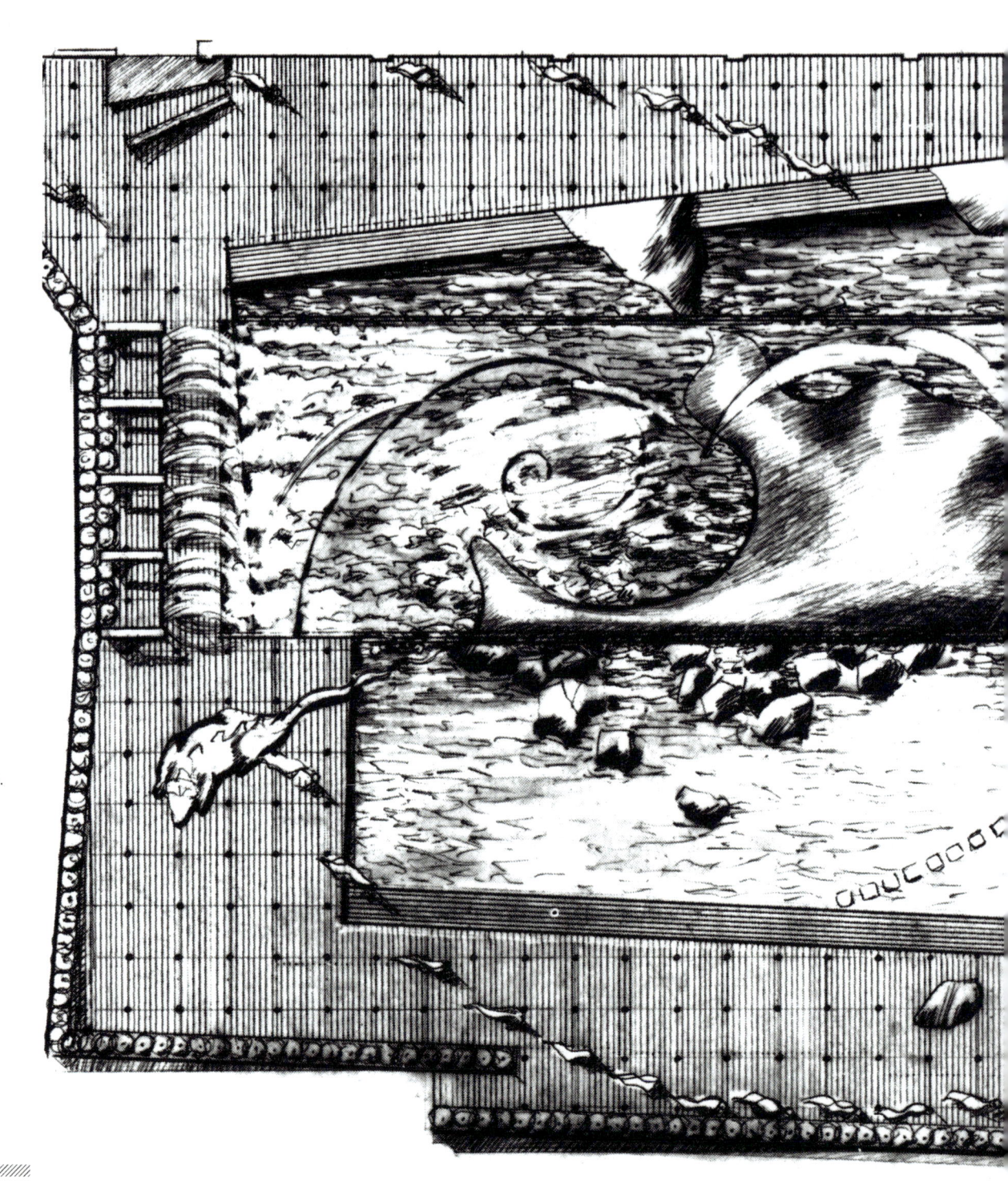

Monika Gora

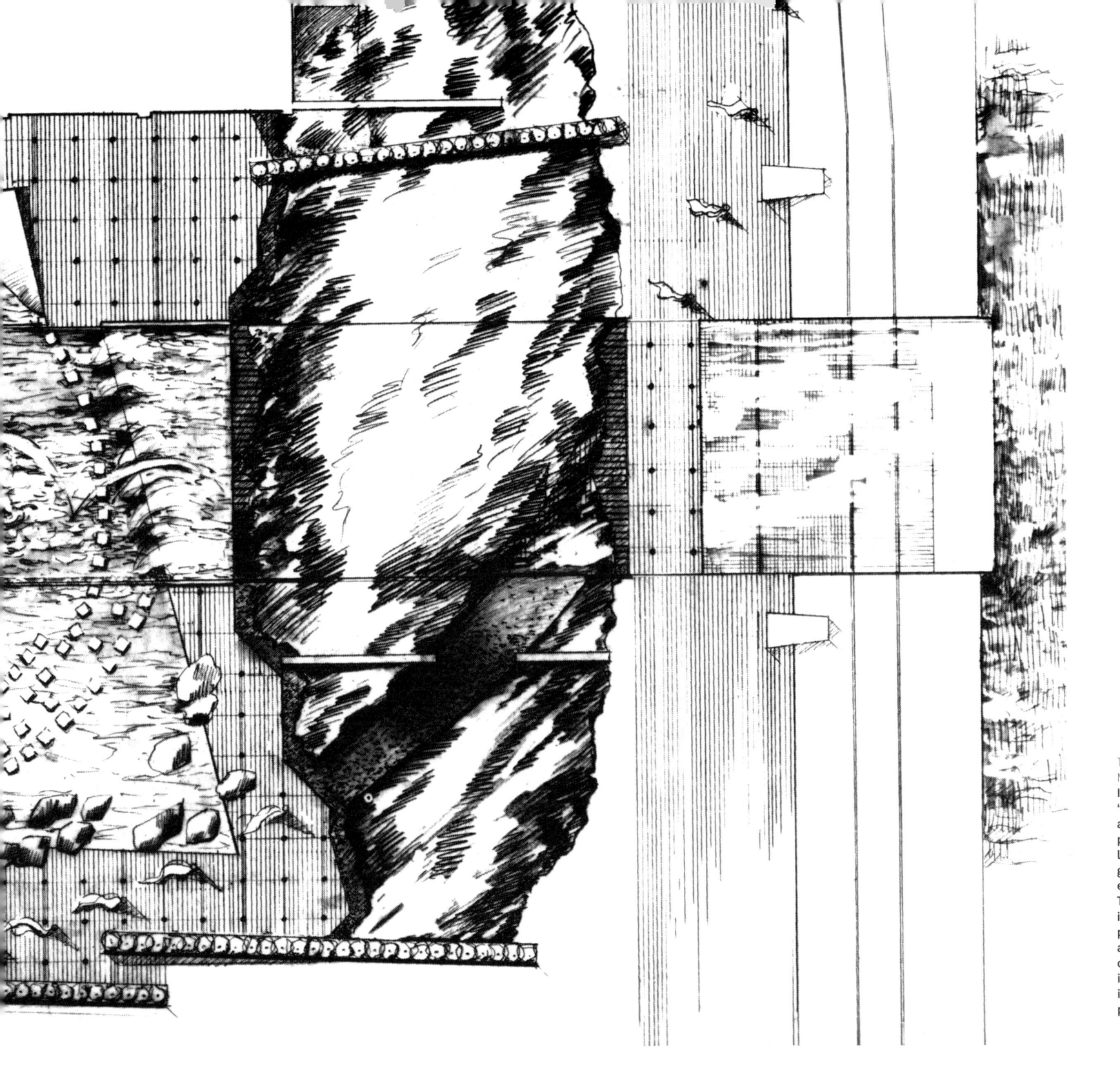

THE PARADISE,
MALMÖ, SWEDEN, 1990
In this sketch for the exhibition 'NordForm 90', held in Malmö, the aim was to show the contrast and the process of transformation between living and dead material. The garden contained images of all four elements: water, air, fire and earth. The watercourse running through the installation started as a waterfall, passed a hovering island, ran under a heap of coal and finally poured over the edge of the quay and down into the harbour basin. The hovering island was situated in the middle of a pond, framed by a wooden deck.

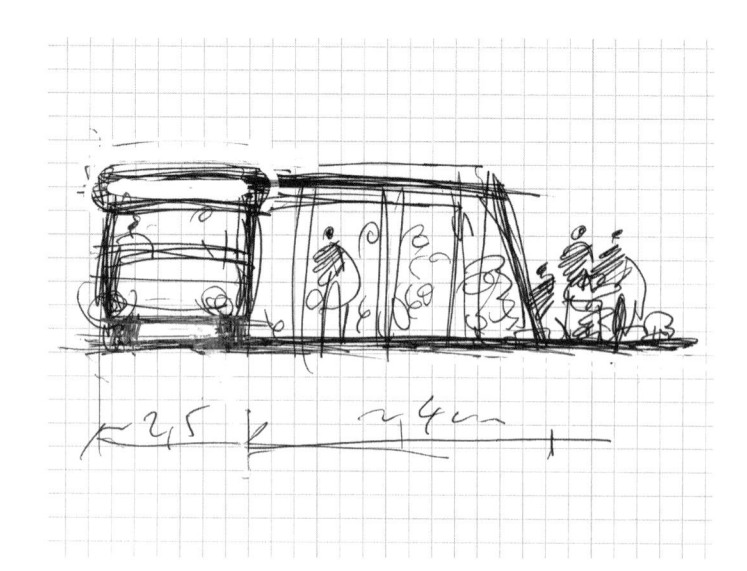

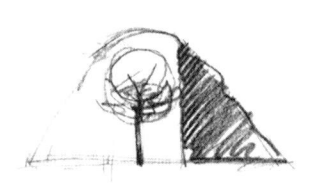

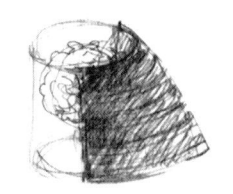

VARIOUS SKETCHES
Early sketches for a variety of projects, including Shelter Tree, Two Piers, Parapluie Kitchen Garden and a ground modulation for a playground.

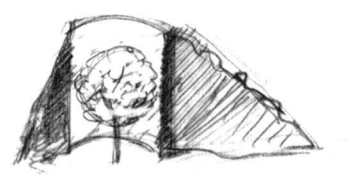

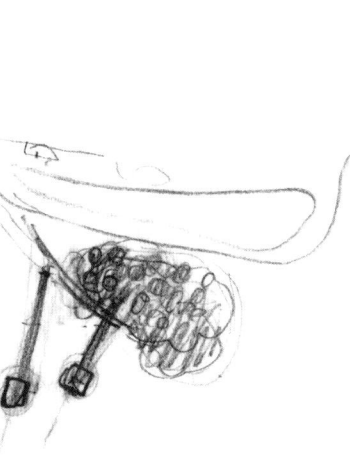

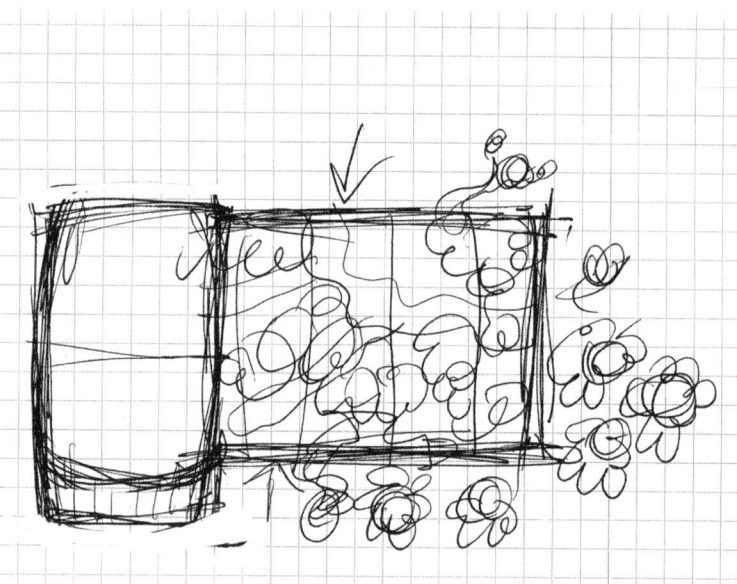

ONCOLOGY CLINIC,
LUND, SWEDEN, 1992
This pencil drawing (above) visualizes the lushness of a garden for the extension of an oncology clinic in Lund. The drawing was used during the building process, along with the motto, 'the house in the forest and the forest in the house', to make sure that everybody involved at the construction site would understand. Many involved liked this illustration and put it on their walls.

DRAWING FOR A
COMPETITION ENTRY, 2010
A pencil drawing with watercolours and models in coloured Styrofoam for a narrow garden (below). This was a quick visualization of a planted area with groundcover plantings and sculptural elements in fibreglass reinforced polyester.

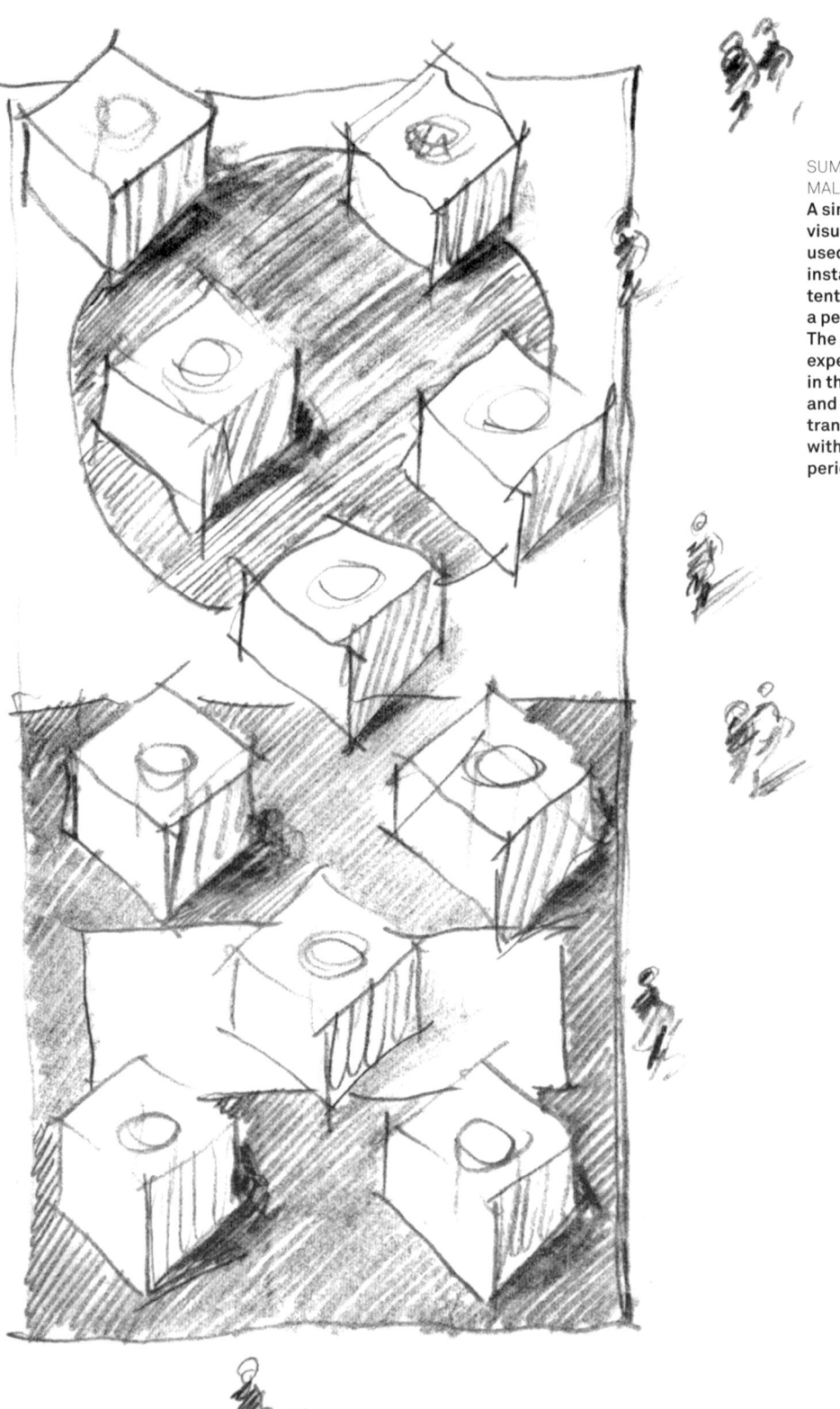

SUMMER AND WINTER,
MALMÖ, SWEDEN, 1998
A simple perspective sketch (left) visualizing the ten blocks of ice used for 'Summer and Winter', an installation that was part of the tenth-anniversary celebrations for a pedestrianized street in Malmö. The project was based on the idea of experiencing minor climate change in the middle of a city in summer, and was also an exploration of the transformative properties of water, with the ice melting slowly over a period of two days.

THE SHELTERED TREE, 1993
A concept study in crayon and watercolours (right), which explored the relationship between man and nature. A solitary tree is planted in an exposed location where it would not normally be possible for it to survive – for example, a lone living orange tree in its own greenhouse on Iceland. It is a symbol of vulnerability and of our need to protect and take care of certain plants and animals.

91

Monika Gora

GreenInc
Randburg, South Africa

The computer-aided designs of GreenInc are proof that hand-drawing is not the only way of producing designs of beauty and immediacy that seem to capture something of the atmosphere of the proposed place, as well as the ideas in the designer's mind. The company notes that ten to fifteen years ago, landscape-architecture graduates did more drawing work than today, but that an understanding of technology is also valuable. Even the simplest drawings published here did not escape a digital moment.

Anton Comrie writes: 'Drawing is design. From initial idea to explaining to contractors how to construct a detail on site, sketching is the main language of communication. Hand-drawings are by nature accessible and economical, so we use them a lot. As the scale and complexity of projects increase in our office, the more we realize the power of sequential or walk-through drawings. They are fantastic communication tools that enable us to simplify complex ideas.

'I prefer fast and dirty design sketches over precise, computer-generated visualizations. Quick drawings made to explore my own ideas are a great help to me when I am working on a number of projects simultaneously. Design should, after all, be a little bit messy. Computer drawings, on the other hand, are slow and tend to suck you into design detail, rather than spatial exploration. Zooming in and out of CGI models can be fun, but it is not helpful at concept-design level.

'With sketching, spatial sequence is more important than the evocation of atmosphere. We are most often in motion when experiencing landscapes, as opposed to being inside buildings. Thresholds and transitions are far more interesting than static environments.'

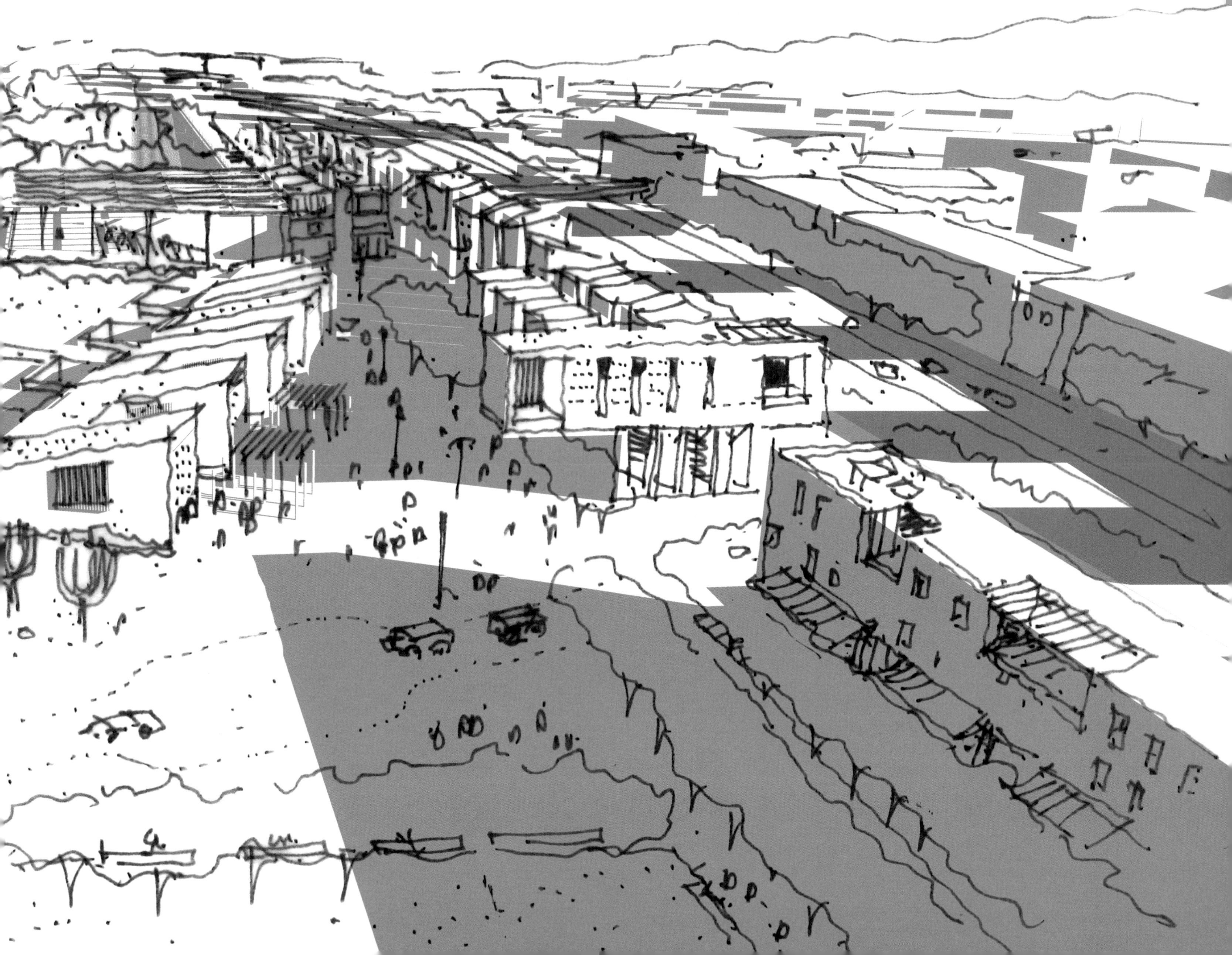

COMPETITION FOR A LANDFILL SITE, ADDIS ABABA, ETHIOPIA, 2014
This series of drawings (these and previous pages) was submitted as part of a competition proposal for the reclamation and redevelopment of a landfill site. A basic 3D model was developed in SketchUp as a guideline for further scaled and spatial development. Felt-tip Artline pens on A1 trace paper were used to sketch in sufficient detail to communicate a sense of place. Drawings were digitally scanned, with SketchUp used to generate shadows for underlay.

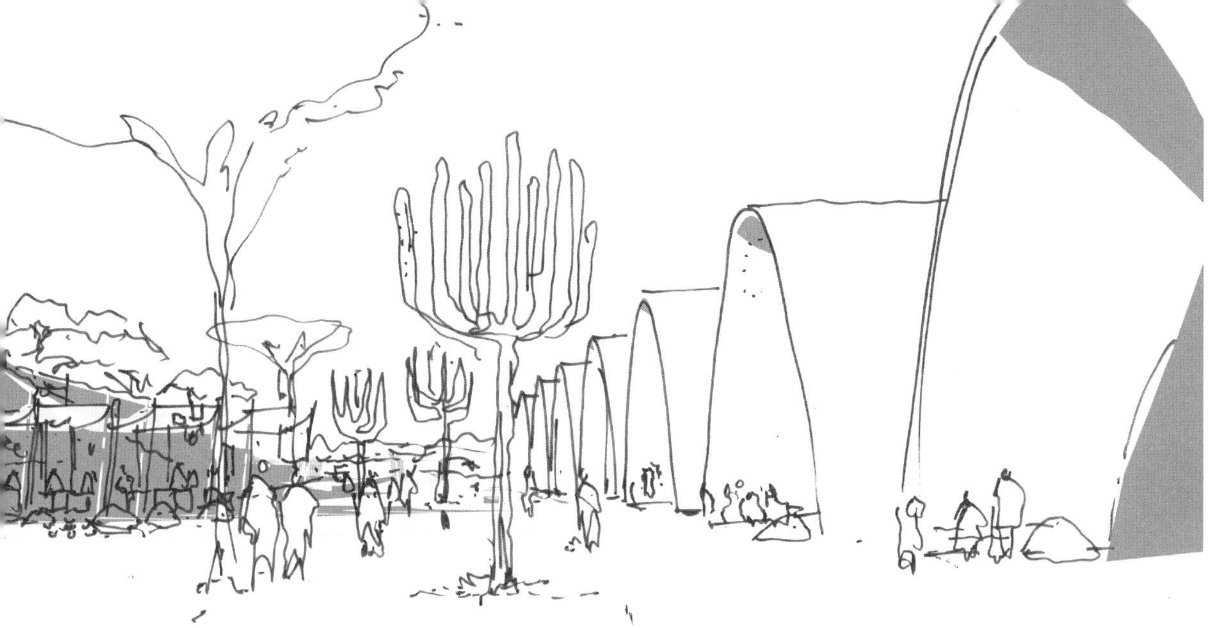
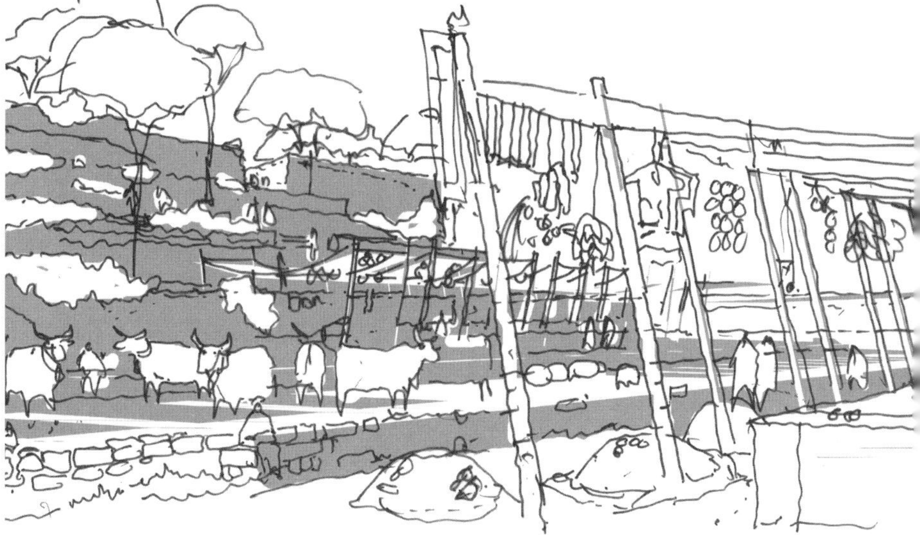
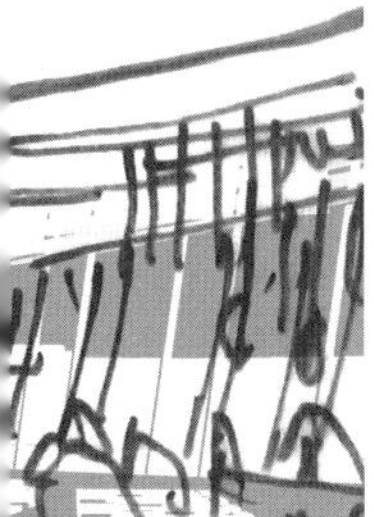
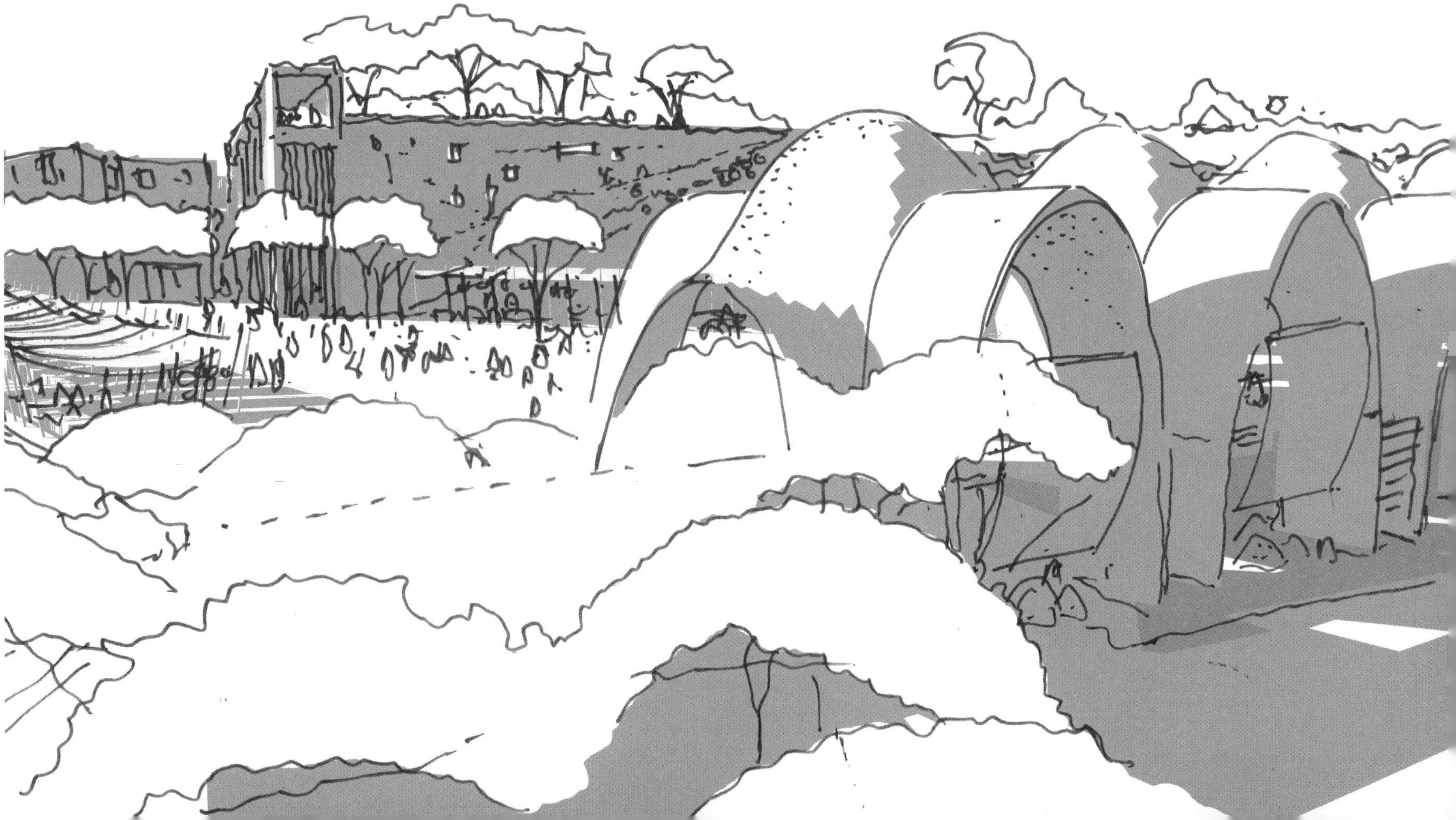

TOURISM DEVELOPMENT STRATEGY, VILANCULOS, MOZAMBIQUE, 2010
These digitally scanned sketches, drawn on trace paper and coloured in Photoshop, were produced as part of a strategy to communicate culturally responsive tourism development for the historic coastal town of Vilanculos. Soft colouring and shadows give the drawings a lightness that works well in A4 document format.

97 GreenInc

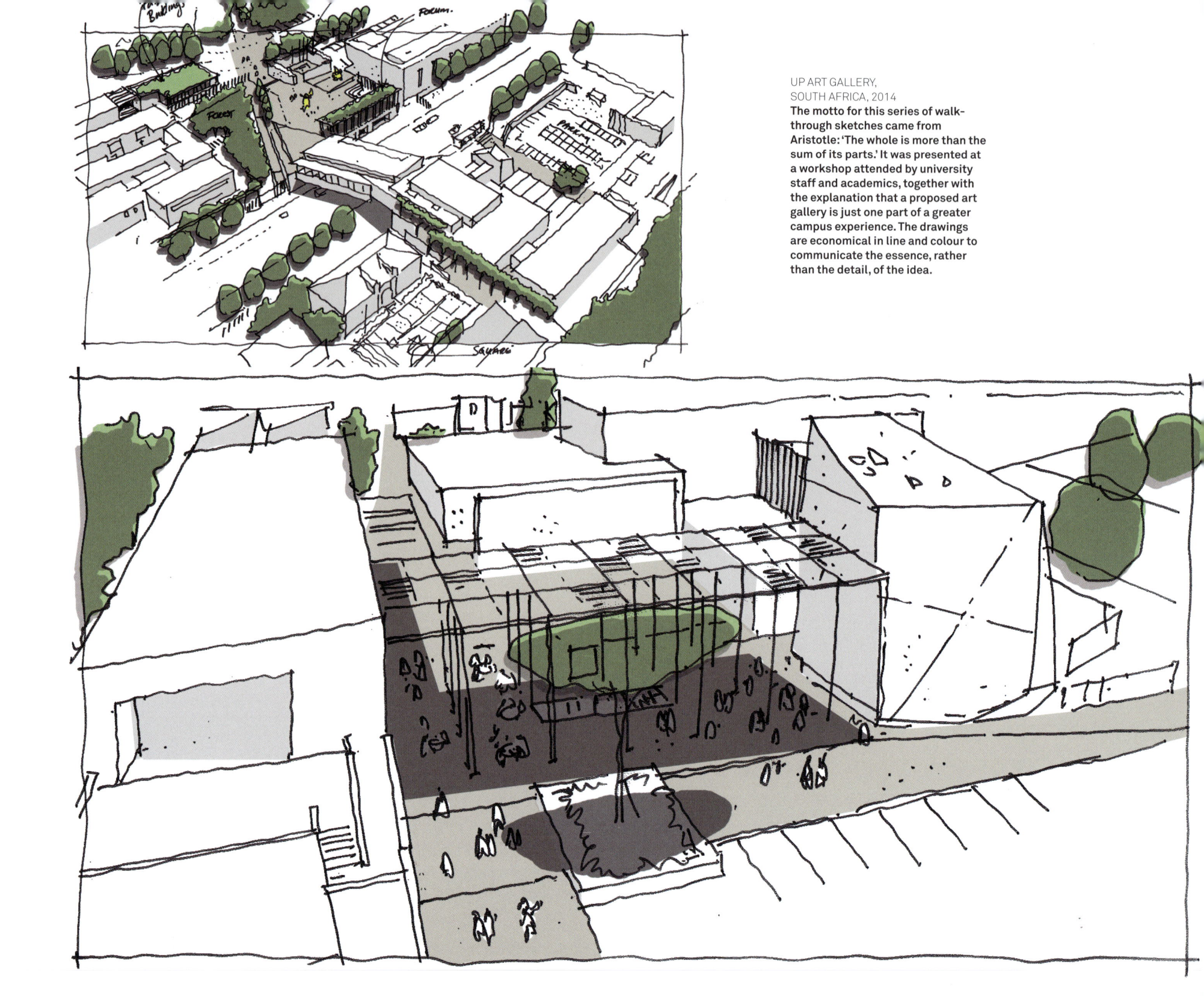

UP ART GALLERY,
SOUTH AFRICA, 2014
The motto for this series of walk-through sketches came from Aristotle: 'The whole is more than the sum of its parts.' It was presented at a workshop attended by university staff and academics, together with the explanation that a proposed art gallery is just one part of a greater campus experience. The drawings are economical in line and colour to communicate the essence, rather than the detail, of the idea.

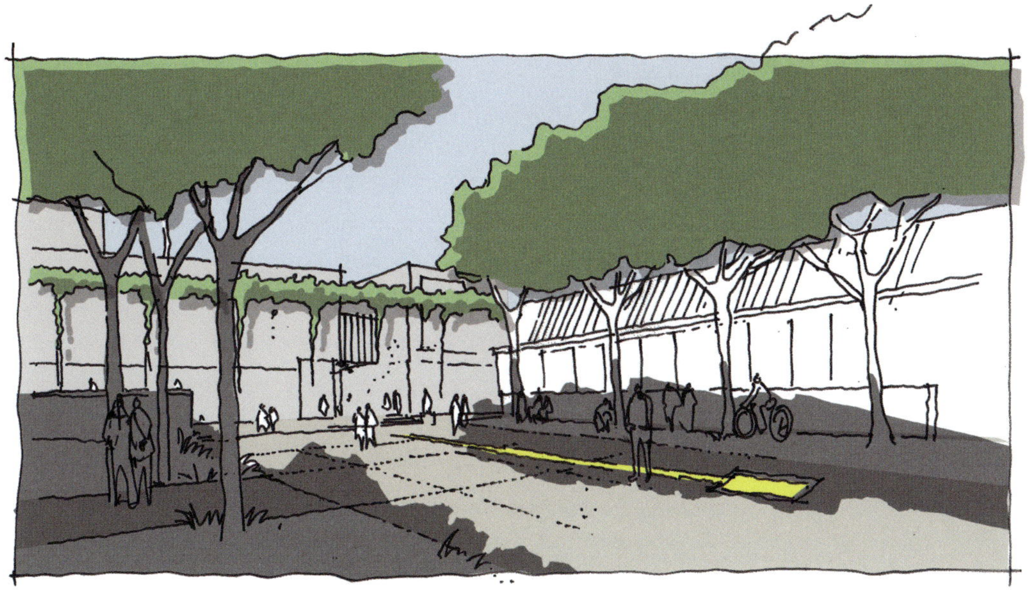

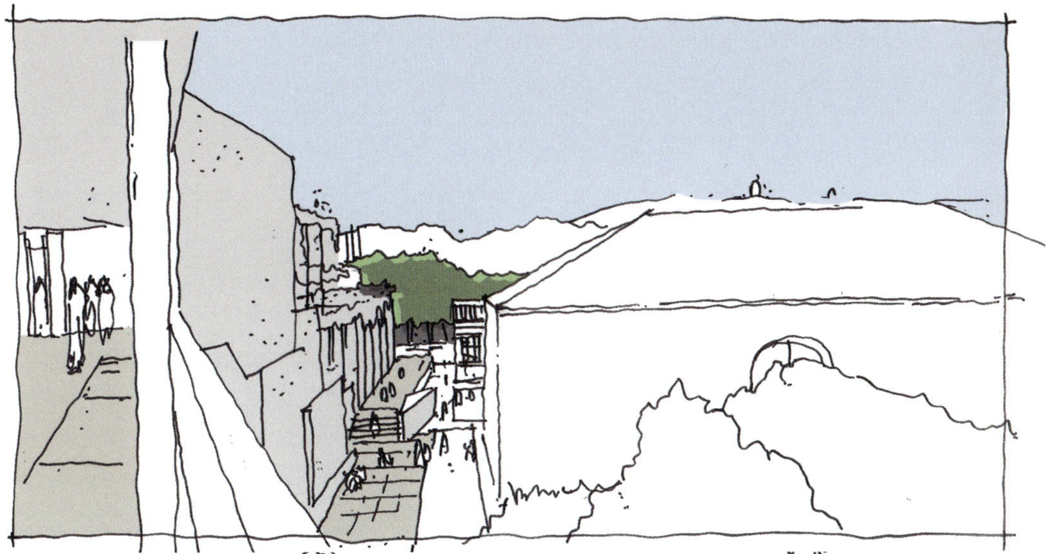

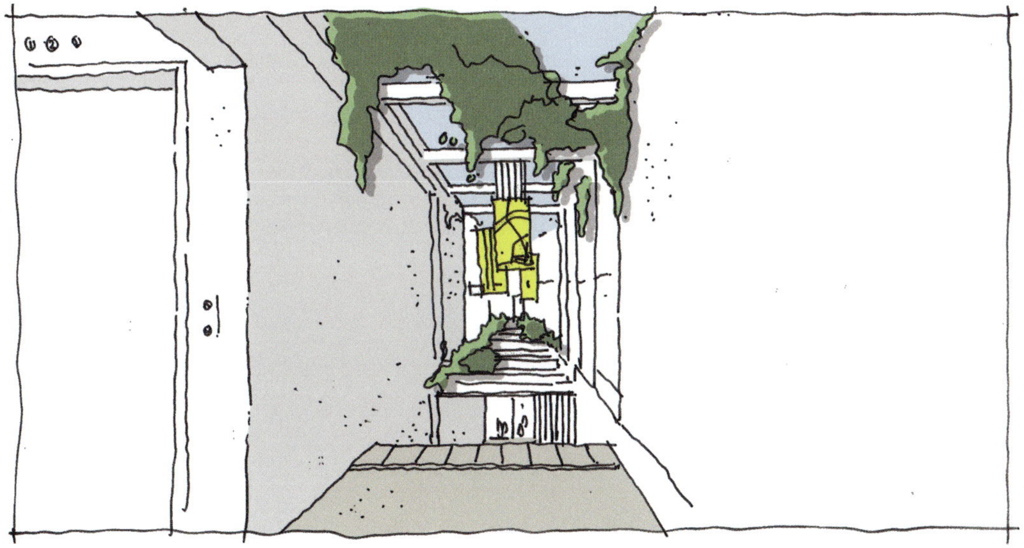

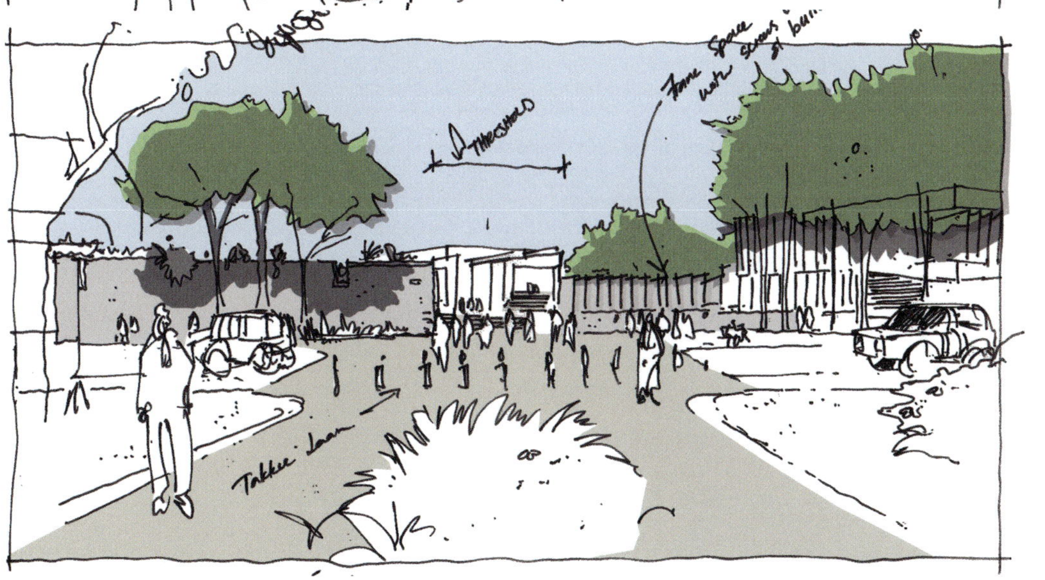

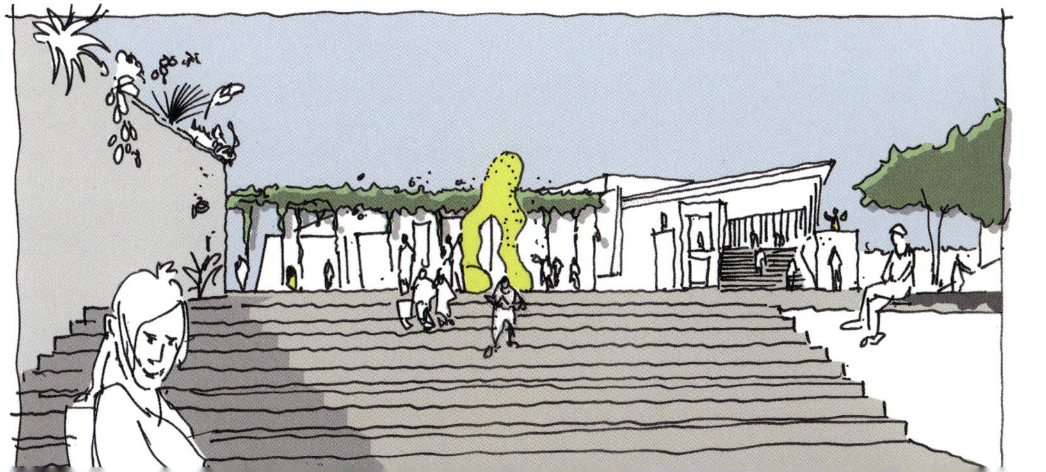

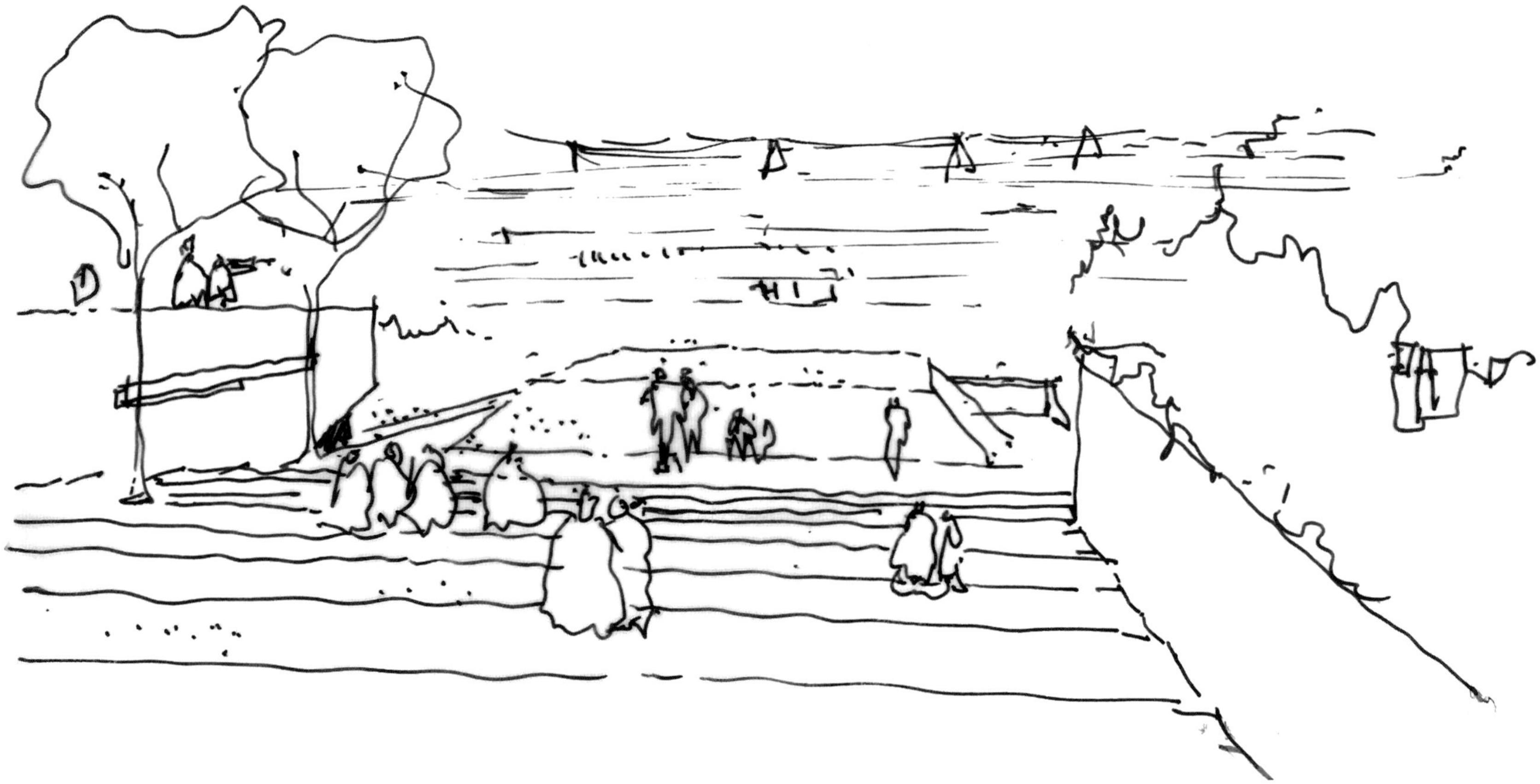

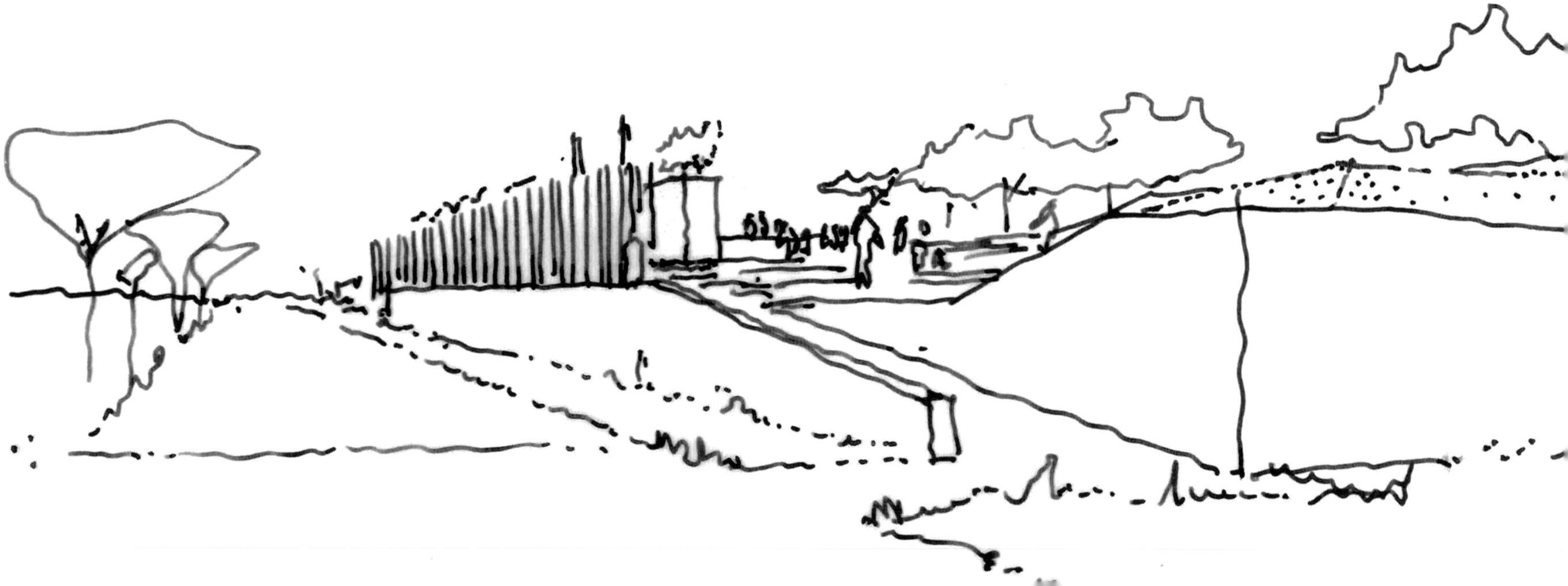

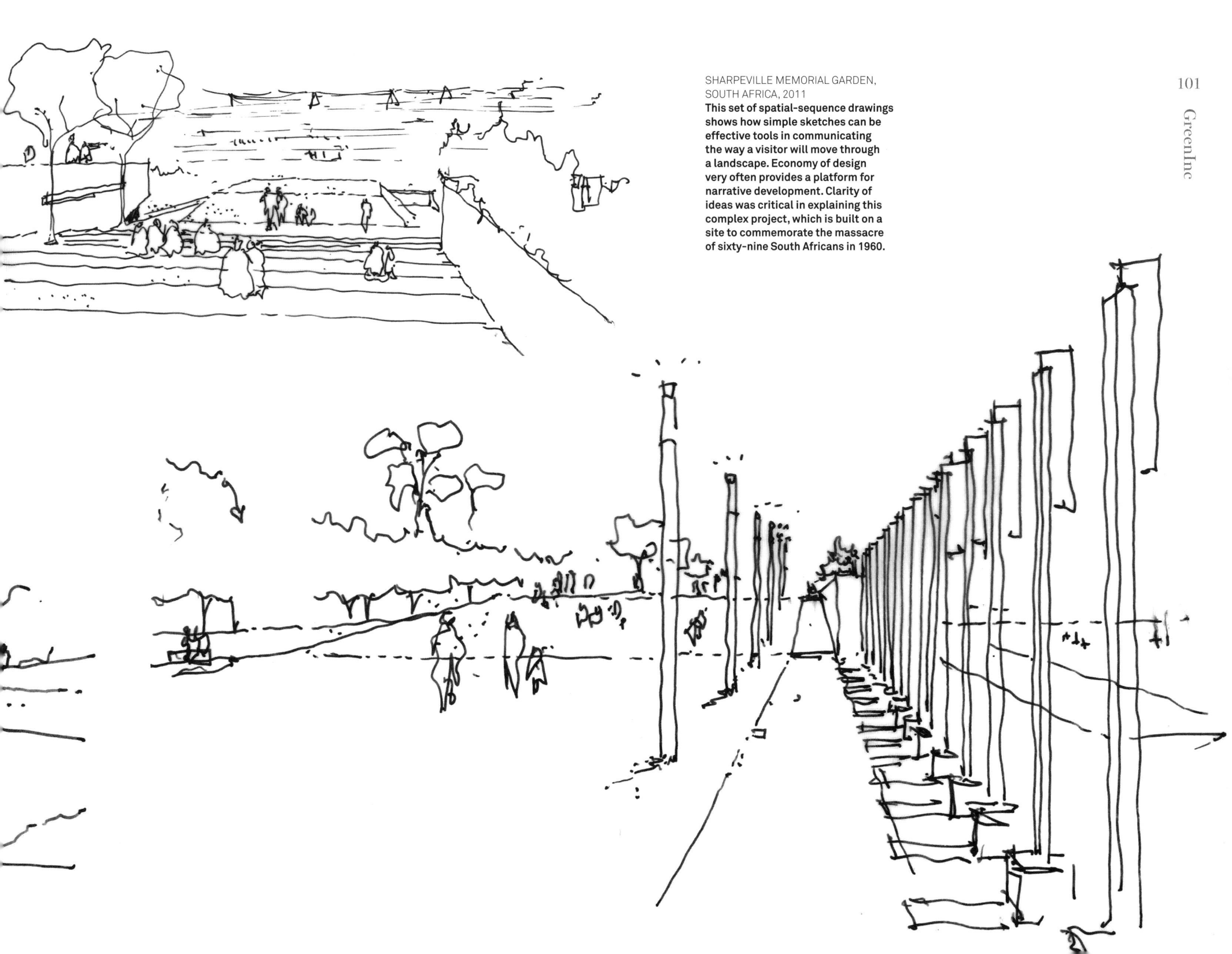

SHARPEVILLE MEMORIAL GARDEN, SOUTH AFRICA, 2011
This set of spatial-sequence drawings shows how simple sketches can be effective tools in communicating the way a visitor will move through a landscape. Economy of design very often provides a platform for narrative development. Clarity of ideas was critical in explaining this complex project, which is built on a site to commemorate the massacre of sixty-nine South Africans in 1960.

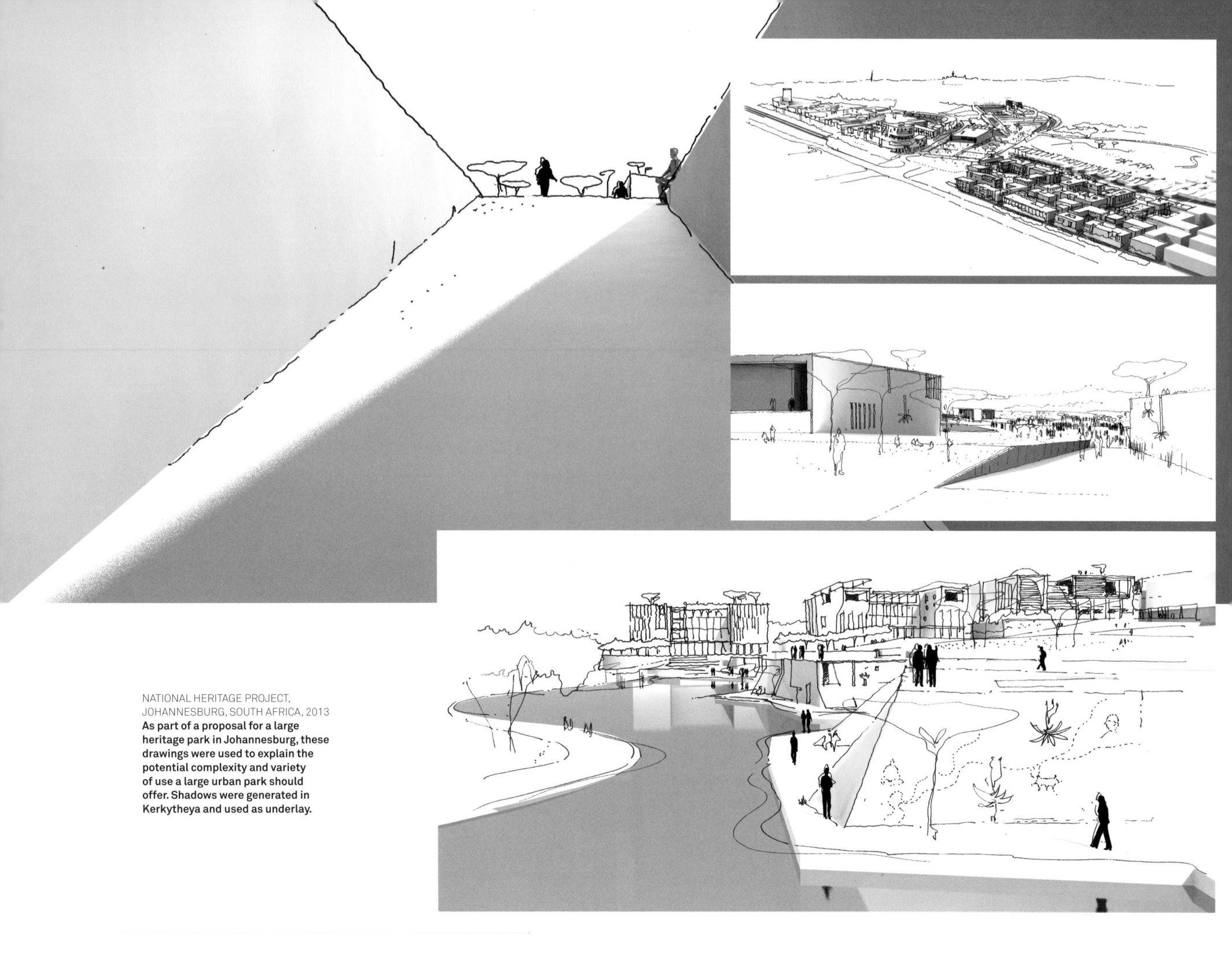

NATIONAL HERITAGE PROJECT,
JOHANNESBURG, SOUTH AFRICA, 2013
As part of a proposal for a large heritage park in Johannesburg, these drawings were used to explain the potential complexity and variety of use a large urban park should offer. Shadows were generated in Kerkytheya and used as underlay.

PROPOSAL FOR A HOUSING
DEVELOPMENT, LE MORNE BRABANT,
MAURITIUS, 2009
Scanned and coloured in Photoshop,
these napkin-sized drawings were
used as part of a proposal for
a high-density development just
outside the core zone of a UNESCO
world heritage site. They illustrate
the fragmentation of architecture
and the mitigation of the scale of
structures that were critical to
the design resolution in terms of
the visual impact on the Le Morne
Brabant peninsula and basaltic
monolith on the southwestern tip
of the island.

Gross Max

Edinburgh, UK

Devoted controversialists and ardent polemicists, Gross Max will always seek to go 'the other way around'. Sometimes it feels like it might be the long way round, but you might see some interesting things on the way. Eschewing the traditional reliance on plan and elevation, Gross Max concentrate on the image that will illuminate their intention with the most clarity and power.

Eelco Hooftman and Bridget Baines write: 'As Giordano Bruno observed in 1591, to think is to speculate with images. Images are speculations of thought. Architectural drawings do not exist in their own right, but only as a leap in the process of making something that is not a drawing. At Gross Max we are not interested in the traditional "before and after", but rather in the "in between", the slender margin between dream and reality, built and unbuilt, past and future. Our imagery is not aiming for the virtual or the actual, but the possible.

'Composing our images layer by layer, we like to capture the project as emotive atmosphere. In our works, the image is not so much artist-impression (presentation) as artist-expression (speculation). In the past, the painted landscape became the direct inspiration for constructed landscape. Today, the pixel is our pigment; the computer screen our canvas.

'Landscape architecture has turned into a truly global profession. We are the children of the Google Earth revolution. We are zooming in and out, telescopic and microscopic, from macrocosm to microcosm. The effect of globalization, shifting economic markets, international exchange, digital technology and worldwide search engines has created an unprecedented international blend of "cut-and-paste" landscape architecture. Planet Earth has become a global garden, the modus operandi for the contemporary landscape architect.'

BOTANIST GARDEN, XI'AN HORTICULTURAL EXPOSITION, CHINA, 2011
Computer-aided visualization (opposite).

GARDEN FOR A PLANT COLLECTOR, GLASGOW, UK, 2007
This installation in Bellahouston Park was inspired by Jean des Esseintes, the plant-collecting protagonist of the novel *À rebours* (1884) by Joris-Karl Huysmans. While inspecting his collection of flowers – which looked like fakes – Des Esseintes proclaimed: 'There can be no doubt, horticulturists are the only true artists left to us nowadays.'

106

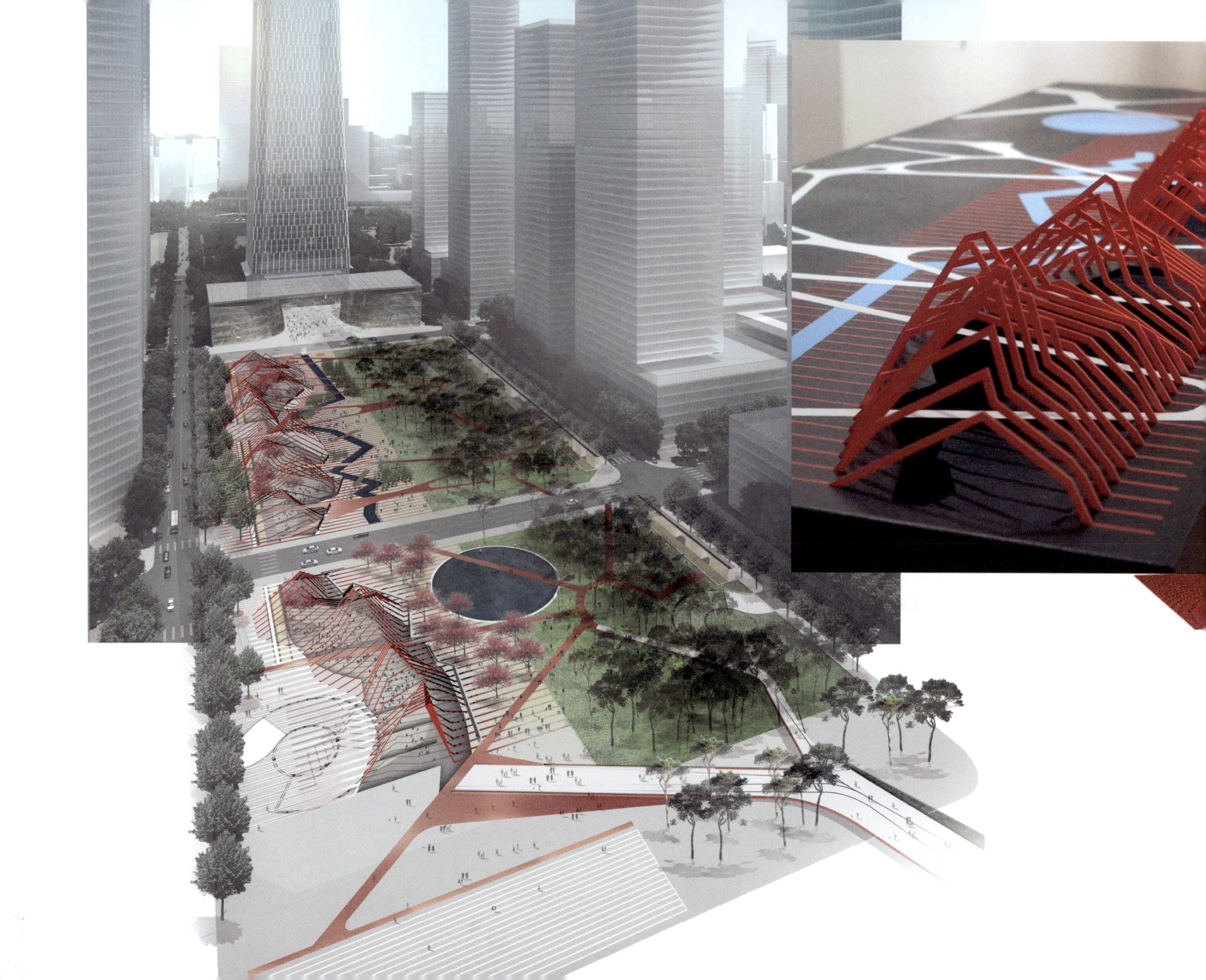

Gross Max

DESIGN FOR A PARK, BEIJING, CHINA
For this linear park in Beijing, the proposal was to represent the silhouette of a 500m (1,641 ft)-long mountain ridgeline: a dynamic configuration composed from angled metal beams, creating an iconic landmark. When seen from different angles, the structure allows for different visual experiences. This exploration involved models, diagrams and computer-generated visualizations.

TEMPELHOF AIRPORT,
BERLIN, GERMANY, 2011

This proposal won first prize in an international competition for the transformation of a former airport into a 380 hectare (939 acre) public park, envisaged as a contemporary prairie for the urban cowboy. Since it opened, the adventurous citizens of Berlin have spontaneously colonized the site with all kinds of high-adrenaline activity sports. The low horizon articulates the site's flatness and focuses the eye on the dramatic sky. The composition is based on a series of overlapping circuits around a central void, not unlike a plane circling in mid-air. A single vertical element, a 60m (196 ft)-high artificial hollow climbing rock, highlights the openness of the space.

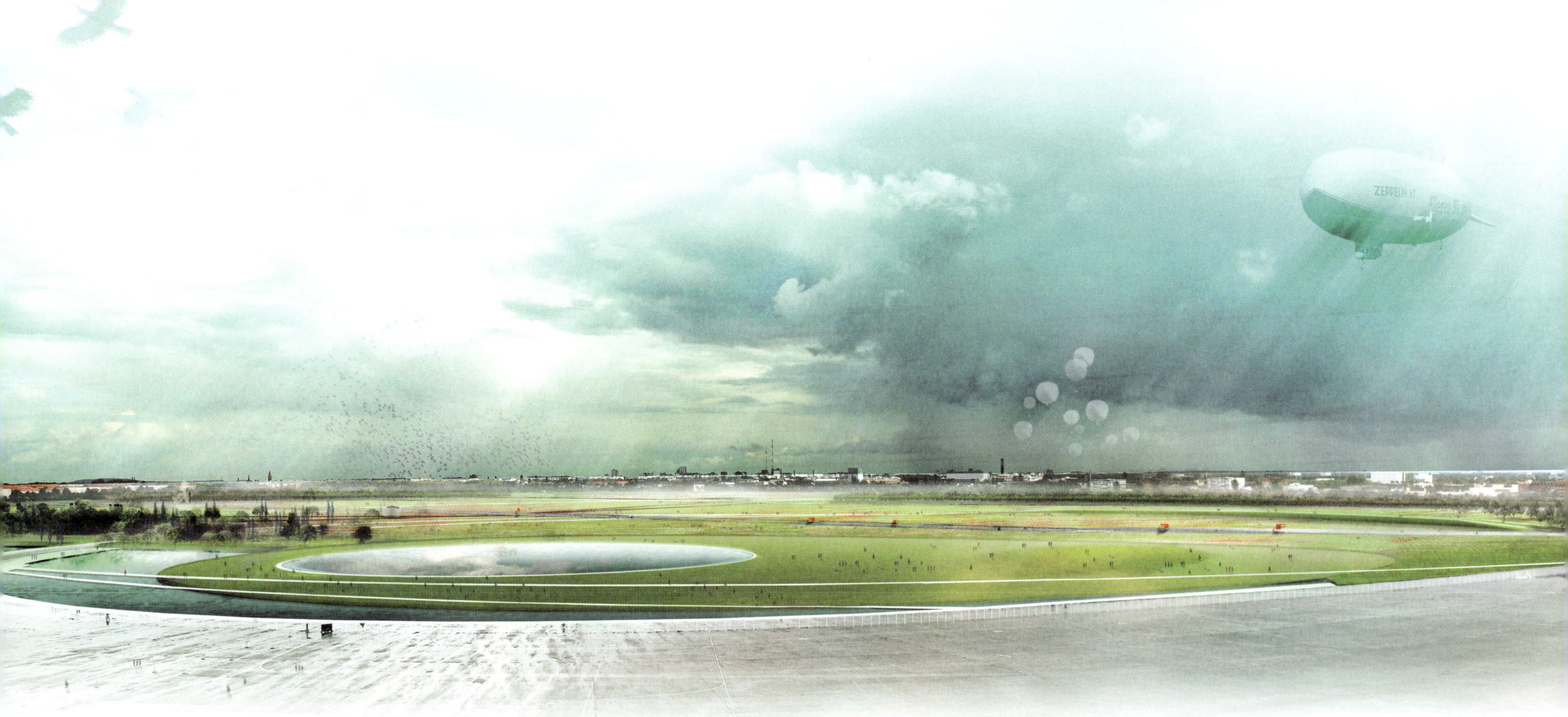
ZEPPELIN NT

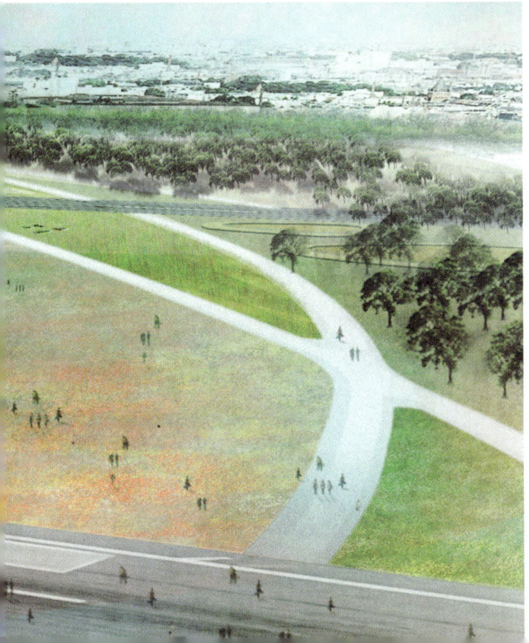

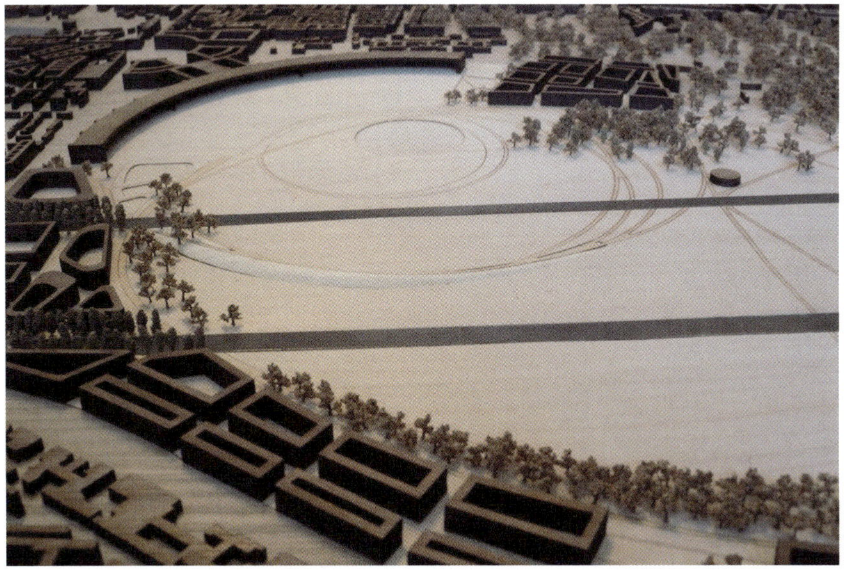

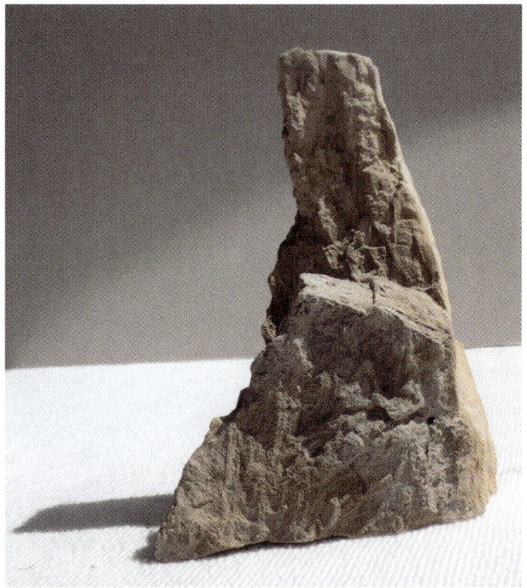

Gustafson Porter
London, UK

Gustafson Porter was formed in 1997, when all initial work was carried out by hand via drawings and models. CAD drawing was used only to create the design in traditional plan, section and elevation. The use of clay to model landscape is a technique that was initiated by Kathryn Gustafson and adopted by Neil Porter and others within the practice. It proved to be a tactile and sensual medium, defining three-dimensional space and sculpting the ground plane, while also freeing the design process from the orthogonal grid.

Gustafson Porter state: 'For the first five years, conceptual drawings were initiated by means of hand-sketches that also incorporated photocopying techniques, transfers, hand-colouring and pencil rendering. From around 2002–3, more of our designs were generated through a combination of working by hand, testing on computer using Rhino and going back and forth between the two methods.

'When working on the Diana, Princess of Wales Memorial Fountain [pp. 120–1], we were able to develop the design from a clay model that was scanned and then worked on using Icem Surf and other specialist computer programs more common in the automobile and aeronautics industry. From around 2004, concept designs were also modelled and visualized in Rhino, which became much more integrated in the development of early ideas.

'Most of our projects now use a combination of hand-sketches, traditional 2D design and 3D modelling. Although our CAD modelling and visualizing techniques have become more sophisticated over the past ten years, we find that clients appreciate the physical embodiment of the design evident in hand-sketches and models. Wonderful things can be achieved with CAD, but traditional drawings have a sensuality about them that is hard to replicate by digital means.'

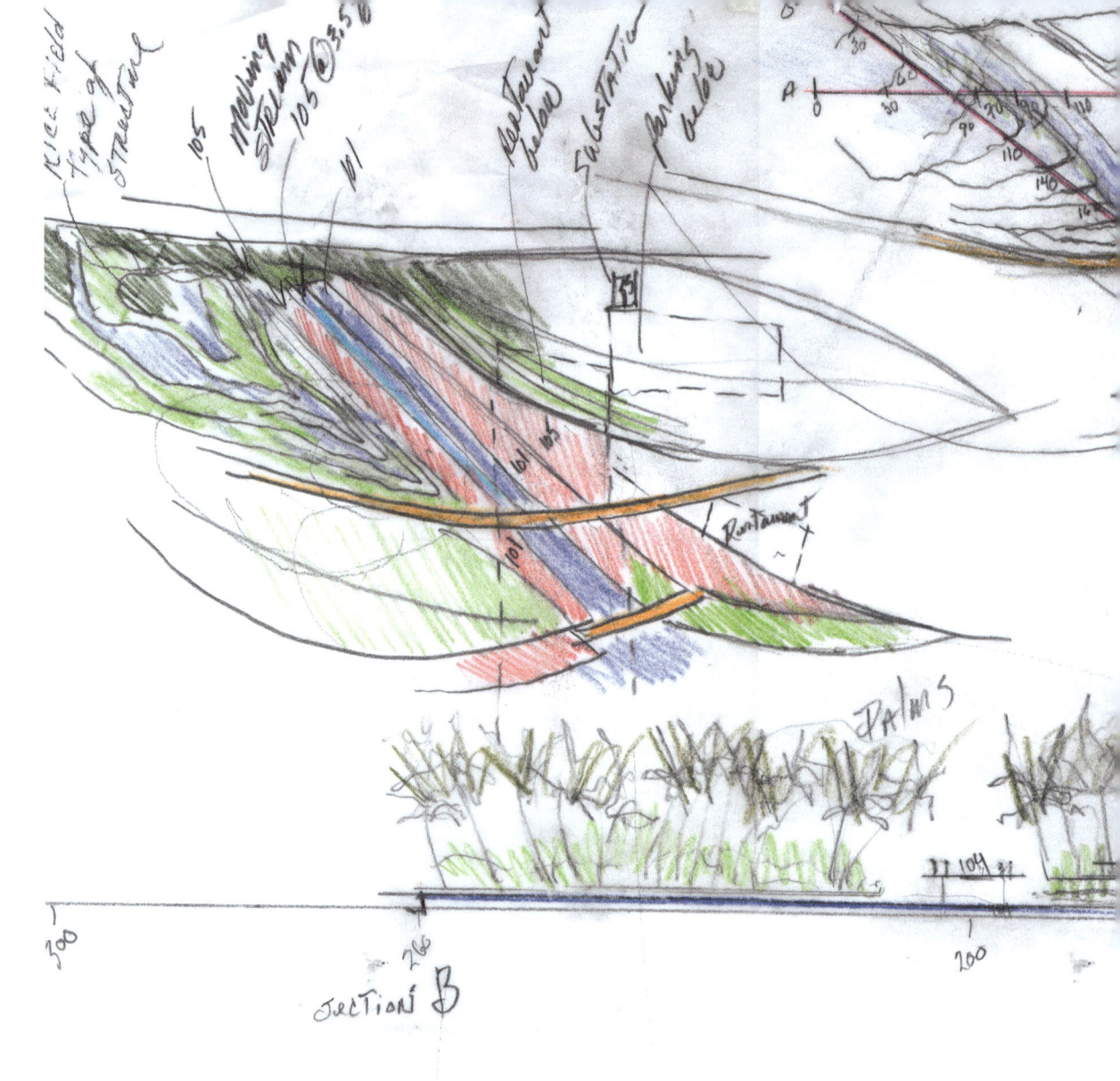

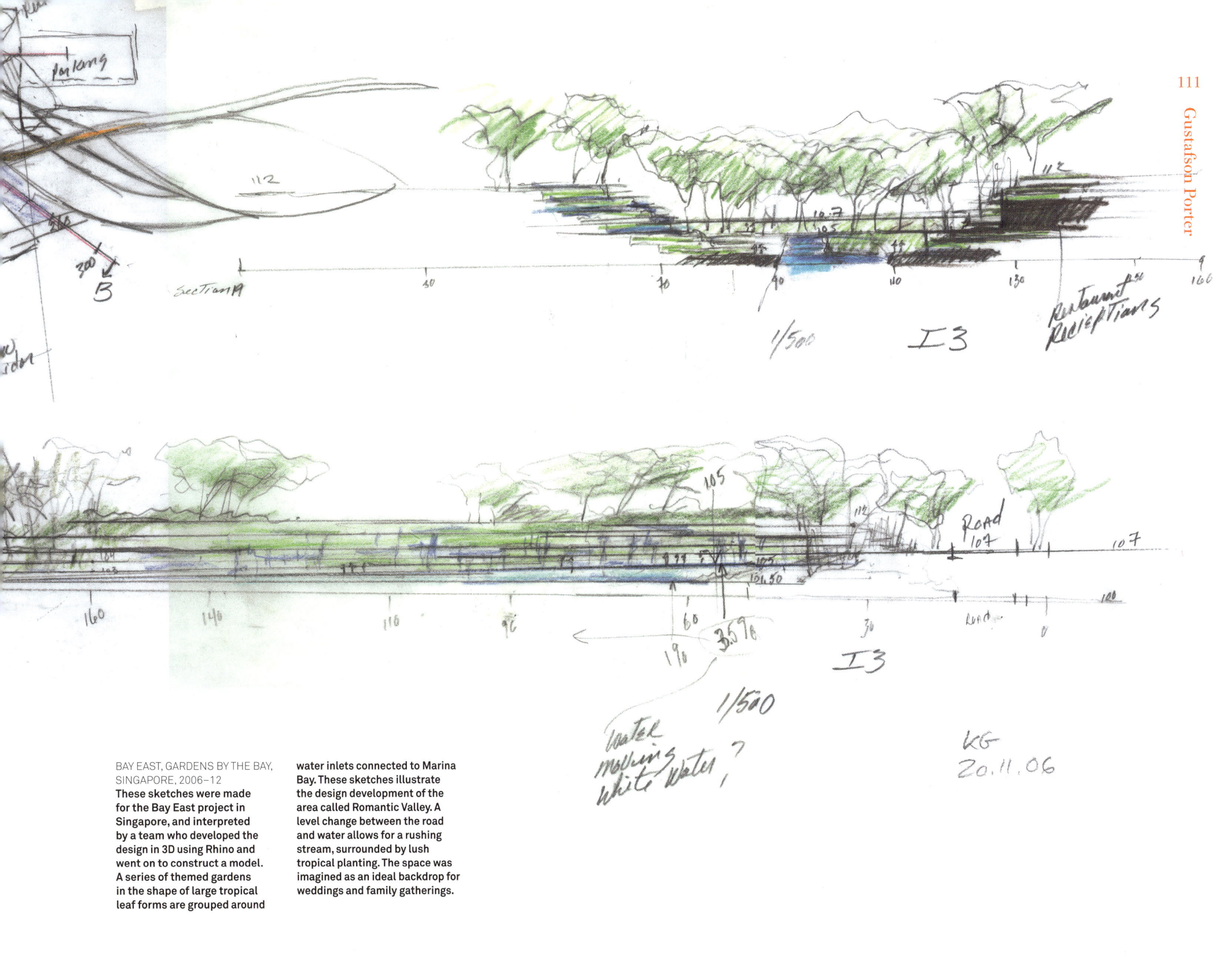

BAY EAST, GARDENS BY THE BAY, SINGAPORE, 2006–12
These sketches were made for the Bay East project in Singapore, and interpreted by a team who developed the design in 3D using Rhino and went on to construct a model. A series of themed gardens in the shape of large tropical leaf forms are grouped around water inlets connected to Marina Bay. These sketches illustrate the design development of the area called Romantic Valley. A level change between the road and water allows for a rushing stream, surrounded by lush tropical planting. The space was imagined as an ideal backdrop for weddings and family gatherings.

BAY EAST, GARDENS BY THE BAY, SINGAPORE, 2006–12

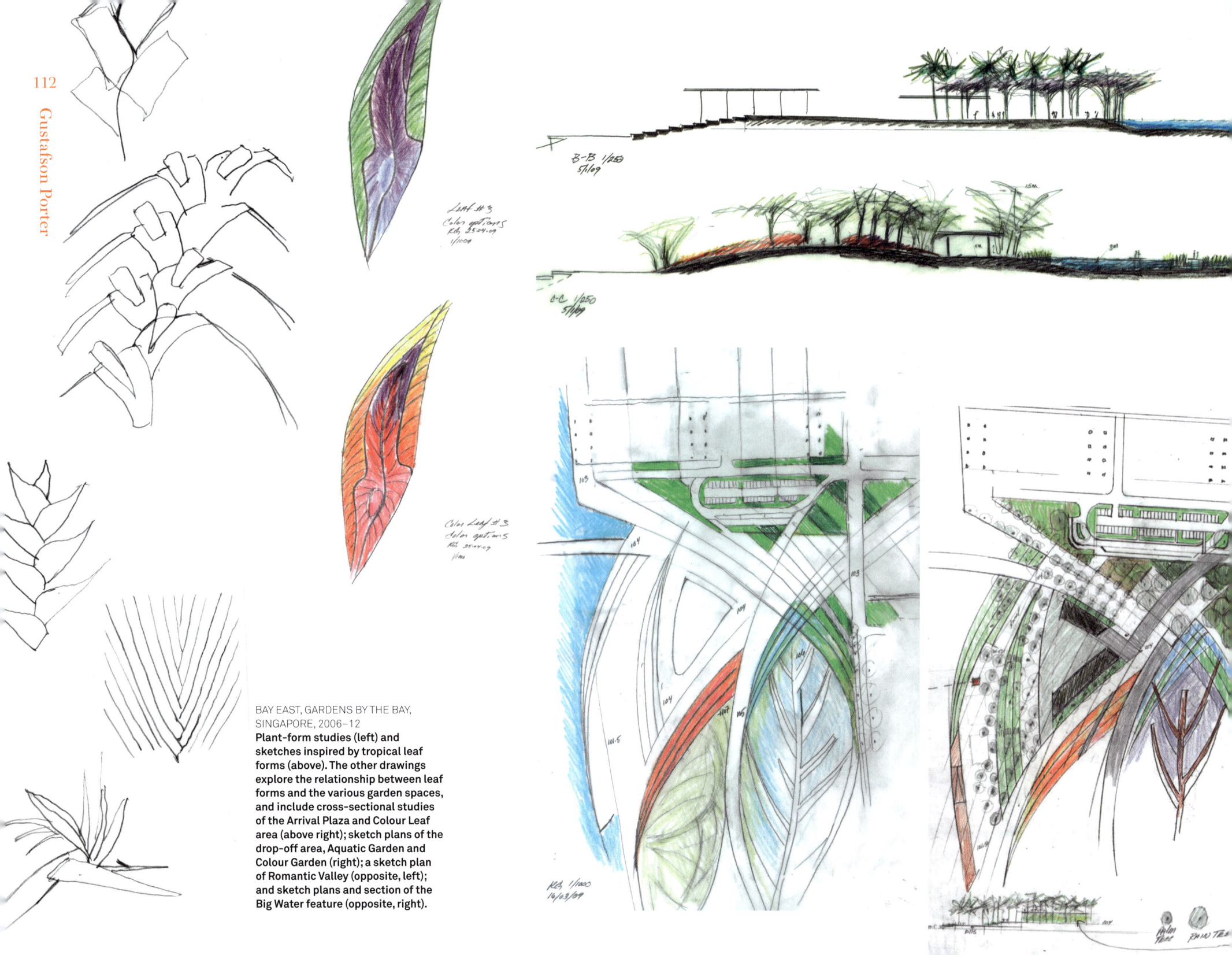

Plant-form studies (left) and sketches inspired by tropical leaf forms (above). The other drawings explore the relationship between leaf forms and the various garden spaces, and include cross-sectional studies of the Arrival Plaza and Colour Leaf area (above right); sketch plans of the drop-off area, Aquatic Garden and Colour Garden (right); a sketch plan of Romantic Valley (opposite, left); and sketch plans and section of the Big Water feature (opposite, right).

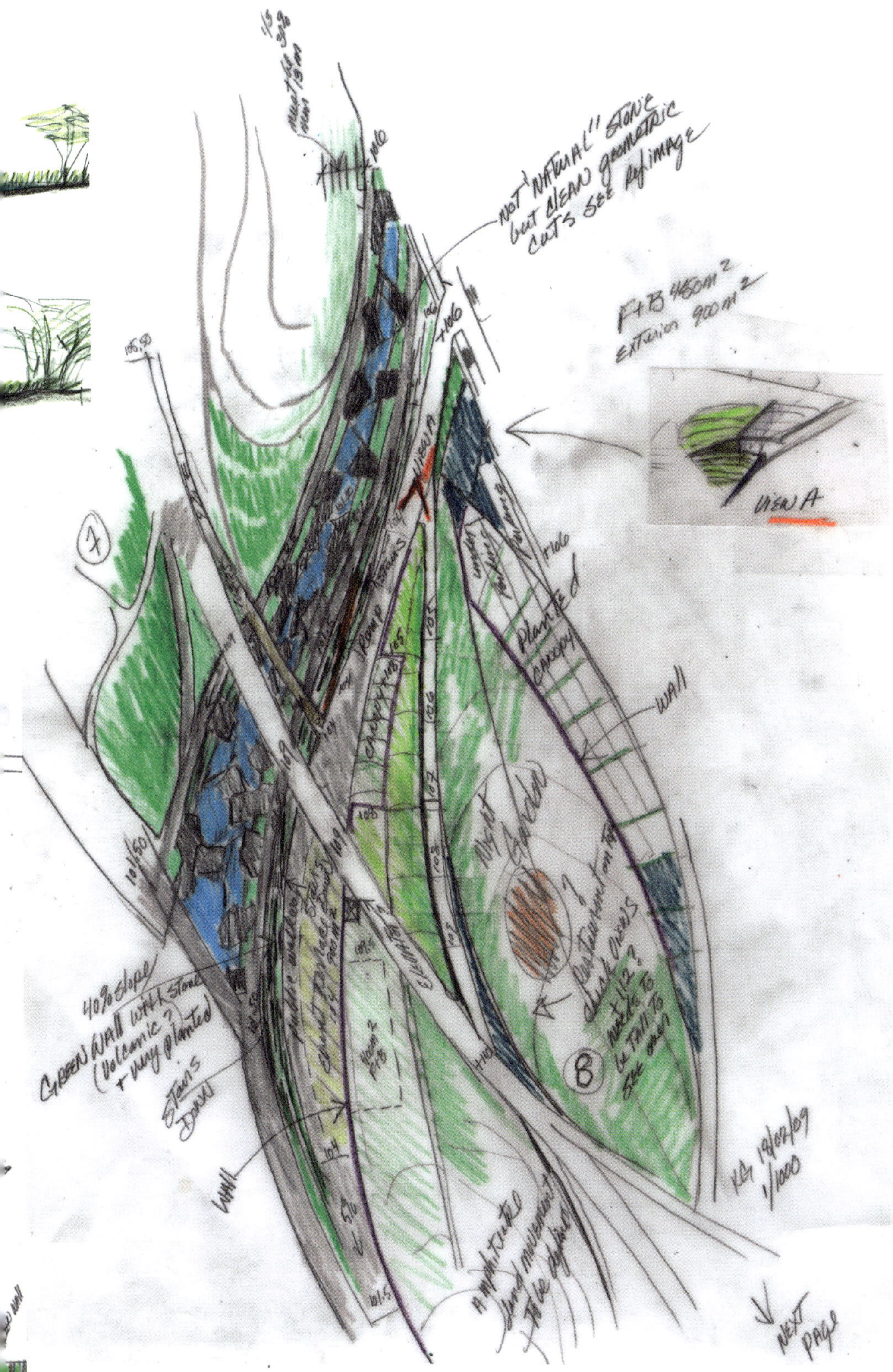
"NOT NATURAL" STONE
but CLEAN geometric
CUTS SEE Ref image
F+B 450m²
Exterior 900m²
VIEW A
Planted canopy
WALL
Night Garden
8
7
40% slope
GREEN WALL with stone
(volcanic?)
+ very planted
Stairs Down
WALL
KG 19/02/09
1/1000
NEXT PAGE

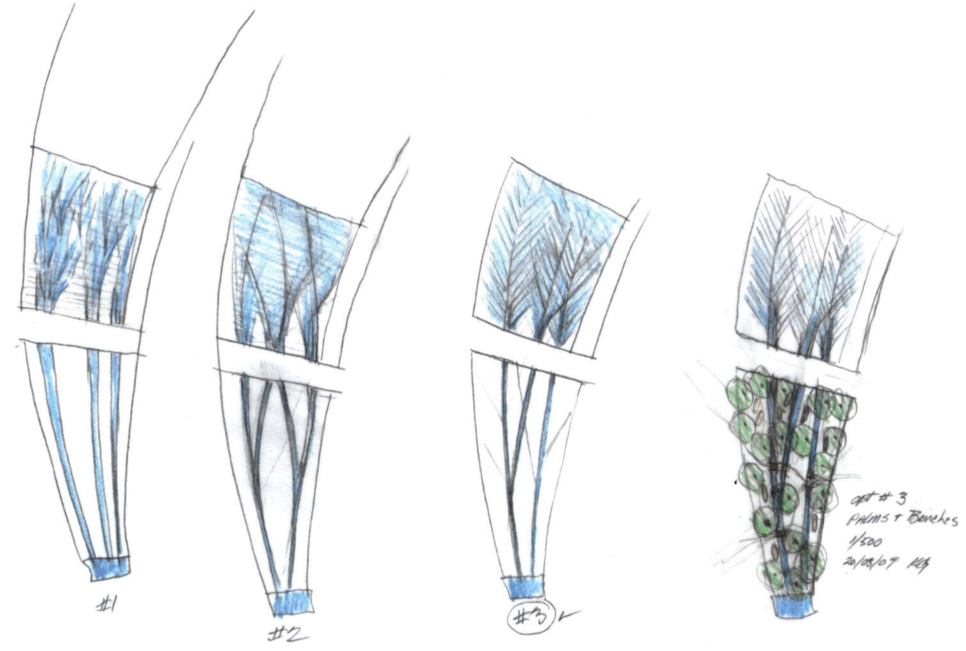
#1
#2
#3
opt # 3
Palms + Benches
1/500
20/03/09 KG

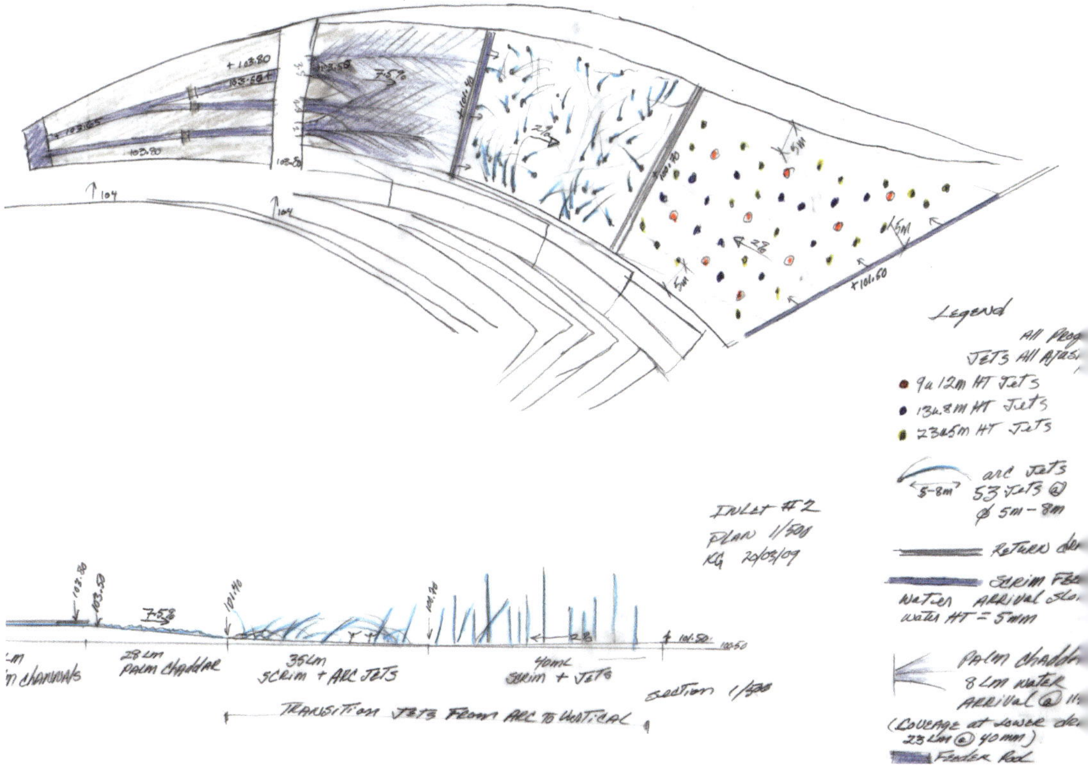
Legend
INLET #2
PLAN 1/500
KG 20/03/09
Section 1/500
Palm chaddar
SCRIM + ARC JETS
SCRIM + JETS
TRANSITION JETS FROM ARC TO VERTICAL
Return drain
Feeder Rod

114

SWISS COTTAGE OPEN SPACE, LONDON, UK, 2006
Sketch showing the central water feature (above left), concept sketch (right) and model showing the recessed water feature and grass amphitheatre (below left). The depressed rectangular space is a sunken five-a-side football pitch.

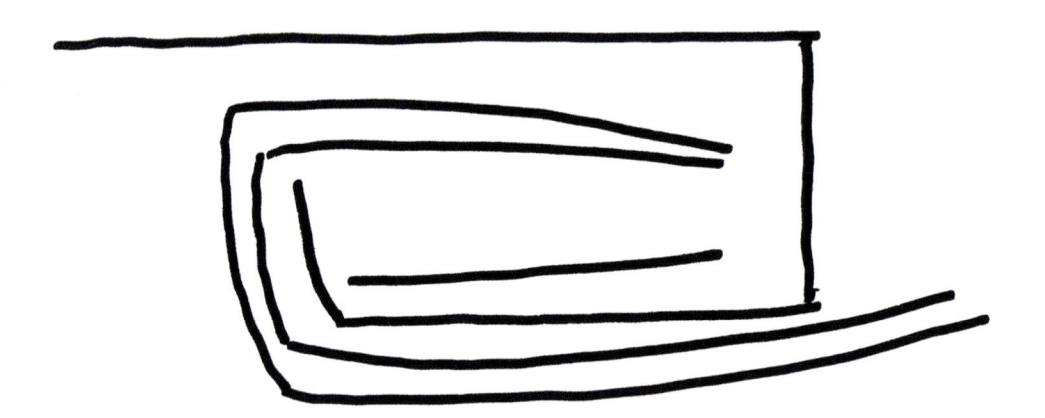

115

Gustafson Porter

116

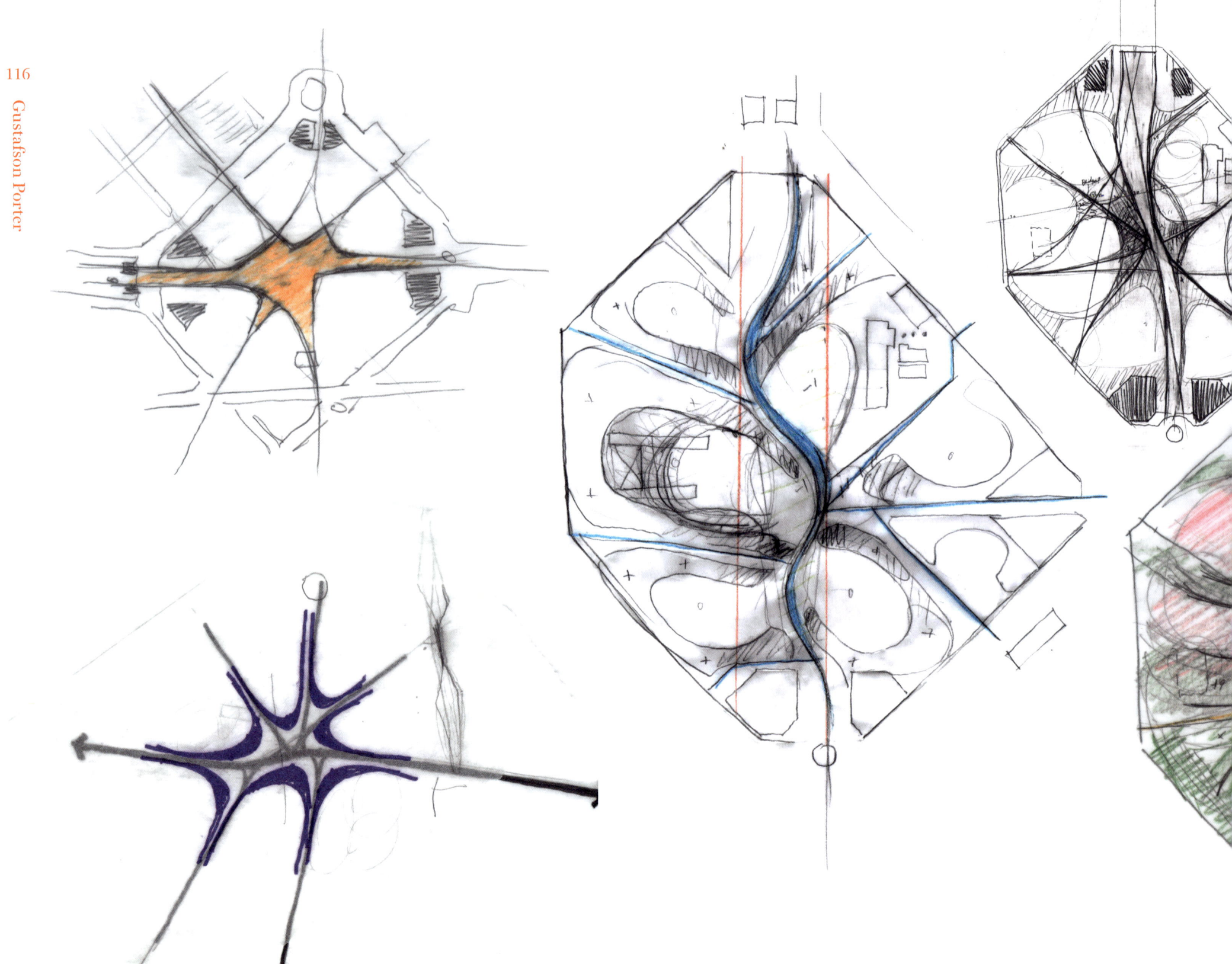

Gustafson Porter

VALENCIA PARQUE CENTRAL,
VALENCIA, SPAIN, 2011
These sketches illustrate the paths converging at the centre and the way landforms define distinct spaces with different uses. The water rills define major paths, while a series of 'bowls' or themed garden spaces is created by landforms.

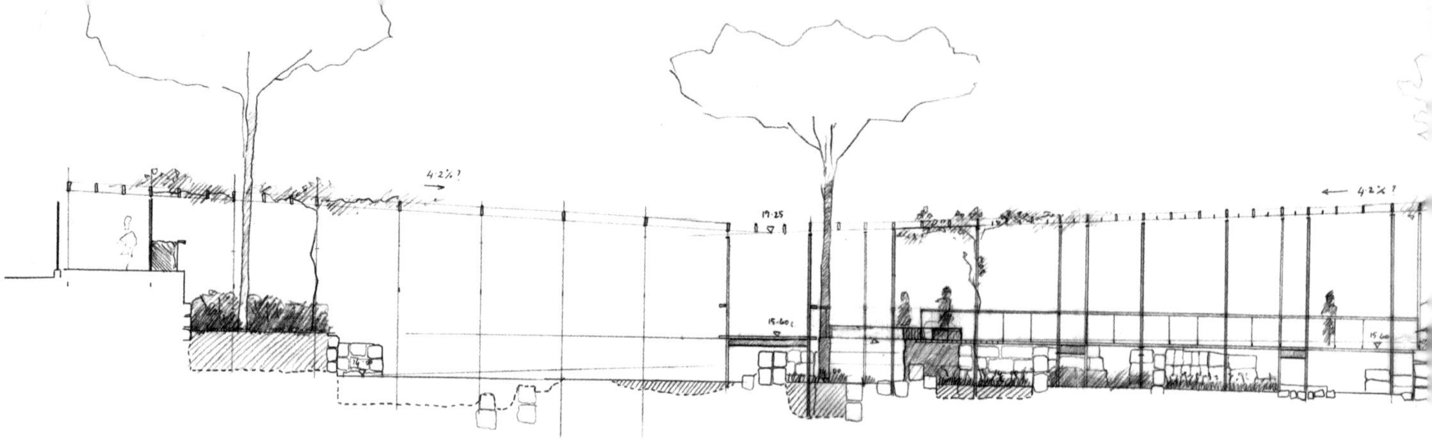

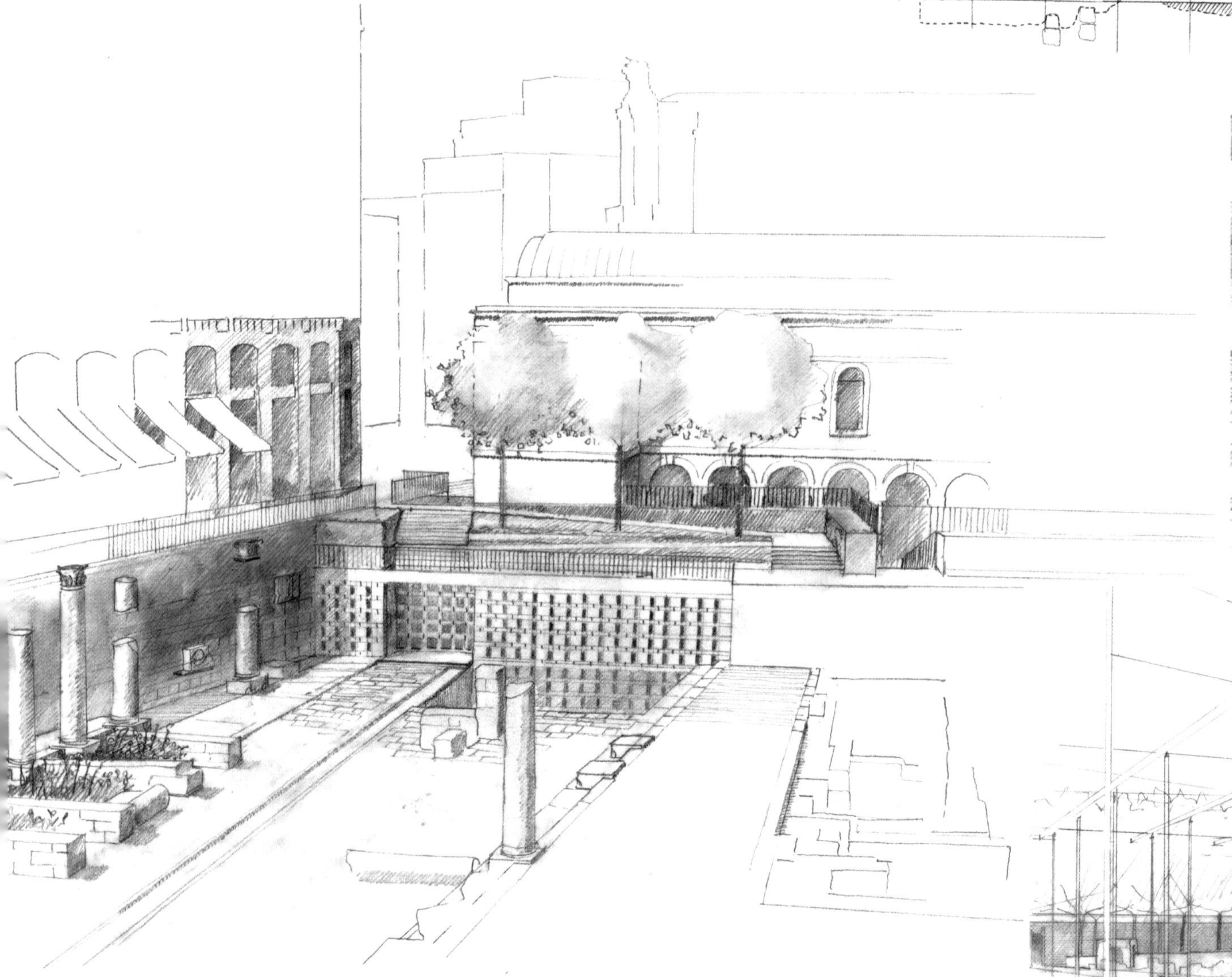

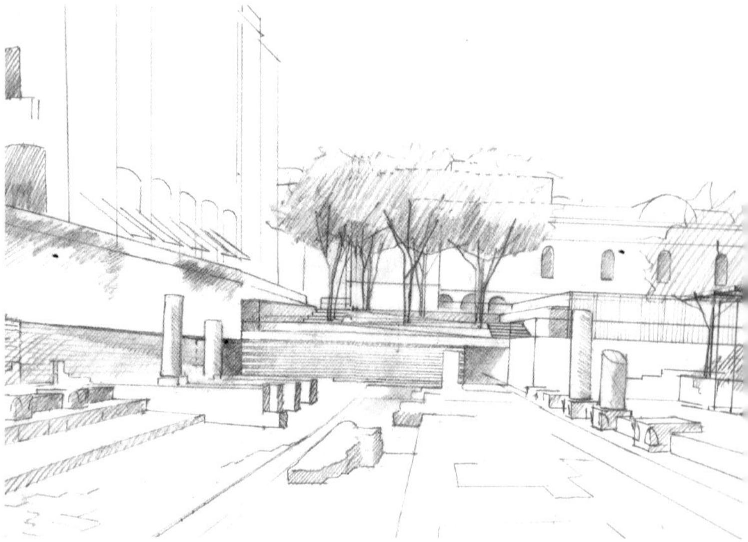

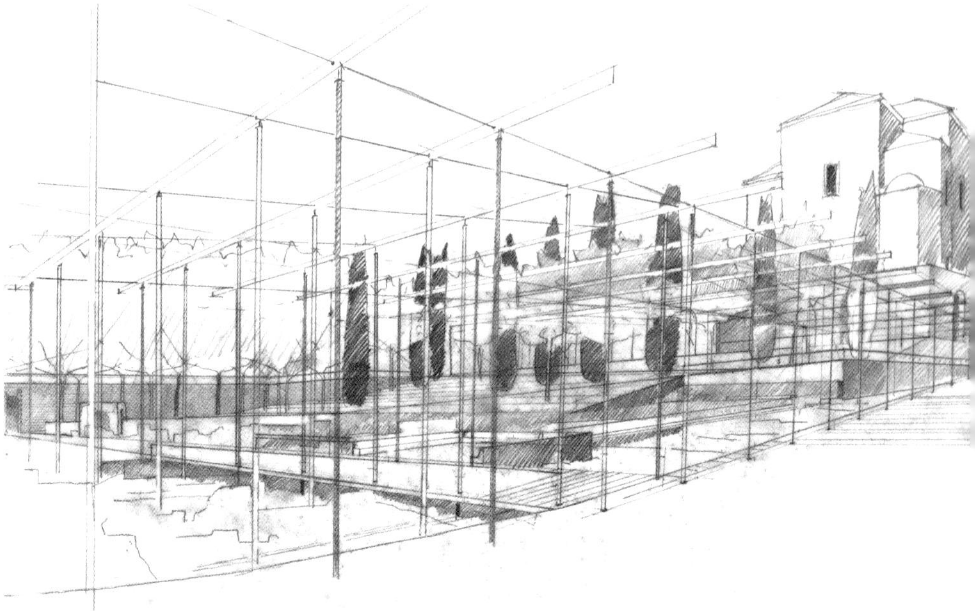

GARDEN OF FORGIVENESS,
BEIRUT, LEBANON, 2003

These drawings explore how new gardens and structures can be brought into close proximity to Greek, Roman and medieval archaeology. New garden paths and terraces facilitate a change in level between new city development and archaeological remains (right). A Roman *cardo*, the principal north–south thoroughfare in a city, runs beneath a viewing terrace overlooking the remains of a bath house (opposite, far left). A pergola garden provides shade over Greek ruins placed on bedrock, with pockets of soil for climbing plants (opposite, below right). Sketches of other proposed gardens and viewing structures (opposite, above right and middle).

Gustafson Porter

DIANA, PRINCESS OF WALES MEMORIAL FOUNTAIN, LONDON, UK, 2004

Several sketches showing the overall plan and sections of the design in Kensington Gardens, which incorporates a circular textured cascade possessed of varying 'moods'. Other sketches describe the early concept and detail of the planting borders, which frame the arrival sequence from West Carriage Drive. The borders were planted with a variety of English roses in memory of the princess.

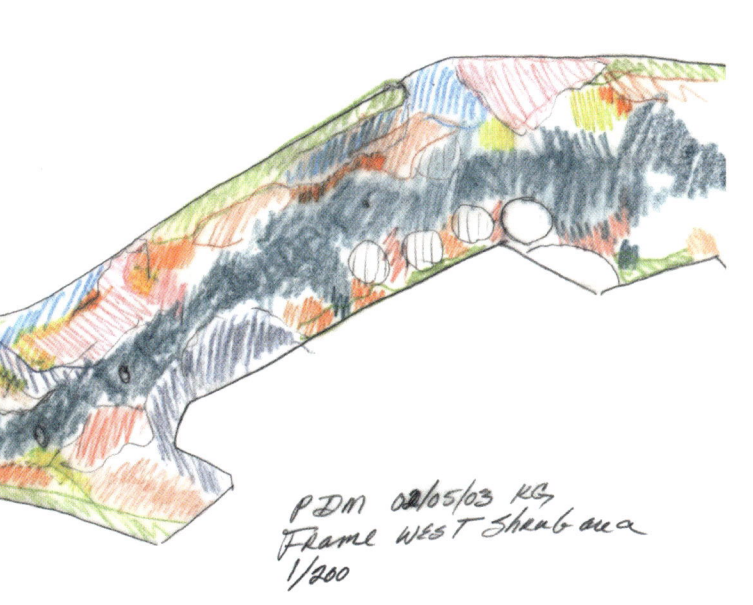

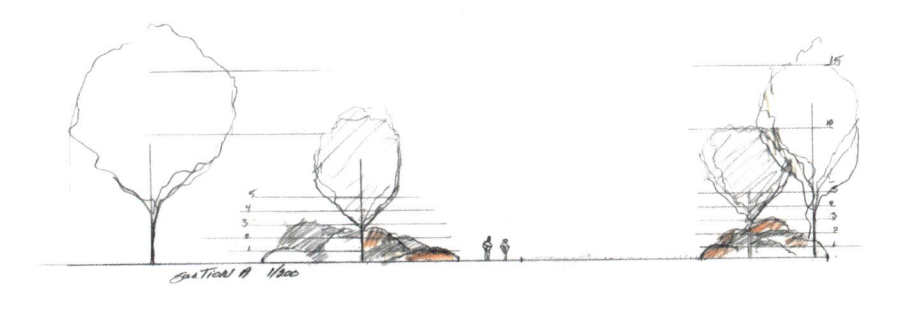

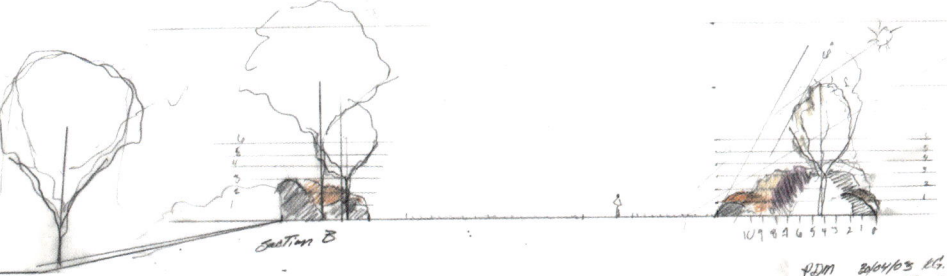

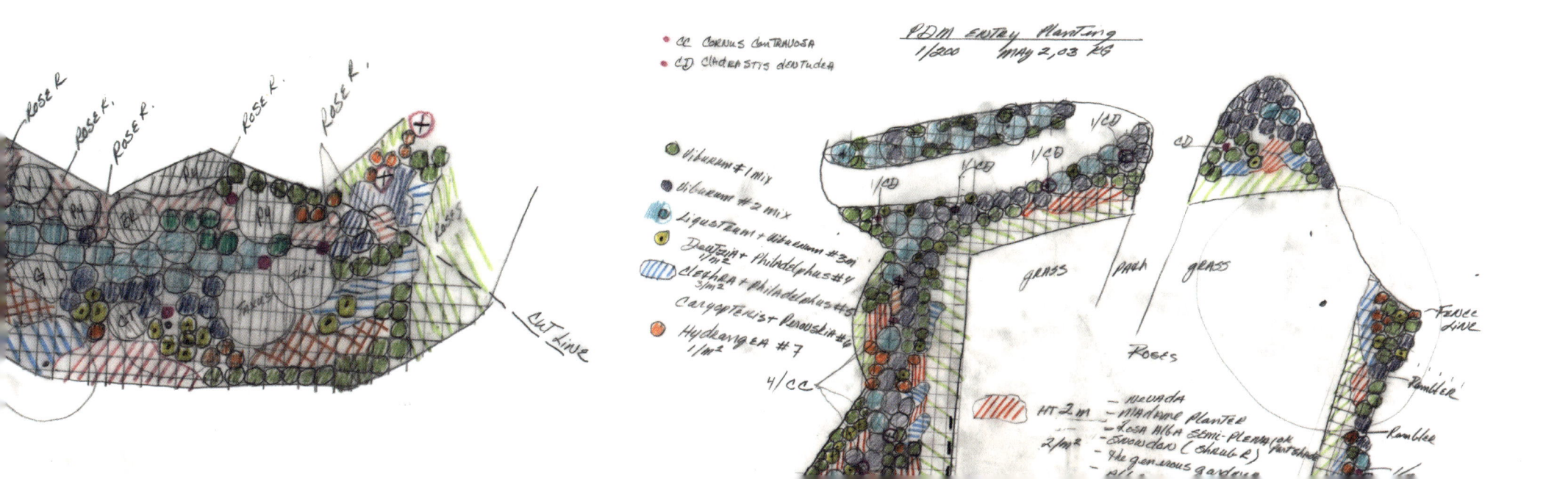

Hassell
Melbourne, Australia

Model-making may or may not be a dying art in the design profession, but its inherent practical and creative value cannot be gainsaid. Hassell is a large design firm working across the disciplines out of multiple international offices, but there is space for model specialist Sharon Wright to work. Her cut-paper models are a long way from the corporate perfection of typical architectural models, but somehow they are surely closer to the reality and spirit of the final result.

Sharon Wright explains: 'The design process starts with in-depth mapping, photographic analysis, historical and cultural research, usually represented in concept models that help to visualize the site's character. These models have to be quick. They are intentionally rough and not overworked. They are a tool designed to get to the essence of a site rapidly in order to find a project's starting point. As a first response to site-mapping, sketch models are used to tease out the story of a site. This is vital in creating schemes that are powerful and contextual, not purely pattern-making exercises.

'The models are mostly made from cut paper and are produced quickly – ten to fifteen minutes, maximum. If they are not working by then, they never will. The models are built from materials that are easily to hand – magazines, paper, even an old model – and rarely from new materials. Working daily in an integrated firm of architects, landscape architects, urban and interior designers, I tend to find that models are a useful way of gauging a colleague's response to a scheme, particularly if it is someone from another design discipline.

'The models are tactile, evocative and easy to alter, remould, reinterpret and then discard. Care is taken when photographing the models by means of exploring different angles and lighting scenarios – anything that might convey the way a site may be experienced in reality.'

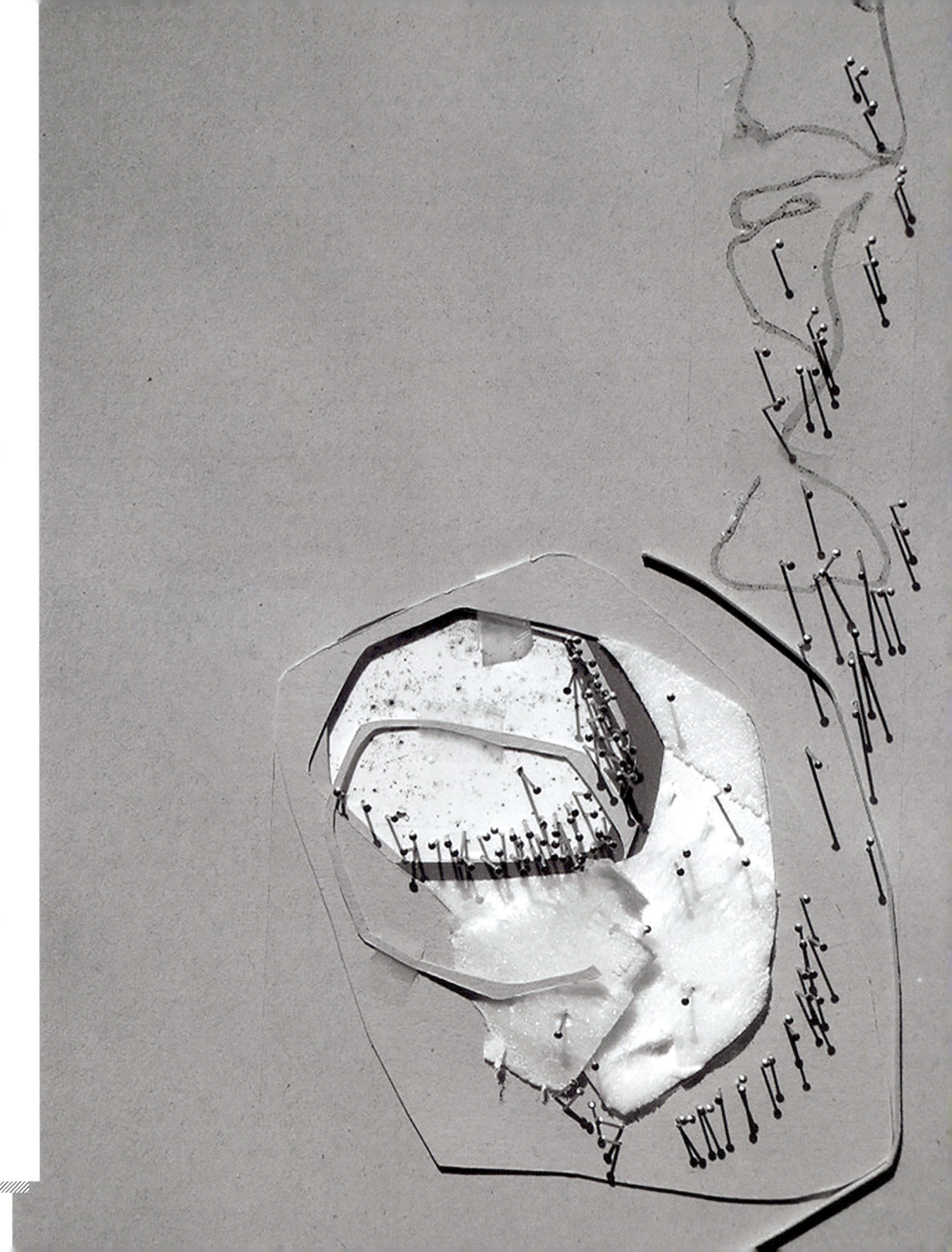

123

Hassell

EAGLE HOUSE,
LONDON, UK, 2012
Projects often begin with a workshop, during which each team member will come up with five conceptual ideas in two hours. The models shown here represent two of these ideas. The first (above and right) drew on the music-hall history of the site, utilizing old pictures of the sumptuous interior, and led ultimately to the selection of materials and colours. The second model (below) recognized the urban context of the site and the desire to soften the streetscape with a miniature woodland. The trees were represented by pins, for speed, which were added and taken away until the team was satisfied with the composition. A year later, the woodland was installed and is now a moment of calm amid the hubbub of City Road.

BOIS CERN, GENEVA,
SWITZERLAND, 2011
For this project, the dramatic setting of the CERN campus – defined by the Jura mountain range to the west of the site – was a major consideration. The sketch model (above and opposite) was used to explore the existing vegetative character of the site, with the strong linear form of the Route de Meyrin slicing through the patterns of forest and fields. A series of clearings in the forest was proposed to define key spaces along the road and across the site. The sketches proved to be a rapid and evocative way of exploring these ideas and of testing spatial relationships, scale and rhythms.

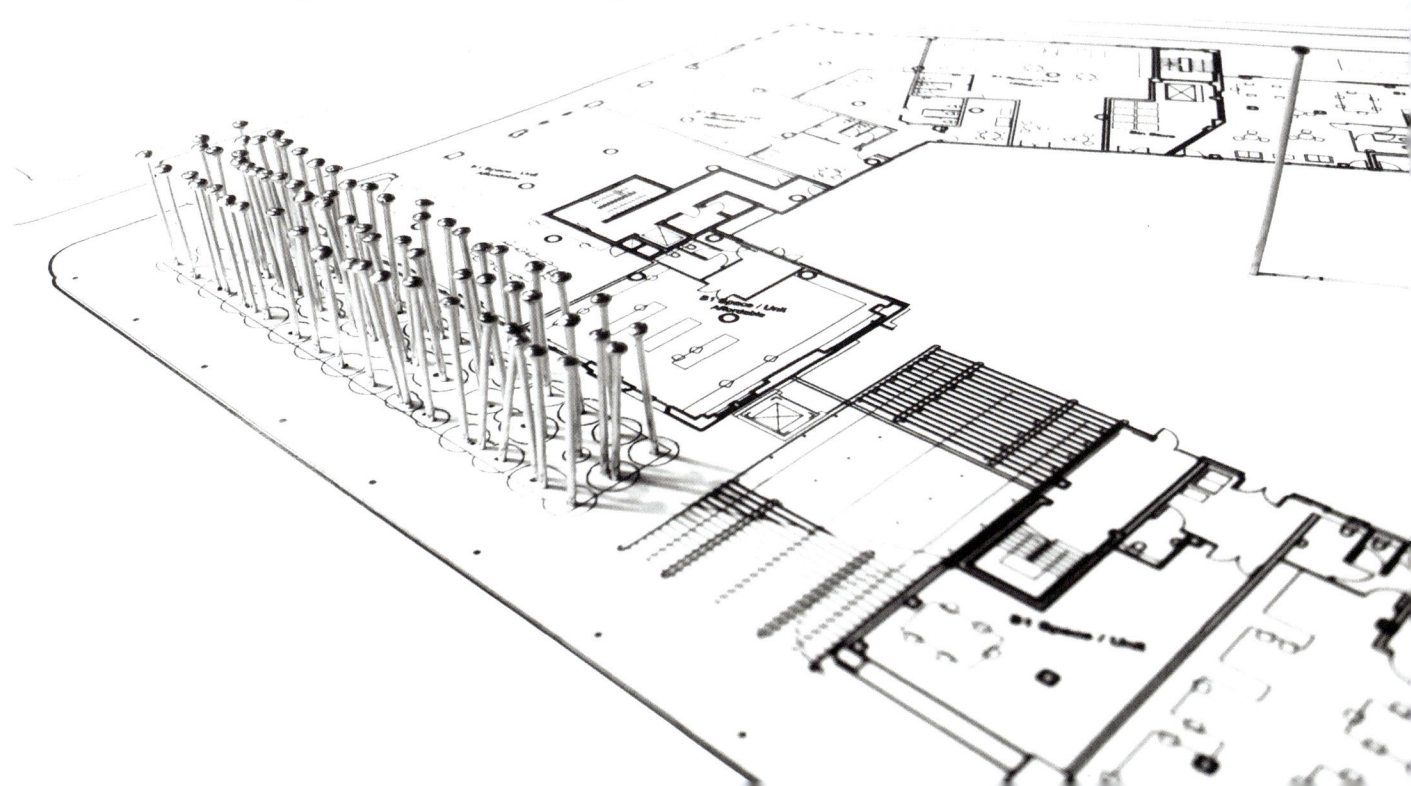

CENTRAL BUSINESS DISTRICT, BRISBANE, AUSTRALIA, 2013
The subject of this competition was a site on the edge of the Brisbane River, flanked by a tangle of elevated roads. This model was a means of exploring different ways of turning the site's significant flooding issues into a positive. It was an expedient way of looking into the way terraces could function at the water's edge in this urban environment. Sharon Wright explored the design of the public spaces and landscape setting with a view to reconnecting Brisbane's business district with the river. The speed of the cuts and the scrappy nature of the card helped to avoid over-thinking the composition.

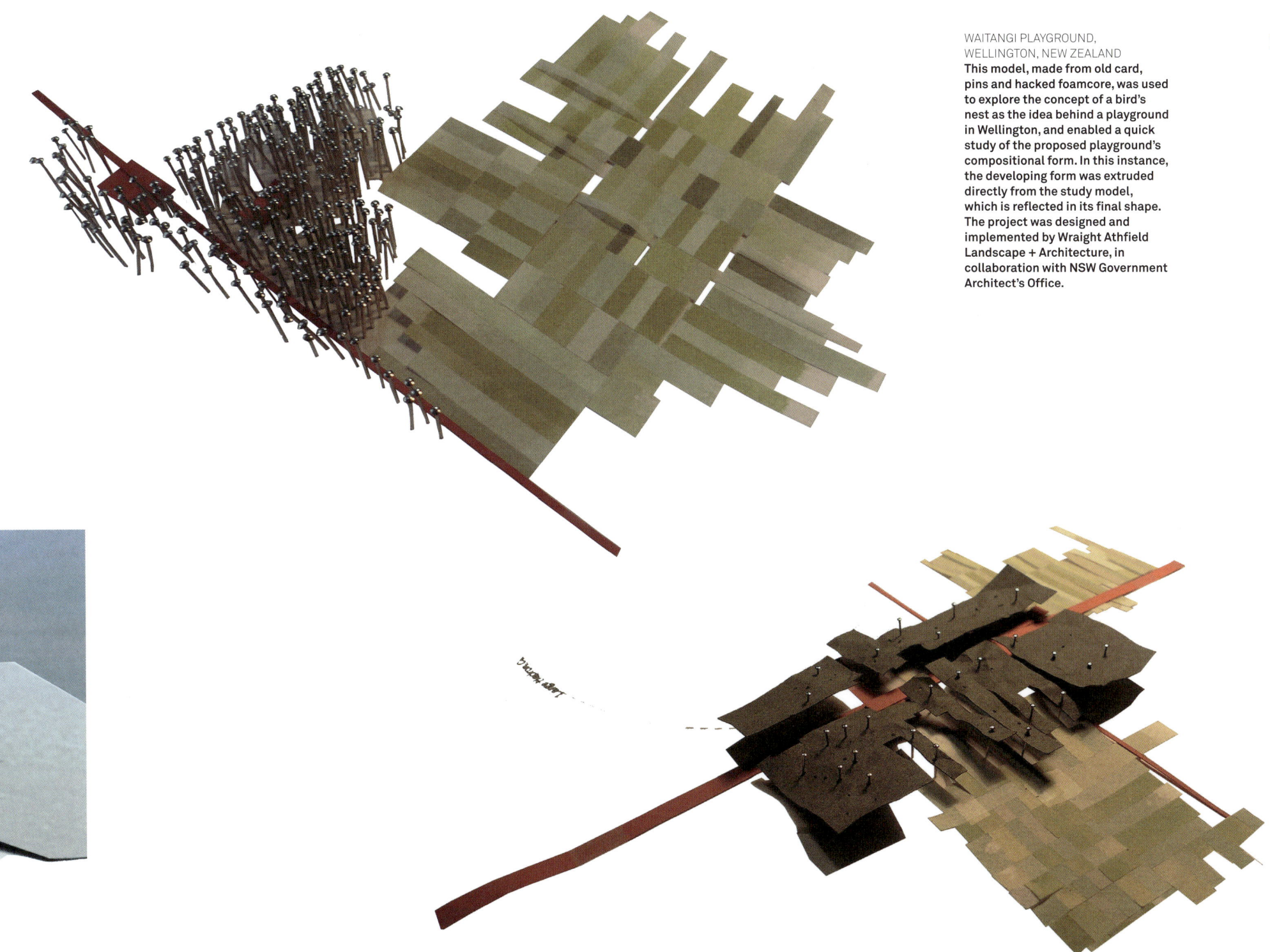

WAITANGI PLAYGROUND,
WELLINGTON, NEW ZEALAND
This model, made from old card, pins and hacked foamcore, was used to explore the concept of a bird's nest as the idea behind a playground in Wellington, and enabled a quick study of the proposed playground's compositional form. In this instance, the developing form was extruded directly from the study model, which is reflected in its final shape. The project was designed and implemented by Wraight Athfield Landscape + Architecture, in collaboration with NSW Government Architect's Office.

Hocker Design
Dallas, USA

Hocker Design president and design principal David L. Hocker has developed a sketching methodology that consists of specific phases, culminating in drawings replete with symbols and notes that are an effective means of communicating with colleagues and potential clients. The intention is clarity of thought and intention, a rationale that is just as valid in its way as the exuberant flights of imagination other designers like to pursue in their sketchbooks.

David L. Hocker writes: 'My process, and subsequently that of the studio, begins with loose, rather noncommittal gestures as a way of visually understanding a site and its contextual influences and overall potential. I use more of a visual note-taking approach to my sketching, in which artistic masterpieces are not the end goal. A more informative dialogue between visual sketches and notation is the result: line drawings mixed with both verbal and numerical information and architectural symbols.

'These pen strokes of visual understanding are distilled down into simple ideas that provide the backbone for the design process. And the ideas are further developed through subsequent sketches. Numerous overlays produce more specific line work, which is ultimately translated by the studio into working drawings.

'Hand-sketching and drawing never stops throughout the design process and project timeline, but the typology continues to evolve, depending on the function of the drawing. Red-line sketches of details – made during conversations with contractors – are more casual, as are process drawings made in early design meetings, as opposed to more illustrative graphics.'

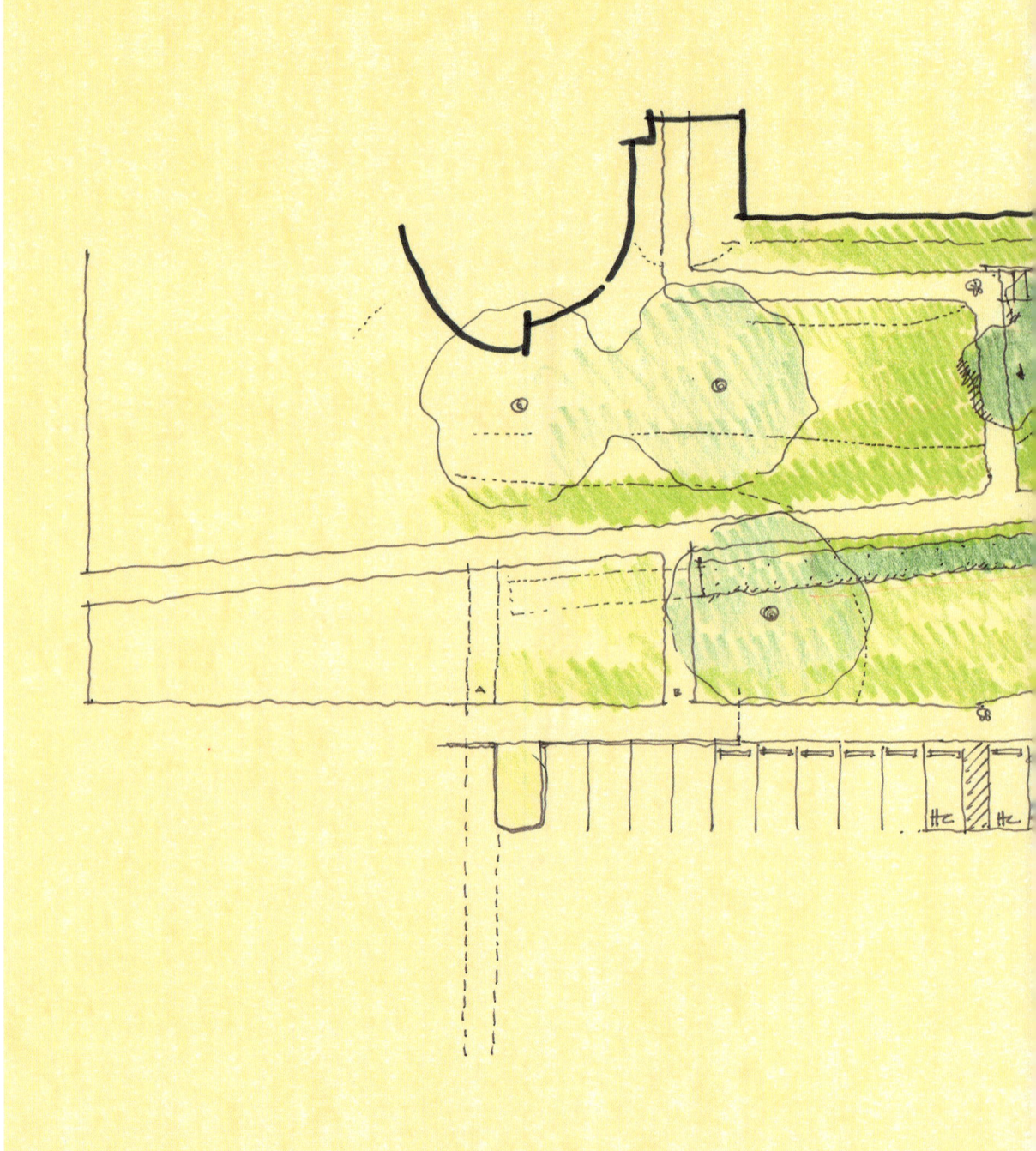

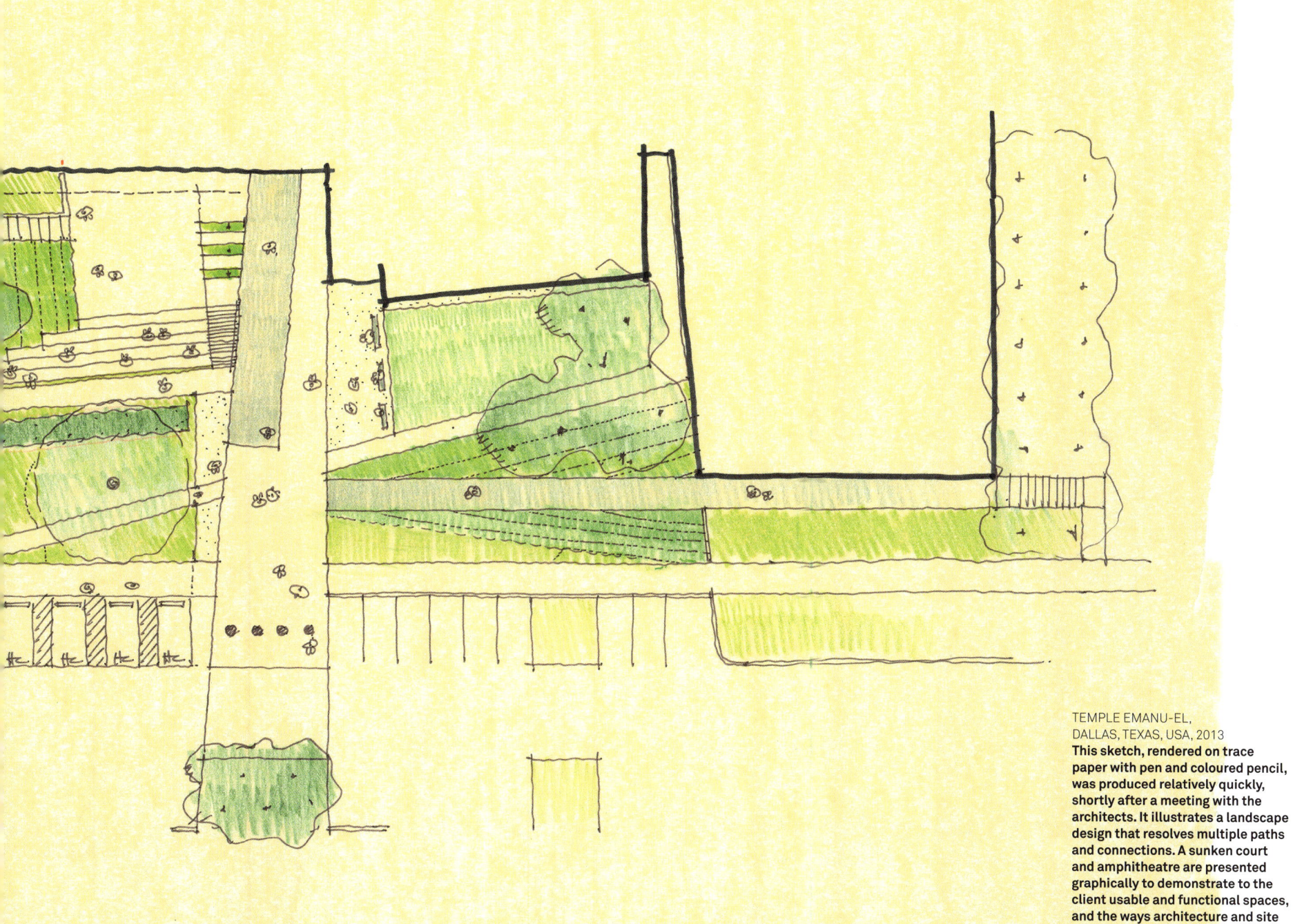

TEMPLE EMANU-EL,
DALLAS, TEXAS, USA, 2013
This sketch, rendered on trace paper with pen and coloured pencil, was produced relatively quickly, shortly after a meeting with the architects. It illustrates a landscape design that resolves multiple paths and connections. A sunken court and amphitheatre are presented graphically to demonstrate to the client usable and functional spaces, and the ways architecture and site might cohere.

128 Hocker Design

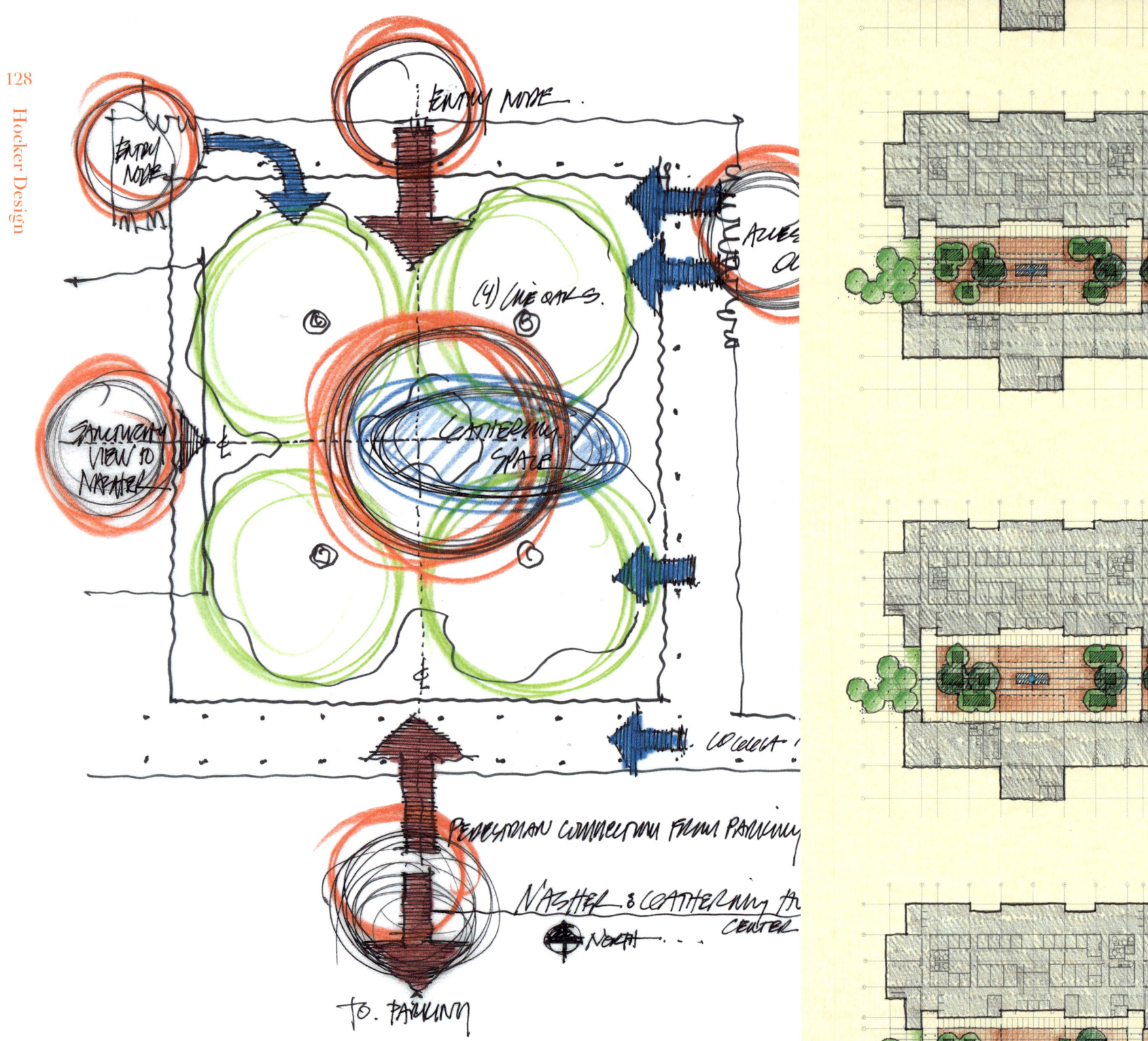

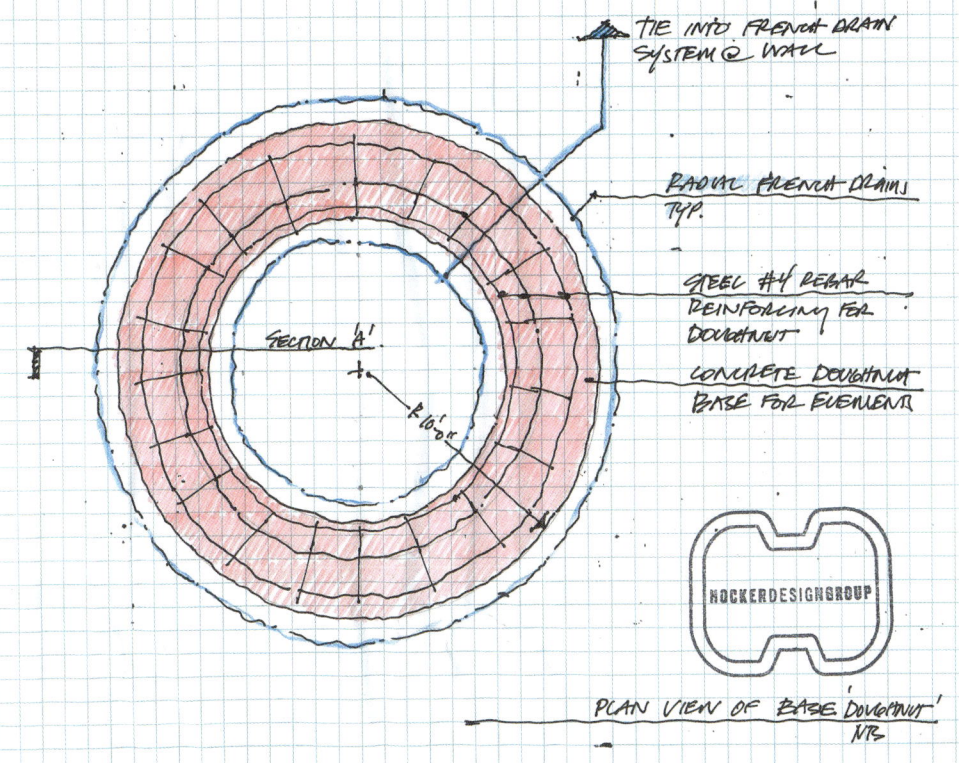

TEMPLE EMANU-EL,
DALLAS, TEXAS, USA, 2013
These fast sketches, all done on trace paper with pen, coloured pencils and marker pens, form a series of visual notes. The entire series dealt with connections across the entire site, new and existing conditions and the development of interstitial spaces between building environments. These visual notes and sketches were then organized and introduced as part of a presentation to the client, reflecting the candid design dialogue that must occur prior to the realization of the actual design.

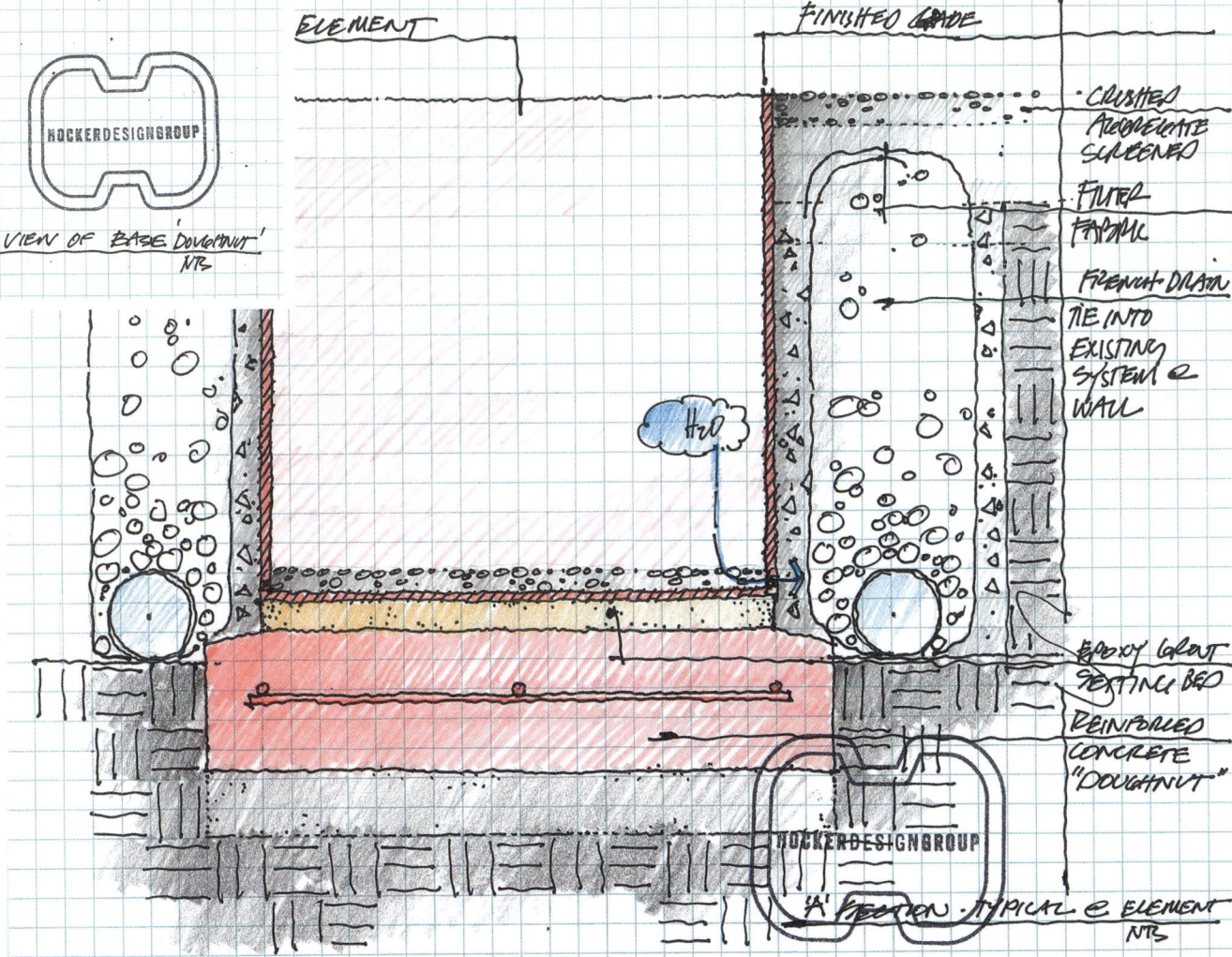

Hocker Design

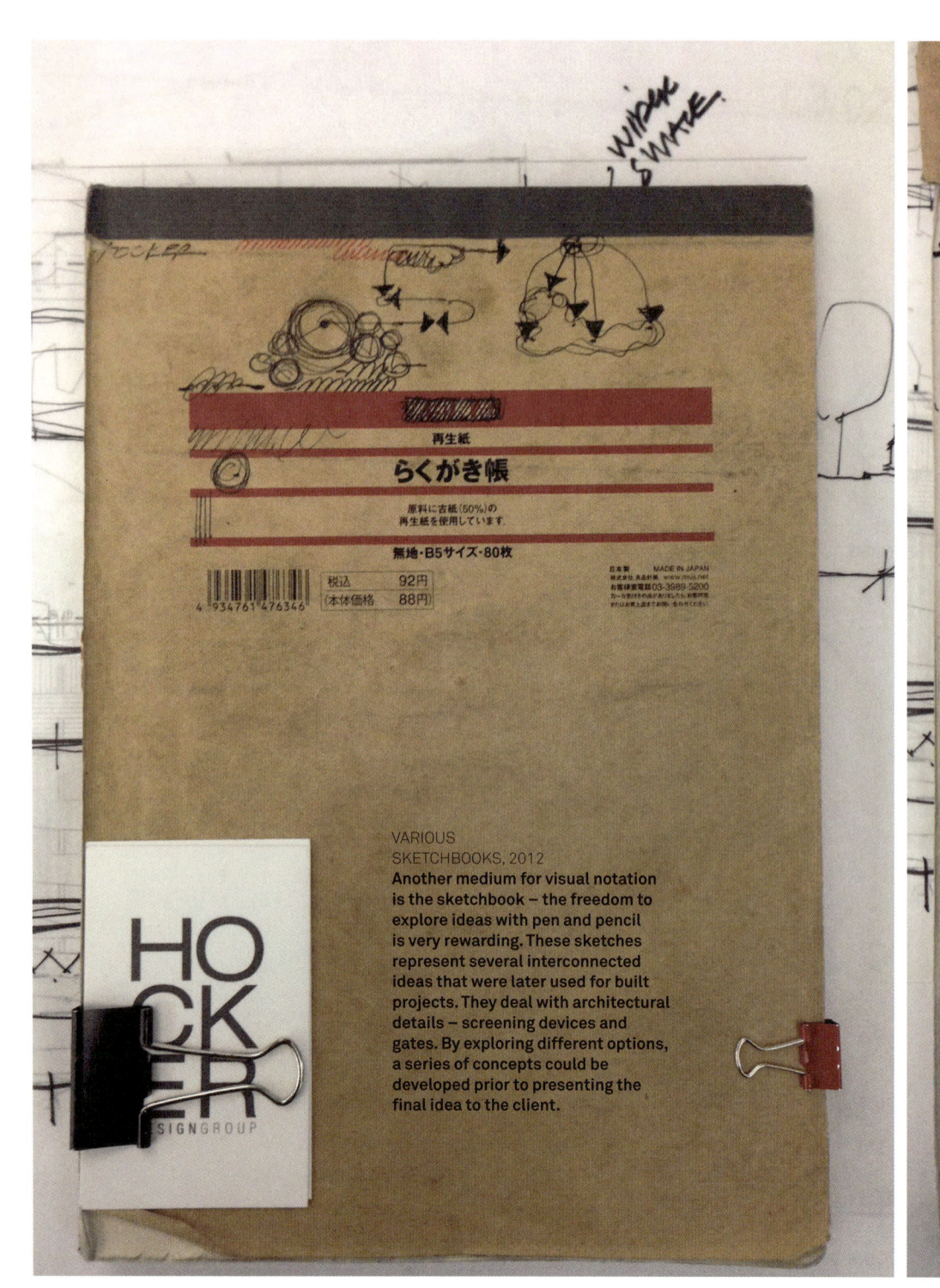

VARIOUS SKETCHBOOKS, 2012
Another medium for visual notation is the sketchbook – the freedom to explore ideas with pen and pencil is very rewarding. These sketches represent several interconnected ideas that were later used for built projects. They deal with architectural details – screening devices and gates. By exploring different options, a series of concepts could be developed prior to presenting the final idea to the client.

Left Page

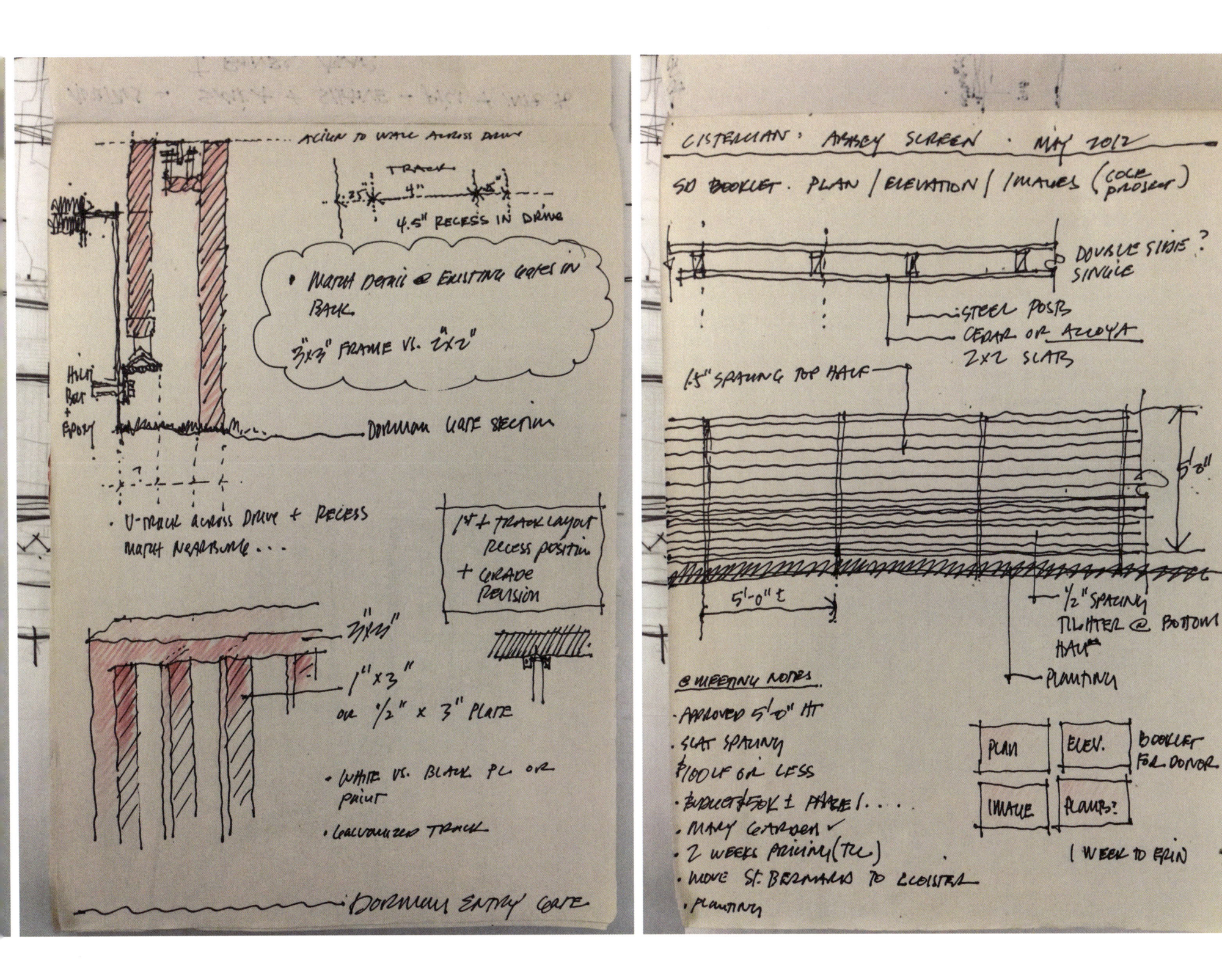

- ALIGN TO WALL ACROSS DRIVE

TRACK
.25" — 4"
4.5" RECESS IN DRIVE

- MATCH DETAIL @ EXISTING GATES IN BACK
- 3"x3" FRAME vs. 2"x2"

HILTI BAR + EPOXY

DORMAN GATE SECTION

- U-TRACK ACROSS DRIVE + RECESS MATCH NEARBUNE...

1st + TRACK LAYOUT + RECESS POSITION + GRADE REVISION

3"x3"
1"x3"
or 1/2" x 3" PLATE

- WHITE vs. BLACK PC or PAINT
- GALVANIZED TRACK

DORMAN ENTRY GATE

Right Page

CISTERCIAN · ABBEY SCREEN · MAY 2012

SD BOOKLET · PLAN / ELEVATION / IMAGES (COLE PROJECT)

DOUBLE SIDE? SINGLE

STEEL POSTS
CEDAR or ACCOYA
2x2 SLAT

1.5" SPACING TOP HALF

5'-0"

5'-0" ±

1/2" SPACING TIGHTER @ BOTTOM HALF

PLANTING

MEETING NOTES
- APPROVED 5'-0" HT
- SLAT SPACING
- $100 LF OR LESS
- BUDGET $50K ± PHASE 1....
- MARY GARDEN ✓
- 2 WEEKS PRICING (TC)
- MOVE ST. BERNARD TO CLOISTER
- PLANTING

| PLAN | ELEV. |
| IMAGE | PLANTS? |

BOOKLET FOR DONOR

1 WEEK TO ERIN

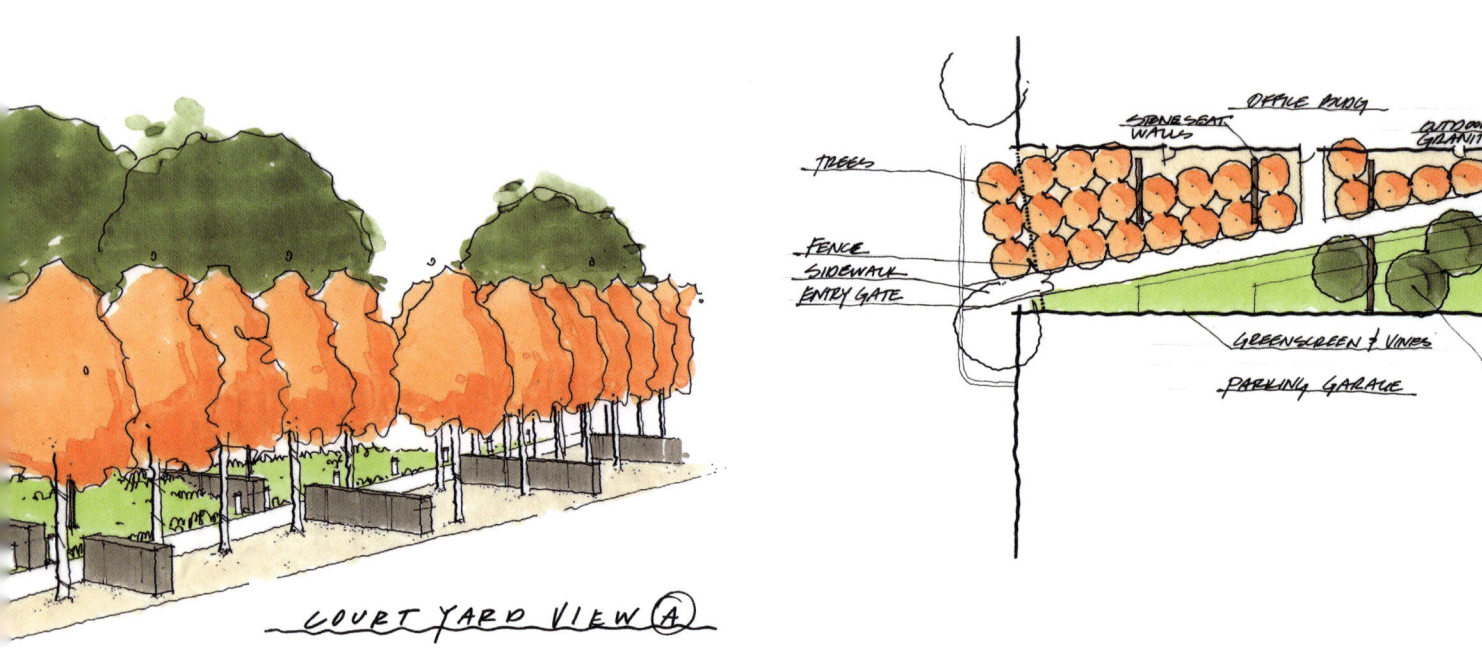

KLABZUBA OFFICES,
FORT WORTH, TEXAS, USA, 2009
All three of these sketches were rendered with pen and marker on trace paper for a design presentation meeting with a client. They introduce a soft and simple use of line-work and colour for the presentation of different perspectives.

COURTYARD VIEW B

COURTYARD VIEW A

IDEA SCHOOLS HEADQUARTERS, WESLACO, TEXAS, USA, 2014
This series of sketches, made on graph paper with pen and coloured pencil, were part of the exploration of a particular detail that addressed the channelling and recapture of rainwater run-off in a large courtyard. These ideas were an important part of the overall design, and the simple illustrations demonstrated the idea to the client.

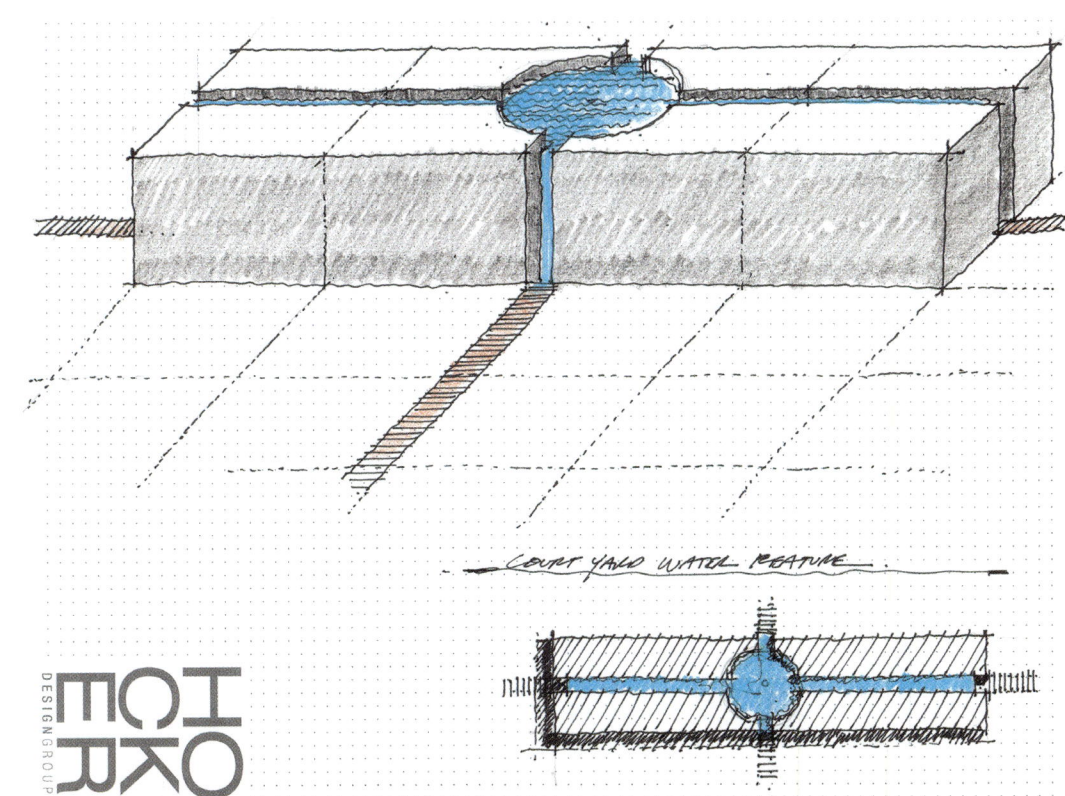

Edward Hutchison
London, UK

A landscape designer whose creative work exists on paper as much as in the world – and who has been consistently valued professionally for this quality – Edward Hutchison imagines a world in which landscape architects may be persuaded to draw daily on paper, just as professional musicians practice their instruments every day. Ultimately, he envisages the soul and sensitivity of the hand combining with the precision of the computer.

Edward Hutchison writes: 'The development of ideas is the quintessence of my practice. Drawing by hand is crucial in the developmental process, to the extent that if only electronic drawing was acceptable, the practice could not be sustained. It is near impossible to sketch ideas on a computer with the same alacrity as by hand. Concepts tumble out as the pencil moves across the paper, giving rise to further thoughts and solutions. The ambiguity of a rough sketch often hints at an unpredictable approach in which serendipity can lead on to an innovative design, a process seldom replicated by the rigidity of the digital medium.

'Landscape is a very sensual subject, and any designer will benefit by exploring ideas in different media to test this sensuality. An initial concept drawn small with a fat 6B pencil can be a very direct way of communicating. At a later stage in the project, using the same pencil to draw details is a good way of testing whether the designs are getting too fussy.

'We have become over-dependent on computers. It is too easy to create images that are very appealing. This imagery draws the design forward, and the consequence is that decisions are based on beautiful, clever renderings and not enough time has been spent on the structural rationale of the design. What is missing in current education and in design offices is the balance of designing using the best of both worlds.'

CHRIST CHURCH SPITALFIELDS, LONDON, UK, 2012
An analysis drawing for a competition (below), showing the contrasts between the sculptural stonework of the eighteenth-century church, the brickwork of nearby houses and the surrounding London plane trees.

GARDEN MUSEUM, LONDON, UK, 2012
This historic site is next to Lambeth Palace (opposite). Analysing the essence of a site by drawing is a more efficient way of communicating its key features than by taking photographs.

RULES FOR THE OPEN SPACE? NO DOGS NO DRUGS NO DRINKING...... SITTING DOWN ON GRASS. TIMBER. PHYSICAL PRESENCE OF CHURCH VERY STRONG
DESIGN CHALLENGE FOR THE NEW SPACE IS IT VERY STRONG - VERY RESPECTFUL
IT CAN NOT COMPETE IN THE SAME LANGUAGE AS HAWKSMOOR?

REDESIGN OF A VILLAGE GREEN, KENNINGTON, LONDON, UK, 2012

Two sketch proposals drawn on site for the redesign of a small village green. Site sketches can be very effective in binding ideas for the landscape into the existing context, as the new and the old can be drawn with the same degree of confidence and vitality. A colourful Fauvist palette used for site-analysis drawings can help present ideas in a distinctive way (opposite). Here, the colours demonstrate the importance of mature trees on a site to be developed by Transport for London. Many have subsequently been cut down.

Re-establishing importance of site

BRIMHAM ROCKS,
RIPON, YORKSHIRE, UK, 2011
The quality of mass, crevices and curiously ordered stacking of these sandstone rocks (below) contrasts with the delicacy of the surrounding trees. Sometimes the abstraction of a subject experienced in situ later lends itself to a surprisingly powerful and intimate engagement with the spirit of the landscape.

ATLAS MOUNTAINS, MOROCCO, AND CHARWELL FIELD, SOMERSET, UK, 2013
Studies on black and grey paper of the Atlas Mountains (right) and Charwell Field (opposite). Few landscape subjects are predominantly white, yet most designers choose white paper, gradually obliterating the whiteness as the drawing progresses.

Edward Hutchison

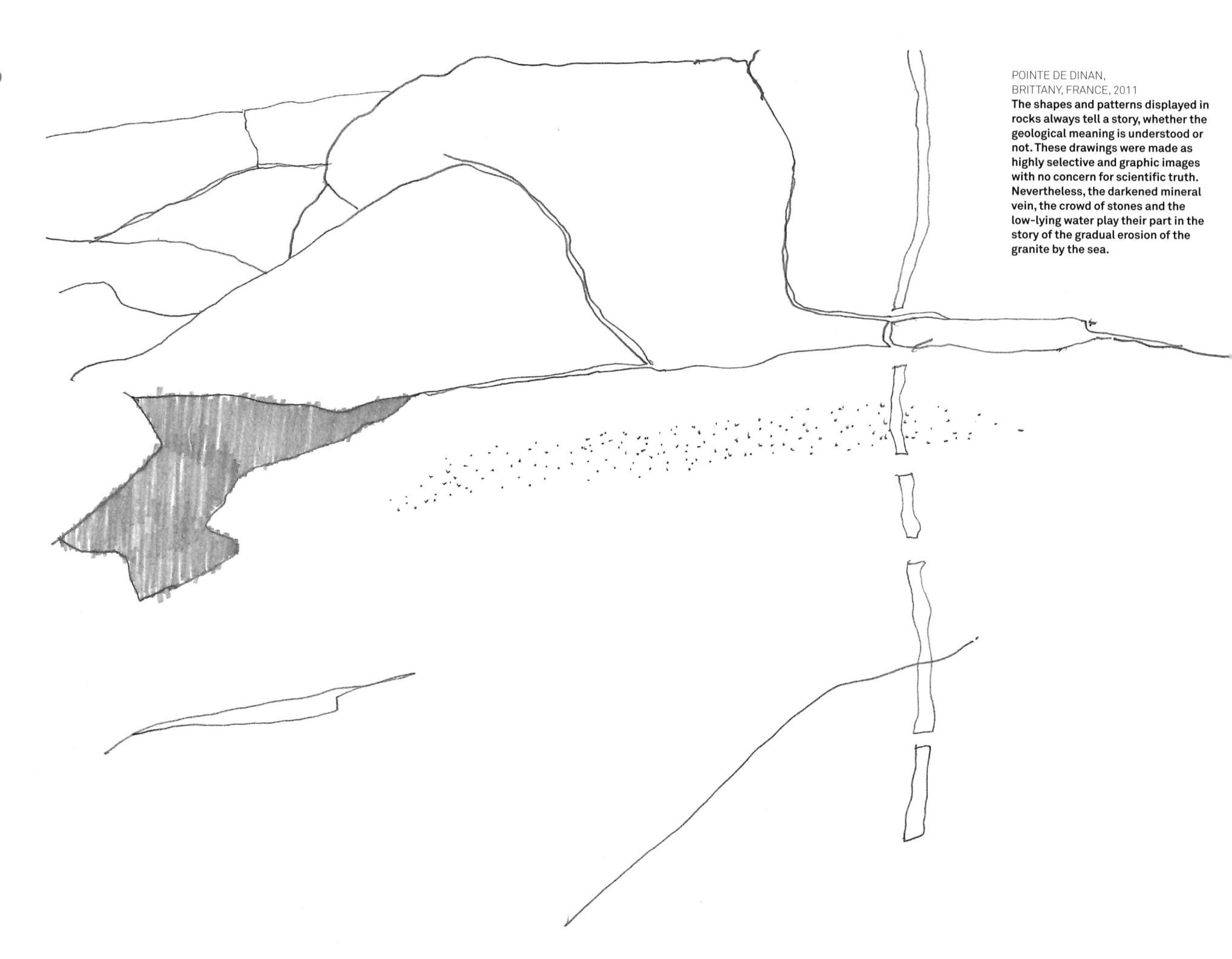

POINTE DE DINAN,
BRITTANY, FRANCE, 2011
The shapes and patterns displayed in rocks always tell a story, whether the geological meaning is understood or not. These drawings were made as highly selective and graphic images with no concern for scientific truth. Nevertheless, the darkened mineral vein, the crowd of stones and the low-lying water play their part in the story of the gradual erosion of the granite by the sea.

141

Edward Hutchison

142

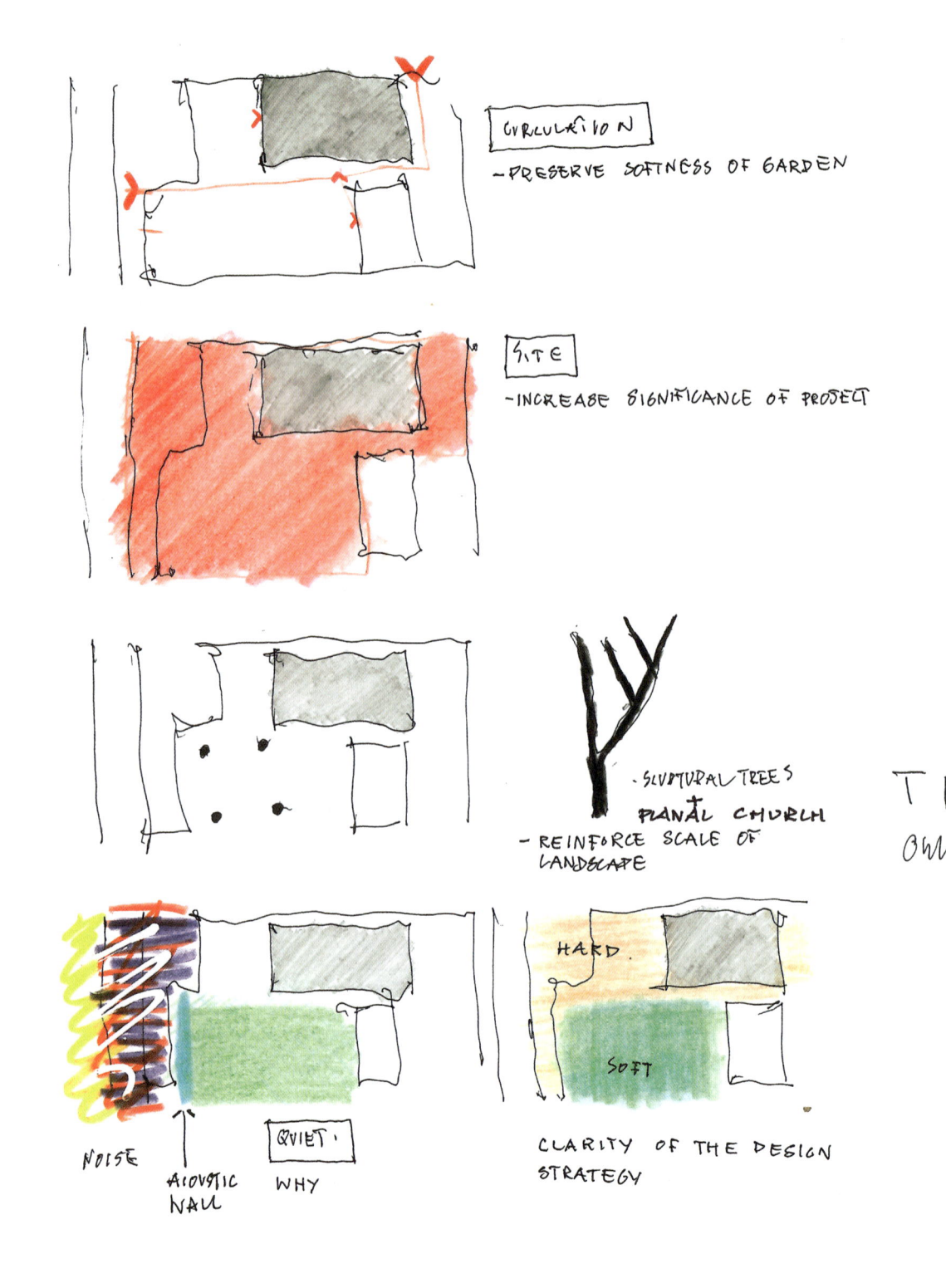

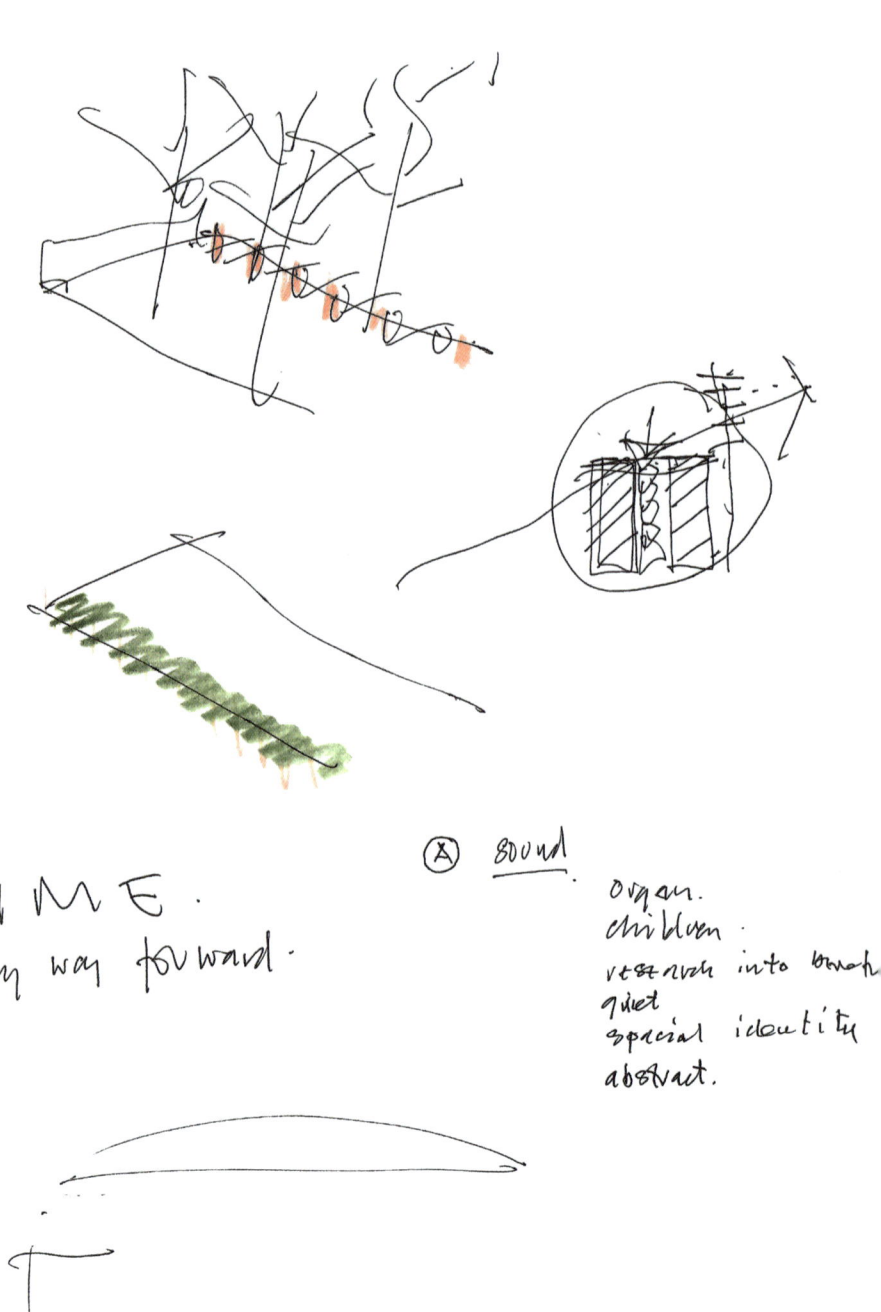

Edward Hutchison

CHRISTCHURCH SPITALFIELDS, LONDON, UK, 2012
Analysis concept sketches (above) for a competition to redevelop the churchyard. Informal coloured-pencil drawings are often less daunting to a client than immaculately drawn plans.

PROPOSAL FOR A PRIVATE HOME, LONDON, UK, 2012
These analysis drawings (opposite) explore the arrival sequence of spaces at a private house in Dulwich.

strategic approach to site

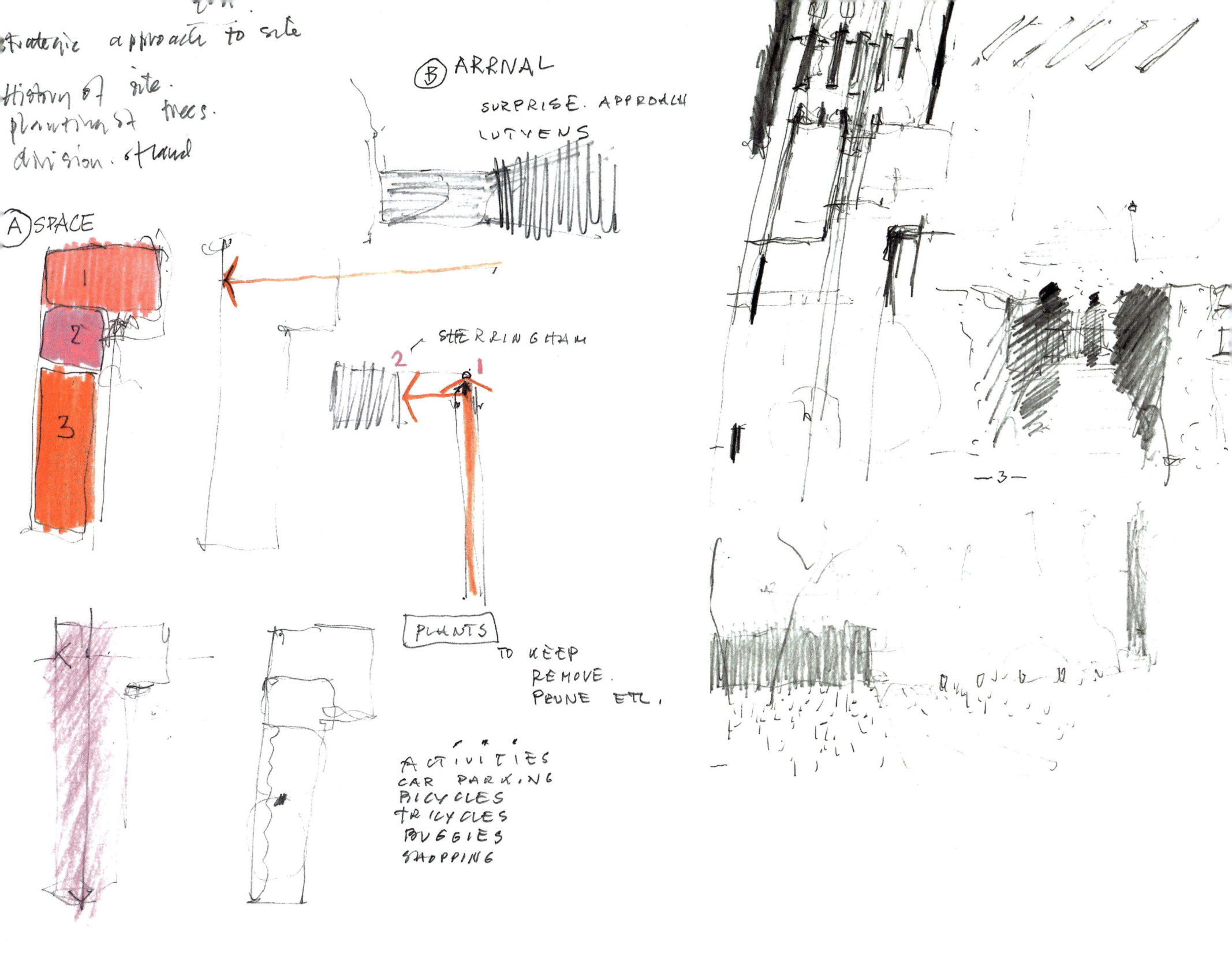

History of site.
planting of trees.
division. strand

(B) ARRIVAL

SURPRISE. APPROACH
LUTYENS

(A) SPACE

1
2
3

SHERRINGHAM
2   1

PLANTS

TO KEEP
REMOVE.
PRUNE ETC.

ACTIVITIES
CAR PARKING
BICYCLES
TRICYCLES
BUGGIES
SHOPPING

—3—

TREGREHAN HOUSE,
CORNWALL, UK, 2014
Drawing well-established landscapes is a good way of learning lessons from the past. The rich variety of tone, texture and bulk of these trees emphasizes the variety of stonework and detailing of this Palladian house.

GRASS? / WATER.

WOLFSON COLLEGE,
UNIVERSITY OF OXFORD, UK, 2014
Philip Powell and Hidalgo Moya
designed the college in the 1960s
on a beautiful riverside site, and
employed no landscape architect.
Half a century later, the brief to the
landscape architect working on the
new extension to the college requires
equal rigour in order to be true to the
original architects' vision.

Raymond Jungles
Miami, USA

It is uncanny when the drawing style of a designer seems to mimic or match the style of the landscape design as realized. (It is something that occurs with noteworthy frequency.) The garden plans of Raymond Jungles reflect the formal exuberance and colour vitality of his work 'on the ground'. The tactility of plants is captured in his drawings, even where they are rendered formulaically. This is something one often notices with the work of garden designers, as opposed to landscape architects.

Raymond Jungles writes: 'I enjoy the process of drawing. I draw on yellow trace paper with Prismacolor pencils and ink. Drawings are work tools and function as one level of presentation. I design in layers. I trace over the site survey, then outline all the architecture and the existing trees. I study the site circulation, and then proceed to grading studies and constructed items first – hardscape including driveways and terraces, pools, water features, and so on.

'I do not draw until I have to. I mull it over and then revise the design through the development phase. I draw as long as I need to and make revisions to make things better. Drawing is a way of thinking about design. It is important because you are communicating with yourself as a designer. It is like a well-written book: you are telling a story. I enjoy the process. Each time I draw, I learn more and begin to see relationships. My drawings make the garden intelligible before it is built.

'Colour is important. It signifies different things, whether a symbol to notate a flowering tree or a water element. I use "grass green" for lawn areas, "peacock blue" for water elements and "lavender" to delineate air-conditioned spaces. I do not design using a computer. Drawing is a tool that I am comfortable with. I think drawings created via computers have merit, but it is only through drawing that I can visualize three-dimensional spaces from two-dimensional drawings.'

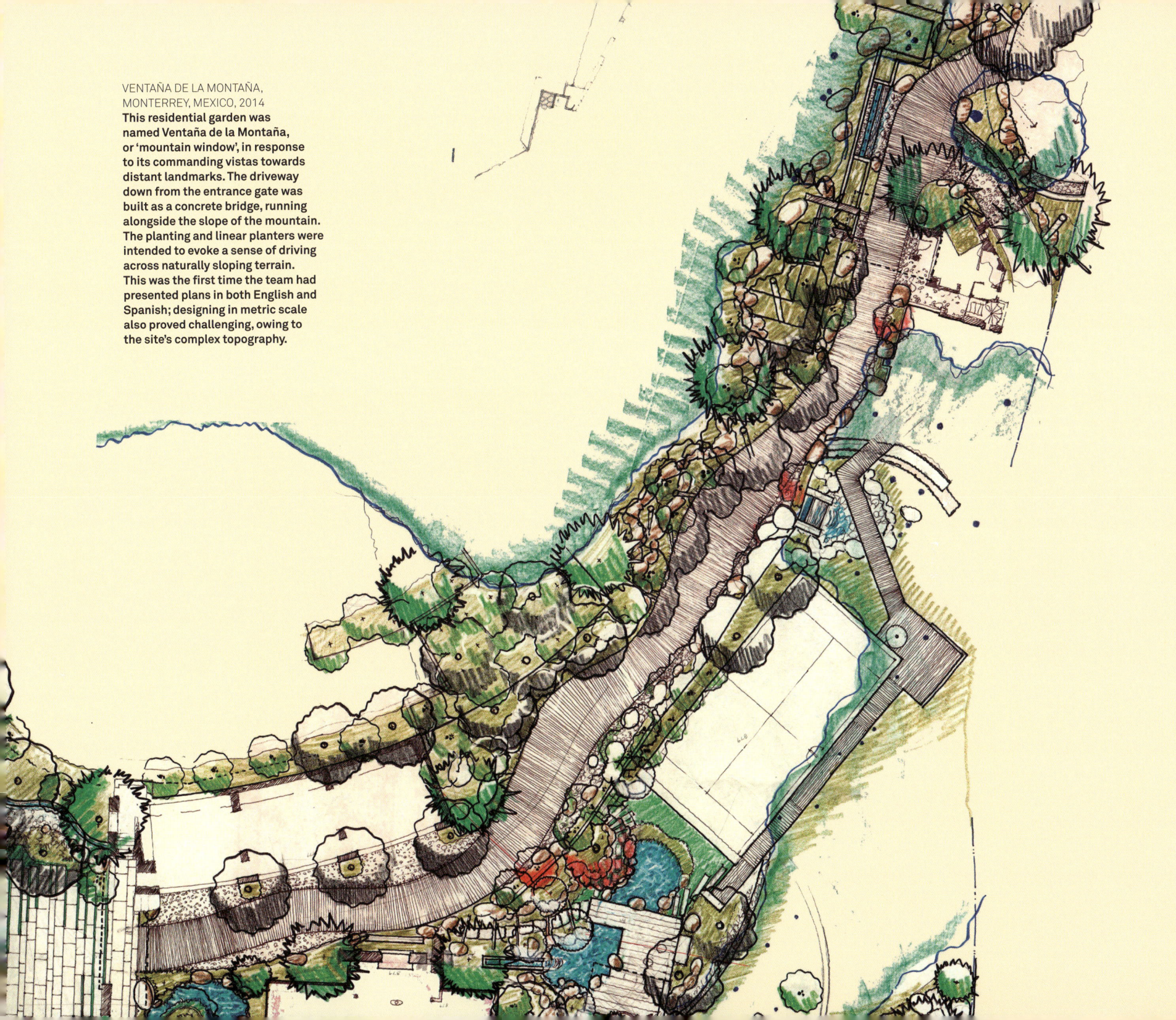

VENTAÑA DE LA MONTAÑA,
MONTERREY, MEXICO, 2014
This residential garden was named Ventaña de la Montaña, or 'mountain window', in response to its commanding vistas towards distant landmarks. The driveway down from the entrance gate was built as a concrete bridge, running alongside the slope of the mountain. The planting and linear planters were intended to evoke a sense of driving across naturally sloping terrain. This was the first time the team had presented plans in both English and Spanish; designing in metric scale also proved challenging, owing to the site's complex topography.

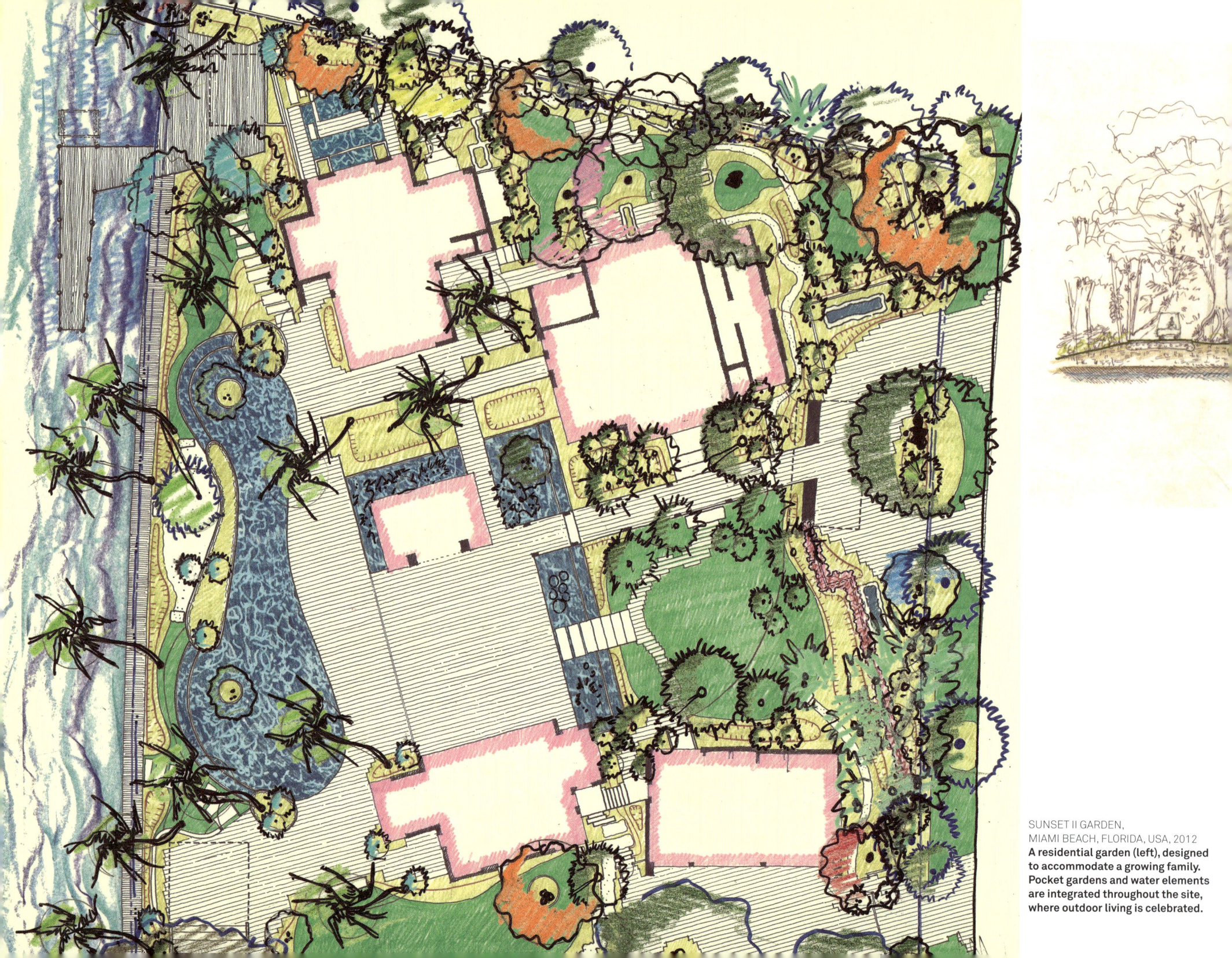

SUNSET II GARDEN,
MIAMI BEACH, FLORIDA, USA, 2012
A residential garden (left), designed to accommodate a growing family. Pocket gardens and water elements are integrated throughout the site, where outdoor living is celebrated.

BRAZILIAN GARDEN,
NAPLES, FLORIDA, USA, 2009
This garden in the Naples Botanical Garden (above and right) was designed to emphasize the prodigious and inventive legacy of the late Roberto Burle Marx. A sense of peaceful drama is created by the garden's focal point, an elevated water garden plaza set against the backdrop of a conserved area of natural vegetation.

CORNFELD GARDEN,
HOLLYWOOD, FLORIDA, USA, 2002
This residential garden was designed to blend into the neighbouring native coppice woodland. Key plantings shown in the sketch include character Sabal palms and legacy canopy trees.

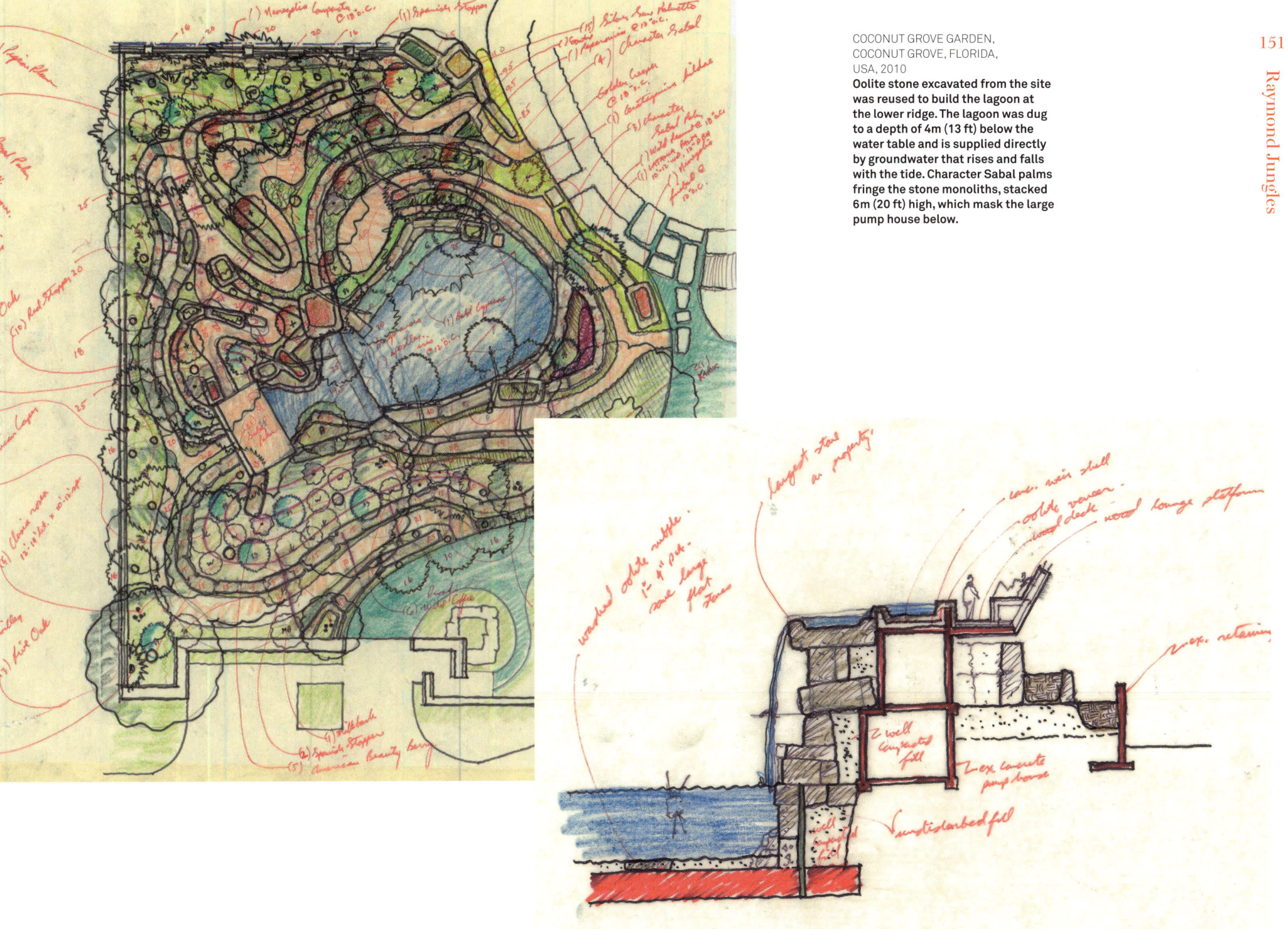

COCONUT GROVE GARDEN,
COCONUT GROVE, FLORIDA,
USA, 2010

Oolite stone excavated from the site was reused to build the lagoon at the lower ridge. The lagoon was dug to a depth of 4m (13 ft) below the water table and is supplied directly by groundwater that rises and falls with the tide. Character Sabal palms fringe the stone monoliths, stacked 6m (20 ft) high, which mask the large pump house below.

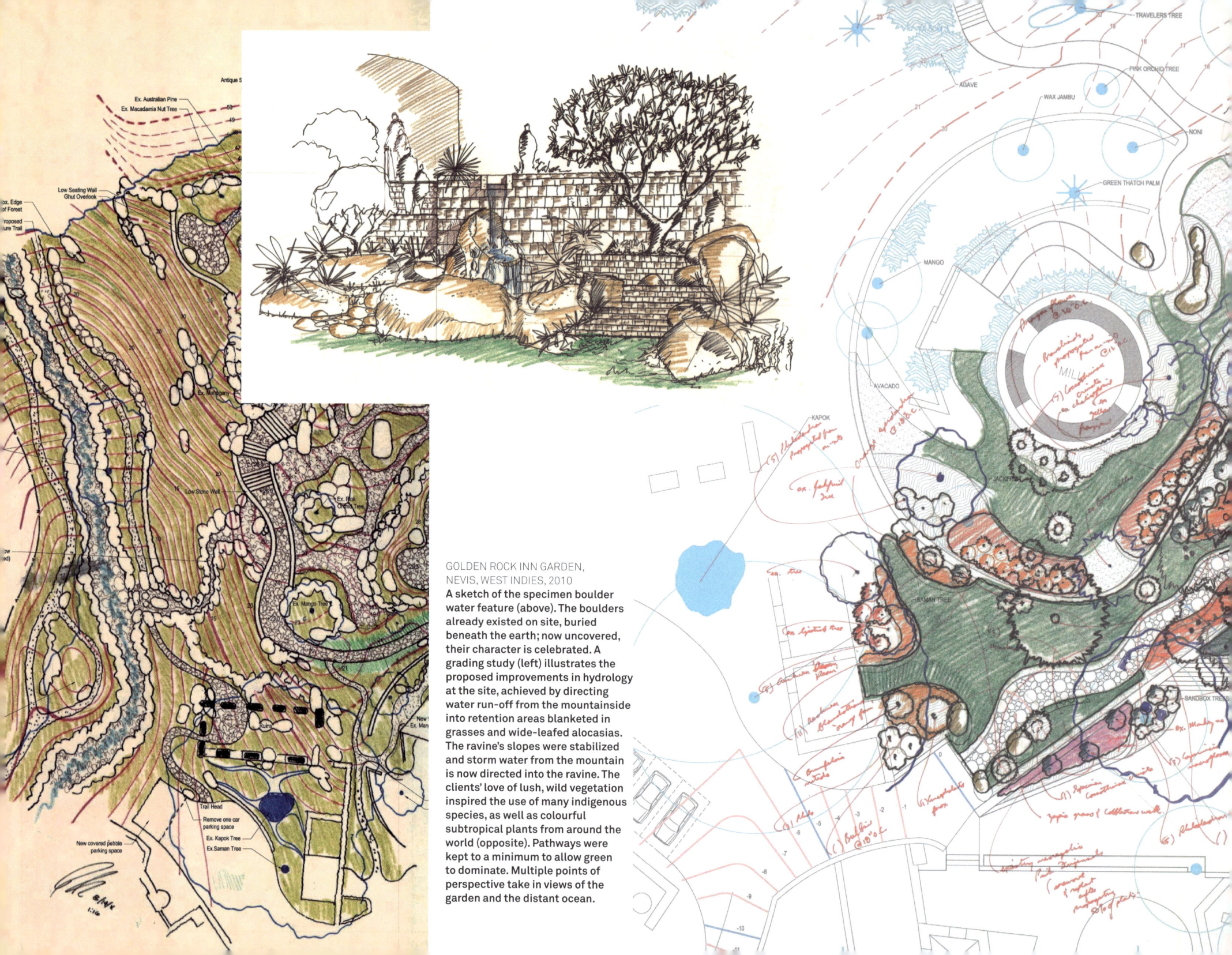

GOLDEN ROCK INN GARDEN, NEVIS, WEST INDIES, 2010
A sketch of the specimen boulder water feature (above). The boulders already existed on site, buried beneath the earth; now uncovered, their character is celebrated. A grading study (left) illustrates the proposed improvements in hydrology at the site, achieved by directing water run-off from the mountainside into retention areas blanketed in grasses and wide-leafed alocasias. The ravine's slopes were stabilized and storm water from the mountain is now directed into the ravine. The clients' love of lush, wild vegetation inspired the use of many indigenous species, as well as colourful subtropical plants from around the world (opposite). Pathways were kept to a minimum to allow green to dominate. Multiple points of perspective take in views of the garden and the distant ocean.

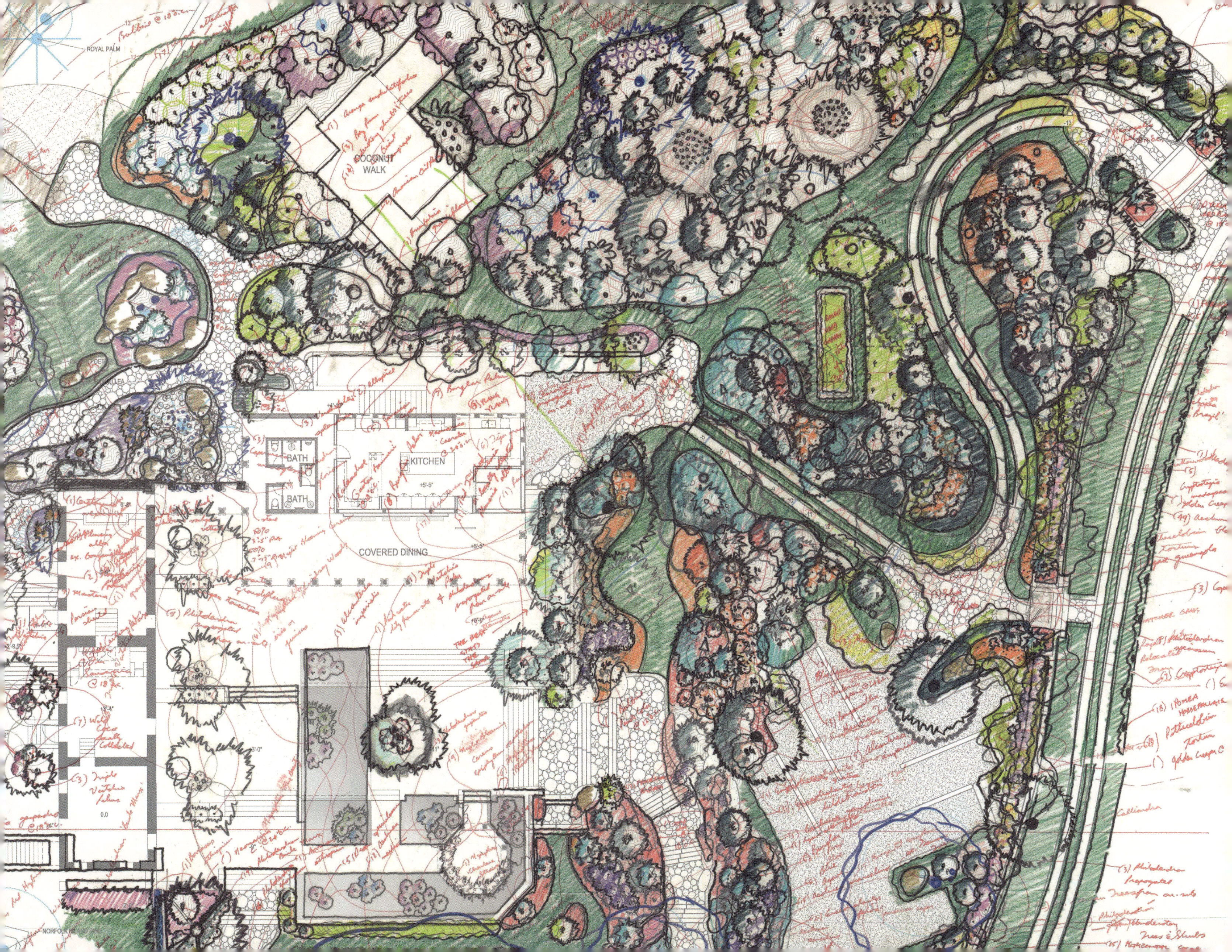
ROYAL PALM
COCONUT WALK
BATH
KITCHEN
BATH
COVERED DINING

1111 LINCOLN ROAD GARDEN,
MIAMI BEACH, FLORIDA, USA, 2010
An early sketch of the sculptural vault, designed to contain the pump equipment for the four water gardens included in the scheme (left). The vault is effectively melded with the plaza by means of a series of platforms, thus reducing its visual impact. This drawing (below) was almost the final design, but the 'Miami Beach red' colouring was ultimately removed. An early sketch (opposite) shows the first ideas for a series of pools in the garden.

Sketch Plan Annotations

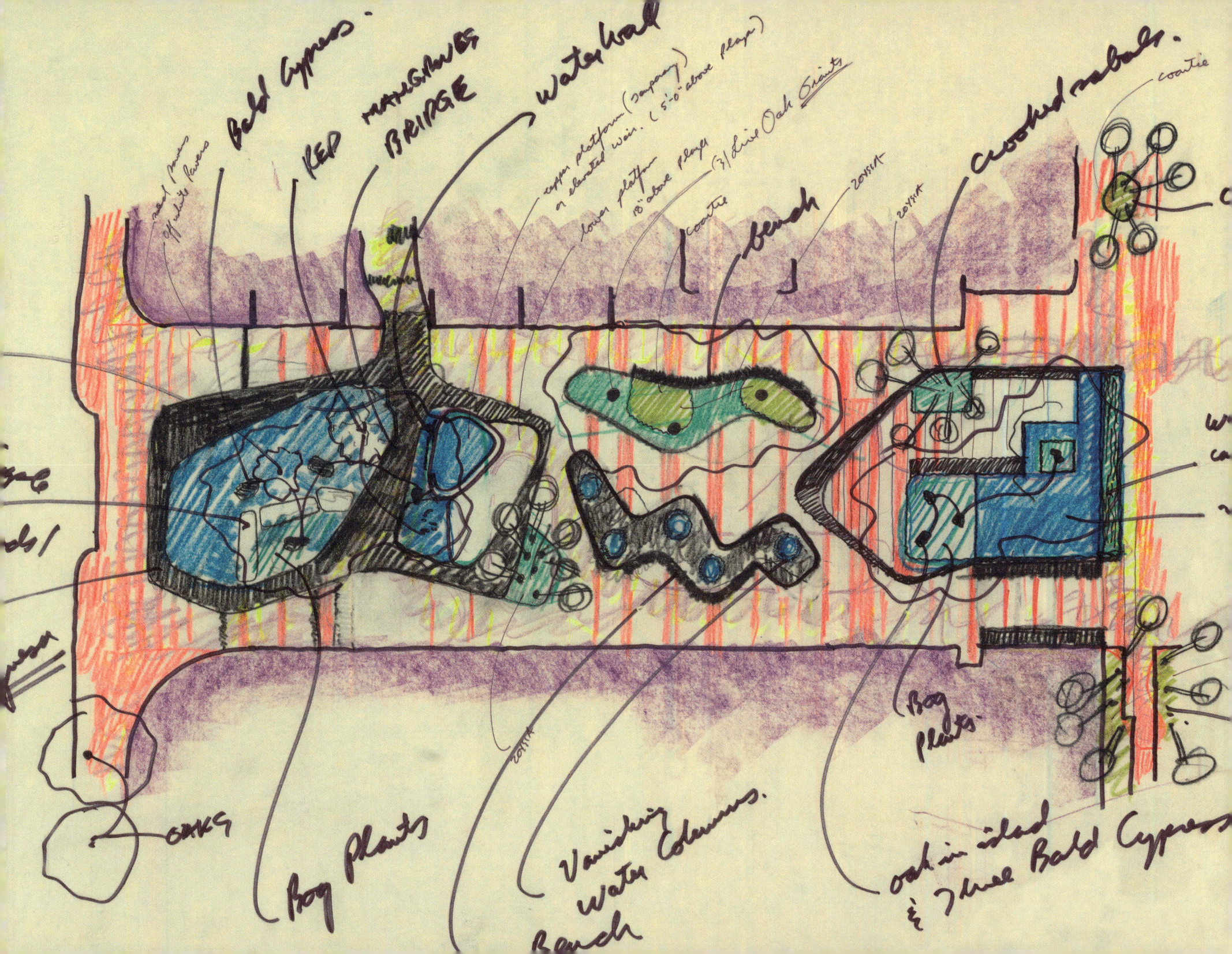

- Bald Cypress
- red roots / Madrone Pavers
- KEP MANGROVES BRIDGE
- Waterwall
- upper platform (canopy) (5'-0" above playa)
- lower platform 18" above playa
- (3) Live Oak Giants
- coatie
- bench
- 20YSIA
- coatie
- 20YSIA
- Crooked nebula
- coatie
- Oaks
- Bog plants
- Vanishing Water Edges Bench
- Bog plants
- oak island & Three Bald Cypress

EL PALMAR,
MIAMI, FLORIDA, USA, 2002
The distinct garden spaces shown in the plan were tailored to the demands of the newly created topography. The intention was for the guest house to be visible across the water garden and grotto. All of the plants, except for the existing baobab trees, were added once the contours of the site had been established.

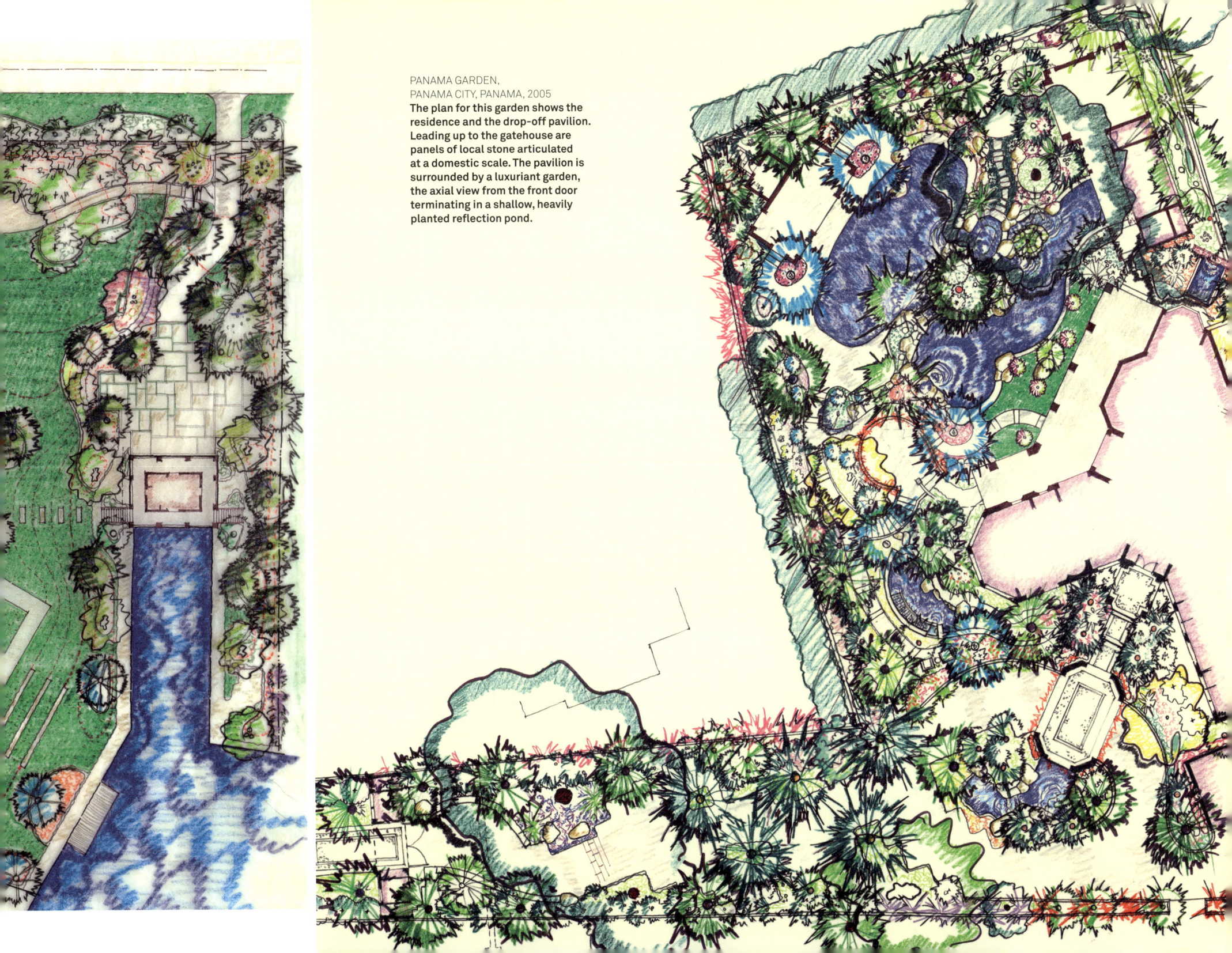

PANAMA GARDEN,
PANAMA CITY, PANAMA, 2005
The plan for this garden shows the residence and the drop-off pavilion. Leading up to the gatehouse are panels of local stone articulated at a domestic scale. The pavilion is surrounded by a luxuriant garden, the axial view from the front door terminating in a shallow, heavily planted reflection pond.

Mikyoung Kim
Boston, USA

For Mikyoung Kim, the language of landscape architecture must embrace the subconscious and the multi-sensory: design cannot rely solely on vision as the primary sensory experience. She reminds us that our bodies are complex organisms that take in information in the landscape through many means, sight being just one of them. Kim believes that designers must address this complexity in their work, suggesting that it is only by using hand-drawing and other 'analogue' methods as an integral element of the design process that this can be achieved.

Mikyoung Kim writes: 'Our most interesting work emerges from an iterative design process that is often frustrating, exhilarating and unpredictable. The word "sketch" is used in jazz to describe improvisation and the development of ideas. This implies products that are incomplete and fresh. Sometimes hundreds of sketches are abandoned during the development of ideas. I believe that these intuitive constructions are a crucial part of invention in design.

'Our work often begins with an understanding of the bodily experience. Choreographed "scores" of the design are developed in hand-drawings and in Photoshop and Rhino. Drawings allow us to define the narrative in spaces. Digital technologies are seductive in their plasticity, but they are only helpful when the ideas are tested alongside materials that resist certain types of form-making. In Rhino, steel can be manipulated like clay, but that is not the case in reality. It is important to use the appropriate physical model-making materials to remain realistic about what can be achieved.

'The danger of working within the boundaries of the computer screen is that it lacks human scale. A purely digital methodology feels inadequate: we are not machines but analogue beings with the full range of sensory capabilities.'

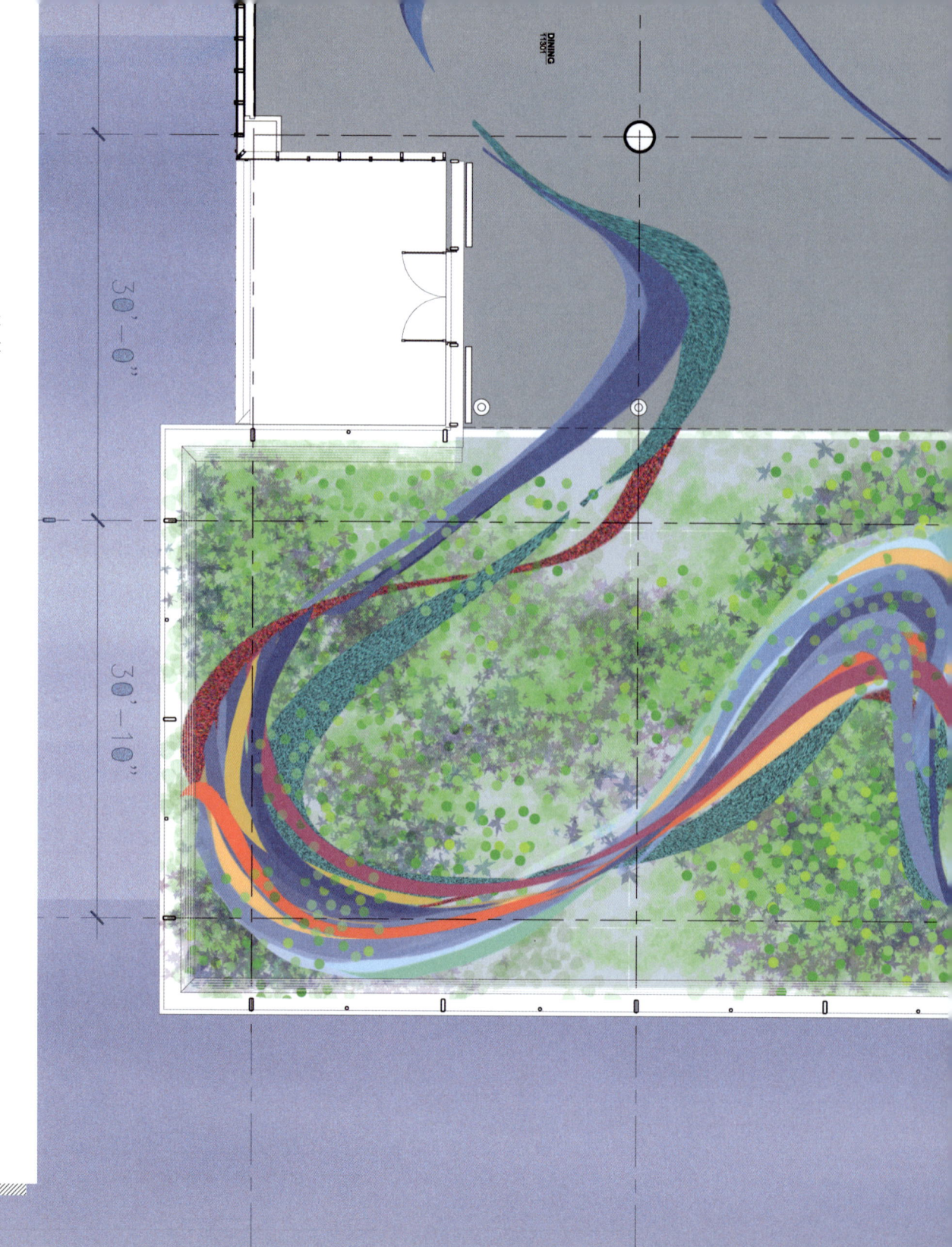

CROWN SKY GARDEN,
CHICAGO, ILLINOIS, USA, 2012
The initial sketch (left) for a garden at the Ann and Robert H. Lurie Children's Hospital was a study in luminosity and colour. The design of the planter walls was developed in Photoshop using digital drawings and a series of hybrid light studies (above and below), which began with resin models pieced together like puzzles, lit from within and tested in Photoshop for scale. Thirty-six physical model studies were created throughout the life of the project in an effort to understand the precise nature of the colour to be used and the layering of materials.

CROWN SKY GARDEN,
CHICAGO, ILLINOIS, USA, 2012
In the design stage, multi-sensory mappings (right) were combined with programmatic diagrams to understand the potential usage and experience of this healing garden. Initial sketches (far right) studied ways in which a canopy of bamboos and resin could create a playful and whimsical experience. Sketches were created with pastel on paper (above) or Photoshop, or as three-dimensional physical models.

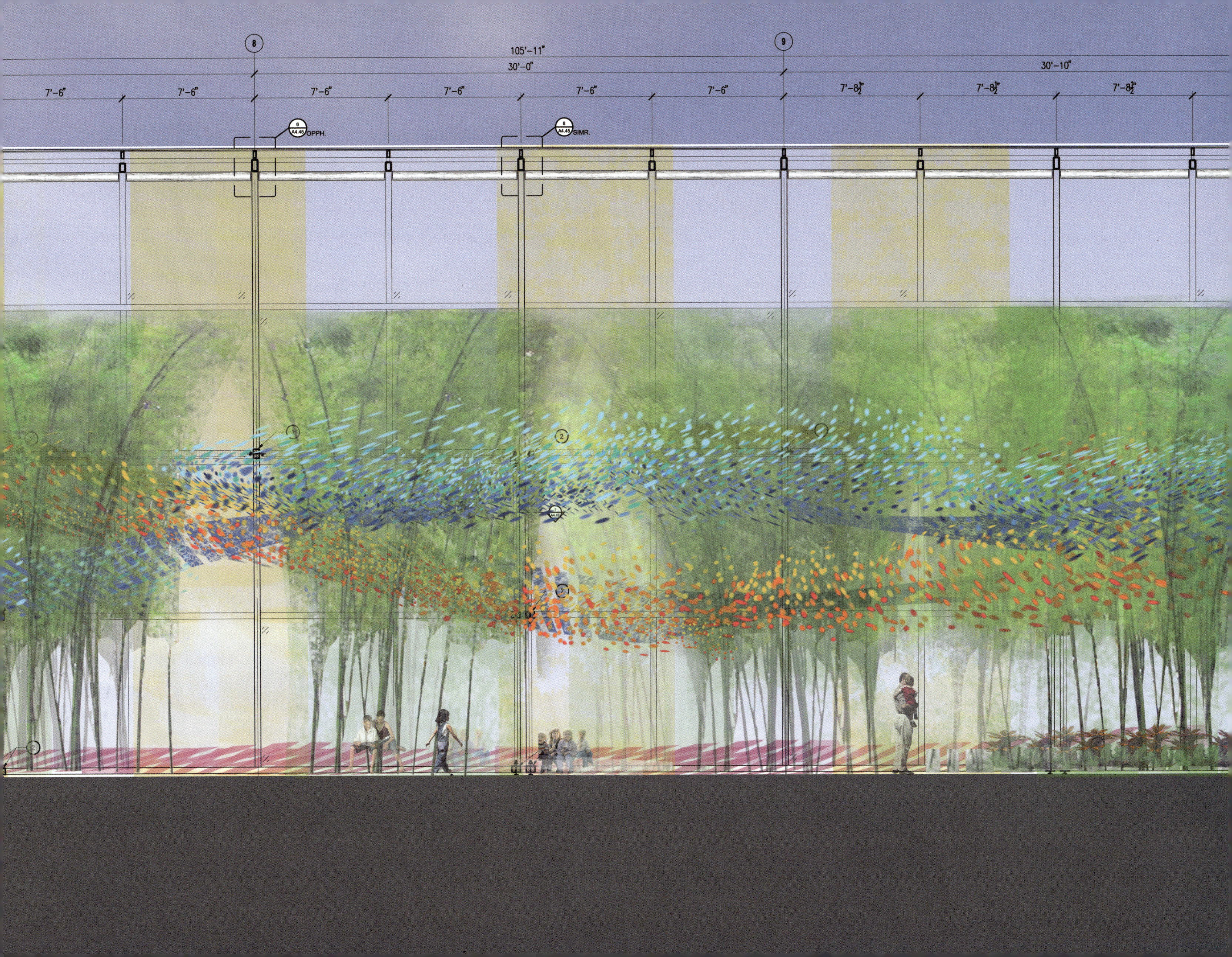
8
9
105'-11"
30'-0"
30'-10"
7'-6"
7'-6"
7'-6"
7'-6"
7'-6"
7'-6"
7'-8½"
7'-8½"
7'-8½"
OPPH.
SIMR.

162

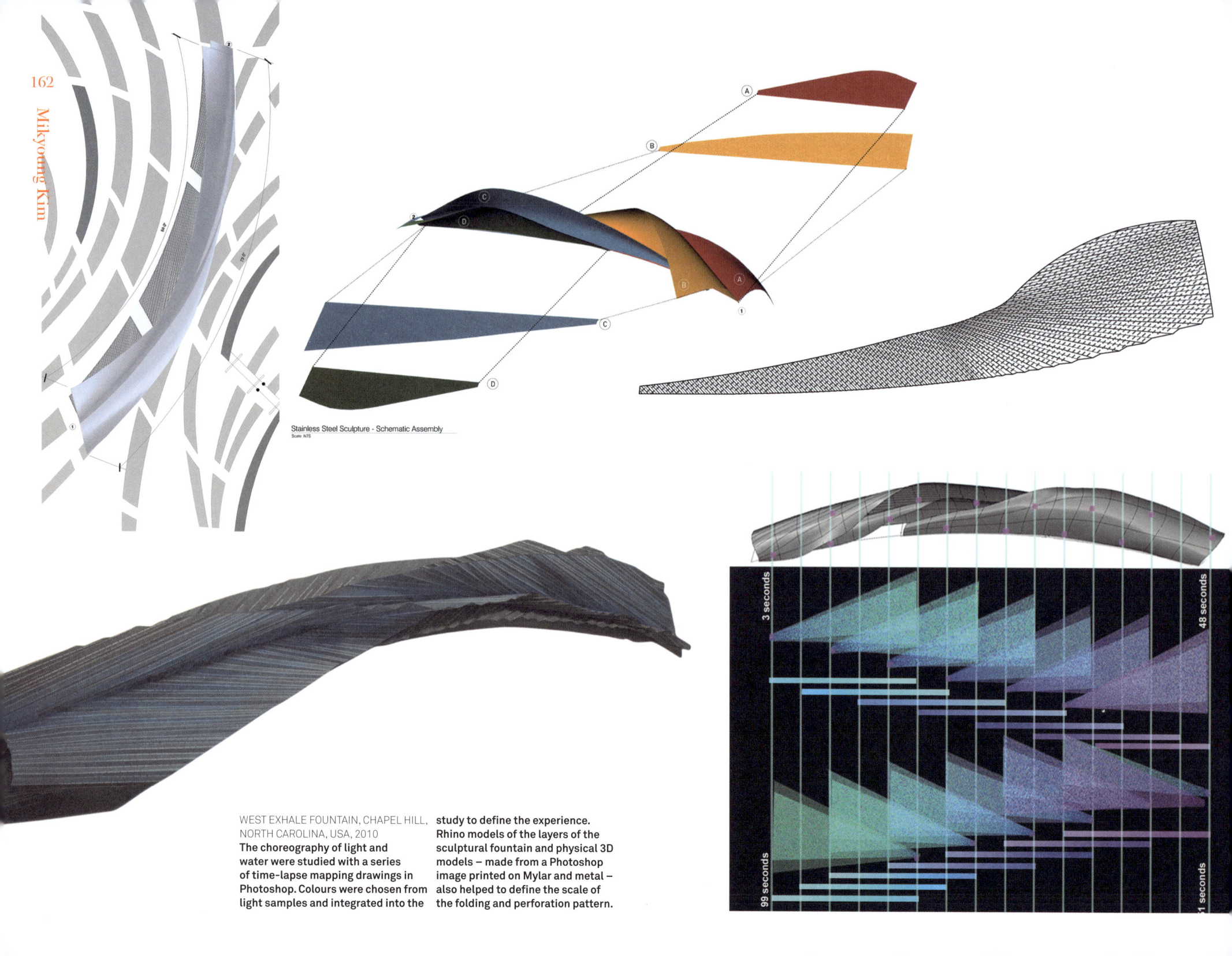

Mikyoung Kim

Stainless Steel Sculpture - Schematic Assembly
Scale: NTS

WEST EXHALE FOUNTAIN, CHAPEL HILL, NORTH CAROLINA, USA, 2010
The choreography of light and water were studied with a series of time-lapse mapping drawings in Photoshop. Colours were chosen from light samples and integrated into the study to define the experience. Rhino models of the layers of the sculptural fountain and physical 3D models – made from a Photoshop image printed on Mylar and metal – also helped to define the scale of the folding and perforation pattern.

SELLWOOD BRIDGE GATEWAY: STRATUM PROJECT, PORTLAND, OREGON, USA, 2012
Inspired by geological maps and imprints from the site, a sculptural gateway forms a series of layers of various metals, including copper, Corten steel and stainless steel. The digital perspective is a combination of a Rhino model studying the folding pattern of the vertical geological totems, with a Photoshop rendering that defines the rain gardens framing each of the totems.

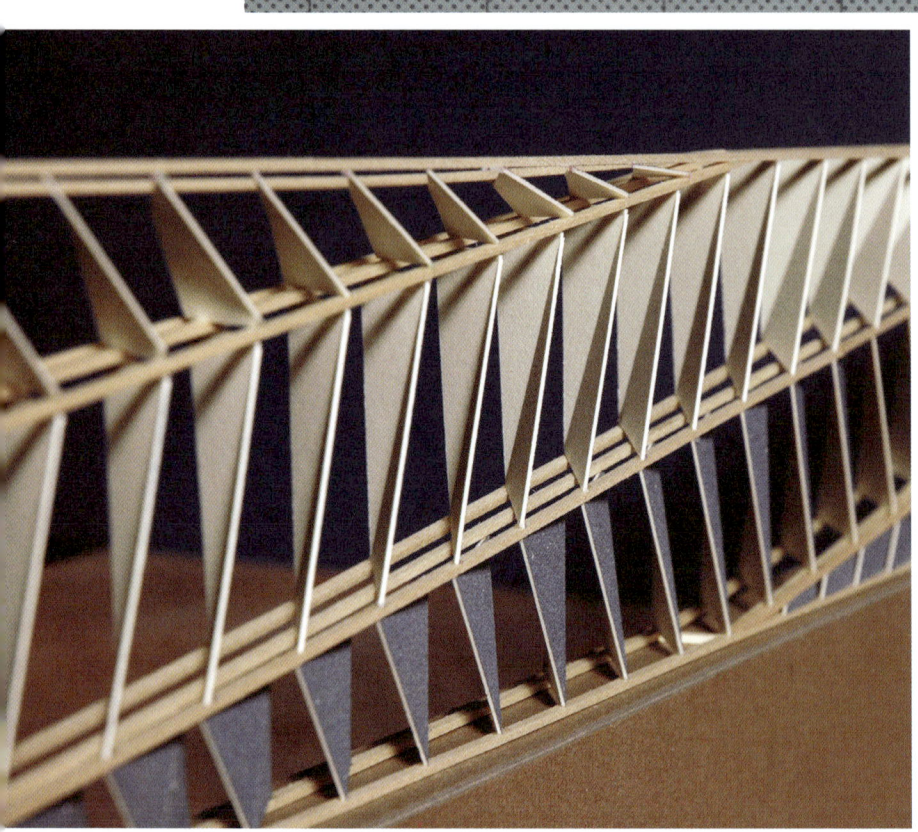

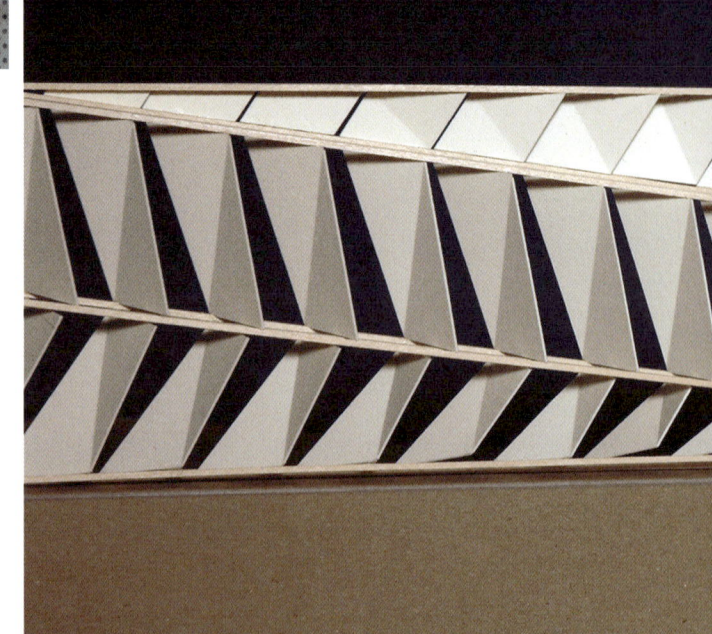

SEATAC INTERNATIONAL AIRPORT, SEATTLE, WASHINGTON, USA, 2011
For this project, a light-screen study began with physical models in chipboard and then moved on to more refined materials, such as museum board and metal. Folding patterns were studied through the various iterations. Rhino models (below) were also developed to study the sequence of experiences from a moving vehicle for each second of time the screen would be in view. The light screens are painted with DayGlo paint and hold the memory of moving vehicles and trains.

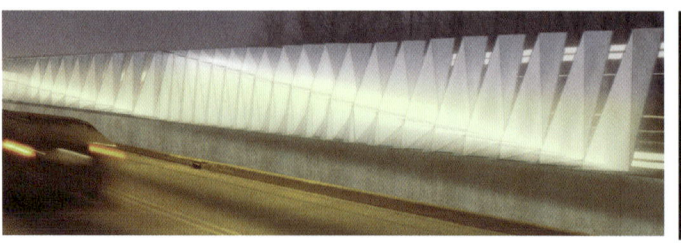

Mikyoung Kim

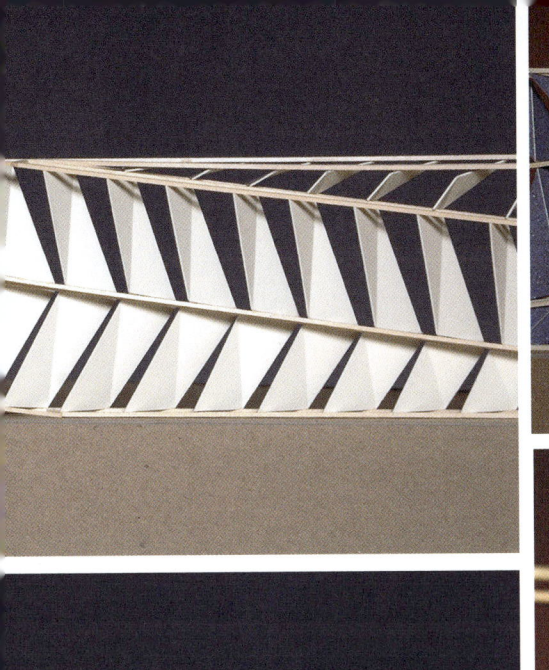

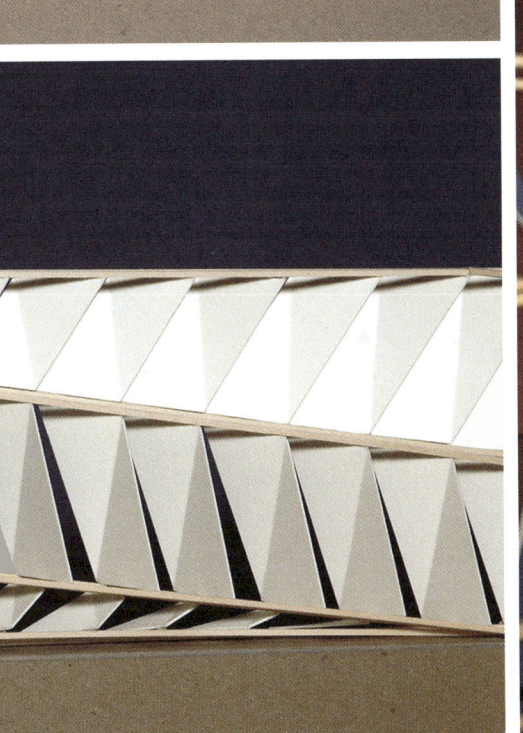

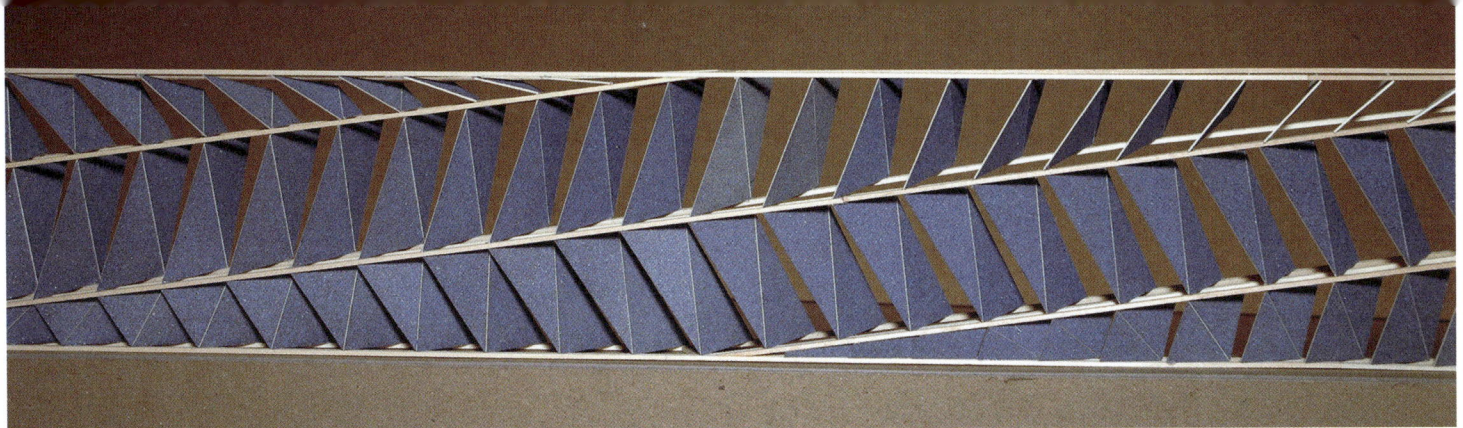

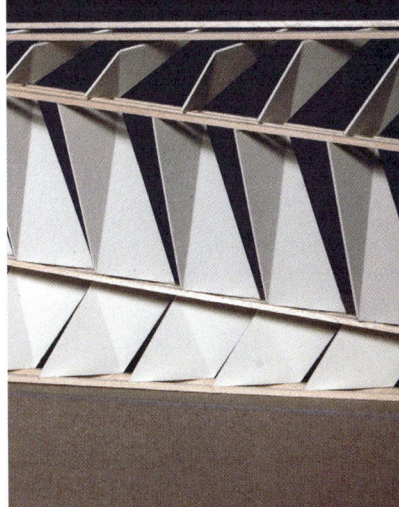

Mikyoung Kim

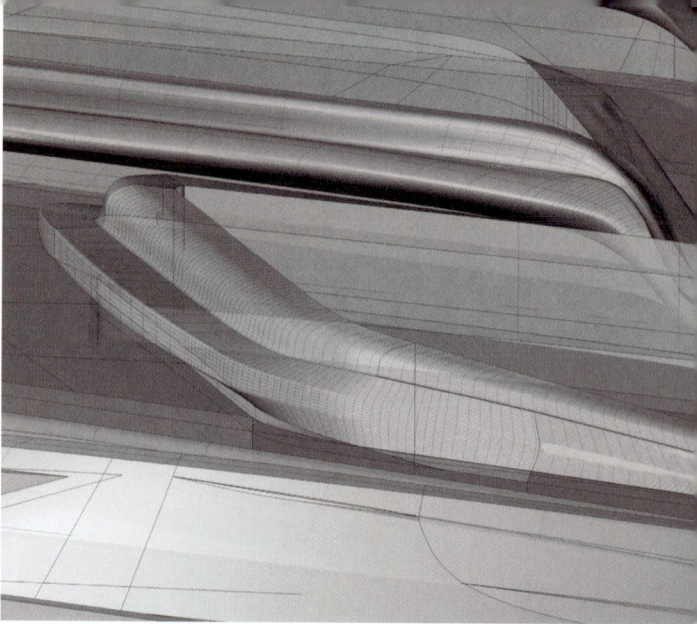

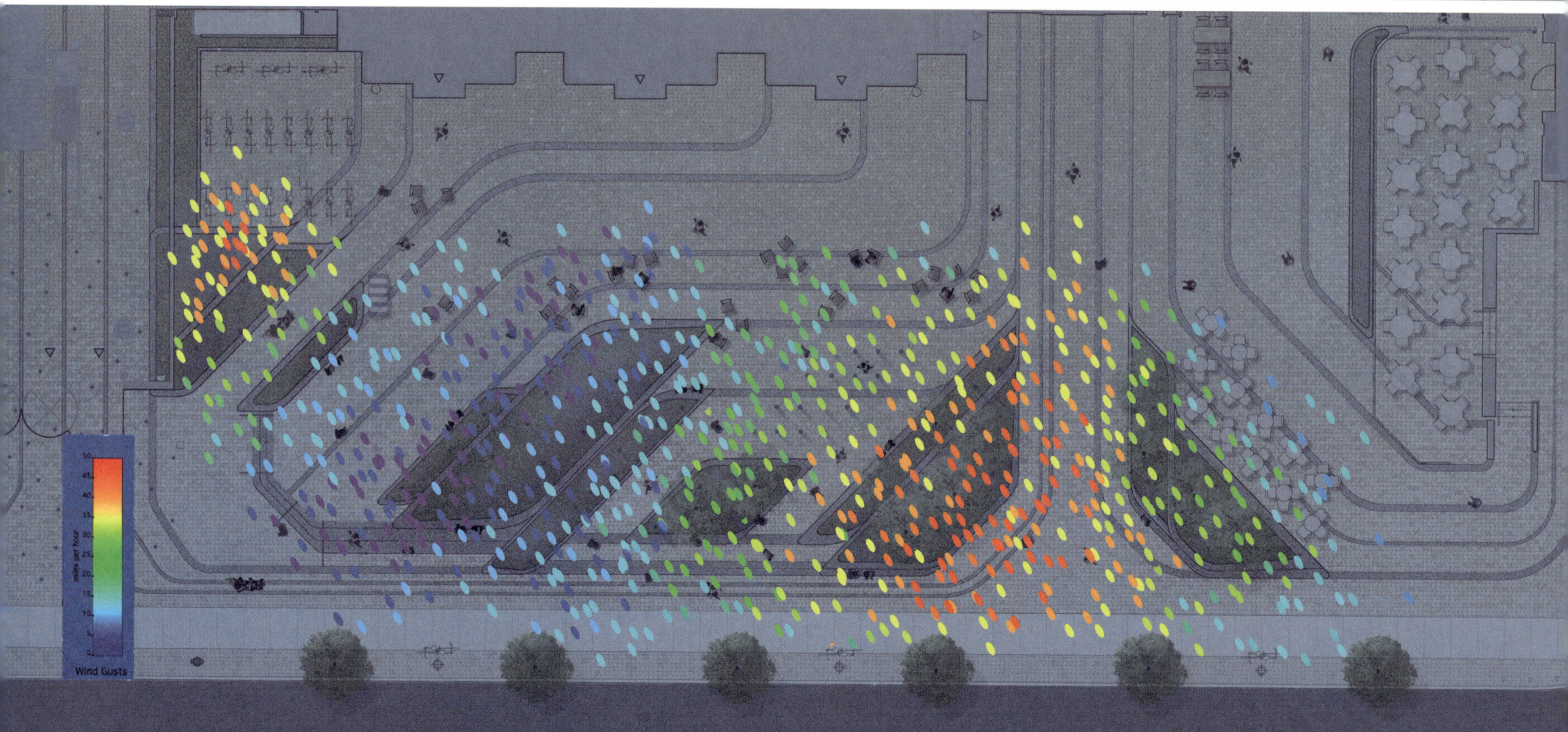

167

Mikyoung Kim

PRUDENTIAL TOWER PLAZA, BOSTON, MASSACHUSETTS, USA, 2014
In this project, the phenomenon of wind defined the scheme. Initial wind studies shaped the design of the planter walls and lighting, and Rhino modelling helped to shape these windswept planters, creating a sense of movement and circulation. Light columns were connected to wind sensors, which emit colours that highlight the intensity of wind. Photoshop and Rhino drawings were made concurrently with physical clay models. Computer-generated perspective of wind columns at night (above); light study of wind speed (right); computer-generated perspective view (opposite, above); modelling of planters in Rhino (above left); study of light and wind (opposite, below).

Cristina Le Mehauté

Buenos Aires, Argentina

Like a number of conceptual landscape designers across the world, Cristina Le Mehauté operates somewhere between the realm of art and design. Her drawings, realized in a wide variety of media, seem to capture with considerable clarity something of the essence of her ideas at the outset. The results are images that are useful both in the personal design process and in communicating the ideas to colleagues and, ultimately, to the client.

Cristina Le Mehauté writes: 'I have drawn ever since I was a little girl. I always look for new techniques, tools and platforms, and I love exploring new places and perspectives with pencils, pens and every other medium that exists. Nowadays I use an iPad, as well. Drawing and model-making is a game that involves entering a fantasy world, in which you dream of a garden. I love to search and discover shapes in the clouds, stones and marks that I find. These can be a good stimulus for creation. When I travel, I enjoy making small watercolours that have nothing to do with my work.

'As for work produced by computer – Photoshop and AutoCAD have no soul. It is handmade expression that captures hearts. I don't like to be asked: "Is that real or is it Photoshop?" We always try to use tenderness in our work, and to make unique and unrepeatable pieces. In my case, I don't use the Internet as a source, as I am afraid it will compromise my freedom and my originality.

'I use drawings at the beginning of the design process – in the ideas stage – and I also return to it at intervals throughout the process. For me, ideas come first in the form of drawings. The language in the design meeting is the sketch, and this can then be used to create Photoshop renditions that are a mix of drawings and pictures. When I am explaining my ideas to a client, my main mode of expression is verbal, backed up by the drawings we present.'

VARIOUS SKETCHES
The design for a city garden (opposite, above) demonstrates how a monolithic red wall interacts with two red benches. In a watercolour of a farmhouse above the Arrecifes River (below), the colours of native flowers are integrated with the materials used in the buildings. Another watercolour (above) is a study of the English garden style, characterized by calm, pale colours lit up by white flowers in every season. In a design for a small garden (right), flowers are placed, like subtle brushstrokes, in reduced numbers to make the most of the space.

170

Cristina Le Mehauté

DESIGN FOR A FIELD PLANTATION, ARGENTINA, 2013
The landscape views (below and bottom right) were made during the design process for a field plantation located 100km (62 miles) west of Buenos Aires. Since any garden would look artificial in this environment, sculptural metal armatures were created as a support for climbing plants (bottom left), so that they would not simply become difficult-to-maintain flowerbeds.

LA RESERVA CARDALES, ARGENTINA, 2013
Sketch created on an iPad for a wild garden (right), 60km (37 miles) from Buenos Aires. The allocated garden space was very small, so a curving pathway was used to create a sense of unity.

THE MARK,
BAHÍA BLANCA, ARGENTINA, 2013
In these iPad sketches (right and opposite, middle row), a red motif was used as a way of unifying the disparate spaces at this housing development.

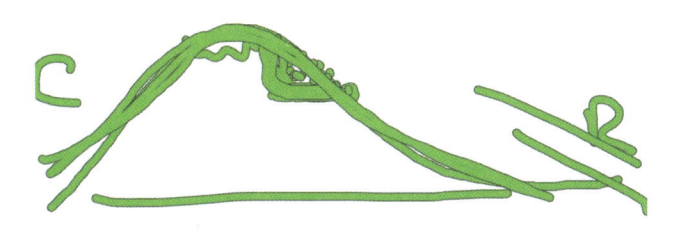

DESIGN FOR A GARDEN,
CHUBUT, ARGENTINA, 2013
This iPad sketch (above left) is for a garden in the mountains in Chubut, where the rocks and indigenous plants help to reconcile the house with the landscape and blend in with its surroundings.

DESIGN FOR A GARDEN,
BELGRANO, ARGENTINA, 2013
This sketch (right) is for a small shady garden in Belgrano, where artificial plants were added to lend character and address the problems of light levels and small size.

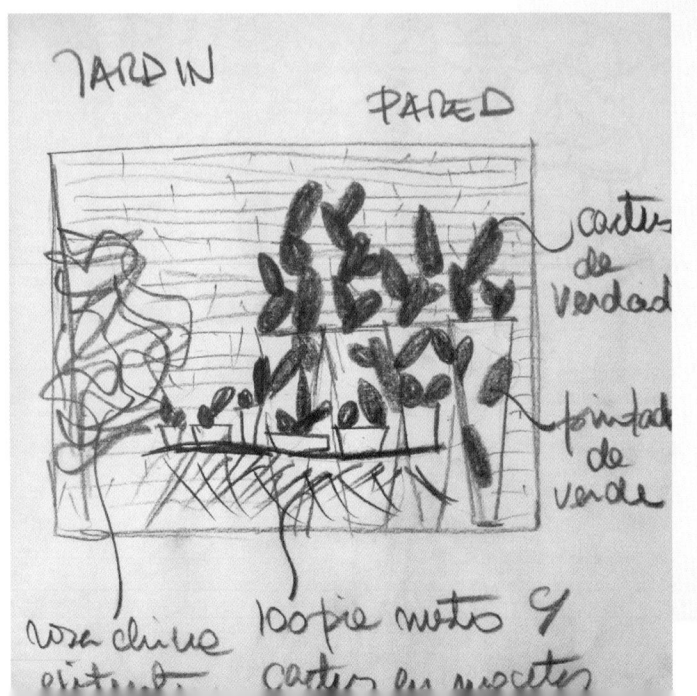

VARIOUS PENCIL DRAWINGS
These drawings from Le Mehauté's sketchbooks represent the initial inspiration and starting point for her designs. Nowadays, the designer's preferred medium is an iPad.

temas
- huellas digitales
- la boca

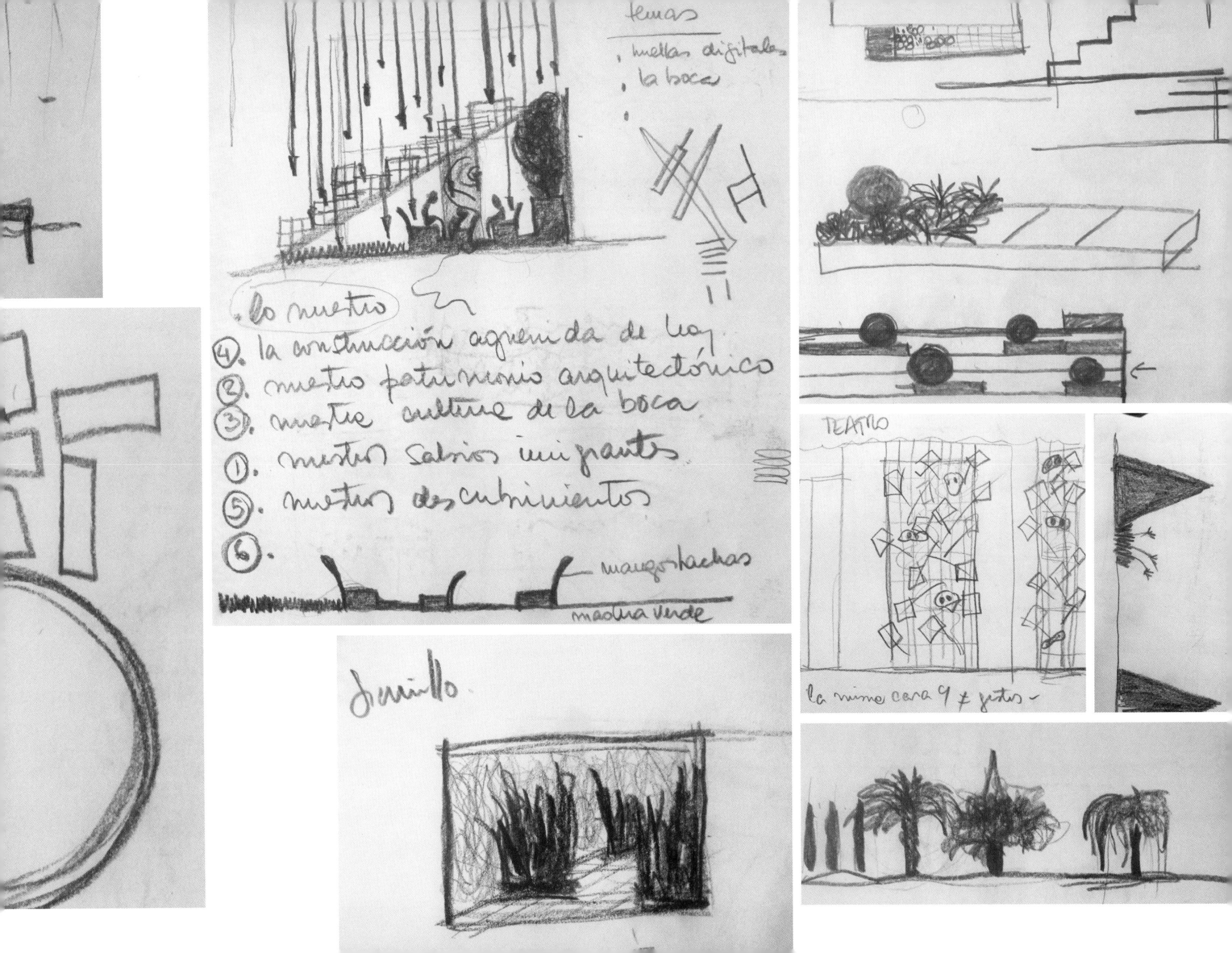

lo nuestro
4. la construcción agendada de hoy
2. nuestro patrimonio arquitectónico
3. nuestra cultura de la boca
1. nuestros sabios inmigrantes
5. nuestros descubrimientos
6.

— mangostachas
— madera verde

Serrillo.

TEATRO

la mismo cara ≠ gestos

Ken McCown

Las Vegas, USA

In this office, drawing is used in specific ways for three different categories of design: urban design, sustainable/resilient design and ergonomics. In McCown's definition, urban design encompasses factors such as light, circulation, landform, seasonal changes and views. In sustainable design, McCown uses diagrams to model processes. For the ergonomic phase, he zooms in through section drawings, exploring how to tune the design to get the scale correct for the number of people who are going to be using a space.

Ken McCown writes: 'The fluency of my hands with drawings and models helps me to get out my ideas in real time, and to explore them quickly to test their viability. I sketch with a felt-tip pen and pencil on bond paper or in small sketchbooks on handmade paper. While one can gain a fluency on computer programs that rivals the fluency of hand-drawing and model-building, the computer is difficult because of its very precision. I can model by hand without having to engage with the exactitude forced upon me by computer programs. The expression of subtleties of light, scale, mass, movement, and so on are difficult using the computer because of lack of capacity to stress one thing above another.

'Drawing is particularly well suited to this field of work because landscapes are big and complicated, and also subject to daily weather conditions and seasonal changes. Landscapes are far more complicated than buildings. One of the most important aspects of drawing is editing. Our minds allow us to distil the information we want to explore. In drawing, we can control the size and complexity of the landscape to help us focus on what we wish to design. If we cannot make it clear what the focus should be in these drawings, we cannot expect users to have an experience that has impact.'

Ken McCown

VARIOUS SKETCHES,
2001
Red-pen drawings represent explorations into how spaces can be defined by means of lines and material changes made on the ground itself, and how these material changes, patterns and repetitions can further define spaces. The black-pen drawings are an examination of how architecture and landscape can merge. The tower (far right) marries the rock emerging from the water, while the ladder is a means of challenging the visitor. Rather than destroy the landscape, the ladder accommodates the body without a drastic change to the form of the landscape. Another drawing (right) is a marriage of landscape and architecture. The ground plantings, topography and trees set a stage for the building. The cut in the façade anchors the composition by pulling the sky into the glass.

TICKLE GRASS
AGROSTIA
INDIAN GRASS
SORGHASTRUM
ALLIUM CERNUUM
AMORPHA CANESCENS
BLUE ASTER
ASTER AZUREUS
COREOPSIS
WHITE OAK
QUERCUS
SHAGBARK HICKORY
CARYA
EARTH
BIG BL
SWITCHGRASS
DICHANTHELIUM
INDIAN GRASS
SORGHASTRUM
LITTLE BLUESTEM
SCHIZACHYRIUM
SKY BLUE ASTER
ASTER AZUREUS
TALL COREOPSIS
COREOPSIS
OATS GRAMMA
BOUTELOUA CURTIP
ASCLEPIAS VIRIDIFLO
WHITE PRAIRIE CLOVER
DALEA CANDIDA
PURPLE PRAIRIE CLOVER
DALEA PURPUREA
AMORPHA CANESCENS
SAVANNAH
BREAKIN
SHOWY GOLDENROD
SOLIDAGO SPE
COMPASS PLANT
SILPHIUM LACIN
PRAIRIE DOCK
SILPHIUM TEREBINTHIN
DOWNY GENTIAN
GENTIANA PUBERU
ROUGH BLAZING STAR
LIATRIS ASP
EUPATORIUM PERF
SILPHIUM TEREB
PHLOX
PHLOX GLABER
BAPTISIA LEUCAN
MOULDING
PANIC GRASS
PANICUM LIEBERG
CLOSED GENTIAN
GENTIANA ANDREWSII
NEW ENGLAND ASTER
ASTER NOVAE-ANGLIAE
SWAMP MILKWEED
ASCLEPIAS
SEDGE
WILD BLUE IRIS
IRIS SH
TURK'S CAP LILY
LILIUM MICHIGANEN

LAYERED
OLD FIELD SUCCESSION
REMNANT ORC

A PRAIRIE SETTLEMENT,
USA, 2001

These drawings are a 'pattern book' for a housing development in the Midwest. The photographs are of local built works, while the pencil drawings illustrate plans and sections as guidelines for their implementation on buildings and landscapes in the prairie settlement.

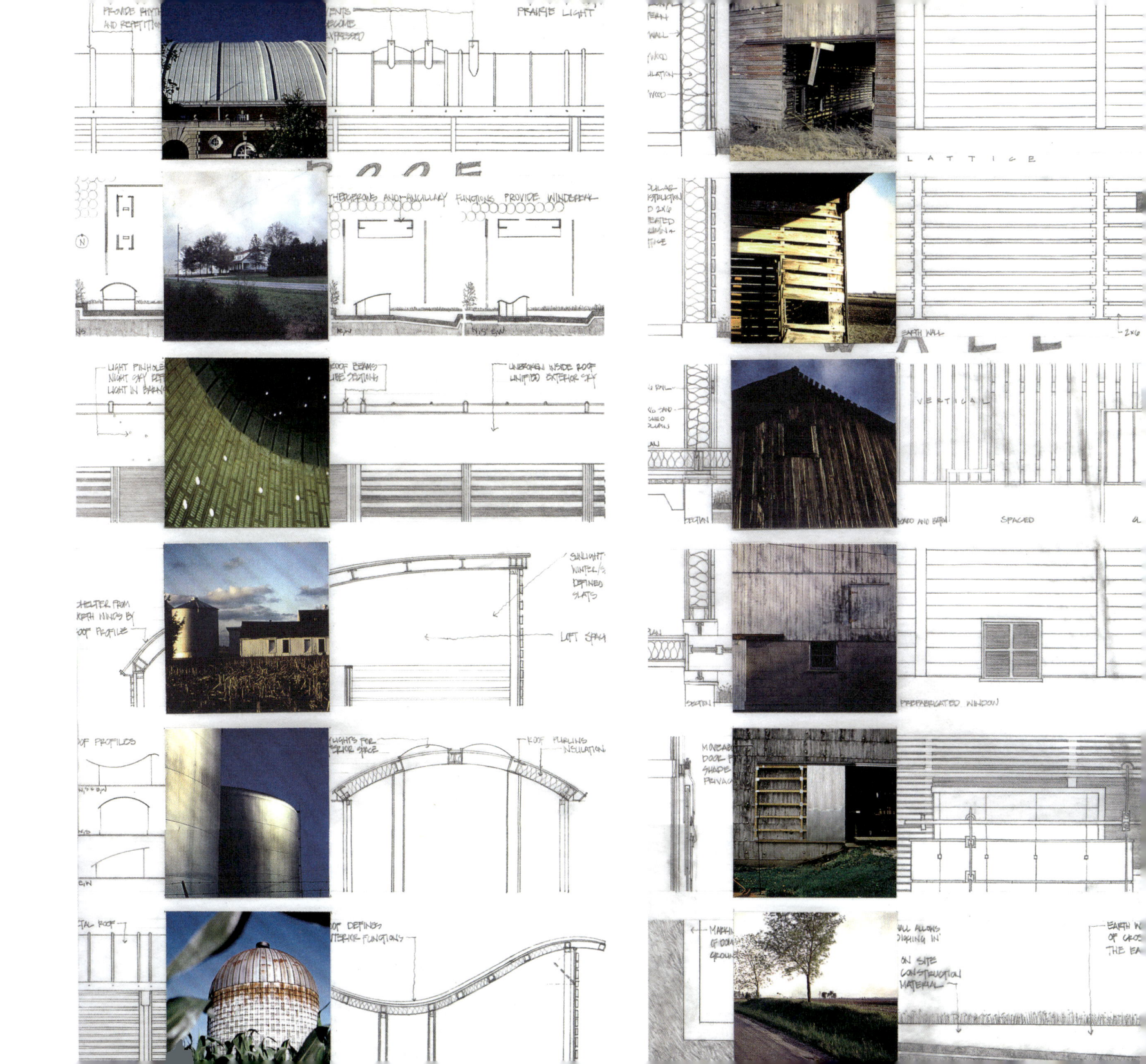

178

Ken McCown

VARIOUS SKETCHES,
2001
These sketches explore the integration of landscape and architecture through sequence, space and tectonics. In this series of works, the buildings are the background elements in both form and minimal detailing. Several of the ideas on this page occur in McCown's other design work, as seen in the sketches for the Prairie Settlement (previous pages and overleaf).

BIG PURPLE CURTAIN

BOOKSHELVES

GLASS WALKWAY

TIMANFAYA

Ken McCown

A PRAIRIE SETTLEMENT,
USA, 2001

Each set of pages in McCown's sketchbook for this project was treated as a 'site.' Under site rules, each spread needed to be a cohesive composition of figure and ground. The fluidity of drawing in this method allowed the ideas to move forward, because areas where there were questions about the design could be spotted quickly. Achieving high density was important, but the design also needed to impact on users by retaining the sense of a landscape beyond.

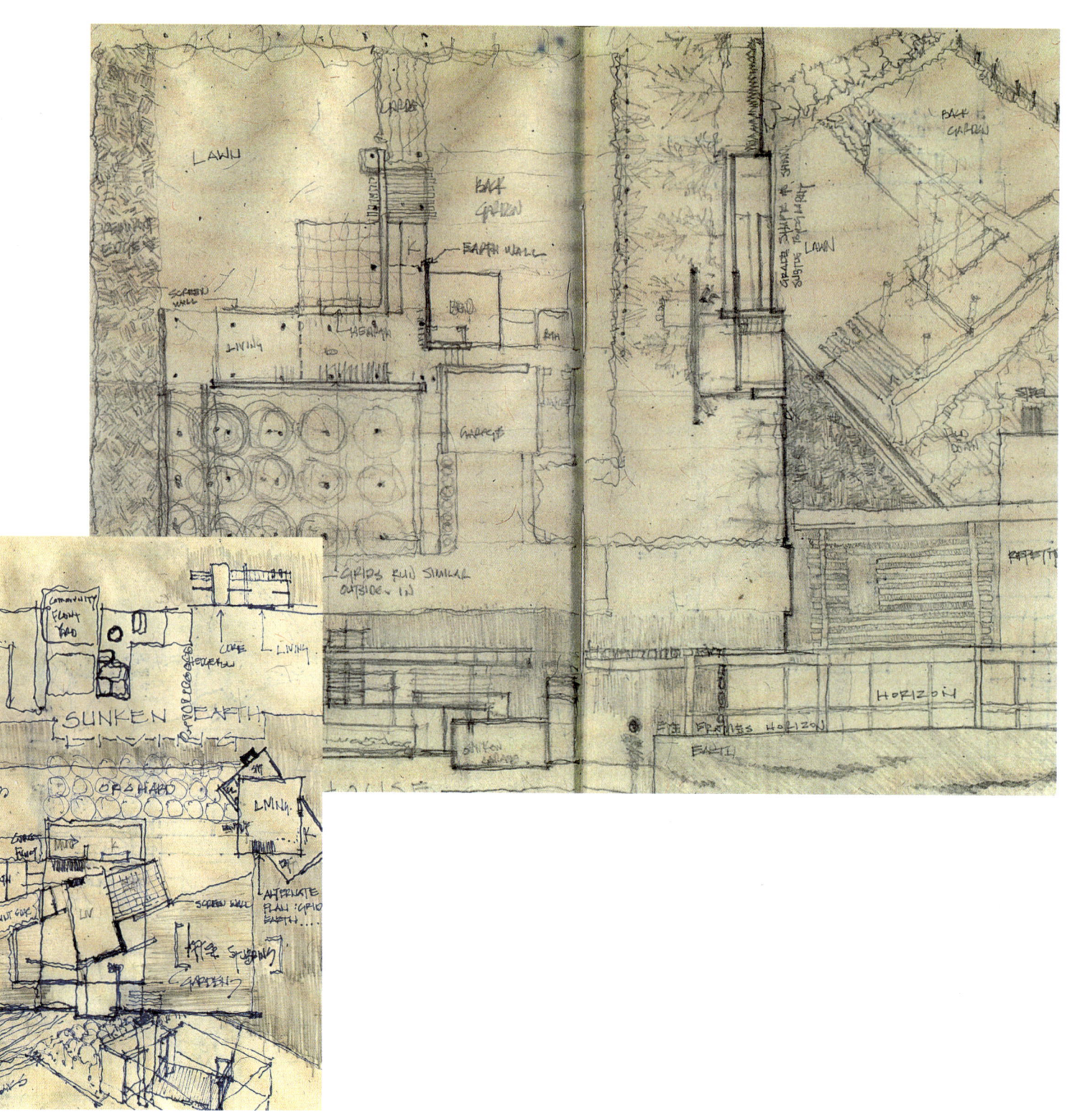

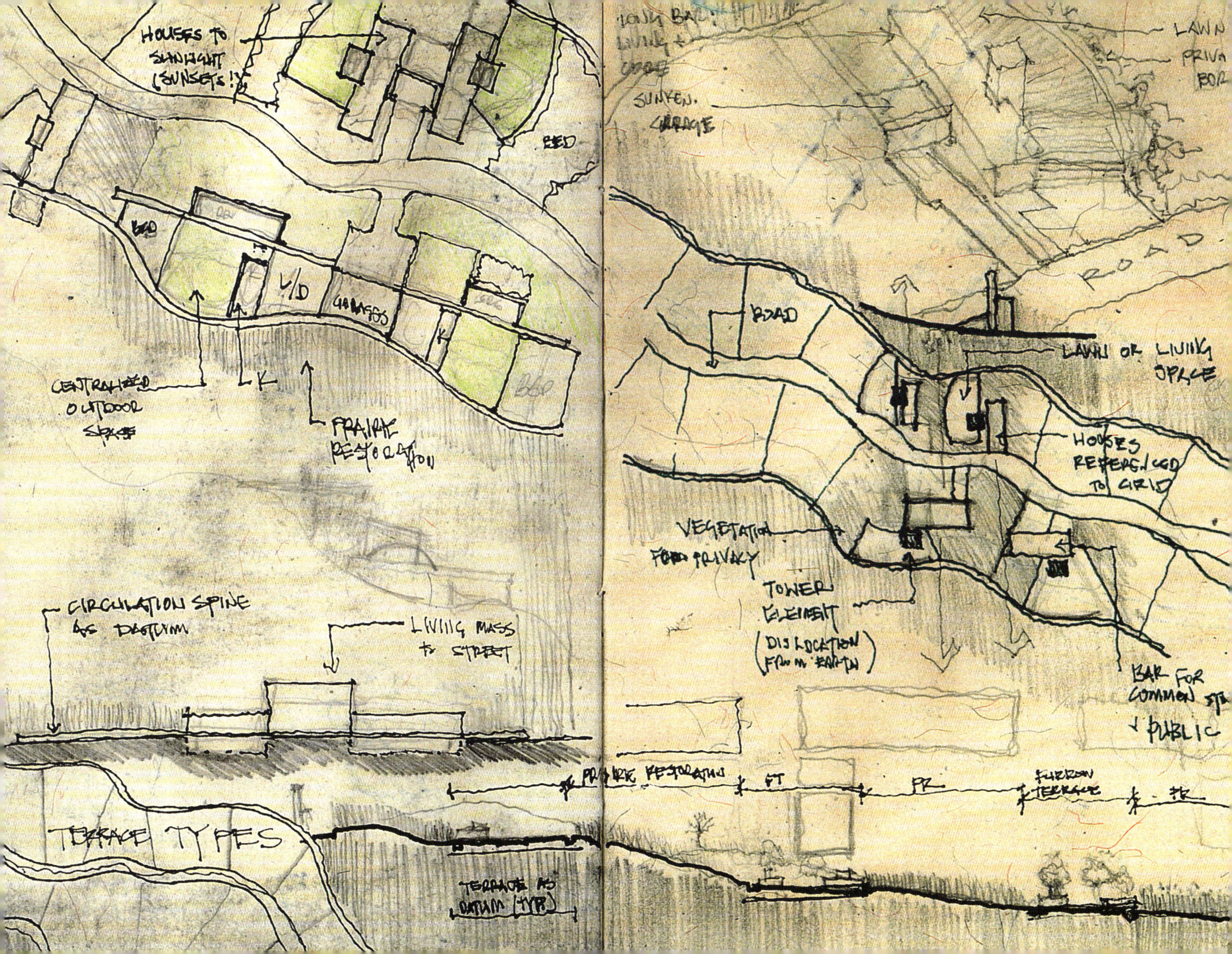
HOUSES TO SUNLIGHT (SUNSETS!)
BED
BED
V/D
GARAGES
K
CENTRALIZED OUTDOOR SPACE
K
PRAIRIE RESTORATION
BED
CIRCULATION SPINE AS DATUM
LIVING MASS TO STREET
TERRACE TYPES
PRAIRIE RESTORATION
FT
PR
FURROW TERRACE
PR
TERRACE AS DATUM (TYP)
SUNKEN GARAGE
ROAD
ROAD
LAWN OR LIVING SPACE
HOUSES REFERENCED TO GRID
VEGETATION FOR PRIVACY
TOWER ELEMENT
(DISLOCATION FROM EARTH)
BAR FOR COMMON
PUBLIC

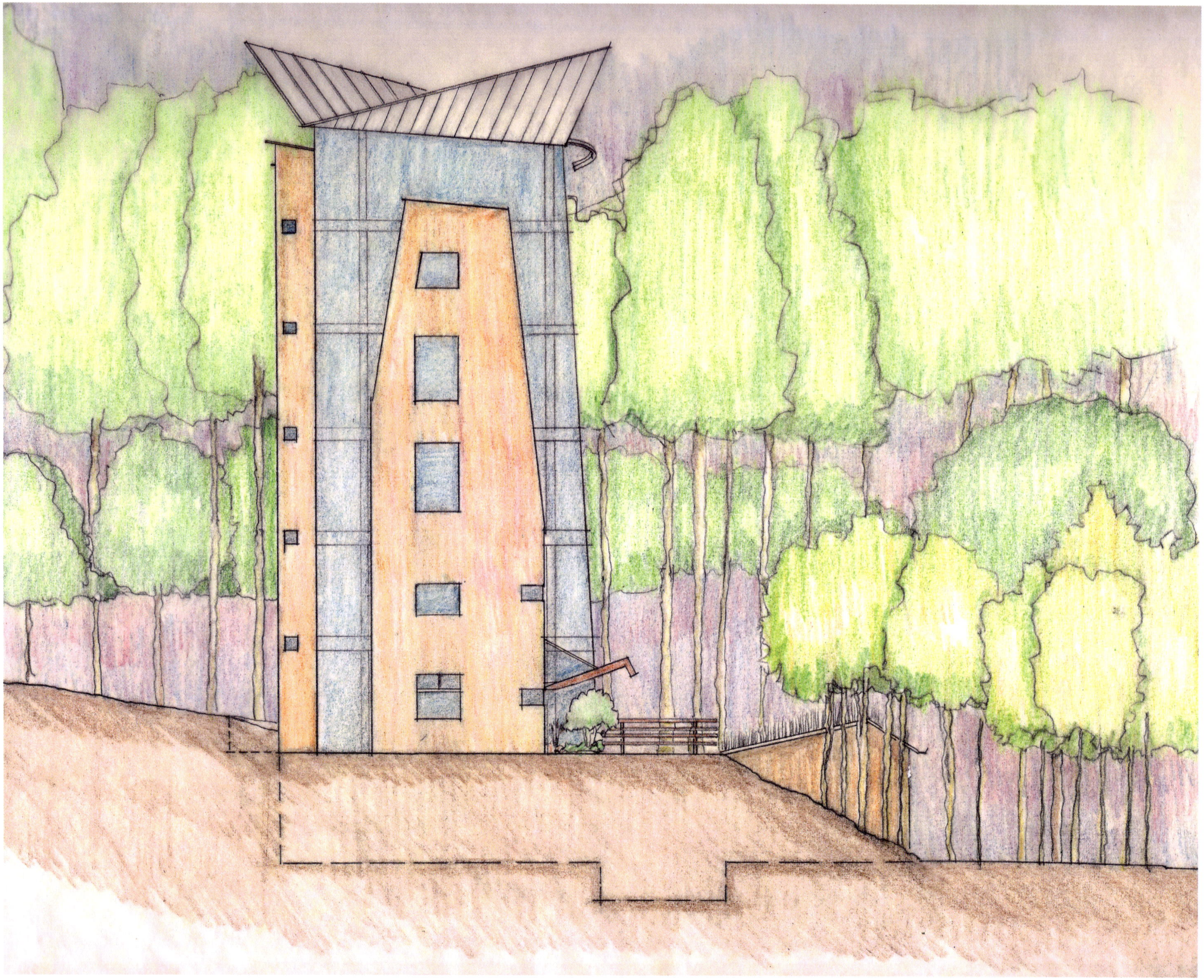

STUDY FOR A HOUSE AND GARDEN, KUNMING, CHINA, 2008
The drawing (opposite) examines the effect of building a house level with the height of the trees, knowing they will grow further to envelop the building. This elevation helped 'lift' the building through the use of a butterfly roof. A curved scupper was added to guide the water down to a rain garden on the other side. To further emphasize the verticality of the house and forest, a tightly planted group of medium-sized trees was proposed. After passing through these trees and up a set of stairs, visitors can look up and see the sky framed by the forest and house.

COMPETITION FOR AN ALGAE BIOREACTOR, 2007
This study (below) was made for a competition, in collaboration with Tyler Stradling, which celebrated the marriage of art and science. Algae needs maximum exposure to sunlight to optimize its capacity to produce resources we use for fuel, and the huge forms of the corn silos would allow great access to light. The drawing explores the idea of wrapping the silos in bags full of algae, with solar roof panels to power the required water system. A wetland with grasses by the silo system could help reduce expenses for water-quality measures.

Helle Nebelong

Copenhagen, Denmark

A leading figure in the natural-playgrounds movement, Helle Nebelong's drawings and sketches are an interesting mix of the visionary and the practical – for playgrounds have to work hard to make play work, but they must also be intriguing and attractive to their users. The challenge is to retain visionary elements of the design – contained in these sketches – even as practical constraints have their effect.

Helle Nebelong writes: 'I love to sketch. It is the most important part of the design process to me, where I examine the possibilities of a place in depth. To sketch is like getting under the skin of a project. I get my fingers and my thoughts deep down into the history of a place and examine its existing elements and qualities. There might be good trees, a special terrain, a building façade, a sculpture or other characteristics. All of this is important and could influence the final design.

'When I sketch, my mobile phone is switched off and my favourite music is on. I'm in a special mood, which might be described as a state of flux, of creative motion. My design expression is quite organic. I draw curves, putting my ideas on lightweight manifold paper using pencils and markers. Suddenly my marks might looks like avocados cut in half, a cat's paw, a ship or just total chaos. At that point, I quickly find a single overall geometric shape that can lie across the chaos, creating some kind of order. When that happens, I know it has worked: I have found the basic idea, the common thread. Thereafter, I work on it and adjust it until I am completely satisfied.

'I always sketch by hand and would never dream of using a computer in that phase. I use a mixture of markers, Lumocolor pens, highlighters, pencils and crayons. I would never sketch directly in AutoCAD. To me, that would be the same as putting on gloves and not feeling the medium and its reality directly.'

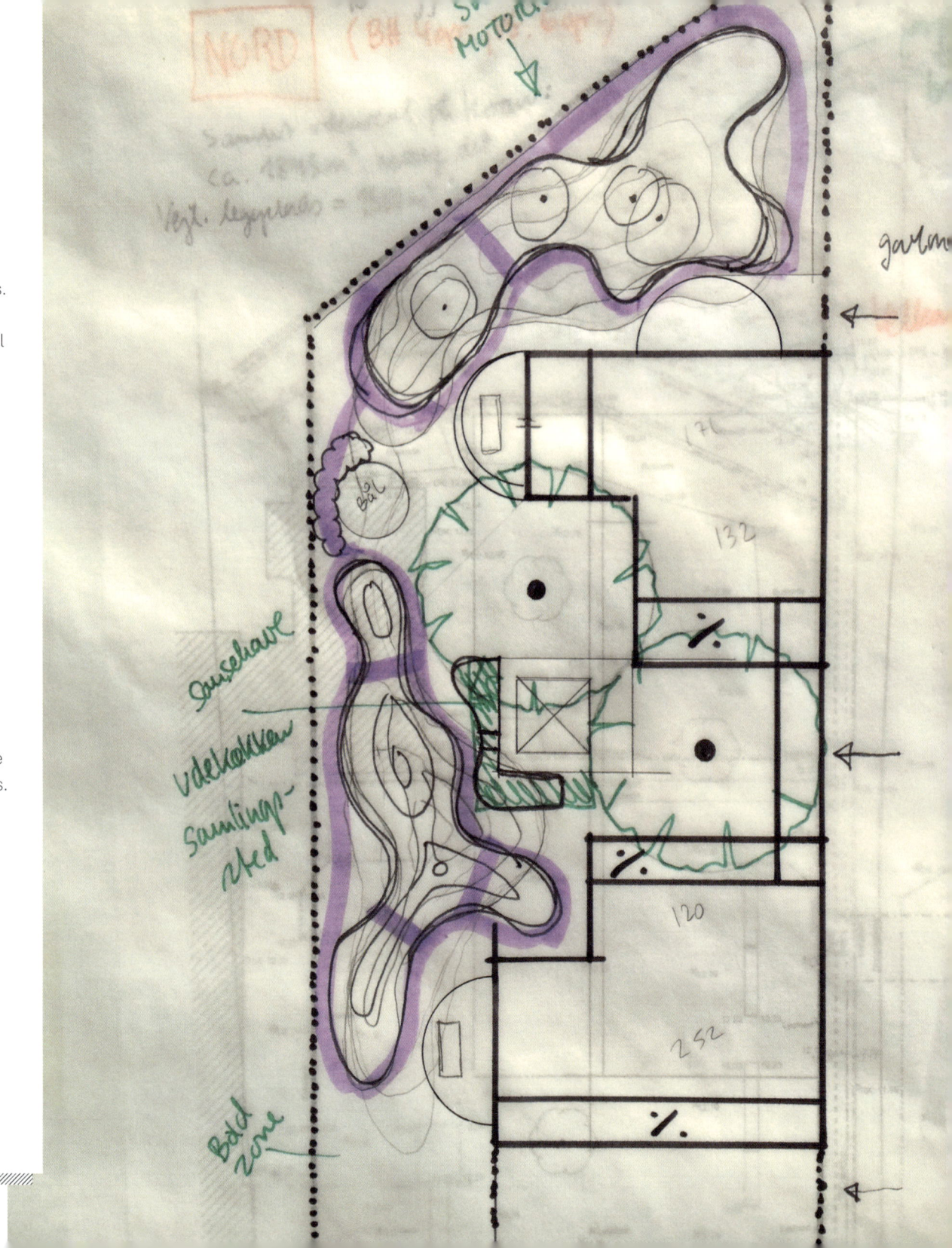

FORFATTERHUSET DAYCARE CENTRE,
COPENHAGEN, DENMARK, 2012
An early competition sketch for a playground for children up to six years of age at a daycare centre in Copenhagen (left). A number of organically shaped hillocks were placed into the space by way of contrast with the geometric buildings. The hillocks provide these urban children with a varied space to play in and to experience the sensation of going up hills. The dotted line indicates a transparent fence surrounding the playground, including two very big, old trees that are to be preserved.

GARDEN OF SENSES,
COPENHAGEN, DENMARK, 1996
The first sketch for this 4,000m² (43,000 sq ft) public garden was drawn during an especially boring lecture, just to get the initial, basic ideas on paper. The meandering path shown in this later drawing (left) was almost exactly realized in the final design. The different patterns indicate the intention to put a lot of different materials and plants with sensory stimulation into the garden.

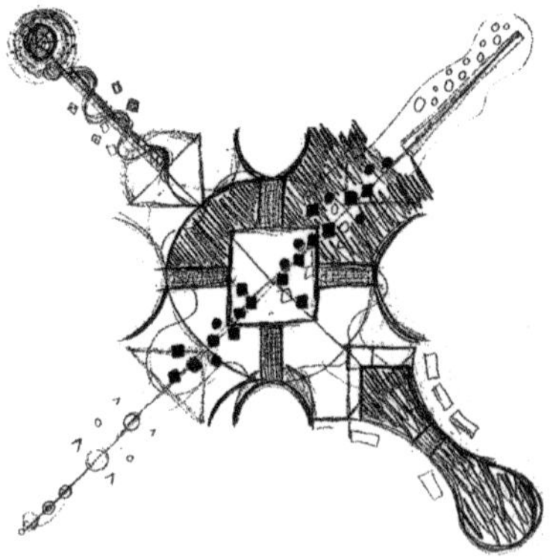

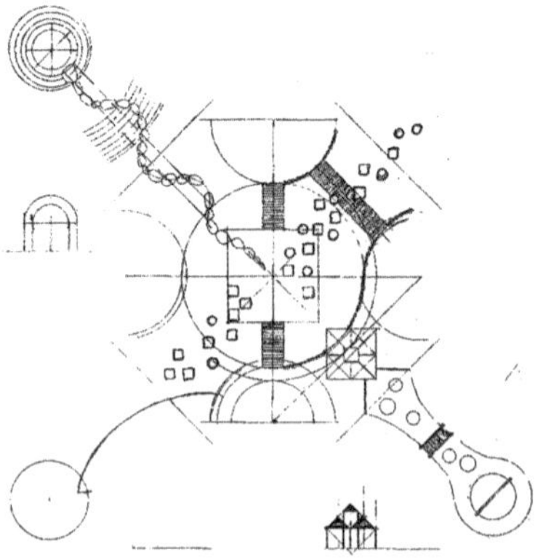

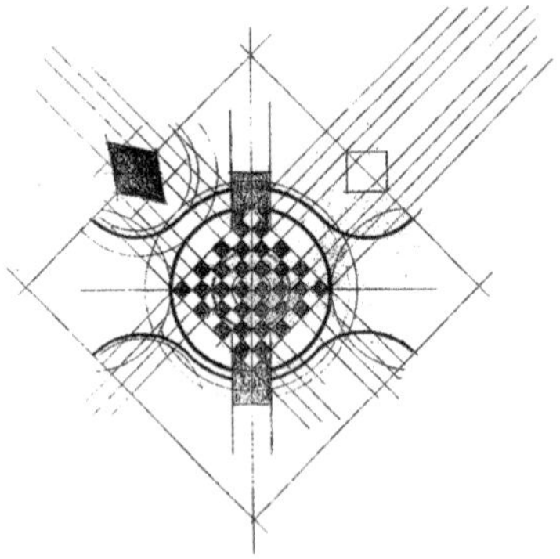

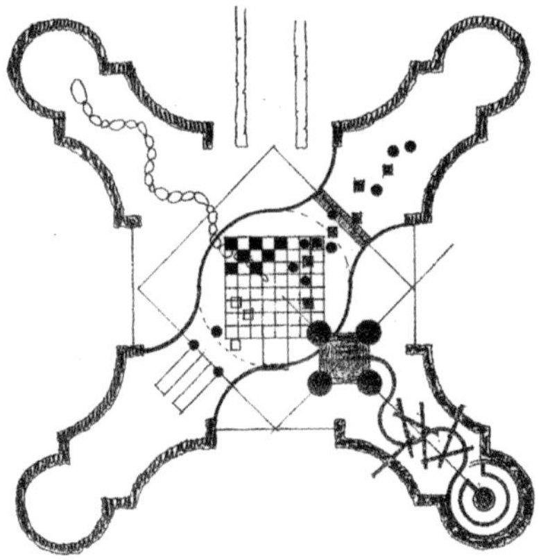

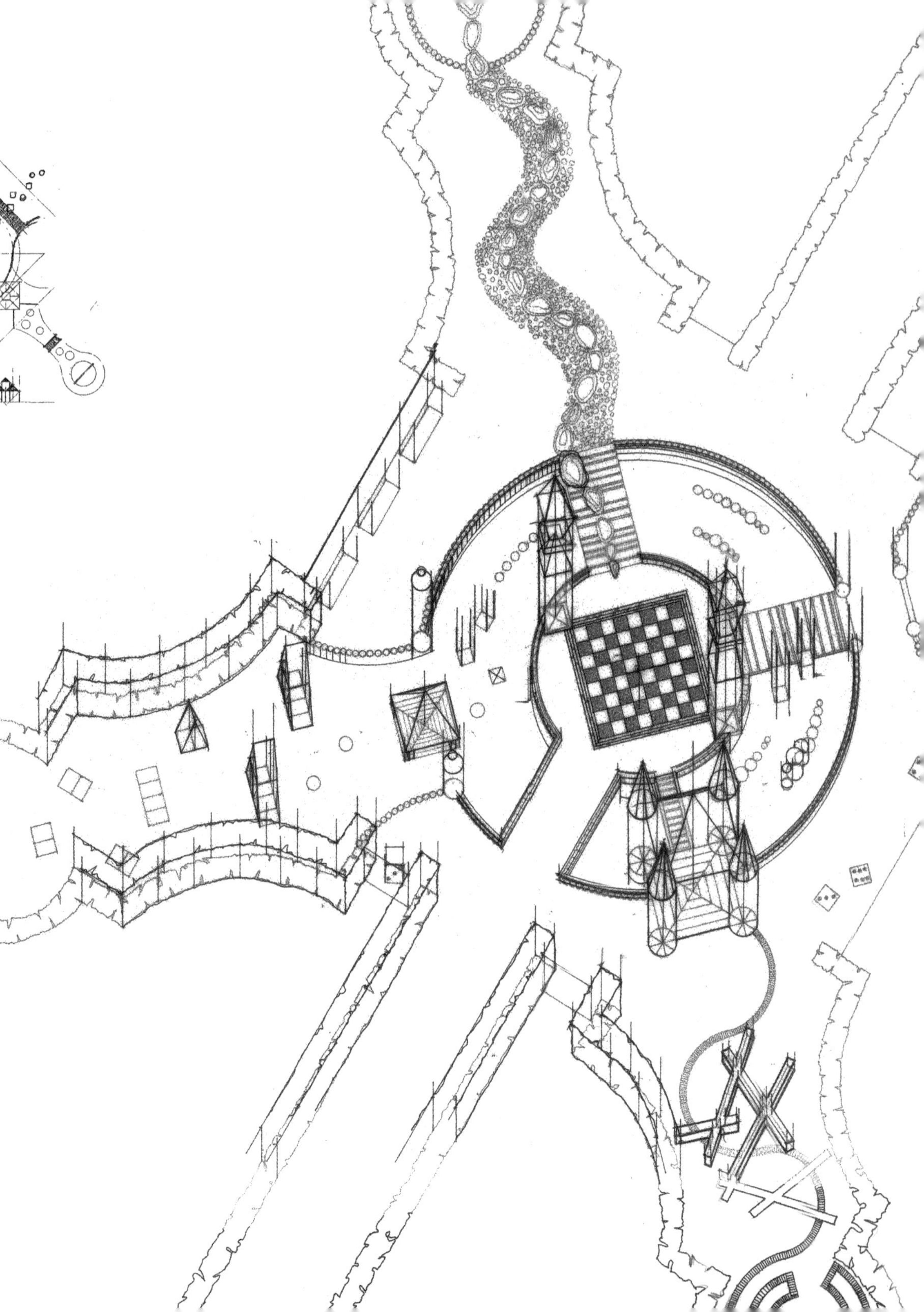

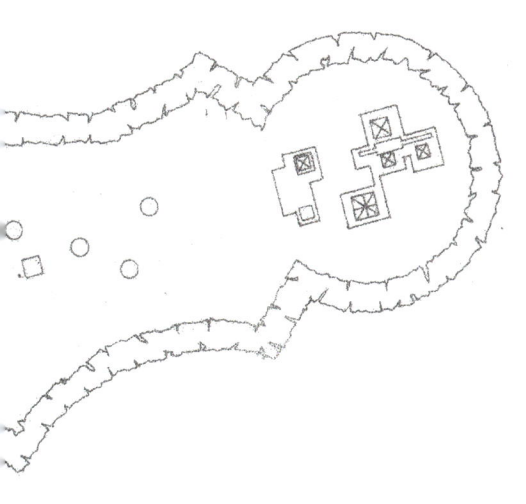

THE KING'S GARDEN,
COPENHAGEN, DENMARK, 1997
Sketch for a design competition for a new playground at Rosenborg Castle (left). The idea was to use a chessboard and chess pieces, oversized and made from wood. Some of the ideas were reused over a decade later in a competition for a playground at Kronborg Castle, in Elsinore.

GARDEN OF SENSES,
COPENHAGEN, DENMARK, 1996
Another sketch for the Garden of Senses (right). It shows a large, sandy area with brick walls that children can run around and between. In the end, there wasn't the budget for brick walls, so wooden palisades were used – although the small island with two wooden bridges was constructed.

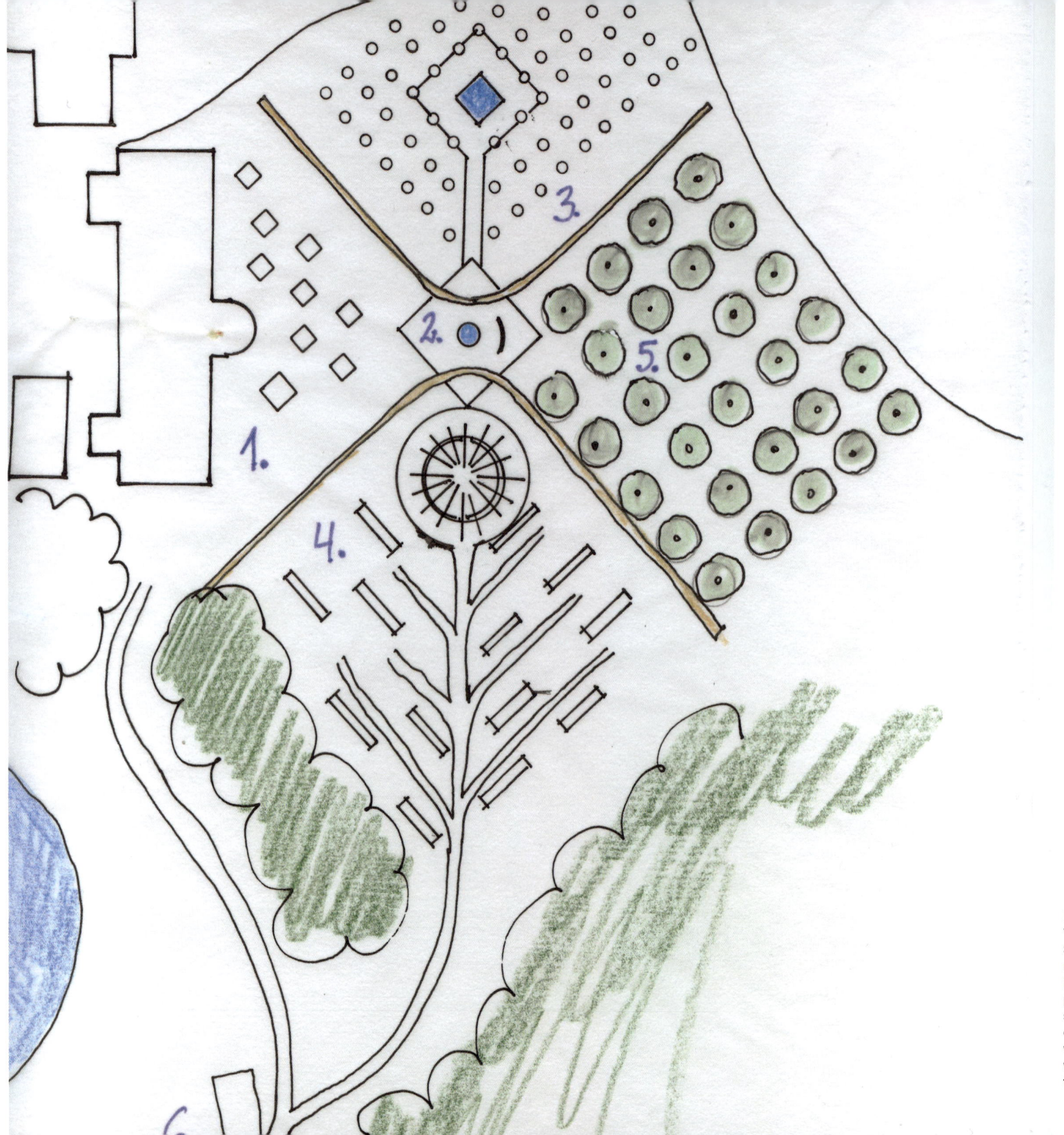

GARDEN FOR ST BRIDGET,
JUTLAND, DENMARK, 2007
The strict geometry of the garden at a monastery in Mariager, Jutland, reflects the rules St Bridget made for the resident nuns and monks. This design includes: (1) a small square garden of herbs and medicinal plants or bulbs; (2) a wishing well in natural stone and a rose trellis; (3) a 'Sisters' Garden' of climbing roses on freestanding pillars; (4) a 'Brothers' Garden' of pillars and trellis with fruit bushes, and a barbecue at the centre; and (5) a traditional apple orchard.

ECOLARIUM ROOFTOP GARDEN,
VEJLE, DENMARK, 2008
Sketches for a 'hanging garden' for relaxation, a temporary rooftop installation (opposite). There were plants in containers, hammocks and shaded sunbeds. It became a garden of soothing sensory experiences, where visitors could relax and no one was allowed to make demands on them, and was very popular.

ØKOLARIET, VEJLE · MARTS 2008
SKITSE TIL PAUSEHAVE I
Helle Nebelong

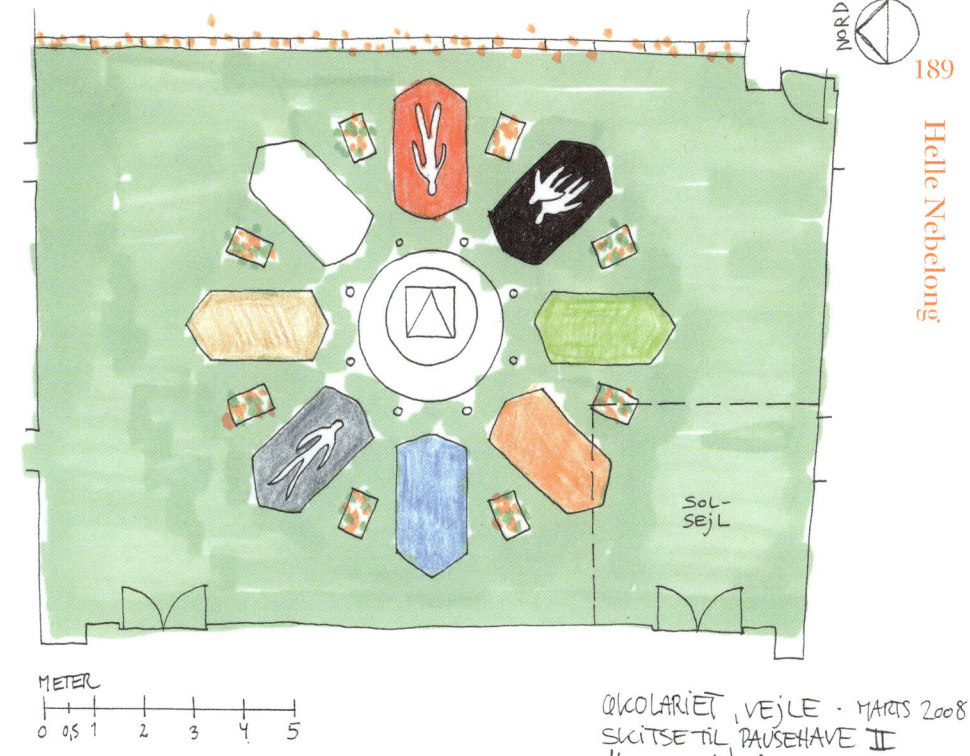

ØKOLARIET, VEJLE · MARTS 2008
SKITSE TIL PAUSEHAVE II
Helle Nebelong

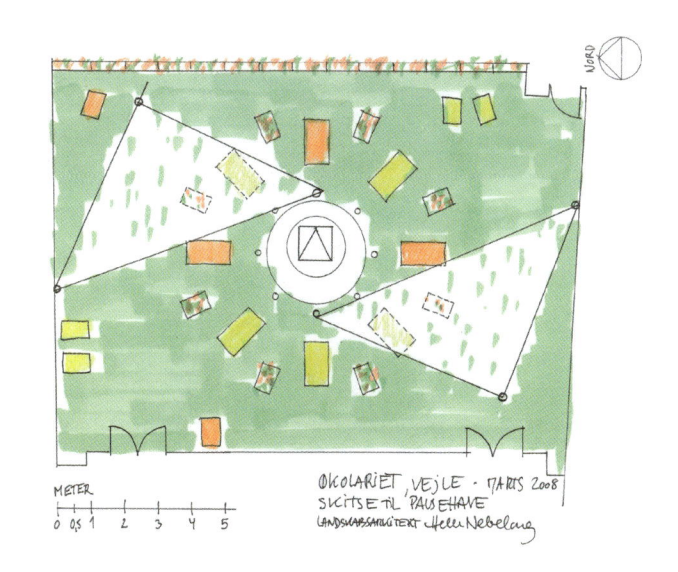

ØKOLARIET, VEJLE · MARTS 2008
SKITSE TIL PAUSEHAVE
LANDSKABSARKITEKT Helle Nebelong

170 m² kunstgræs á 100 kr.	17.000
4 stk. headdemoch, lime, Fatboy á 3.499,-	13.996
4 stk. —"—, orange, —"— á 3.499,-	13.996
17 plantekasser á 100,-	1.700
Blomsterhave, solsikker, jord 5,6 m²	1.000
8 robiniapæle m. spiretop á 2.000	16.000
16 fuglekasser, plywood, grøn og orange á 169,-	2.704
	66.396

Bambus
nælder
vand
under duftplanter
sejl

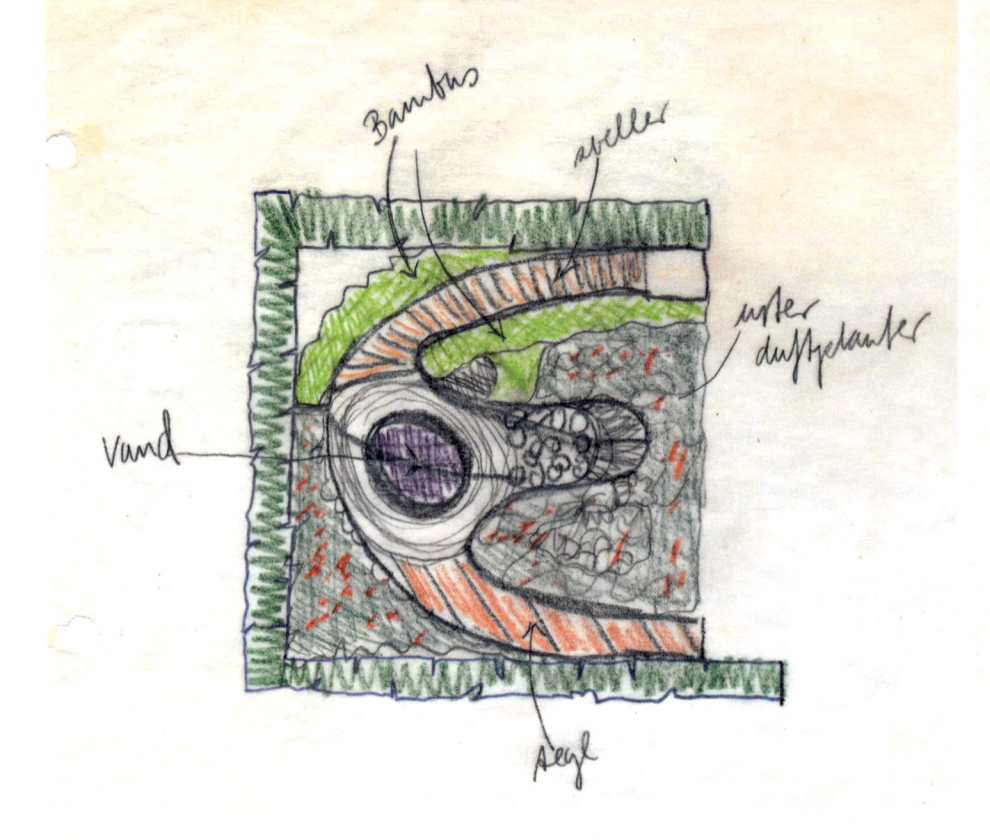

II 9/3-93

I - 9/3-93

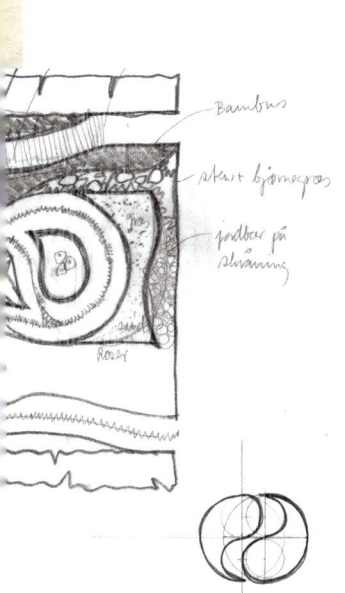

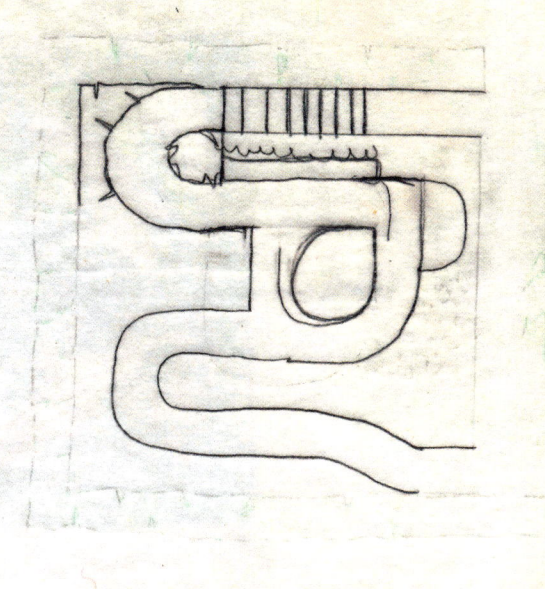

GARDEN IN AALBORG,
JUTLAND, DENMARK, 1993
A series of quick sketches, ideas for a garden at a home for young deaf-blind people. The area was very small – barely 200m² (2,153 sq ft) – and surrounded by a beech hedge, which is shown in all of the sketches. It was difficult to find the right shape for a path that would offer the residents a continuous flow of sensory experiences through their feet, using lots of different materials in the surface and several small wooden bridges.

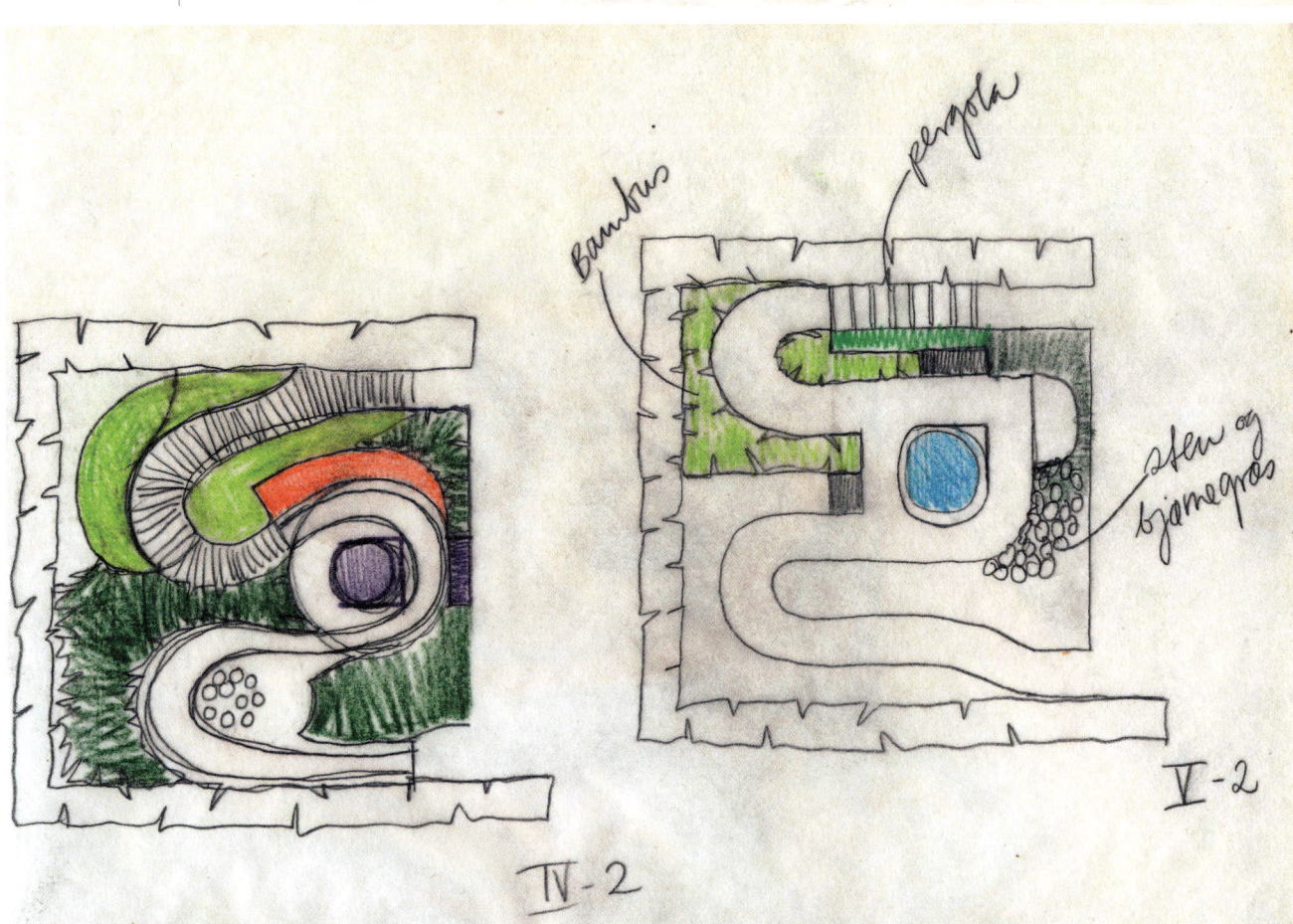

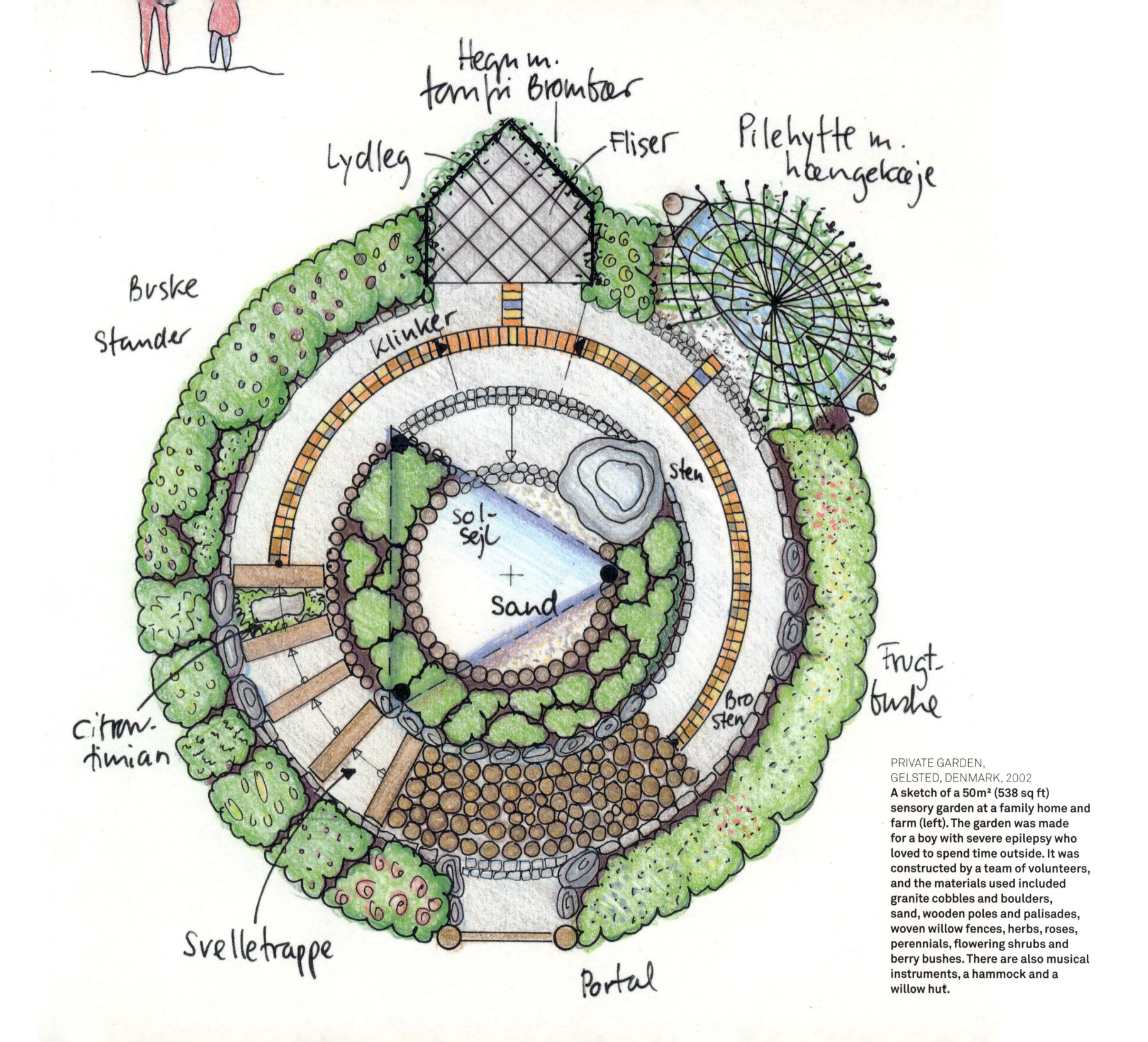

PRIVATE GARDEN, GELSTED, DENMARK, 2002
A sketch of a 50m² (538 sq ft) sensory garden at a family home and farm (left). The garden was made for a boy with severe epilepsy who loved to spend time outside. It was constructed by a team of volunteers, and the materials used included granite cobbles and boulders, sand, wooden poles and palisades, woven willow fences, herbs, roses, perennials, flowering shrubs and berry bushes. There are also musical instruments, a hammock and a willow hut.

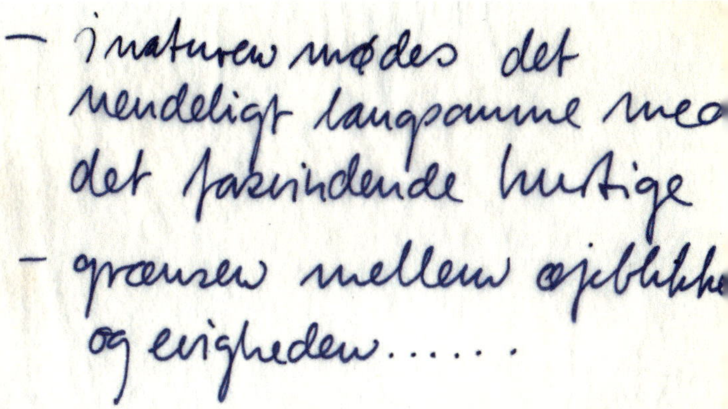

VALBYPARKEN,
COPENHAGEN, DENMARK, 1995
Preliminary sketches for the masterplan for seventeen themed gardens in Valbyparken, the basis for a garden show in 1996. Several ideas were tried, but in the end a series of variously sized circular gardens was constructed, located along a winding path like a string of pearls. The site was eventually made permanent, although the themed gardens change.

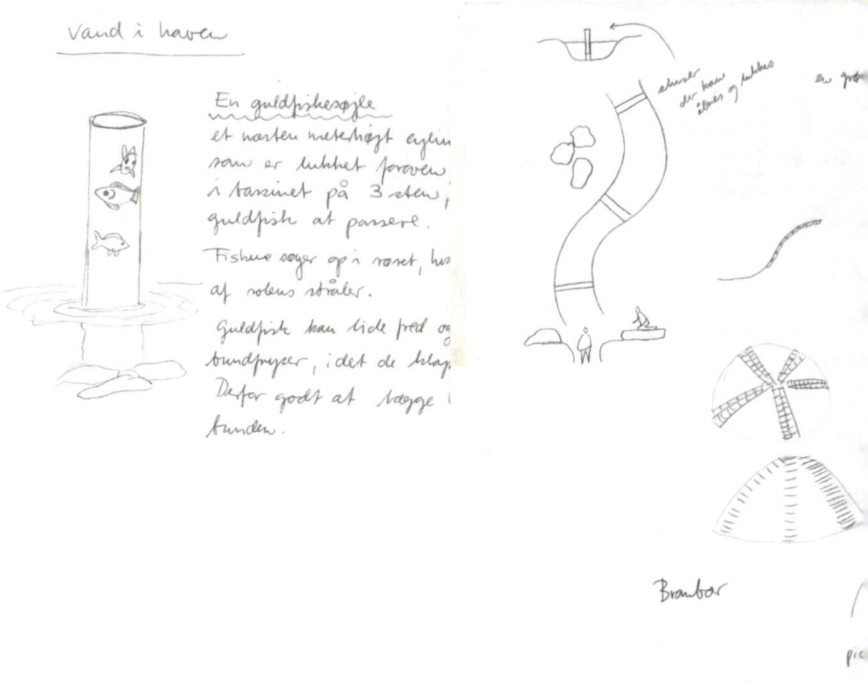

Piet Oudolf
Hummelo, Netherlands

Leader of the 'New Perennials' school of planting design, which promotes the use of large, rhythmic drifts of perennial flowers and grasses, Piet Oudolf has developed a unique way of making planting plans. The plans themselves are of artistic merit and were the subject of a solo exhibition in 2014. The fact that the colour codings used are not related to the colours of plants in nature is testament to the fact that it is form and structure, rather than colour, which is the main design motivation.

Piet Oudolf in a dialogue with the author:

What does drawing mean to you personally, and what part has it played in your development as a designer/artist? It is a slow process. While doing it, it gets you in the right mood. Even though the colours don't represent the plant in my plans, one can feel the rhythm and see whether all is in balance.

How is work done by hand 'different' to that produced by computer? Planting design by computer is impossible for me. Working by hand, I can feel the rhythm. It stimulates the process in the right direction.

Do you use drawing at the beginning of the design process – the 'ideas stage' – or is it something you return to at intervals throughout the project? In my case, the theme or big idea is essential before starting to draw. After the idea, I start with a plant palette that I can choose from.

Do you use drawing primarily as a way of envisaging a potential atmosphere or creating a sense of space and scale, or perhaps for showing the habits and forms of trees and plants? The drawing is more or less exact and on scale. It is also needed in order to calculate plant numbers and for the gardeners to lay out the plants.

What does drawing allow you to do that other modes of expression do not? Contemplation. It is very much about yourself and the action of that moment.

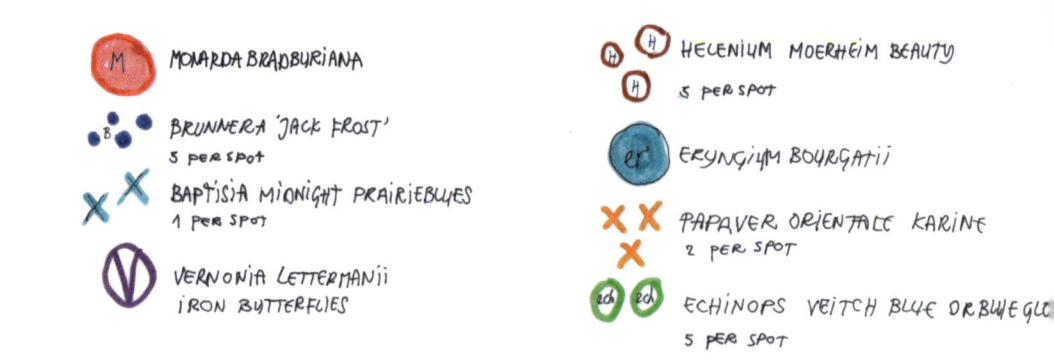

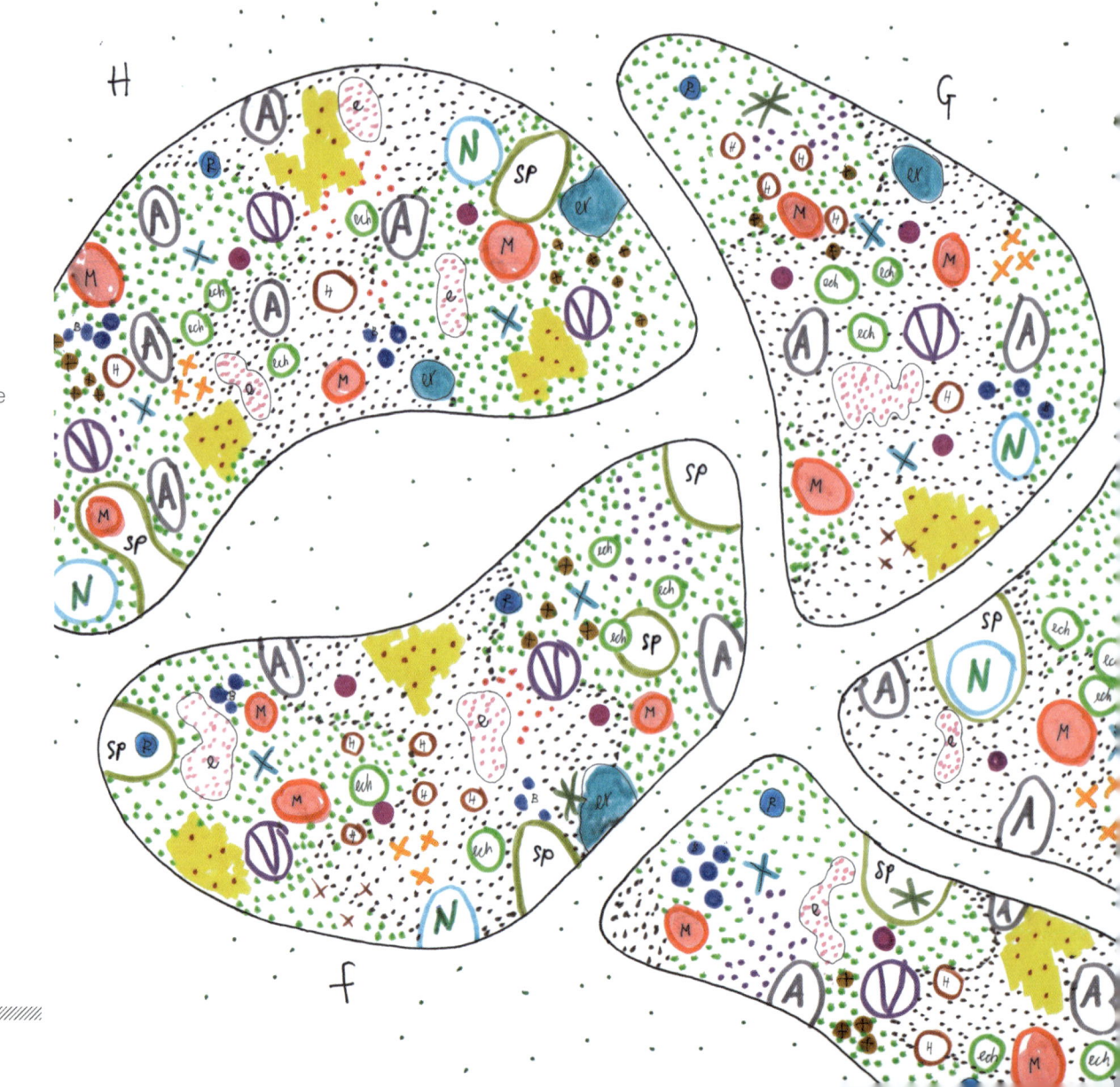

ACHILLEA 'TERRACOTTA' + SEDUM MATRONA
50%   50%

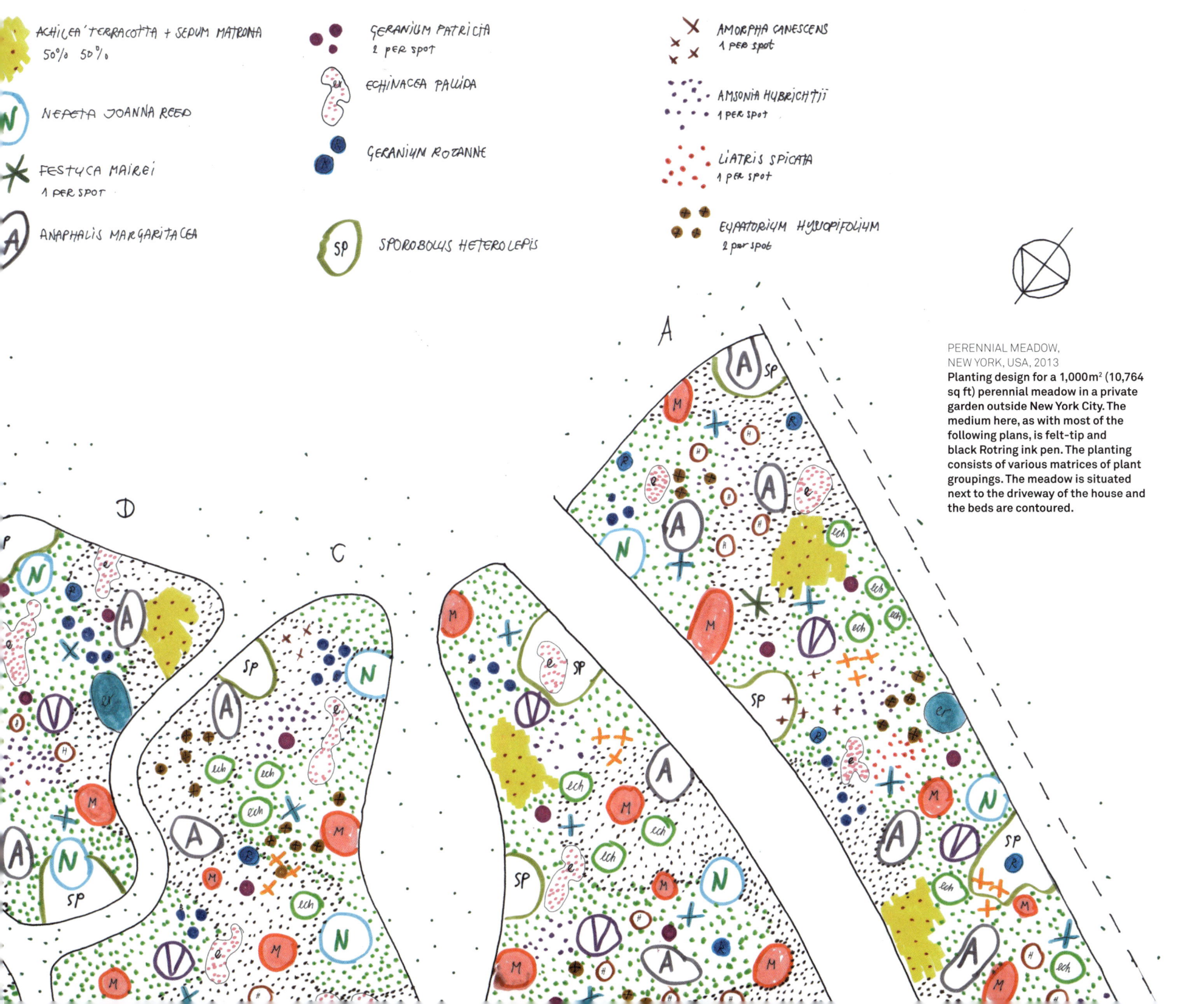

N NEPETA JOANNA REED

✱ FESTUCA MAIREI
1 PER SPOT

A ANAPHALIS MARGARITACEA

GERANIUM PATRICIA
2 PER SPOT

e ECHINACEA PALLIDA

GERANIUM ROZANNE

SP SPOROBOLUS HETEROLEPIS

✕ AMORPHA CANESCENS
1 PER SPOT

AMSONIA HUBRICHTII
1 PER SPOT

LIATRIS SPICATA
1 PER SPOT

EUPATORIUM HYSSOPIFOLIUM
2 PER SPOT

PERENNIAL MEADOW,
NEW YORK, USA, 2013
Planting design for a 1,000m² (10,764 sq ft) perennial meadow in a private garden outside New York City. The medium here, as with most of the following plans, is felt-tip and black Rotring ink pen. The planting consists of various matrices of plant groupings. The meadow is situated next to the driveway of the house and the beds are contoured.

Piet Oudolf

MAXI PARK,
HAMM, GERMANY, 2011
Planting plan for a public park around an ex-industrial site; the different coloured markings represent plant varieties. This sketch (right) was made to ascertain if there was the correct balance and rhythm within the scheme. A second-stage sketch (opposite, above left) shows the labelled plant groupings. Colour-coded plant names were added to early sketches (opposite, below left). Another sketch (opposite, right) details the contours of the planting beds and specifies the position of interspaced plants, such as eupatorium, between the larger groupings.

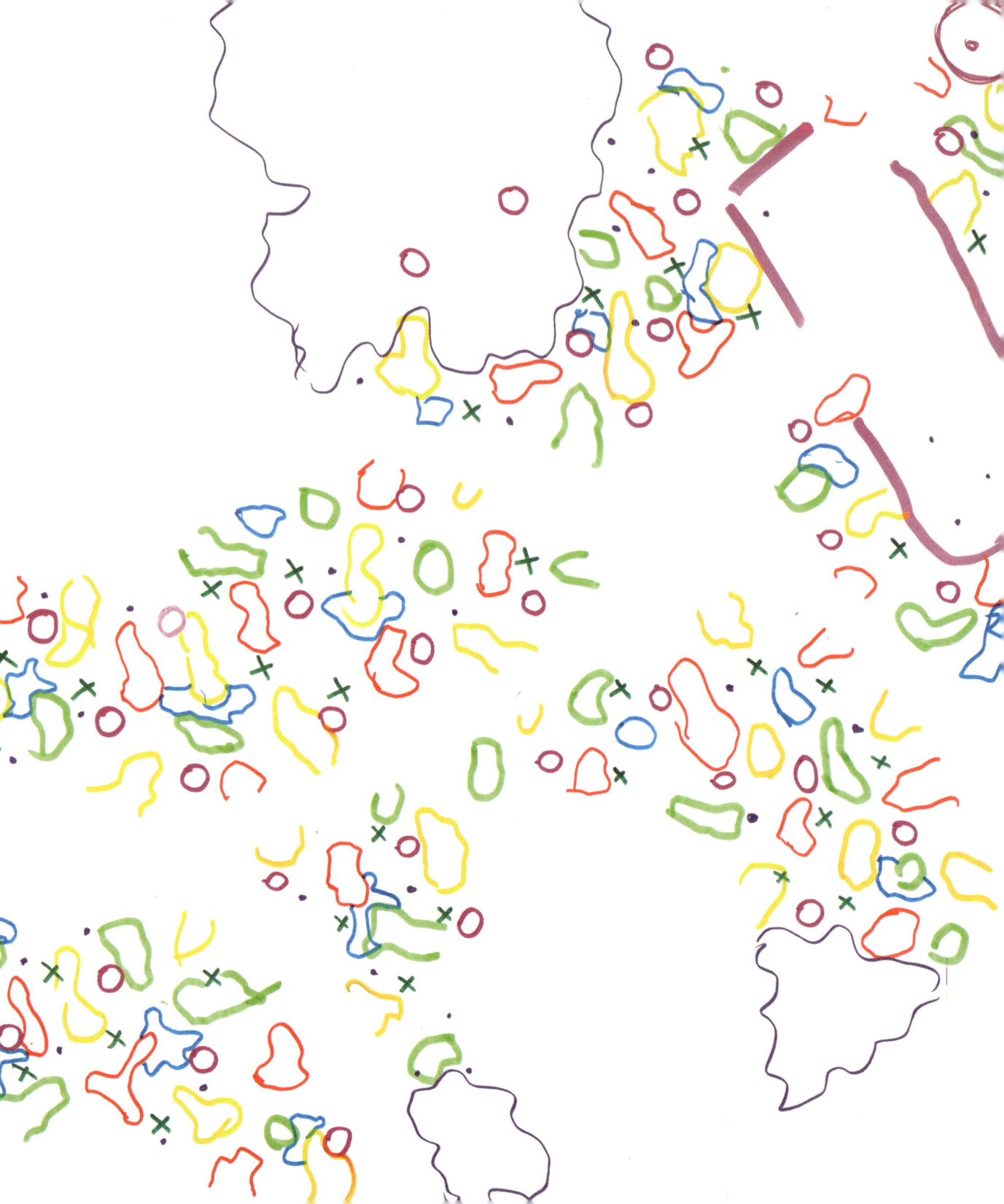

Piet Oudolf

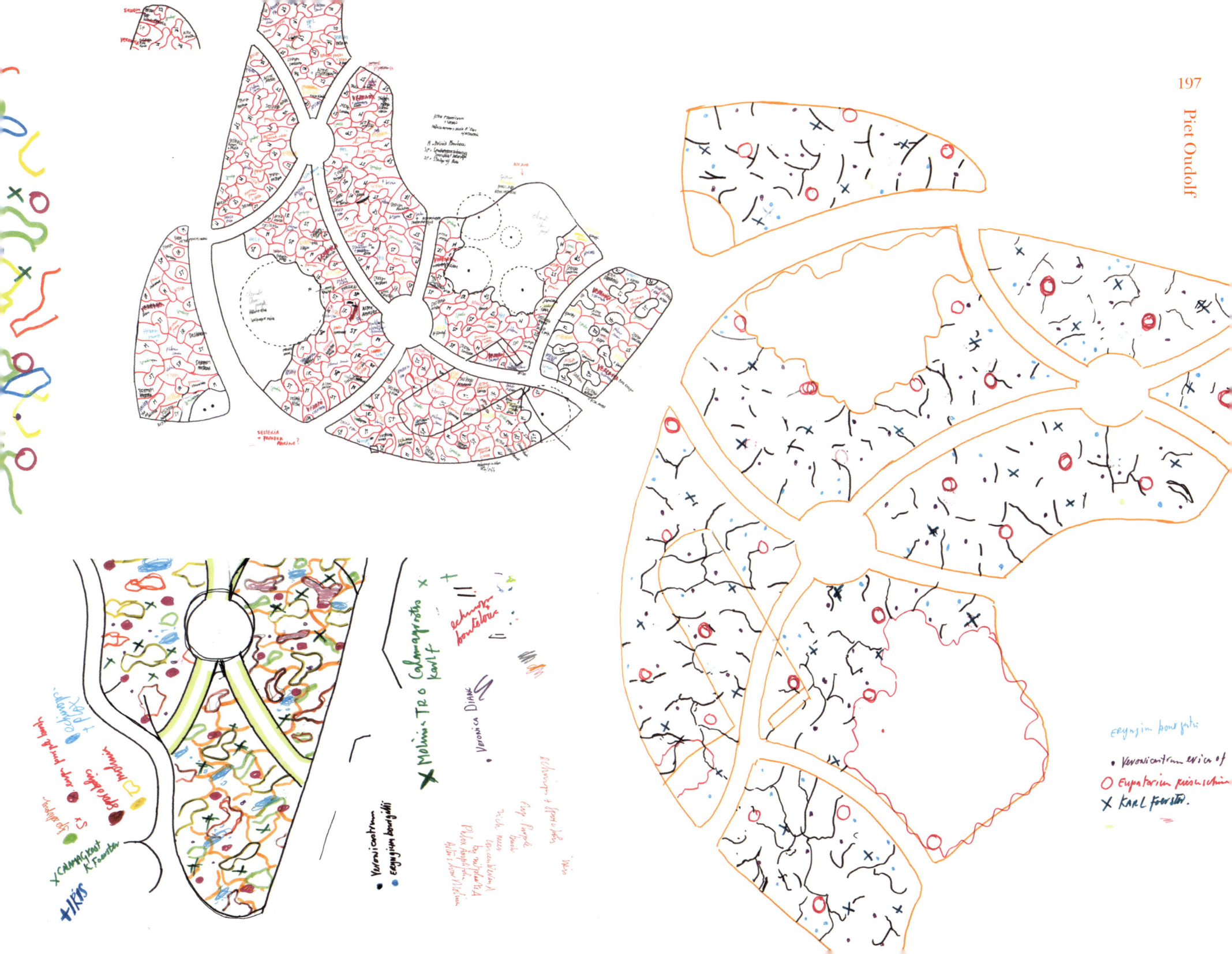

TOWER
DEPOT
IL GIARDINO D
THE ARSENAL
RYE
TANK
TREE
UNKEPT AREA
GRADED LAWN
WALKING AND SITTING AREA
GARDEN AND PLANTING DESIGN (FINAL)
PIET OUDOLF 2010
EUPATORIUM MAC. ATROPURPUREUM
MOLINIA TRANSPARENT
HELENIUM RUBINZWERG
ECHINOPS TAPLOW BLUE
ASTER N-A VIOLETTA
ANEMONE ROBUSTISSIMA
PERSICARIA ORANGE FIELD
AGASTACHE BLUE FORTUNE
ACONITUM ARENDSII
PENNISETUM VIRIDESCENS
1:100
0 2 4 6 8 10m

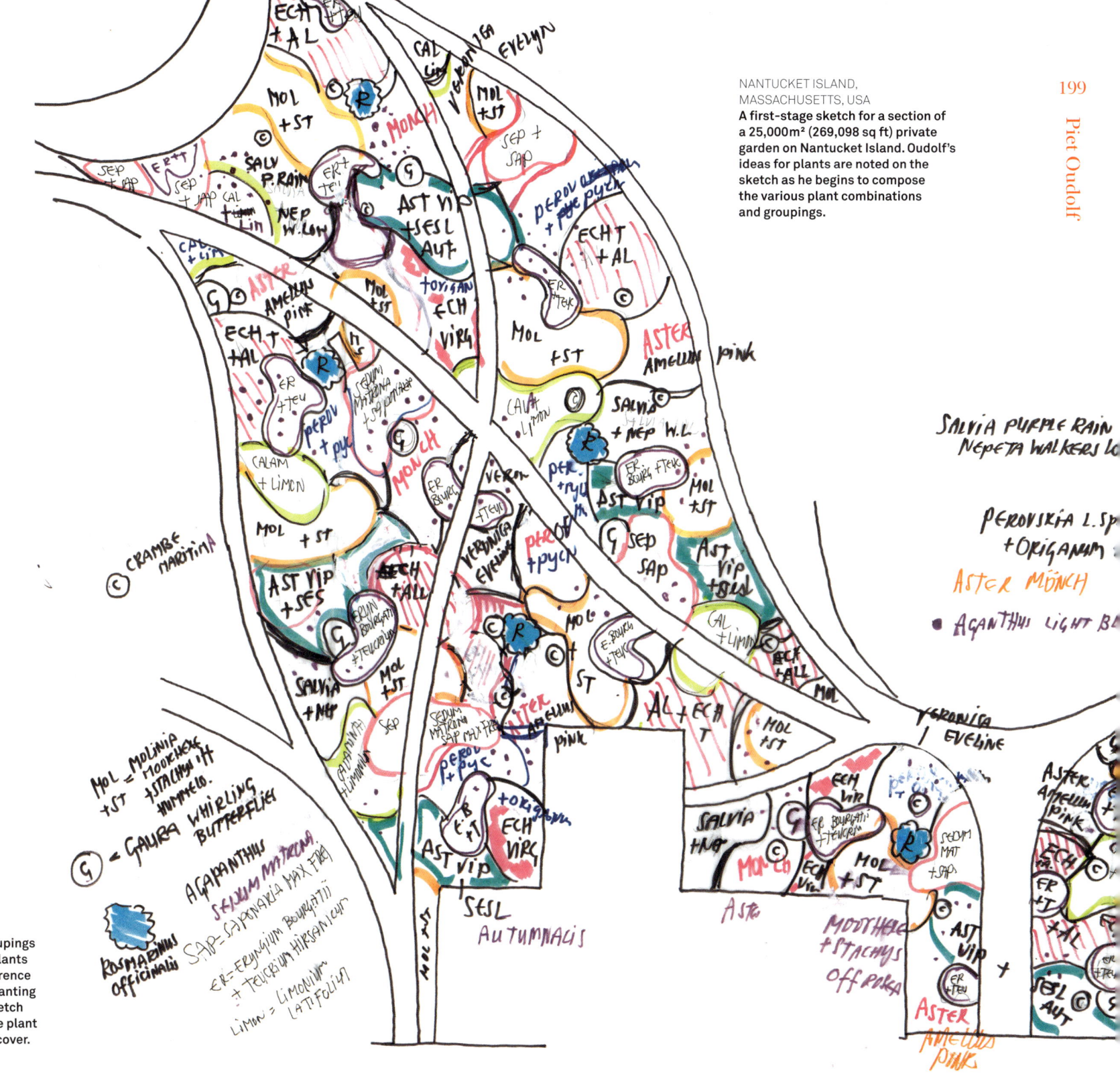

NANTUCKET ISLAND, MASSACHUSETTS, USA
A first-stage sketch for a section of a 25,000m² (269,098 sq ft) private garden on Nantucket Island. Oudolf's ideas for plants are noted on the sketch as he begins to compose the various plant combinations and groupings.

Piet Oudolf

IL GIARDINO DELLA VIRGINI, VENICE BIENNALE, 2010
In this design (left), plant groupings are interspersed with taller plants that interact and create coherence and a sense of volume. The planting area at the top right of the sketch has a matrix, or basis, of three plant species that serve as groundcover.

DESIGN FOR AN APARTMENT BLOCK, DEHAAF, NETHERLANDS, 2009

Early sketches for an unrealized planting design around an apartment block. Specific plant names begin to be introduced as plant groupings and matrices are gradually built up for the variously shaped planting spaces available.

**ROOFTOP GARDEN,
NEW YORK, USA, 2012**
Part of the planting design for a rooftop garden in New York (above), designed with Jonathan Caplan. Here, the plant names are used as a kind of palette that can be worked with on the sketch.

**SERPENTINE GALLERY,
LONDON, UK, 2011**
Planting design for the interior of Hortus Conclusus, Peter Zumthor's pavilion at the Serpentine Gallery, in Hyde Park (below). This garden was created to stay in situ for one summer only. The planting is dense and consists of many varieties that grow to different heights, so that it appeared instantly mature and was interesting to look at throughout its short existence. For this sketch, coloured pencils were used in addition to felt-tip and black pens.

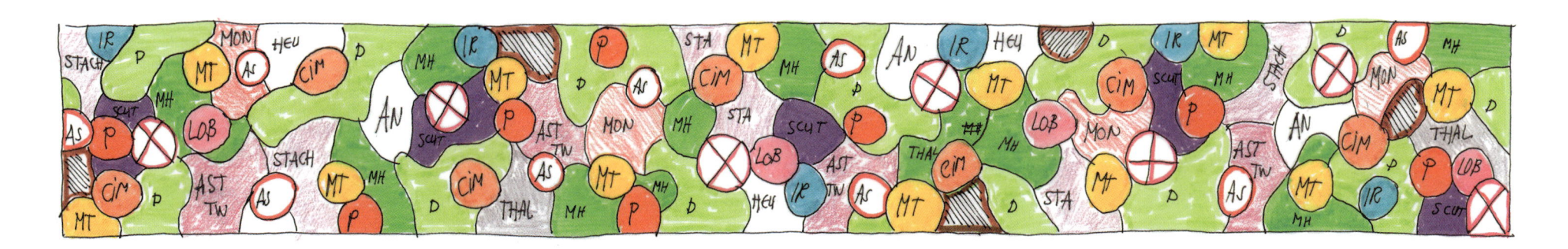

PENSTHORPE NATURE RESERVE, NORFOLK, UK, 2009

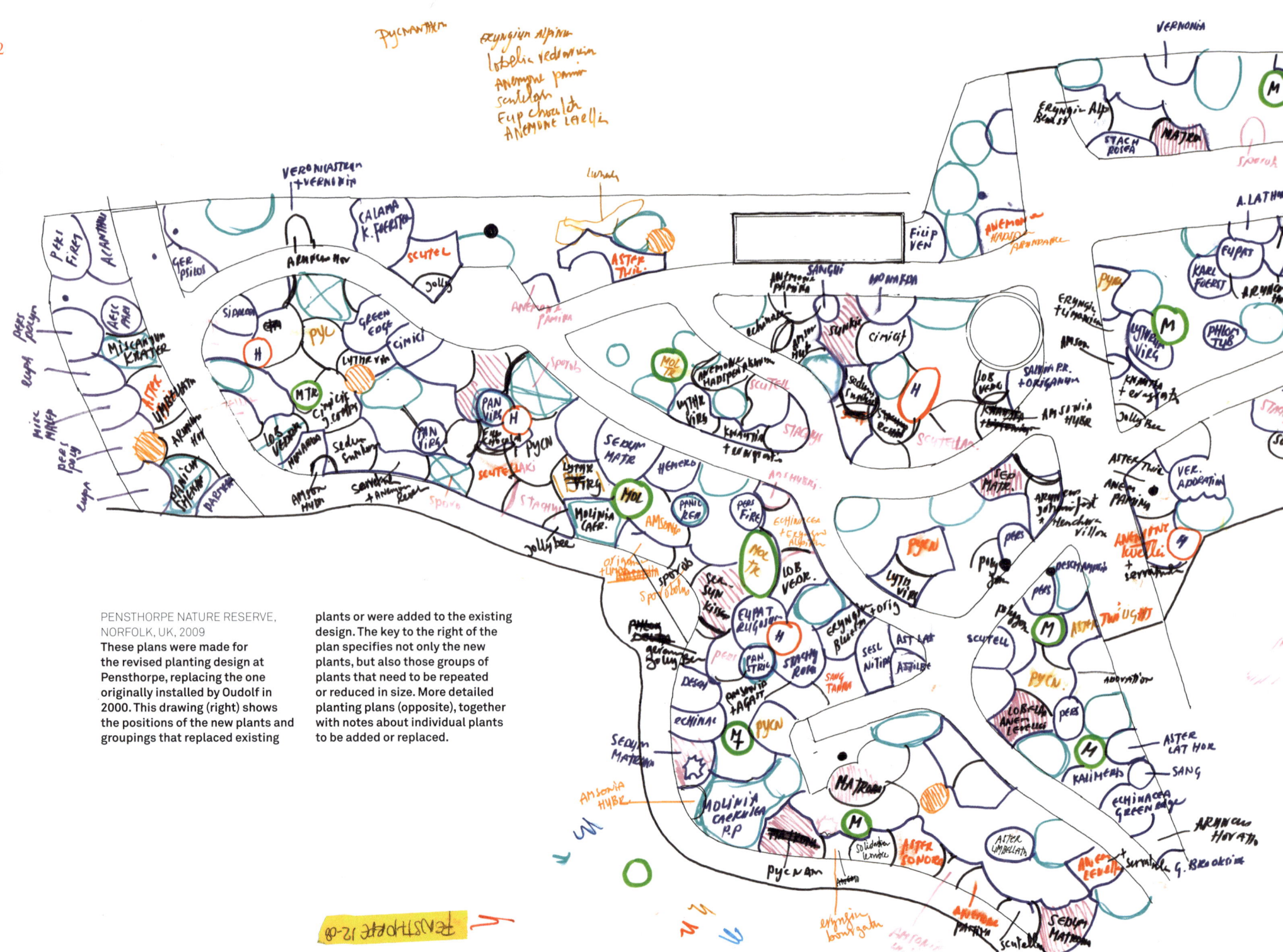

These plans were made for the revised planting design at Pensthorpe, replacing the one originally installed by Oudolf in 2000. This drawing (right) shows the positions of the new plants and groupings that replaced existing plants or were added to the existing design. The key to the right of the plan specifies not only the new plants, but also those groups of plants that need to be repeated or reduced in size. More detailed planting plans (opposite), together with notes about individual plants to be added or replaced.

Piet Oudolf

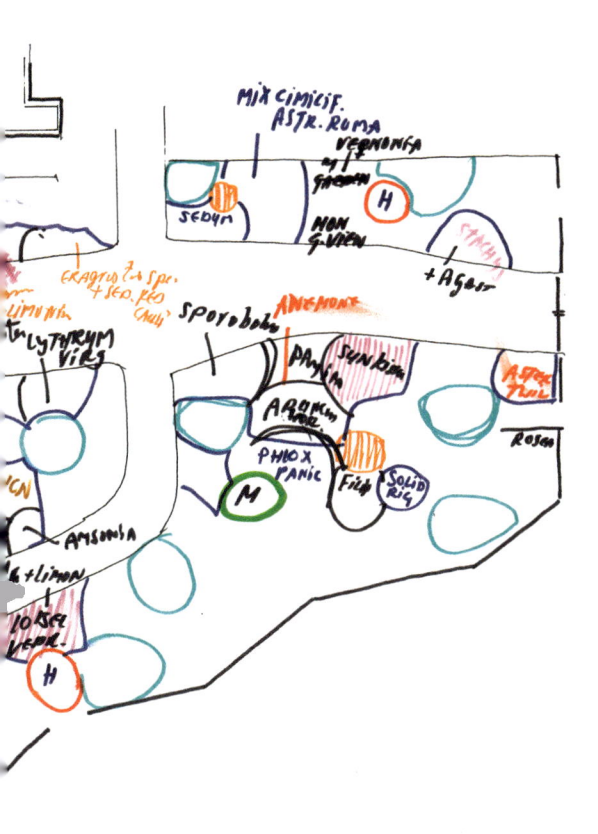

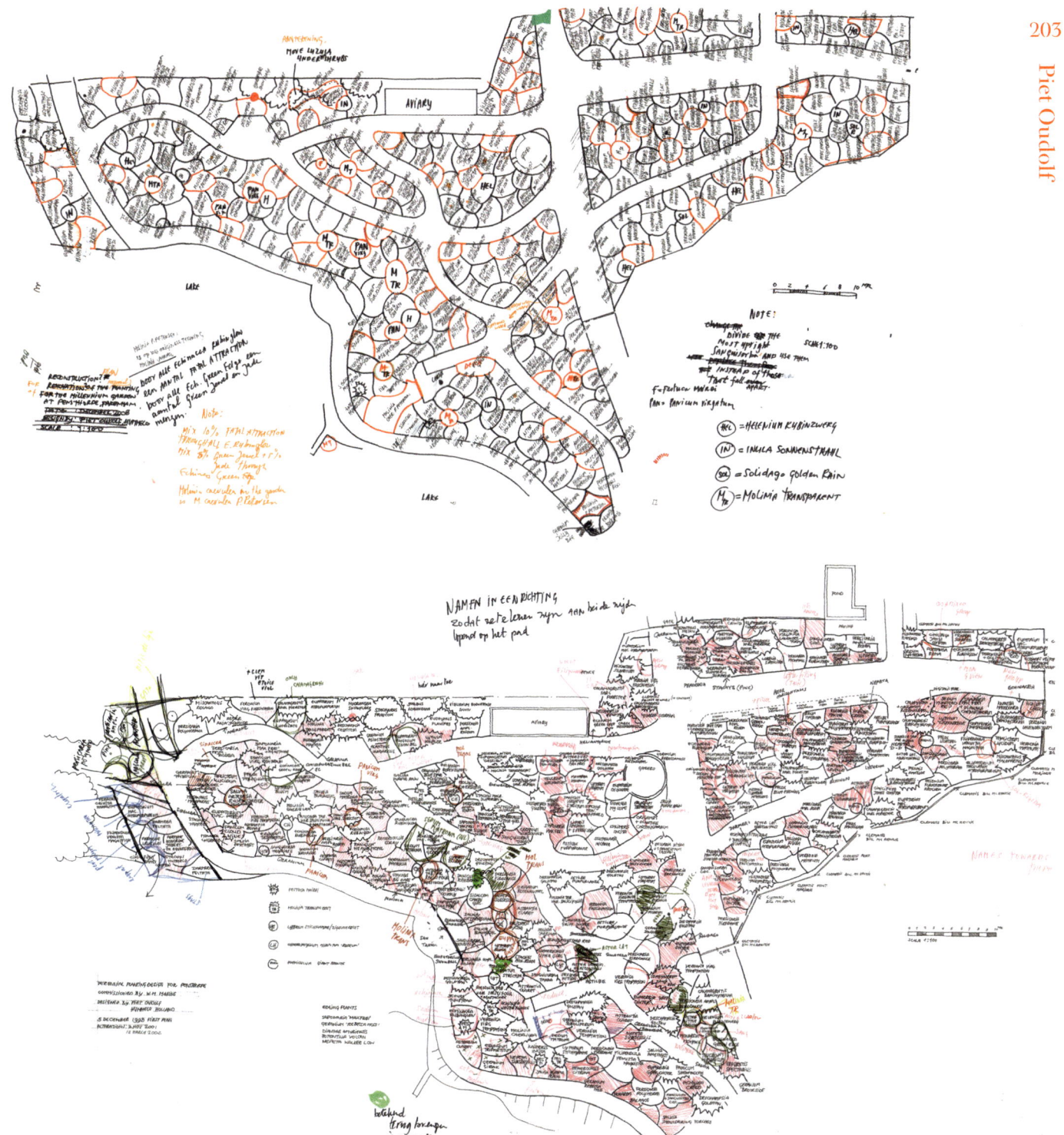

204

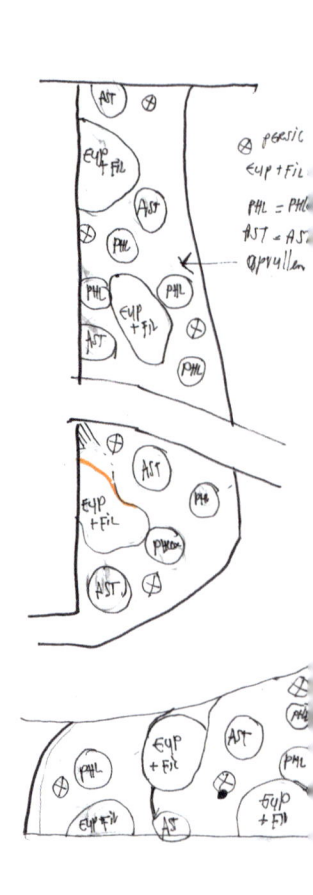

Piet Oudolf

SKÄRHOLMEN PERENNIAL PARK, STOCKHOLM, SWEDEN, 2007
The first sketch (opposite, above) contains the idea of circular drifts, each defined by a combination of plants that can create its own rhythm and change through the seasons. In the centre of the plan is a water feature and seating area. The second sketch (opposite, below) is more worked out. A coloured plan (top) utilizes a colour key to the palette for each planting area. It shows a part of the park shaded by trees, and uses ferns and other repeated plant groups. A pen-and-ink sketch (above) shows the same area with more robust plants, which is at the edge of the park and shuts off the view on the road. A sketch with detailed notes about the plant combinations (left).

Péna & Peña

Paris, France

Michel Péna takes his three pencils (2H, HB, BB) and his notebook wherever he goes. For him, even the most advanced digital tablets are not as quick, portable and easy to use. Since 1982 he has accumulated forty-six identical notebooks, all purchased from Sennelier, in Quai Voltaire, Paris. His three techniques are pencil drawings, writing and collages, and he calls the result his 'imaginary museum'.

Michel Péna writes: 'I practice three stages of pencil drawings. The first stage is that of the free spirit – imagination and creation, pleasure without restraint, which often connects sketches of ideas with writings. The second stage is the expression of "first desires". All of my embryonic dreams for projects are scrawled in these notebooks. The third stage is the expression of landscapes.

'The fastest way to simulate a landscape emerging from a project is to take a photograph of the site to be transformed. My drawing table is equipped with a pantograph, a mechanical device that creates multiple versions of the same drawing. I start with A3 trace paper, my three pencils, a razor blade, a good eraser and tape. I rigorously add the architectural elements to the image, then find the vanishing point and horizon. Using my 2H pencil, I enter the soft contours and the outlines of trees and structures.

'Next come the broad strokes of my HB, and then it's back to 2B. This process creates the image of a landscape of simple contrasts, shadow and light, and textures. I stick the tape onto the too-dark areas and then peel it off to clarify. I also "draw" using an eraser. The advantage of using extremely thin trace paper is the impossibility of reworking the same lines. It is better to throw the plan away and start again, simply to retain the expressive strength of the image.'

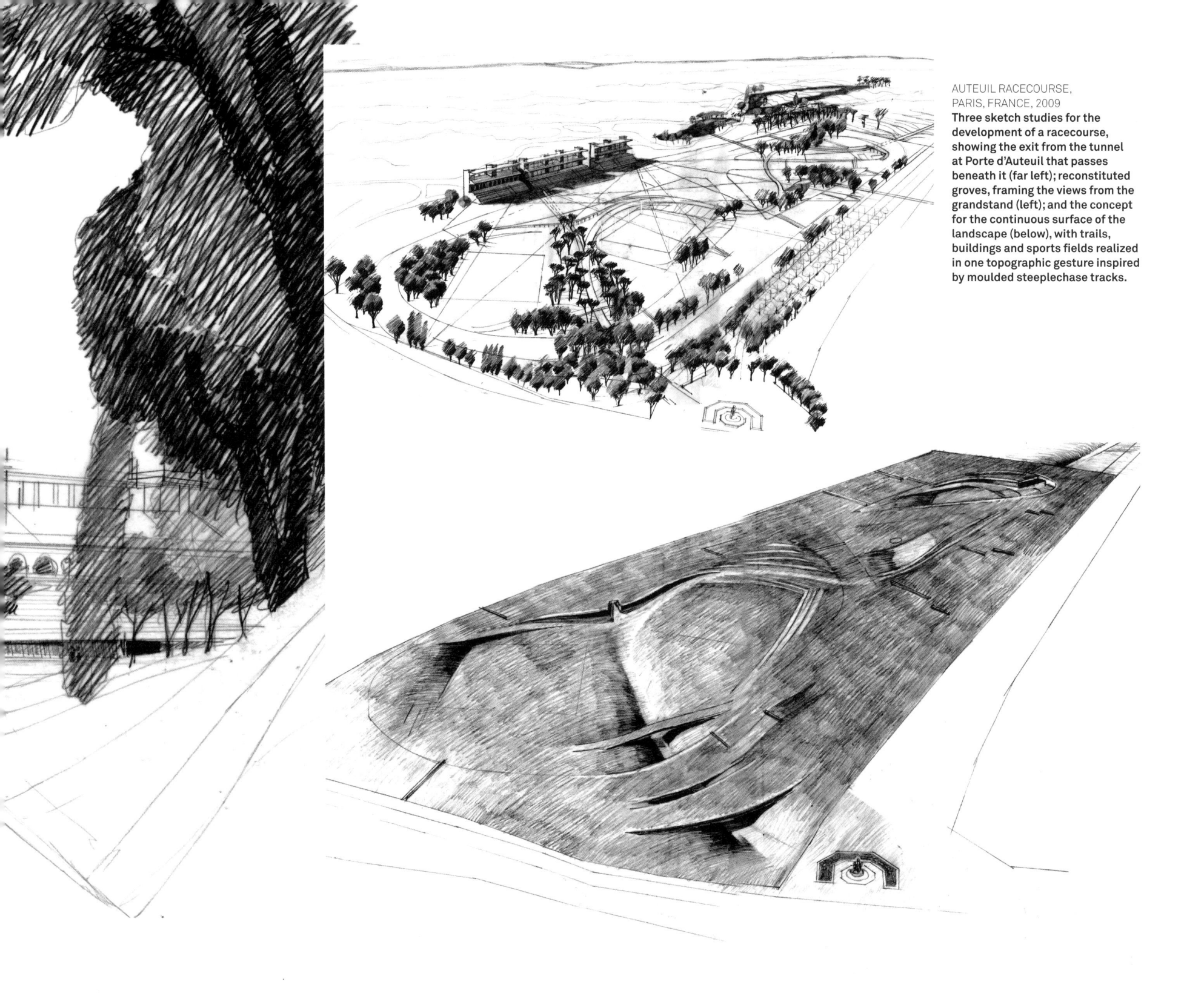

AUTEUIL RACECOURSE,
PARIS, FRANCE, 2009
Three sketch studies for the development of a racecourse, showing the exit from the tunnel at Porte d'Auteuil that passes beneath it (far left); reconstituted groves, framing the views from the grandstand (left); and the concept for the continuous surface of the landscape (below), with trails, buildings and sports fields realized in one topographic gesture inspired by moulded steeplechase tracks.

VARIOUS SKETCHBOOKS, 1986–90
Drawing of Place de la Concorde (above left): a sensual plaza, a clearing in Paris, surrounded by moats; Napoleon plants 'his' gold-tipped obelisk. Searching for the right colour for a red tree seen in the fields from the Paris–Bordeaux train (below left). Sketch study of the texture and theatricality of the rocks at Pornichet, near Nantes (below), research for a 'rocky' staircase created for the Jardin d'Atlantique.

VARIOUS SKETCHBOOKS, 1987–2002
Sketch representing the first vision of the Jardin d'Atlantique (right), an imaginary garden that might land above Gare Montparnasse, in Paris. The sketch reflects a vision for an extraordinary and fantastical world, a contradiction with the very cold, geometric and regulated existing site. Study of the texture, colour and sensuality of plant forms (below). Musings for a stone path in the forest of the Cévennes mountain range (below right).

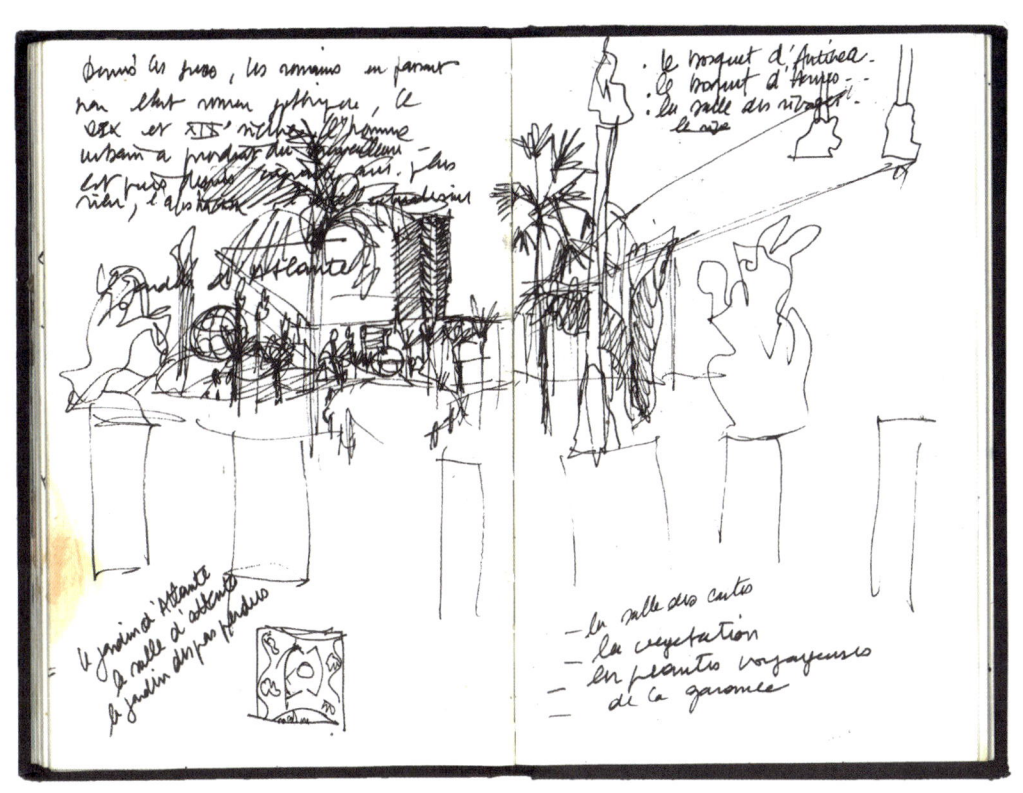

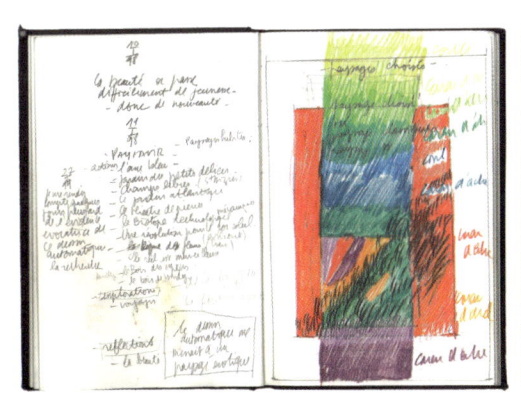

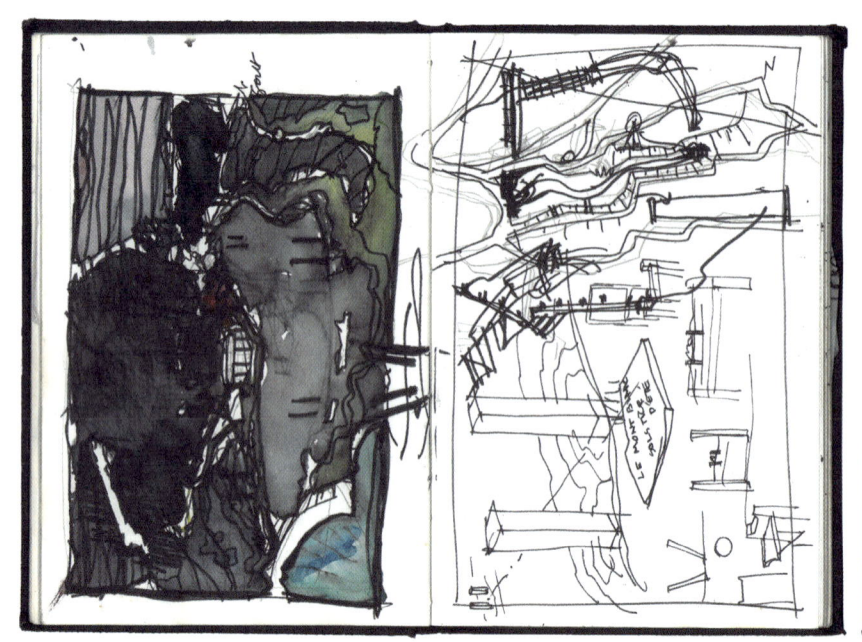

VARIOUS SKETCHES, 1986–2000
Watercolours and drawn studies for a pond in the Cévennes (left); sketches of the beach at Collioure and the skies of the eastern Pyrénées (below); research for development of the Gonesse triangle, north of Paris (bottom left); India ink used to frame notebook research studies (bottom right); sketch in coloured pencils (opposite), made as research for a pond in the Cévennes.

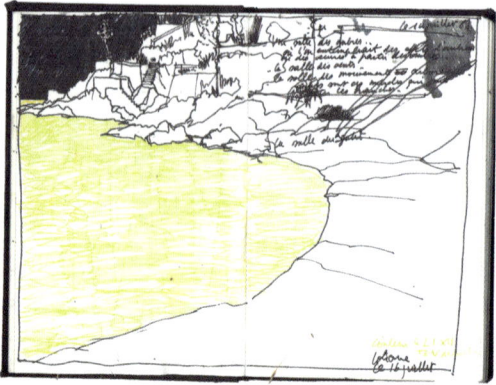

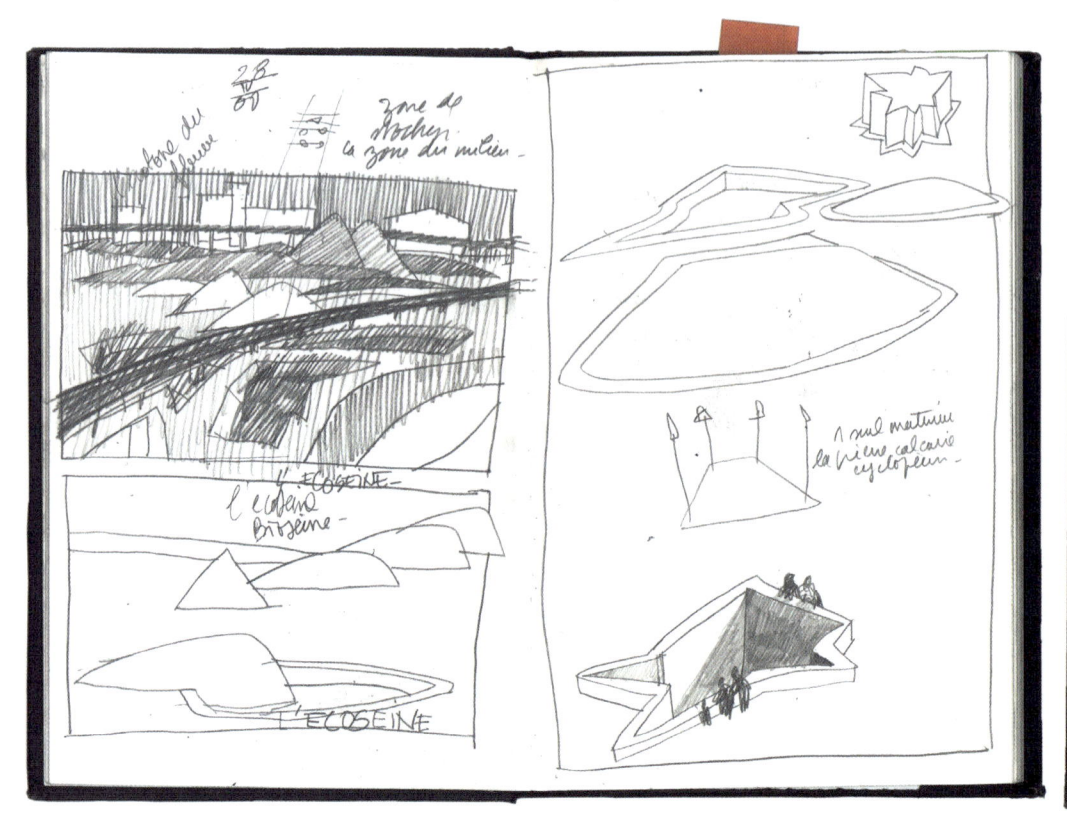

M.P. 03
8/1
LE MIROIR.

PEDESTRIAN PATHWAY,
VALLON-PONT-D'ARC, FRANCE, 2003
Study for a pedestrian pathway, in the Ardèche.

NOISY-LE-GRAND,
MARNE-LA-VALLÉE, FRANCE, 2003
The first vision (above) – almost scribbles – for a new sensual garden in a difficult neighbourhood.

LANDSCAPED CEMETERY,
LA BAULE, FRANCE, 2005
Sketch showing the meditation and contemplation space bordering the canal at a cemetery in La Baule (top).

COURROUZE ECOLOGICAL DISTRICT,
RENNES, FRANCE, 2003
Development sketch (right) for the Courrouze ecological district.

PLATEAU DES CAPUCINS,
BREST, FRANCE, 2005
Sketches at a former women's prison. The vegetation below a new footbridge over a former slipway recalls the extraordinary journeys taken by sailors from the Arsenal in the Capucins district. The sketches show how the plantings will develop.

DRAVEIL ACTIVITIES CENTRE,
PARIS, FRANCE, 2008
Theoretical drawing for an outdoor activities centre near Paris. A suspended wooden bench slips (or sneaks) between the trees.

Pola

Milan, Italy

For Pola, the act of drawing is akin to telling a story about the spirit of the space, as opposed to merely describing or understanding its limitations and borders. Landscape design operates in between these areas of understanding, between 'real' reality and the imagination. The team at Pola believes that drawing occupies the same territory.

Jörg Michel writes: 'The experience of landscapes and gardens creates individual worlds within us. In our practice, the goal of a drawing is not to show a realistic image of a space to be designed, but an understanding of feeling, atmosphere and vision. To me, sketching is seeking out the boundaries of space, while drawing is floating in time. I draw to show the soul of a design.

'Knowing that feelings and memories are even stronger than what has triggered them, emotions continue to exist as real even when we have left the original site. Imagination is often stronger and lasts longer than reality; we carry the landscape of our childhood vividly with us, even though it may not even exist any more. The feeling survives, not the built reality. This is the way I understand the concept of sustainability.

'It takes only few minutes of sketching to get the spatial idea of a place, to clarify my ideas about its design. But it can take days of endless drawing to find out the story of the particular space I want to tell. To me, drawing is floating in time in search of the particular atmosphere of the place, its temperature, heartbeat and story.

'Sketching and drawing are less about tracing barriers and more about feeling, sound and emotion. They are not about skills; they are about atmosphere, spirit and shade. I draw, too, to create a sense of distance from the atmosphere and the emotions I want to create and provoke.'

217
Pola

CLOUDBURST, BRANDENBURG GARDEN SHOW, GERMANY, 2013
This garden (these and previous pages) was designed to celebrate the joy and instability of being. Seasonal changes and temperature fluctuations are visible, noticeable and appreciated. This is not a garden of built reality, but of emotional outpouring. The garden represents the essence of poetic gardening and beauty, and the idea of cultural and emotional resonance that is central to the firm's work.

219

Pola

GLEISPARK 1 RAILWAY PARK, OELSNITZ, GERMANY, 2012

For this competition entry, a reduced design was produced to show the elementary parts of a post-industrial site in Saxony. The region was also the birthplace of German Romanticism in the late eighteenth century. Pola suggests that this aesthetic, exemplified by the paintings of Caspar David Friedrich, has much in common with contemporary landscape design: 'Ruins of Gothic churches and neoclassical pavilions were the settings for scenes of romantic transfiguration, just as landscapes featuring abandoned railway tracks or damaged factory buildings are today's "reused landscapes"'.

221
Pola

Patrizia Pozzi

Milan, Italy

For Patrizia Pozzi, nothing can replace the power of the initial sketch. For her, the stronger the image, the stronger the idea and soul of the project. Pozzi will often draw during an initial inspection of the site, and use this first artistic reaction later to convince a client to commission the work. Many other designers use their drawings in a similar way, because they can be extremely persuasive and compelling – even more so than the most advanced computer renderings.

Patrizia Pozzi writes: 'In this discipline, sketching is much more important than it is for an architect. In our job, the overall vision is so important, and drawings – sometimes associated with photography – can capture that vision better than any other technique. Hand-drawing has been a part of my life since I was a little girl, when it became my way of approaching and learning about the natural world. Later, this become the inspiration for my work and, especially in the first years of my career, drawing was my most important resource. Freehand drawing remains an integral part of my work, and I think it will remain so.

'By hand-drawing, I mean all the techniques that are related to it, including pencils and watercolours, which allow you to add colour – not the actual colours as they appear, but as a way of intensifying ideas. By contrast, drawing using a computer produces an artificial and incomplete vision. We sometimes use the computer to reinforce our freehand drawings, and it is very often complementary. Drawing is particularly important in the initial phases of the design process, when you have to communicate your ideas and persuade the client.

'But even in the later phases, hand-drawing can be used as part of the design process – especially in the construction phase, where by means of a simple paper-block and a pencil you can better specify your intention to the artisan or contractor through the use of a graphic.'

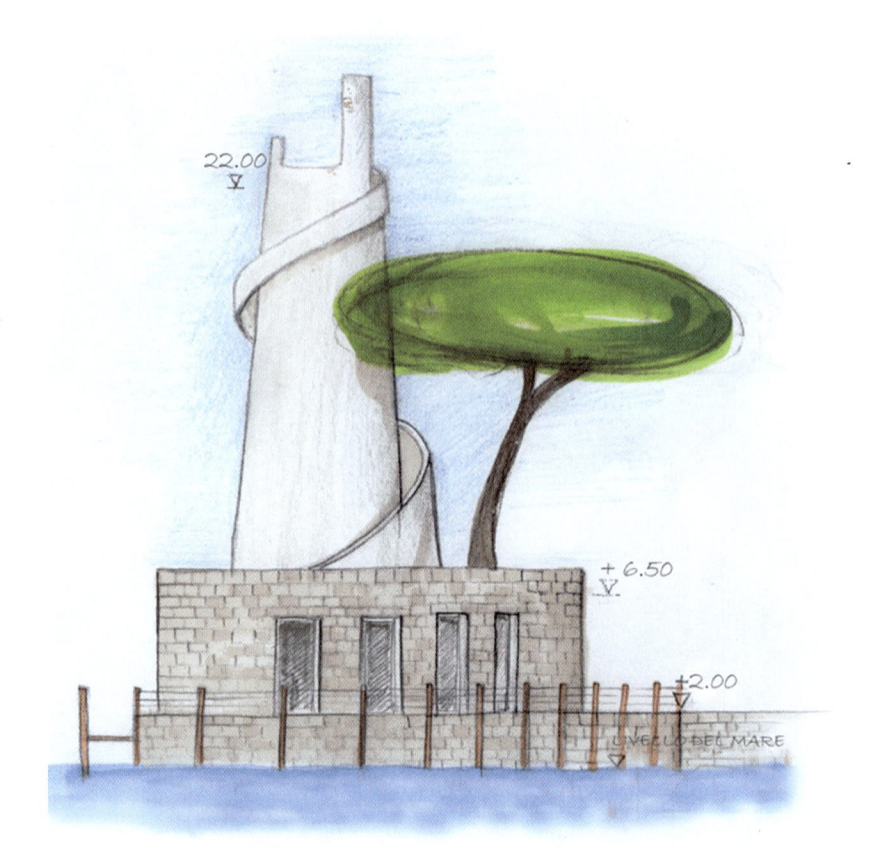

DESIGN FOR A HARBOUR,
VALONA, ALBANIA, 2004
Soft pencil sketches with Pantone colour markers of the landscape design for a new harbour. The distinctive shells of the region were discovered on a first site visit and came to form the basis of the design of residential units and a lighthouse tower, sited among the Aleppo pines and tamarisks that bend in the strong winds. The units are positioned at different levels to mimic the natural scattering of shells along the beach.

DESIGN FOR A COURTYARD,
SAN COLOMBANO, ITALY, 2001

Sketches in pencil and Pantone colour markers, showing a new design for a courtyard in front of a sixteenth-century house in northern Italy. This is a neo-Baroque garden with a twist, in that it develops both horizontally and vertically by means of the interplay between ornamental parterres of box hedges and surfaces of split stone, pebbles and grass laid out in geometric patterns. The sketches show different iterations of the rotated parterre (below) and the 'parterre fence' (right).

① TIPO "PORCINAI" - TOPIARIA

② TIPO GIARDINO ALL'ITALIANA - TOPIARIA

③ TIPO "CLASSICO"

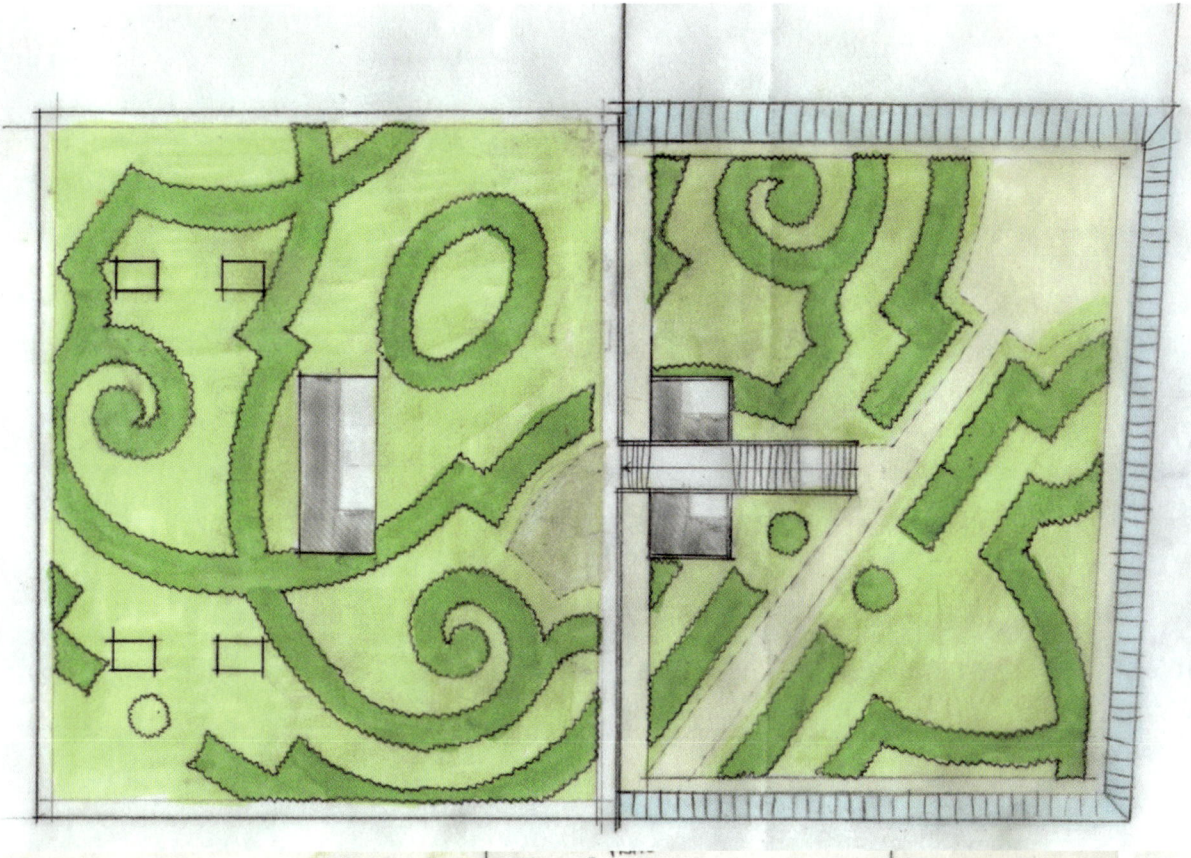

L'ORÉAL ITALIA,
MILAN, ITALY, 2013
These sketches, also in pencil and Pantone colour markers, show a magnified and rotated Baroque parterre design for L'Oréal Italia. The parterre comprises gravel paths of crushed yellow granite and four species of plants that flower in different seasons: heather (*Erica vulgaris*) in autumn, horned violet (*Viola cornuta*) in winter, primrose (*Primula vulgaris*) in spring, and New Guinea impatiens (*Impatiens hawkeri*) in summer. The drawings illustrate the different proposals formalized within the open space on two levels connected by a staircase.

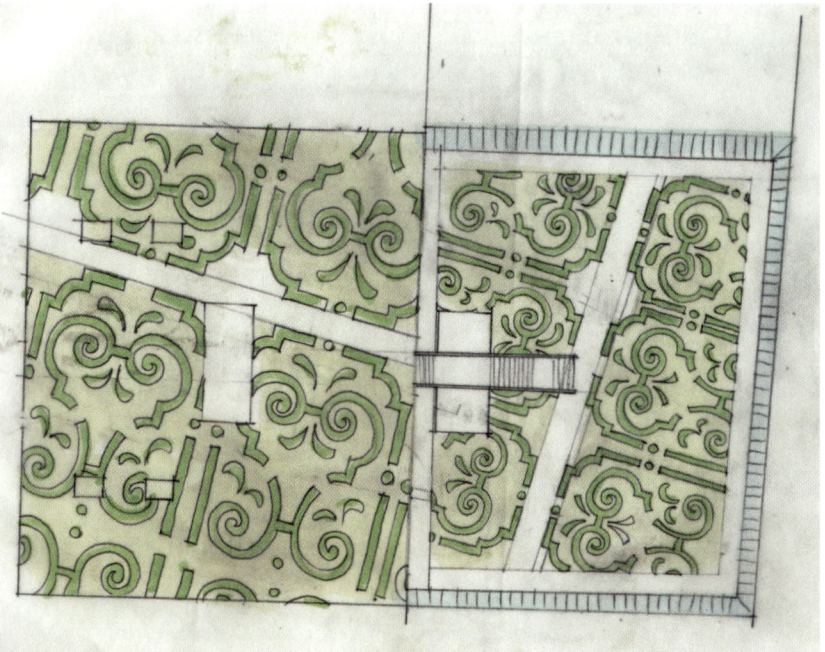

H. sempre 2016
la vista

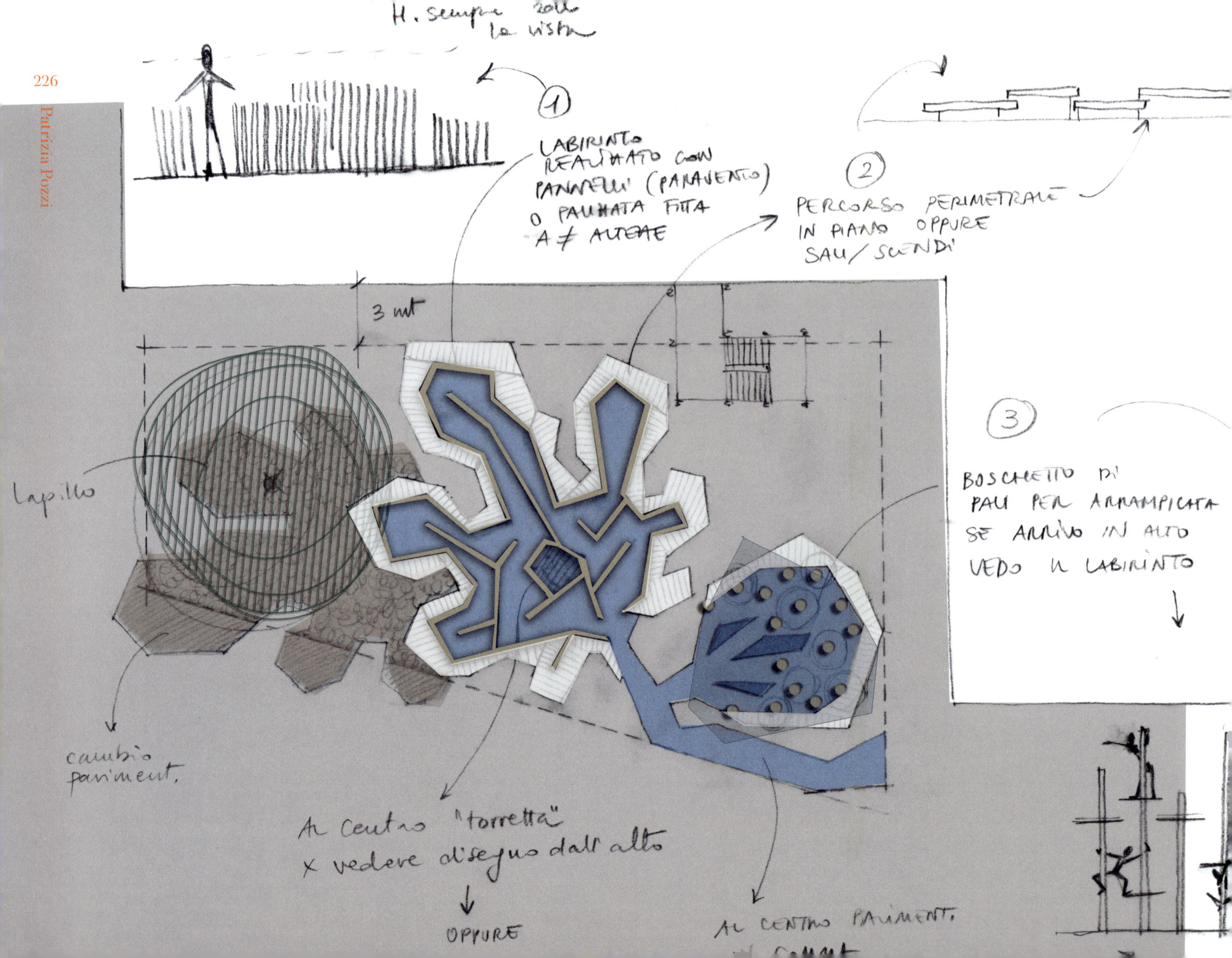

① LABIRINTO REALIZZATO CON PANNELLI (PARAVENTO) O PALIZZATA FITTA A ≠ ALTEZZE

② PERCORSO PERIMETRALE IN PIANO OPPURE SALI/SCENDI

③ BOSCHETTO DI PALI PER ARRAMPICATA SE ARRIVO IN ALTO VEDO IL LABIRINTO

3 mt

Lapillo

cambio pavimenti

Al centro "torretta" x vedere disegno dall'alto
↓
OPPURE

Al centro pavimenti.

IL FICO,
CATANIA, ITALY, 2010
Preparatory studies for a garden for a new Ikea store in Catania. The fig tree – its leaf and fruit – was the underlying concept for this design. One early sketch (opposite) shows how the 'leaf' part of the design defined the boundaries of the garden, while the 'fruit' part became a children's play area. The other sketches show how the motif was used for various parts of the design – for example, as an outdoor exhibition space and as entrance orientation.

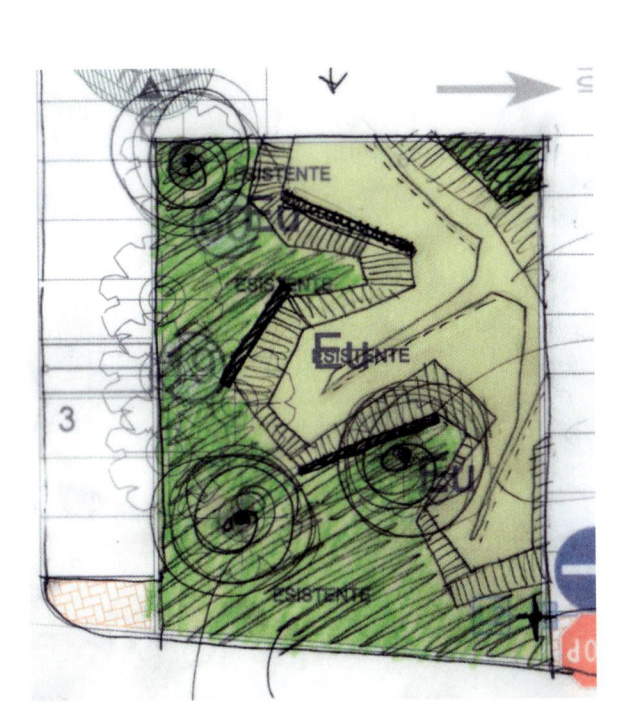

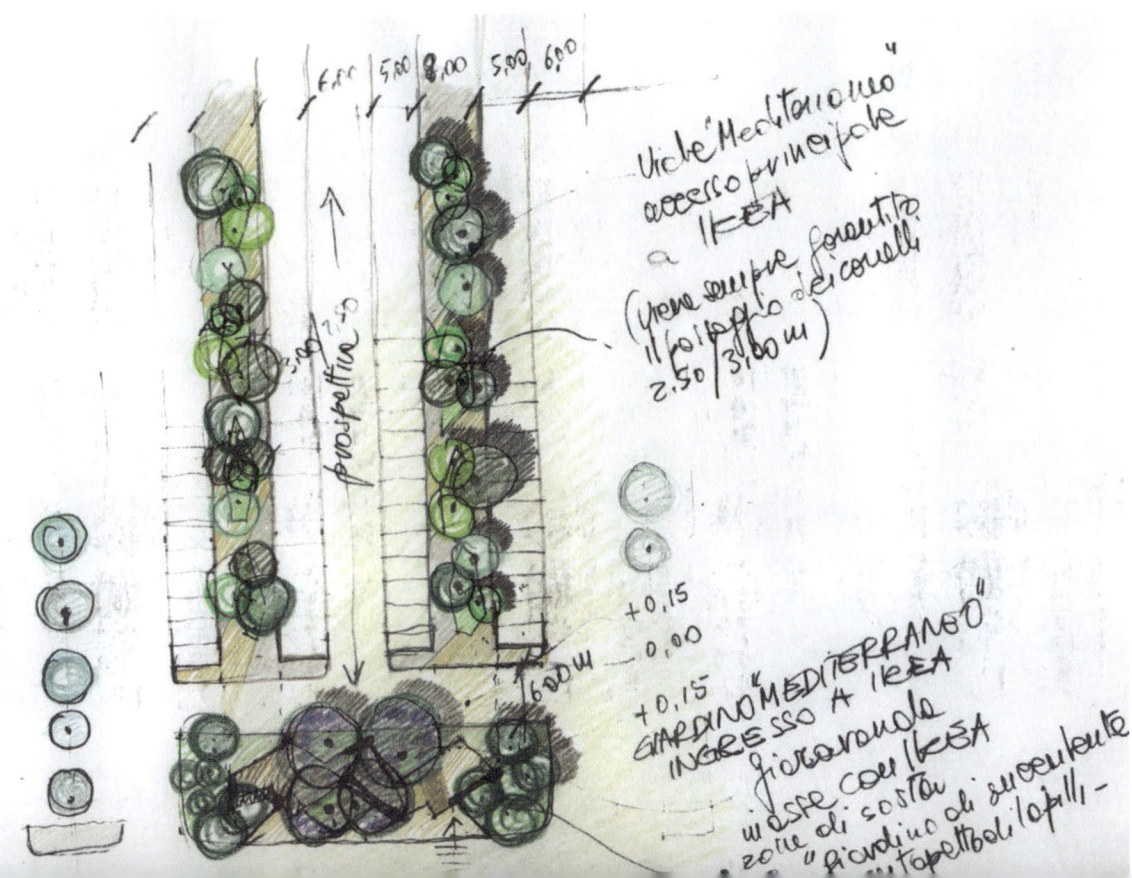

PIAZZA LE TRE TORRI,
MILAN, ITALY, 2009
Studies for the creation of a large new piazza as part of the redevelopment of the old trade-fair district of Milan. The piazza is connected with the surrounding park at different levels by a system of ramps and staircases to form a 'gash' in its compact fabric. The edges of the gash, which form the roof of the commercial area below, are animated by green areas and ponds. A small grove of trees in the middle of the piazza recalls the green character of the area, emphasized by the presence of climbing plants trailing over the façade of the commercial centre.

229

Patrizia Pozzi

Sarah Price
Monmouthshire, UK

Many designers rely on drawings early in their career as a way of 'selling' their ideas – because they have few finished projects to show. Sarah Price is among those who have not abandoned drawing, even as the practice has expanded. For her, sketching has become a more private activity, often undertaken at speed – especially at the beginning of the design process, when sketching and note-making still sets the direction and tone of projects.

Sarah Price notes: 'It can be difficult trying to explain initial ideas through words. Sketching feels intuitive, a way of translating my ideas directly to the page. It's so immediate: there is nothing between your pencil and your ideas. The time you take to observe and then to commit your thoughts to the page (or to a material model) is invaluable creative-thinking time. Everyday observation provides ideas and insights, and these can often be subconscious until you pick up a pencil.

'When designing planting schemes, I often draw cross-sections of my plant selection on cheap trace paper. Simple squiggles represent a simplification of the main plant forms: umbels, spires, button-like dots and low, mounded hummocks. I usually draw to the same scale, so I can see how different layers combine and interact visually. I like to test my planting schemes to make sure I have enough variety in plant forms.

'I feel confined by the size of a computer monitor; landscapes and garden spaces are expansive and complex, and suited to rolls of trace paper that you stick together to form a series of panoramas. I don't like the predictability of conventional computer rendering, as it can control the design process and dictate the final outcome. On the other hand, computer programs such as SketchUp and Photoshop are incredibly powerful. When treated as another tool, they can help designers produce fantastical and often unexpected outcomes.'

HEEM PARKS, AMSTELVEEN, NETHERLANDS, 2009
Ink sketches of clipped and pollarded Salix (willow) forms and marginal vegetation, observed in the 'heem', or 'habit', parks at Amstelveen. Price notes: 'During the design process, my scribbles of planting combinations usually take on a looser style, as they confirm the composition in my head. I want plants to take centre stage, so that their shapes, forms and patterns create the underlying compositional elements. Drawing helps imprint the habit and form of trees and plants in my mind, and extends my visual vocabulary.'

DAILY TELEGRAPH GARDEN,
CHELSEA FLOWER SHOW,
LONDON, UK, 2012

Initial concept sketches (right and below), exploring the relationship between two square pools and a surrounding composition of stone. Each sketch imagines a pattern of stone inset within the pools and escaping as a ground-pattern detail. This pencil and pastel sketch (opposite) explores the composition of stone, water and planting within the show garden. Despite being a very loose sketch, this plan view formed the basis of the final design, which evoked the beauty and romance of wild places in the British countryside.

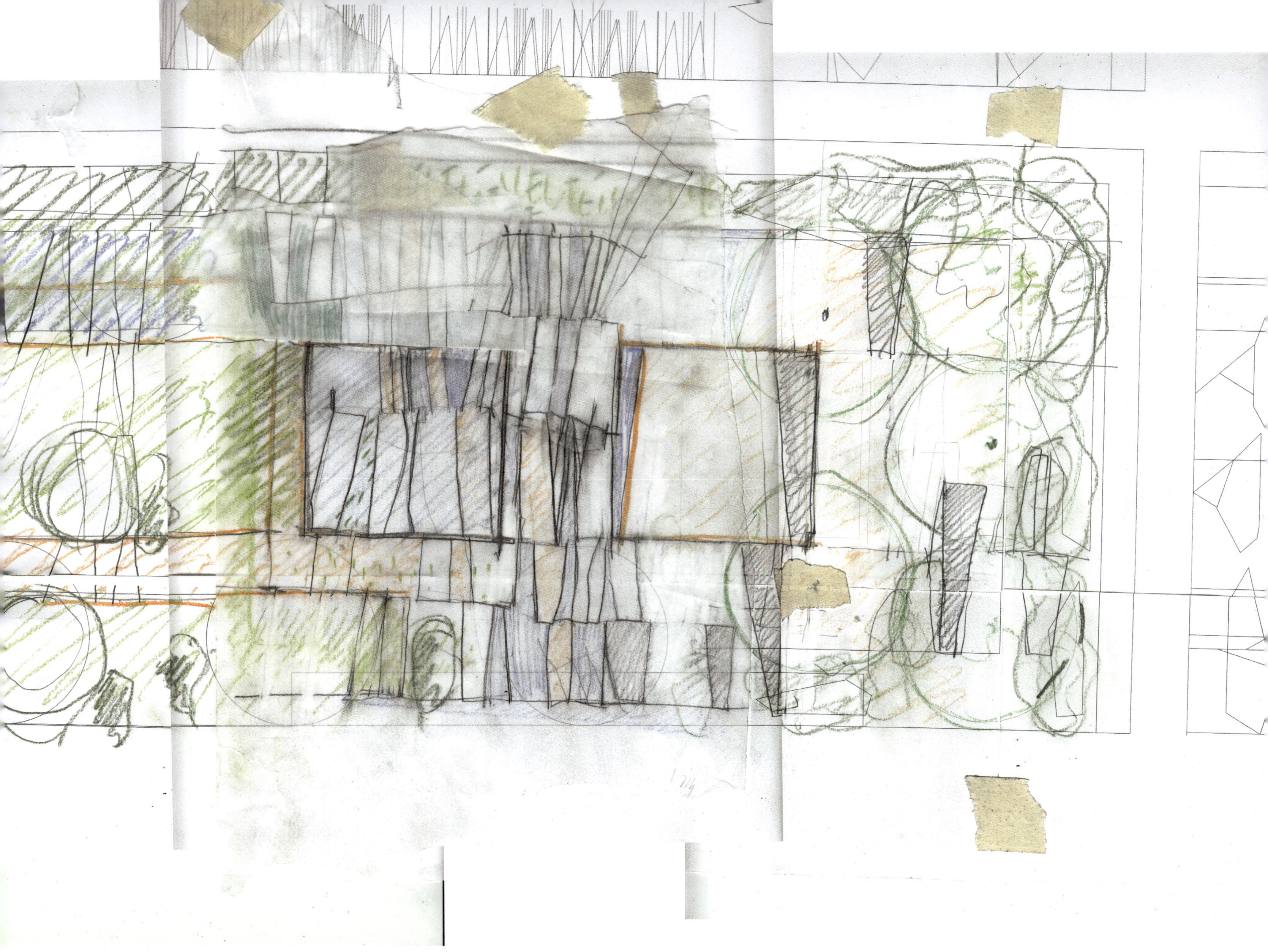

234

Sarah Price

BAPTIST CHAPEL, ABERGAVENNY, MONMOUTHSHIRE, UK, 2014
Concept sketches in pencil and wash on paper with Photoshop collage for a new garden at a renovated Baptist chapel, now an arts, performance and café space. The garden was built like an evolving 3D collage, using reclaimed materials (mainly stone slabs and setts) collected from the renovation works.

COMMUNITY CENTRE,
UNIVERSITY OF CAMBRIDGE,
UK, 2013

Proposed views, created using SketchUp and Photoshop, for a new community centre in Cambridge. The view from the hall towards the landscape beyond (left) is framed by three 'dancing' trees and domed evergreen shrub forms. The private courtyard garden (below) is intended to be a contemplative space, conducive to meditation or tai chi. The design is focused around a mature magnolia tree, which grows in the shelter of the south-facing brick wall. The theme of play is introduced through the use of of mounded levels, rolling evergreen cloud hedging and closely planted copses of birch trees (right). These elements form a 'green veil', separating the garden from the play space behind. Both spaces benefit from the sense of light and depth this introduces.

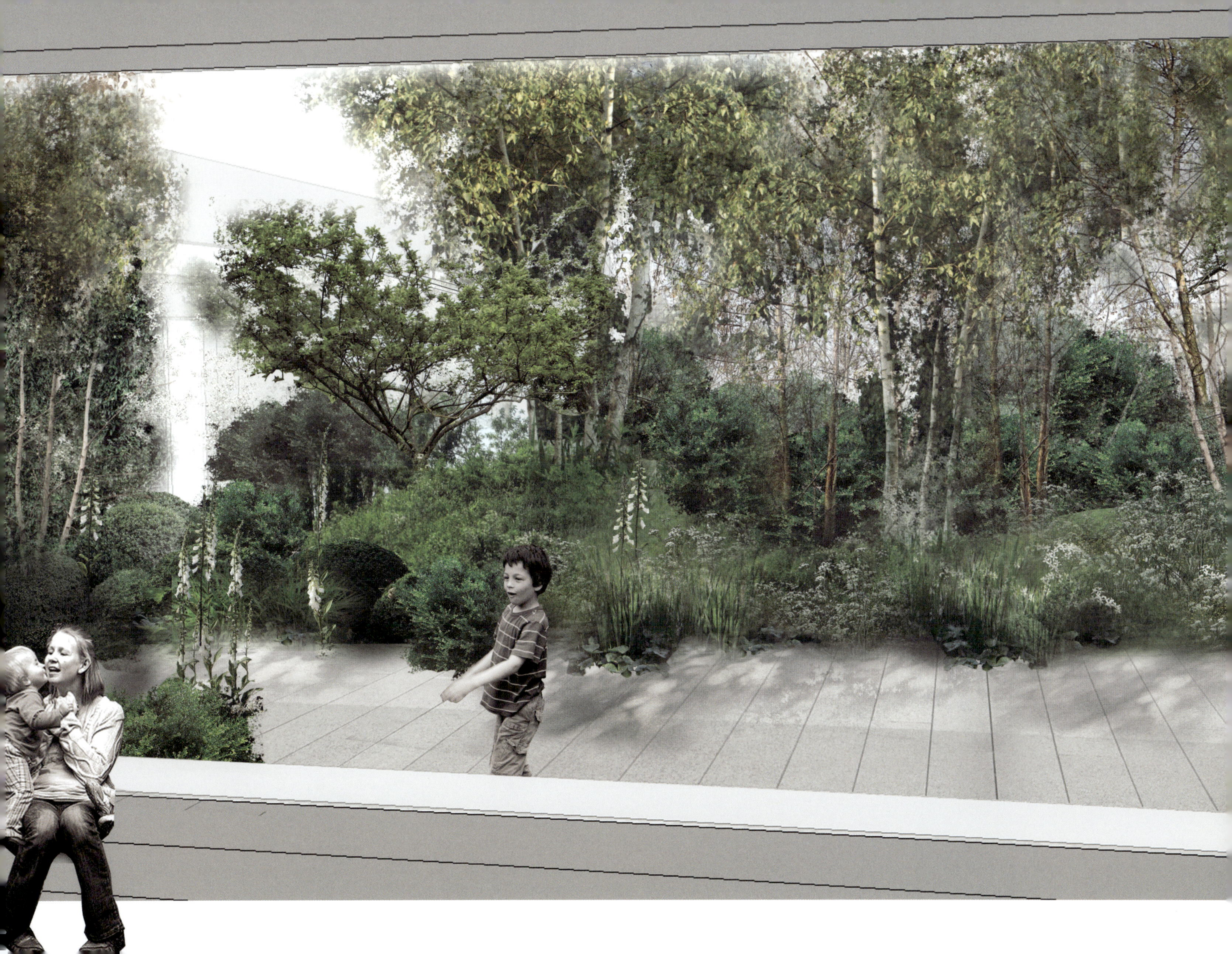

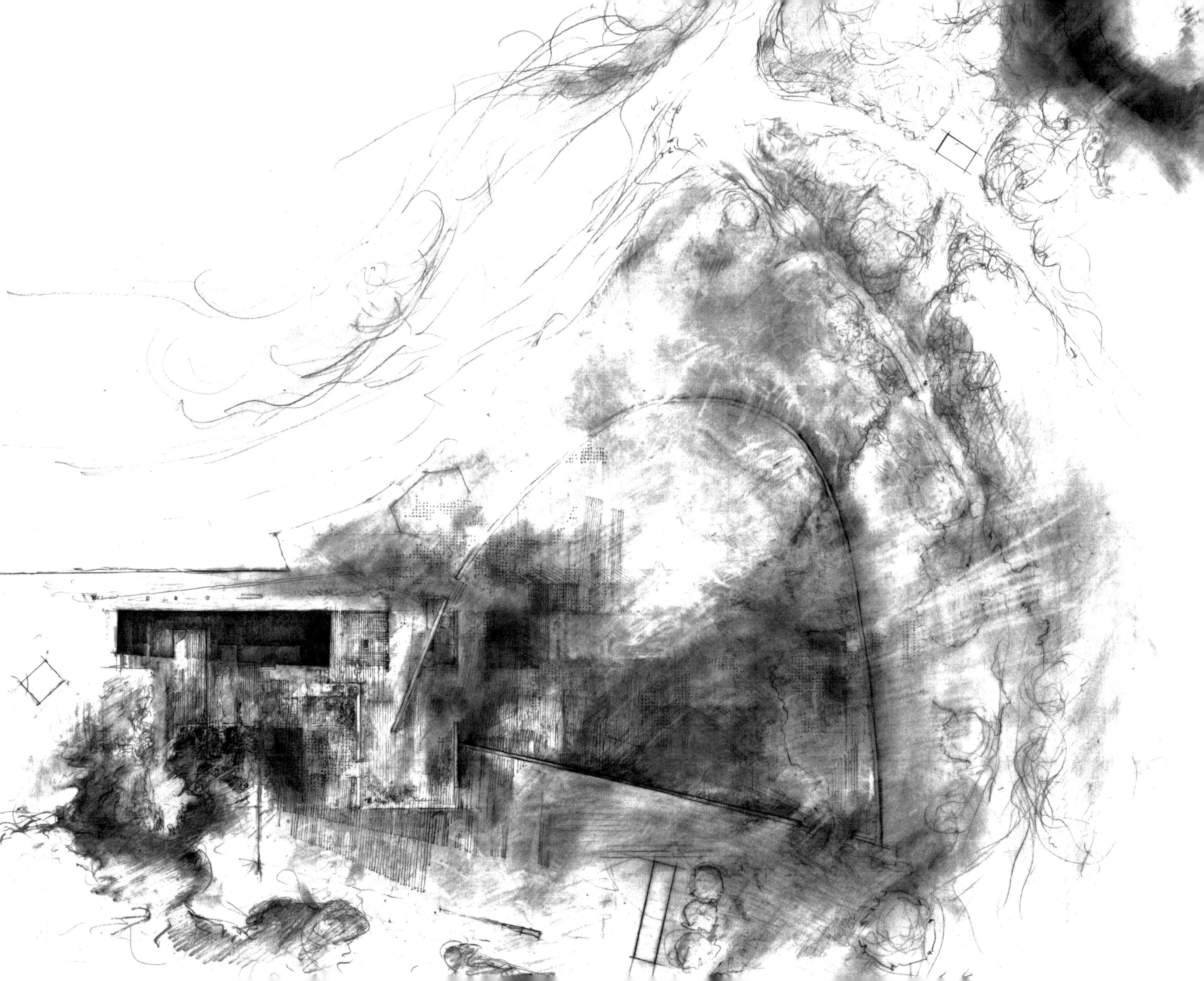

HADSPEN GARDEN,
PITCOMBE, SOMERSET, UK, 2009
In winter, water floods the low side of the pool and this walled garden is transformed. The drawings show the area as a series of flooded water rooms and the walled parabola as a meadow, with intensively gardened patches, planted 'overlays' and hard interventions kept to a minimum. Although dreamy in atmosphere, the drawings would have formed the basis of a detailed planting plan. The different qualities of the marks represent the different plant groupings: small dots, for example, represent key linking species that form seasonal overlays connecting the different areas. The overlay was formed of plants with near-leafless stems, so that sunlight could penetrate to the lowest levels. The designs were not implemented by the client.

Proap
Lisbon, Portugal

João Nunes of Proap makes no clear distinction between drawing as a form of artistic expression and drawing as an instrument of work – it has both analytical and aesthetic capabilities. He also understands hand-drawing as a complement to computer-aided design, though each has its particular strengths and weaknesses. Despite the precision and capability of the computer, he says that, ironically, drawing is a much faster way of getting an idea down on paper. He also feels it is a more effective communication tool, both with others and with oneself, as the designers seek to clarify an idea.

João Nunes writes: 'I have always enjoyed drawing. Every aspect of the act of drawing – the solitude and intimate companionship with oneself; the smell of the paper, graphite and ink; the noises, gestures and inevitable honesty of a medium that exposes one's own errors and flaws. Drawing allows me to isolate an aspect of thought that is particularly interesting at any given moment of the design investigation. I can reflect on light, texture, scale or on any formal aspect without having to represent everything else. Drawing can be considered an analytical instrument in the design process.

'What matters is the way in which a drawing allows us to create a dialogue with ourselves. The precision or "accuracy" of the drawing is not important; what matters is the ability to be precise about a specific theme. The precision required by technical drawing can be added later, and for that the computer is much more effective. Of course, it is possible to emulate hand-drawing using a computer, but the sense of freshness and speed will be lost.'

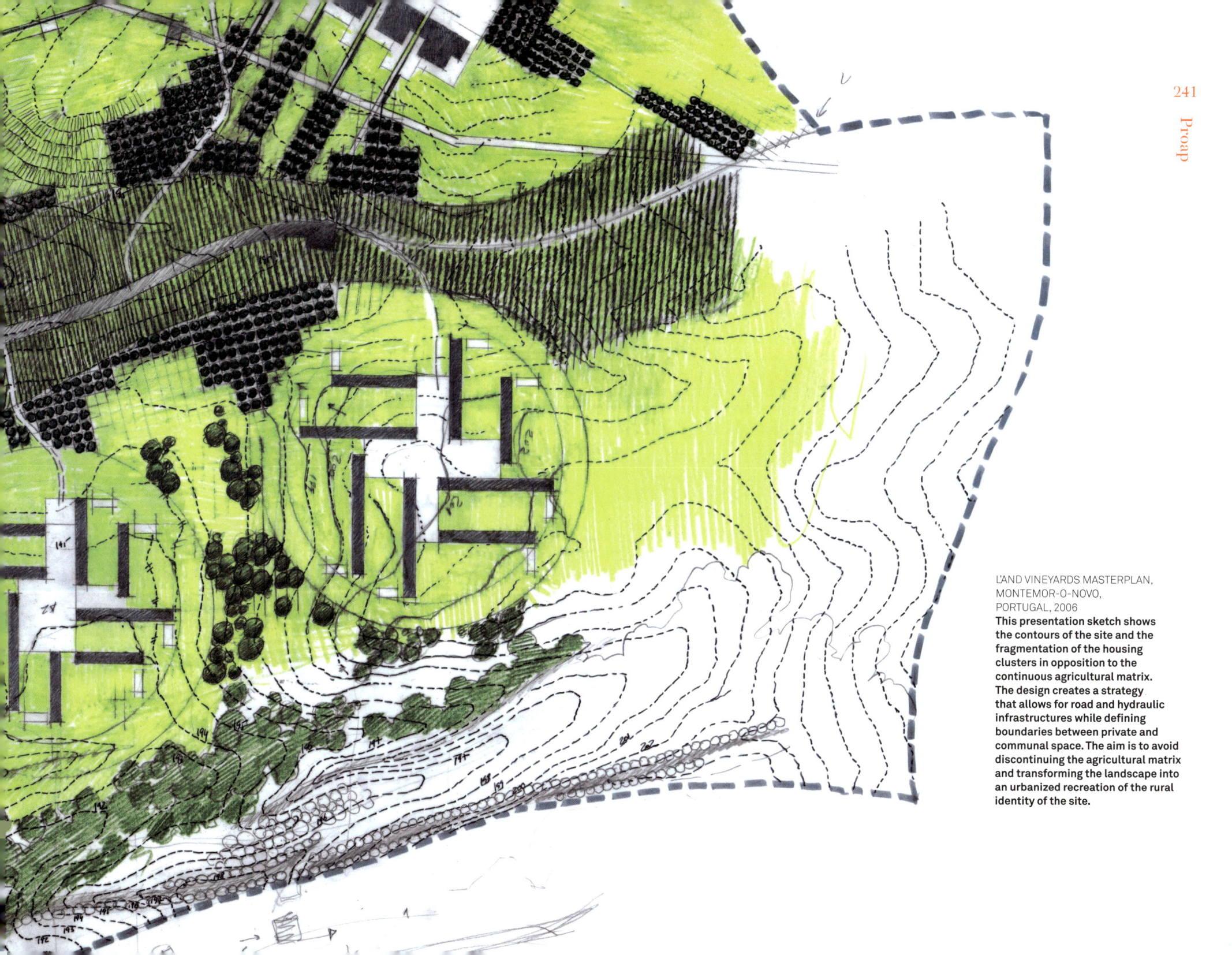

L'AND VINEYARDS MASTERPLAN,
MONTEMOR-O-NOVO,
PORTUGAL, 2006
This presentation sketch shows the contours of the site and the fragmentation of the housing clusters in opposition to the continuous agricultural matrix. The design creates a strategy that allows for road and hydraulic infrastructures while defining boundaries between private and communal space. The aim is to avoid discontinuing the agricultural matrix and transforming the landscape into an urbanized recreation of the rural identity of the site.

EL HIERRO,
CANARY ISLANDS, SPAIN, 2012
Presentation drawings, which express ideas for the creation of a new tourist industry on the island of El Hierro. A lack of sandy beaches (almost the entire island is surrounded by steep coastal cliffs) precludes large-scale beach tourism. The landscape emerges as the determinant for its unique touristic appeal within the context of the Canaries.

243

Proap

ACADEMIC PARK,
NINGBO, CHINA, 2013
Work-in-progress sketches and plan overviews, showing a proposed new system of water circulation designed to create a new dynamic of flows.

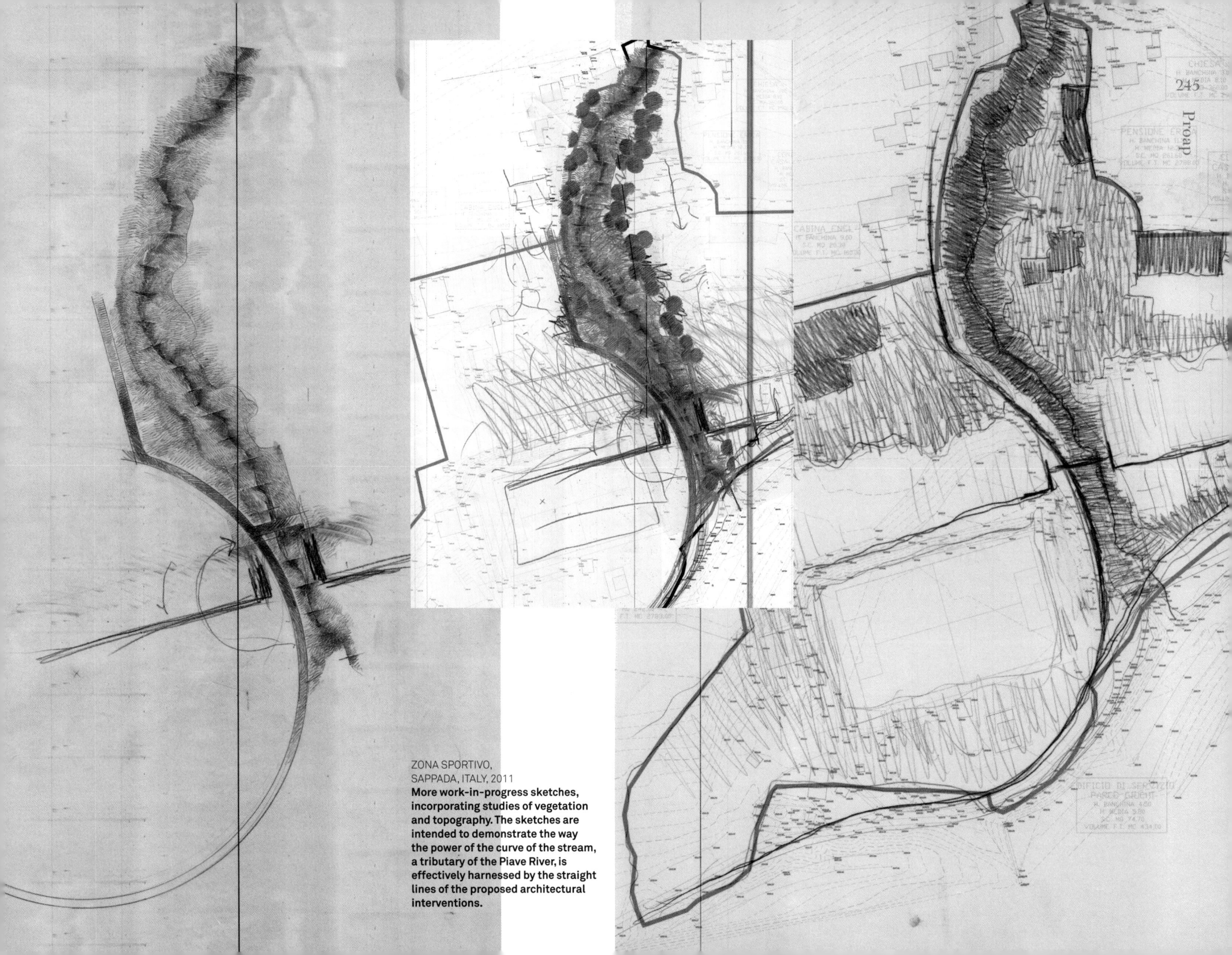

ZONA SPORTIVO,
SAPPADA, ITALY, 2011
More work-in-progress sketches, incorporating studies of vegetation and topography. The sketches are intended to demonstrate the way the power of the curve of the stream, a tributary of the Piave River, is effectively harnessed by the straight lines of the proposed architectural interventions.

246

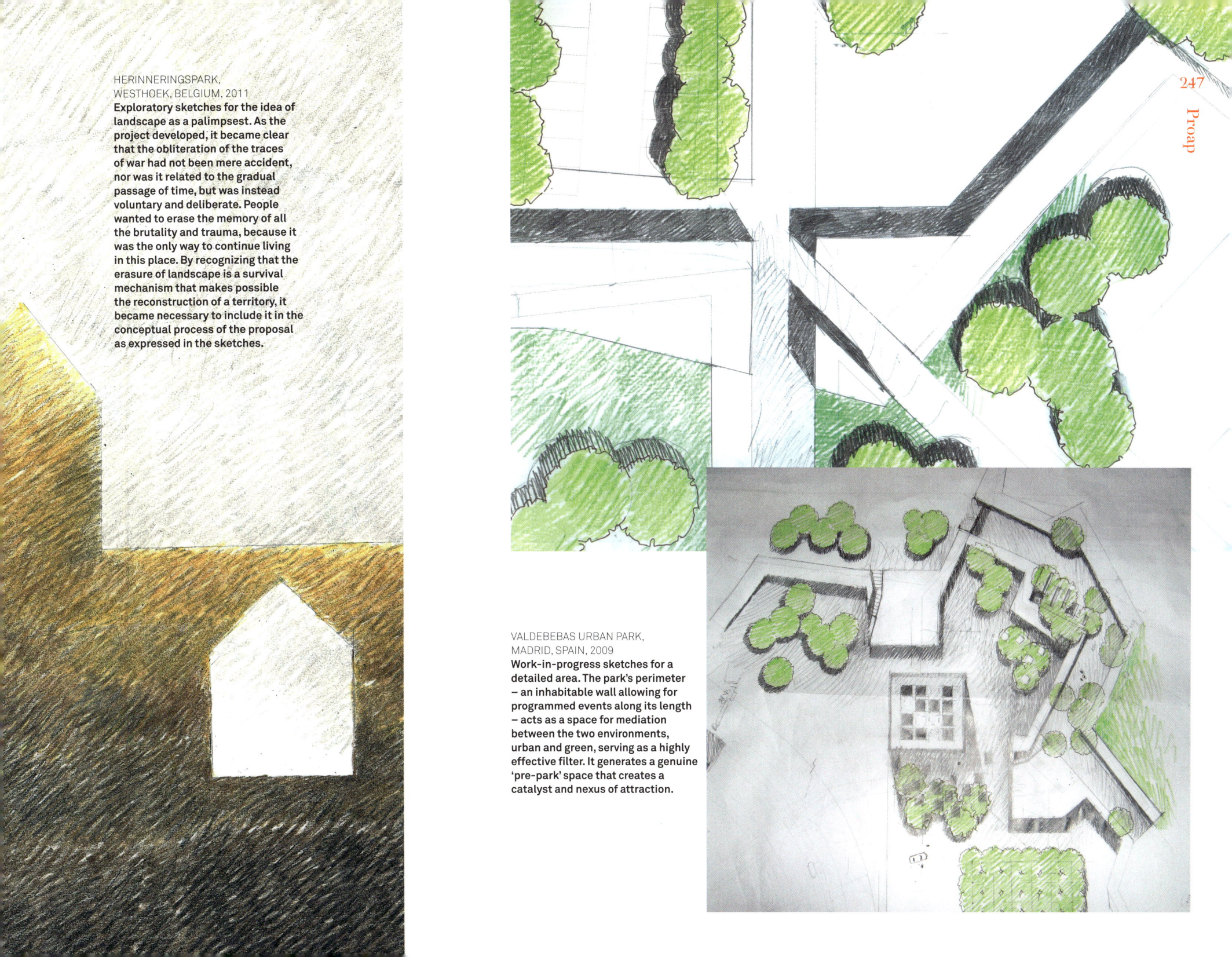

HERINNERINGSPARK, WESTHOEK, BELGIUM, 2011
Exploratory sketches for the idea of landscape as a palimpsest. As the project developed, it became clear that the obliteration of the traces of war had not been mere accident, nor was it related to the gradual passage of time, but was instead voluntary and deliberate. People wanted to erase the memory of all the brutality and trauma, because it was the only way to continue living in this place. By recognizing that the erasure of landscape is a survival mechanism that makes possible the reconstruction of a territory, it became necessary to include it in the conceptual process of the proposal as expressed in the sketches.

VALDEBEBAS URBAN PARK, MADRID, SPAIN, 2009
Work-in-progress sketches for a detailed area. The park's perimeter – an inhabitable wall allowing for programmed events along its length – acts as a space for mediation between the two environments, urban and green, serving as a highly effective filter. It generates a genuine 'pre-park' space that creates a catalyst and nexus of attraction.

Daniel Roehr
Vancouver, Canada

Daniel Roehr is Associate Professor in Landscape Architecture at the School of Architecture and Landscape Architecture, University of British Columbia, where the technique of on-site sketching and note-taking is taught on sketching tours to places of architectural and design interest, such as Iran, Italy or Germany. Analytical sketching, in particular, deploys the whole palette of drawing tools, from orthographic diagrams to perspectives. This practice helps to elevate hand-drawing from simple referential sketching of what exists at a site to an analysis and documentation of its conditions. For Roehr, hand-drawing is a visual tool that documents the thinking process of the brain, and is the basis of any design education.

Daniel Roehr writes: 'It is time for the reintroduction of a rigorous education in hand-drawing skills. Students should learn the processes of seeing, editing and documenting through drawing at the beginning of their design careers. Training the eye, brain and hand to draw will stimulate the development of creative designers. Hand-drawing is the language of design communication. It's a language that everyone understands; it is universal and internationally adaptable. The flood of images on the Internet, in publications and in movies can be overwhelming. Hand-drawing leaves the decision to the executor, who decides how much needs to be drawn in order to visualize and interpret the site and to develop a new design idea. It is this visual literary and editing process that needs to be learned.

'Hand-drawing on paper is the fastest method for developing an idea. The new flat computer screens, however, allow drawing on the screen with a stylus. The drawing movements are digitized in tight pixel lines, resulting in a hand-drawn image. This is a link with traditional hand-drawing teaching methods and reinforces the need to practice this skill.'

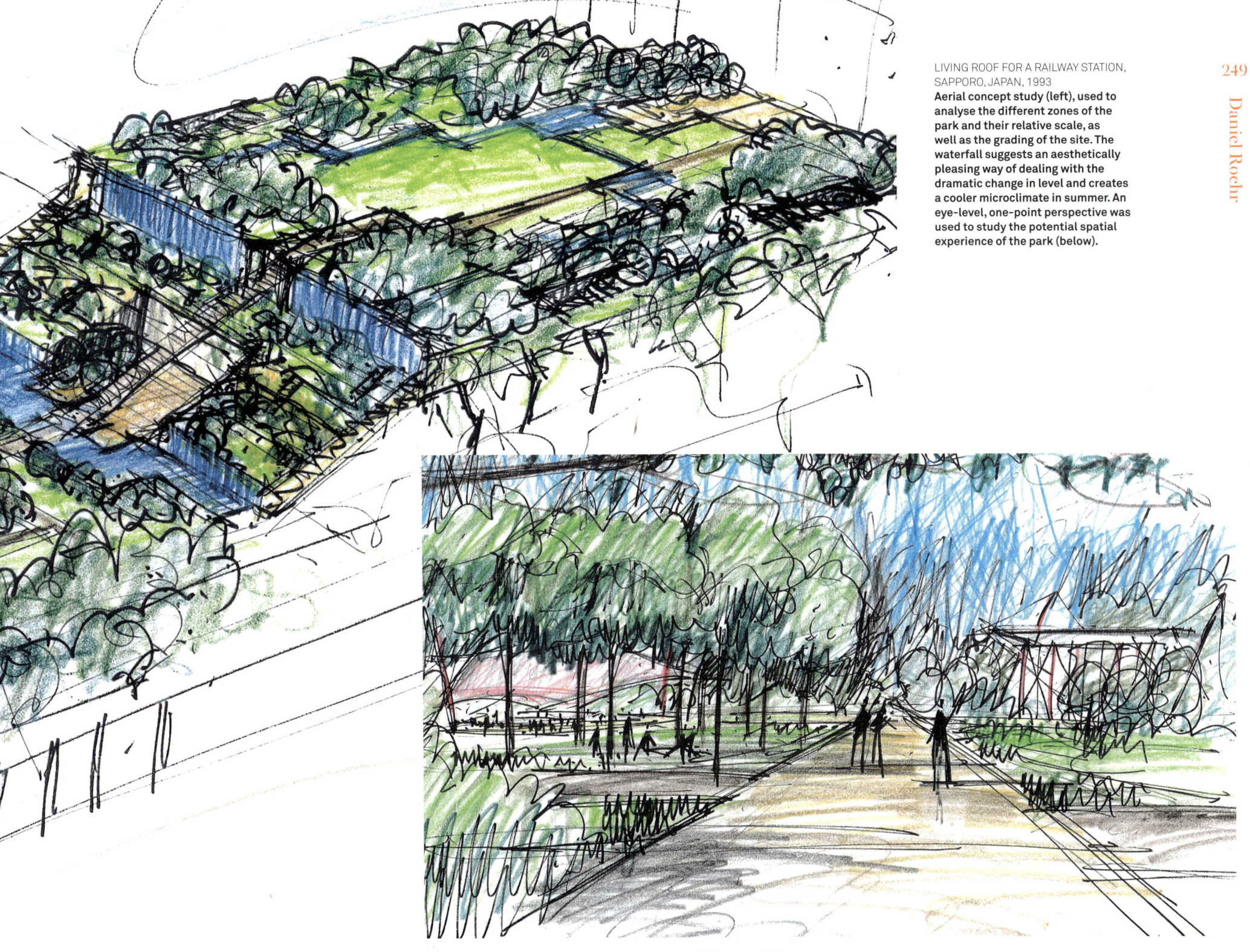

LIVING ROOF FOR A RAILWAY STATION, SAPPORO, JAPAN, 1993
Aerial concept study (left), used to analyse the different zones of the park and their relative scale, as well as the grading of the site. The waterfall suggests an aesthetically pleasing way of dealing with the dramatic change in level and creates a cooler microclimate in summer. An eye-level, one-point perspective was used to study the potential spatial experience of the park (below).

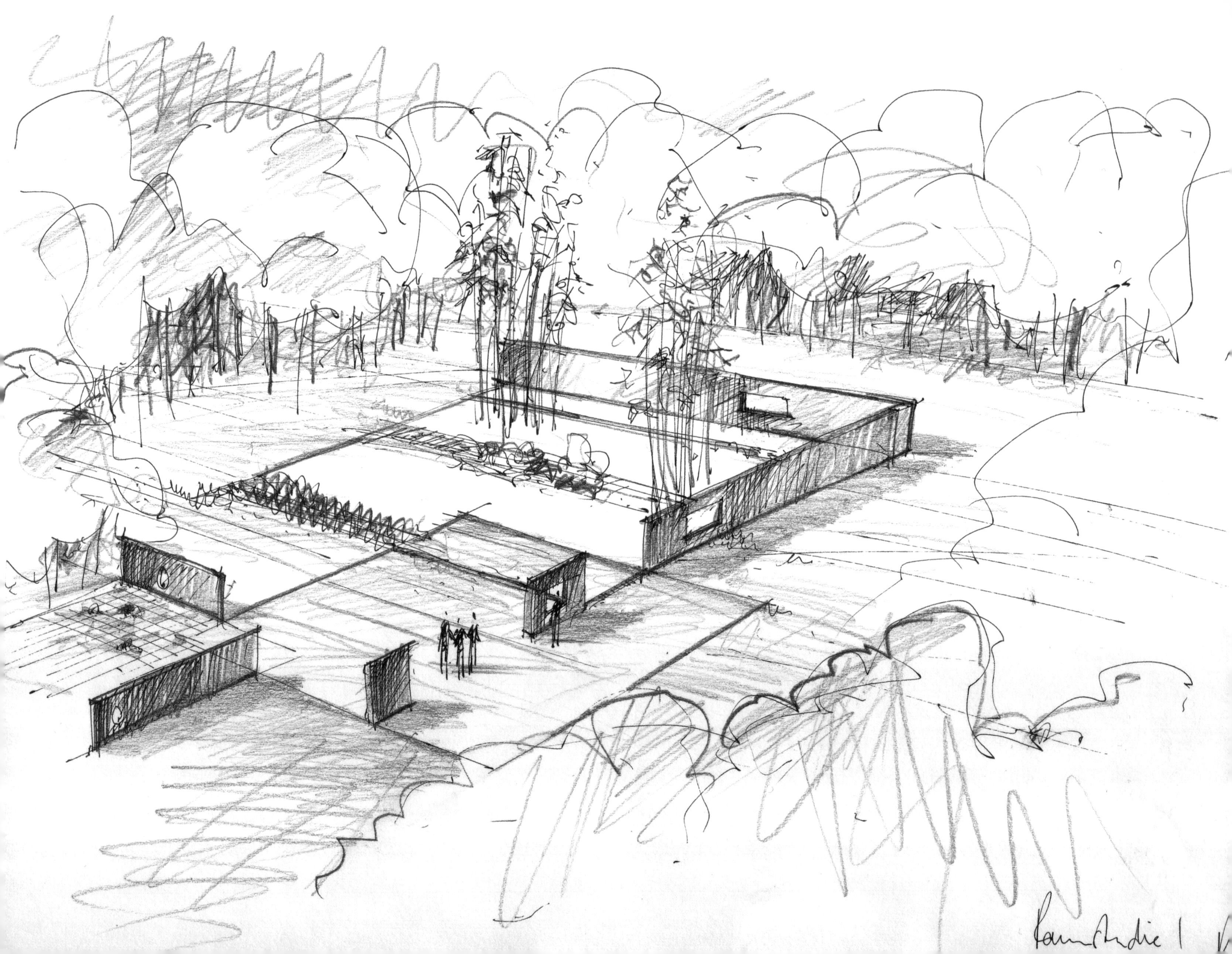

251

Daniel Roehr

VARIOUS SKETCHES,
2013–14
The top three drawings (left) are 'memory sketches', made on an iPad after visiting a site or seeing a work of art. Memory sketches can stimulate the mind, honing observation skills and adding the signature of reinterpretation to a subject. From top: the Californian coast; sketch inspired by a Lawren Harris exhibition at the Vancouver Art Gallery; Whistler, British Columbia. The bottom sketch was a planting idea for a competition for the National Holocaust Monument in Ottawa and was drawn on a plane.

PRIVATE GARDEN,
BAVARIA, GERMANY, 2003–4
Drawings made from multiple perspectives can be effective in showing the proposed landscape around a building. In one sketch (below right), the building's lines and proportions are used to develop a swimming pond, parallel with the house. It was made to persuade the client that the terrace and the pond might relate to the vertical and horizontal lines of the façade. Another sketch (above right) responds to the historic façade with a traditional herb-garden layout.

THEME GARDEN IN A PARK,
SUZHOU, CHINA, 2005
This spatial aerial study (opposite) was drawn in black and white first, with colour added later on a scanned copy to explore different colour themes in the plantings.

Daniel Roehr

Lunch 'Plaza' Concept
Shinjuku Tokyo

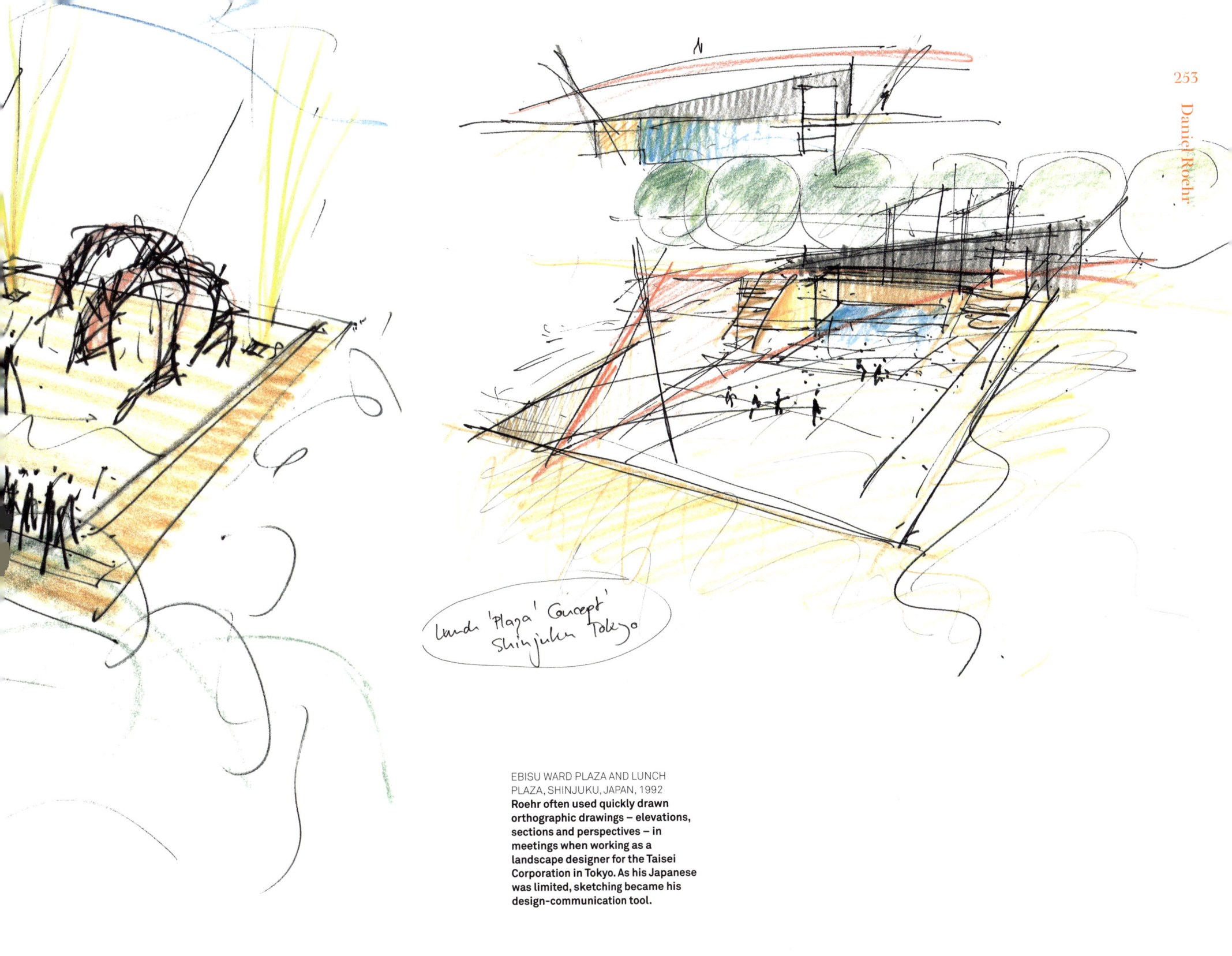

EBISU WARD PLAZA AND LUNCH
PLAZA, SHINJUKU, JAPAN, 1992
Roehr often used quickly drawn orthographic drawings – elevations, sections and perspectives – in meetings when working as a landscape designer for the Taisei Corporation in Tokyo. As his Japanese was limited, sketching became his design-communication tool.

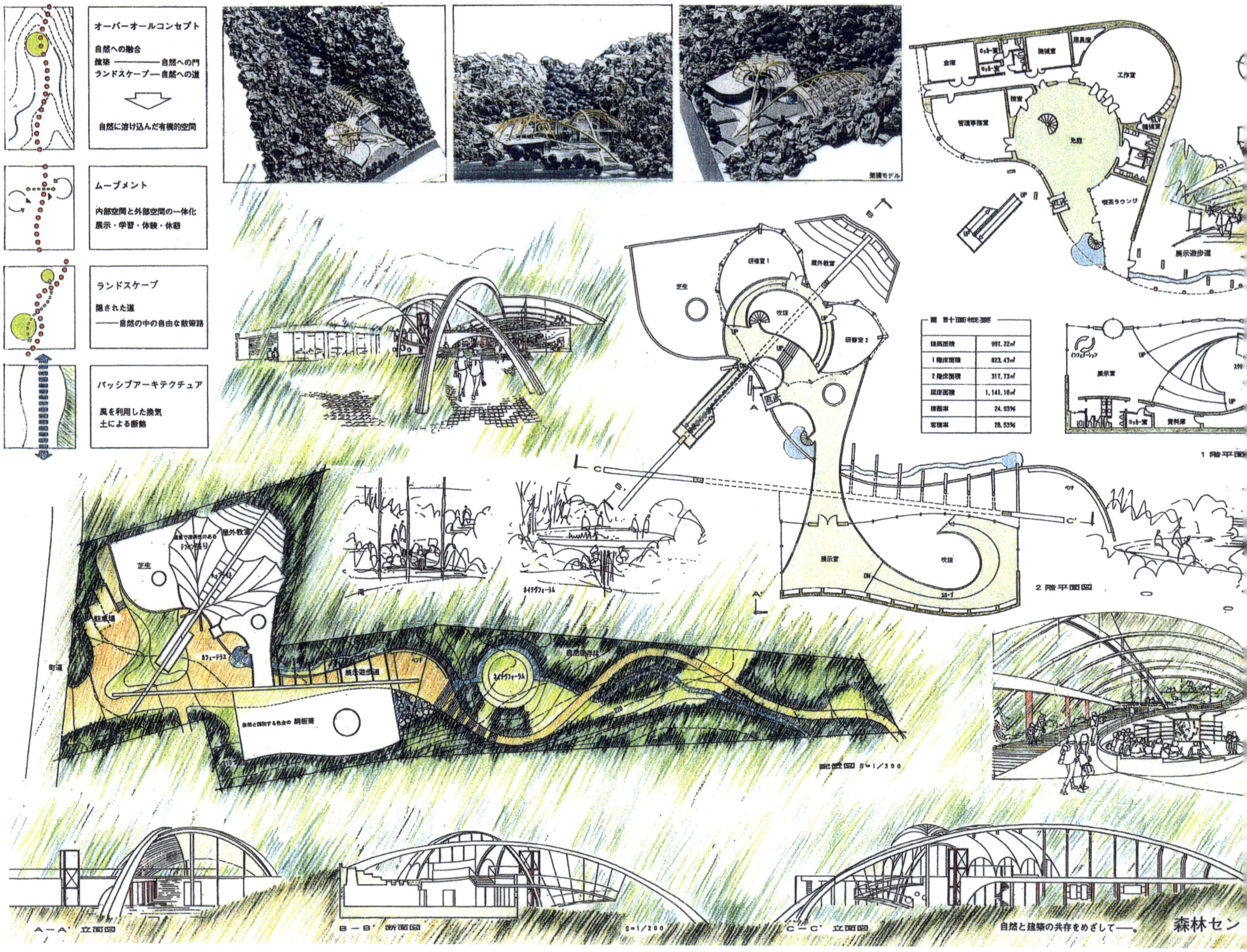
オーバーオールコンセプト
自然への融合
建築 ———— 自然への門
ランドスケープ— 自然への道
自然に溶け込んだ有機的空間
ムーブメント
内部空間と外部空間の一体化
展示・学習・体験・休憩
ランドスケープ
隠された道
——— 自然の中の自由な散策路
パッシブアーキテクチュア
風を利用した換気
土による断熱
架構モデル
計画概要
建築面積 997.22㎡
1階床面積 823.43㎡
2階床面積 317.73㎡
延床面積 1,141.16㎡
建蔽率 24.93%
容積率 28.53%
芝生
研修室1
屋外教室
吹抜
研修室2
展示室
2階平面図
配置図 S=1/300
駐車場
カフェテラス
展示遊歩道
自然研究林
町道
A—A' 立面図
B—B' 断面図
S=1/200
C—C' 立面図
自然と建築の共存をめざして——。
森林セン

FOREST CENTRE,
TOKYO, JAPAN, 1993
Freehand drawings combined with an abstract concept model on a presentation board illustrating ideas for a forest information centre outside Tokyo. Although this method of presentation was very different to that of Roehr's Japanese colleagues, his line drawings helped to provide a focus on specific parts of the design. They are also a useful editing tool for a designer.

HAIKU GARDEN, SCHLOSS IPPENBURG GARDEN FESTIVAL, GERMANY, 1999
Following a study of the principal structures of Japanese Haiku verse, these drawings were a first spatial impression of the concept and an attempt to visualize the rhythms spatially. The red of the garden boundary represents the temple *torii* gates. In the Shinto tradition, gates mark the transition from the profane to sacred; in this case, it was the garden space that was sacred. Colour can be used to highlight a particular design element or enhance the drawing spatially.

PARISER KOMMUNE, BERLIN, GERMANY, 1993
This design for a plaza along Karl-Marx-Allee (right) was made while Roehr was working in the office of Stephan Haan. An off-centre, one-point perspective focused on the pergola structure that framed the play area. Such drawings are a useful way of exploring the ways different materials can be combined to achieve a consistent and balanced space, while also immersing the viewer in a site.

257

Daniel Roehr

SLA

Copenhagen, Denmark

The work of SLA is centred on the aesthetic power of nature, but not just in terms of visual imagery. Their aesthetic concept also embraces the full sensory repertoire – all of our senses and feelings. As such, nature is the focal point of everything the studio develops, draws and thinks. The aim is to make each sketch a hands-on exploration of the aesthetic power of nature.

SLA state: 'Our approach rests on the fundamental realization that nature's "grown environment" and the built environment are complementary. The two are fundamentally incompatible, but together they form a holistic architecture. Nature is what is living and growing, and constitutes the very foundation of life. For us, architecture, masterplanning, urban spaces and landscape must learn from nature's processes. Nature constantly develops, grows and changes from one state into another. As such, a city is never finished (or rather, a finished city is a dead city).

'How do you sketch and illustrate your work under these circumstances? When you know that there are no finished images to show, only changing states? Or when you are convinced that it is not how a project looks that is important, but how it feels? Our solution is to use sketches as an exploration of the sensuous – how you might perceive the different materials and spatialities of a site; how you might absorb them; what you will associate with them; what they make you remember; how they make you feel. Our sketch work more often than not includes many different forms and materials, from pencil drawings, watercolours and site-specific collages to material studies, clay figures, biotic material collections, and so on.

'The aim is to make each sketch a hands-on exploration of the aesthetic power of nature, and to engage the viewer in a dialogue about the true meaning of a given project.'

YELLOW MUD GARDEN,
XI'AN, CHINA, 2010

The first sketches for a garden at a horticultural expo in China. The project took initial inspiration from drawings made by Stig L. Andersson, founder and creative director of SLA, with his daughter Xenia. The sketches convey the atmosphere and the aesthetic feel of the garden, which later informed more finished plan drawings.

YELLOW MUD GARDEN, XI'AN, CHINA, 2010
The sketches were made in many different forms and materials, from drawings using the convention of the vertical format common to Chinese art (opposite, left) to abstract sculptural studies in red clay (opposite, right), which allude both to Chinese garden rocks and to the reddish soil commonly found in Xi'an. The clay figures were later reproduced in large-scale form in the garden.

261

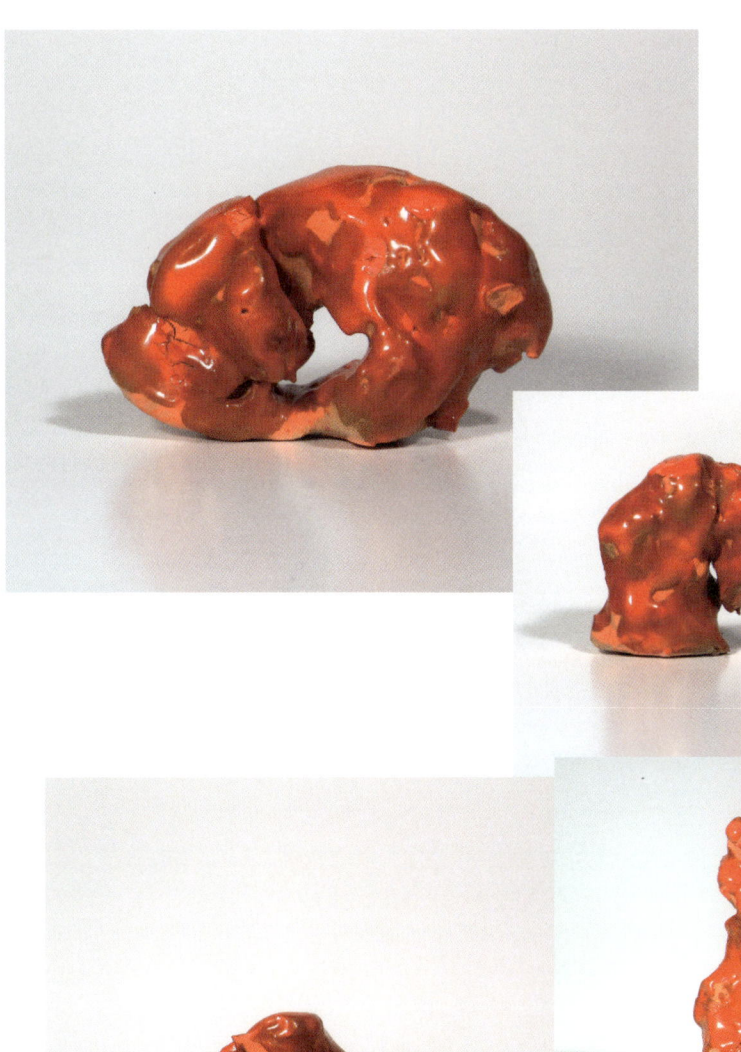

262
SLA

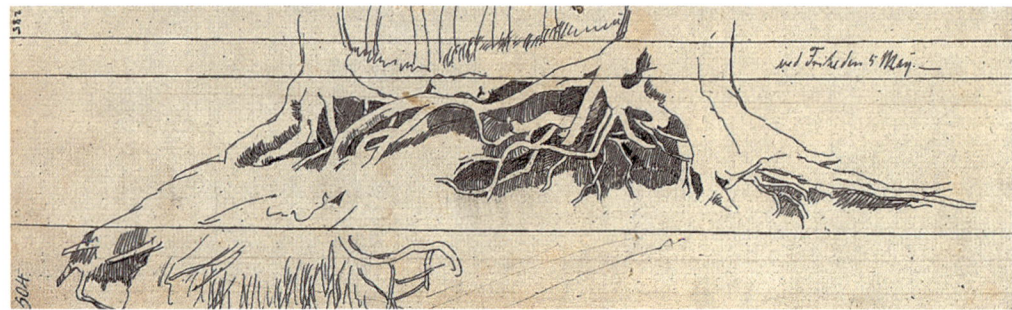

DANISH PAVILION,
VENICE ARCHITECTURE
BIENNALE, 2014
Conceptual work for the Danish Pavilion included multiple sketches and material experimentation with the aim of achieving a correlation between the exhibition's theoretical and aesthetic elements. Working with the full range of human sensibility, the sketches are not concerned chiefly with how the exhibition would look, but with how it would feel.

Ken Smith

New York, USA

An 'ideas man', Ken Smith acts quickly when the mood takes him, jotting down ideas on anything to hand so they will not be forgotten. Anyone in the creative professions knows that telling yourself that 'this time' you will remember a particular thought never happens. Ideas sketched out in this way can take on totemic importance as the 'soul' of a piece – perhaps why this designer has saved and archived these sketches, while at the same time professing their lack of importance.

Ken Smith writes: 'Quite frankly, I don't sketch a lot. My affinity is much more with montage, so I do most of my drawing on the computer, using Photoshop. I'm quite good at drawing with a mouse. As a student, I never developed the discipline to rigorously carry a sketchpad around with me at all times, so I never seemed to have a proper drawing medium when I needed it.

'When I want to draw or sketch, I typically use whatever paper is available, whether it is the margin of a newspaper or a paper placemat or napkin. When I travel, I stick those complementary hotel notepads in my pocket and use them as my sketchbooks. I always carry a black Paper Mate Flair pen. I like the line weight a lot – not too fat, not too thin. They are cheap and disposable, so I don't worry about losing them. The hotel notepads, of course, are free, and have the added benefit of being monogrammed to remind me later of where and when I made a sketch.

'I wouldn't really describe what I do as drawing or sketching. It's more a matter of notation. Mostly, I do diagrams (really, more like cartoons) that help me sort through the design ideas that I'm thinking about. These are sufficient to remind me later of the idea, which I will develop into something more thought out or perhaps abandon in hindsight as not worthy.'

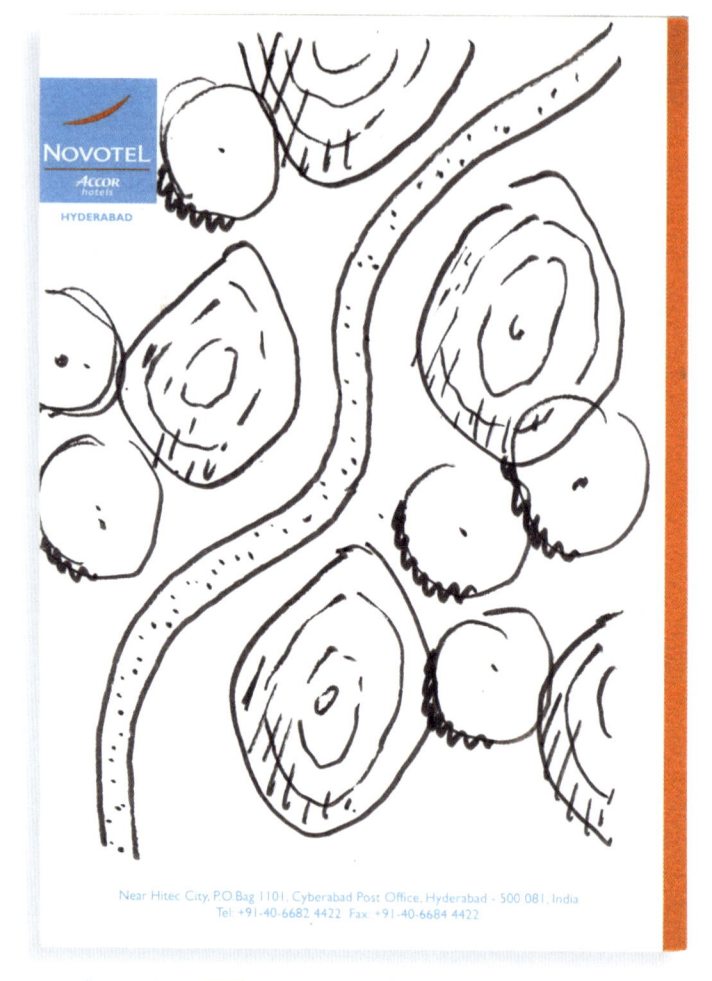

VARIOUS SKETCHES

Smith notes: 'Often I will diagram a landscape concept, like the serpentine path and series of berms and trees I was thinking about in Hyderabad, India (left), or a more formal quincunx of trees with an intersecting diagonal path on an Amsterdam Best Western Hotel notepad (opposite, left). In Denver, Colorado, I was working on an idea for a floating boardwalk edge (below), and in Washington, DC, on a GSA pad (opposite, below right), I was working on a glacial boulder escarpment for a corporate campus. While I was in New Orleans, I have no idea why I drew what looks like some kind of weird TV table (opposite, above right).'

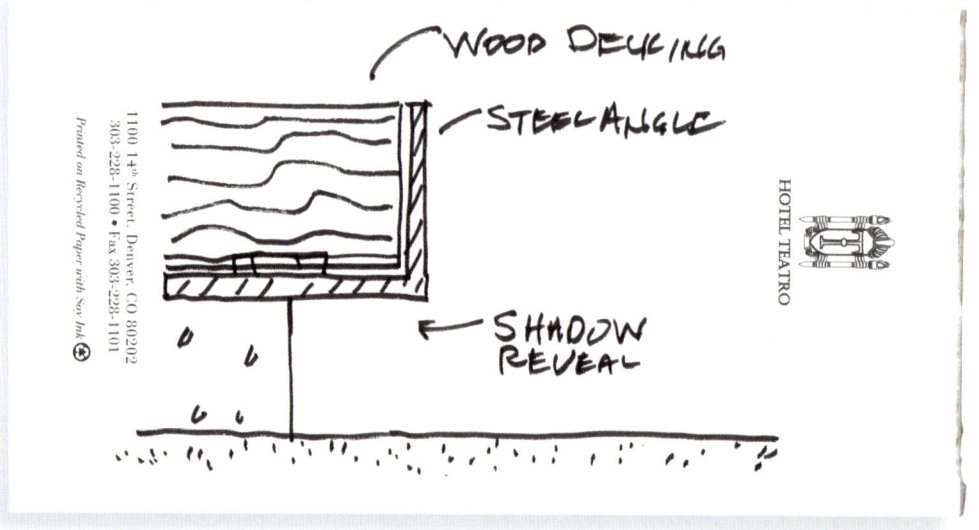

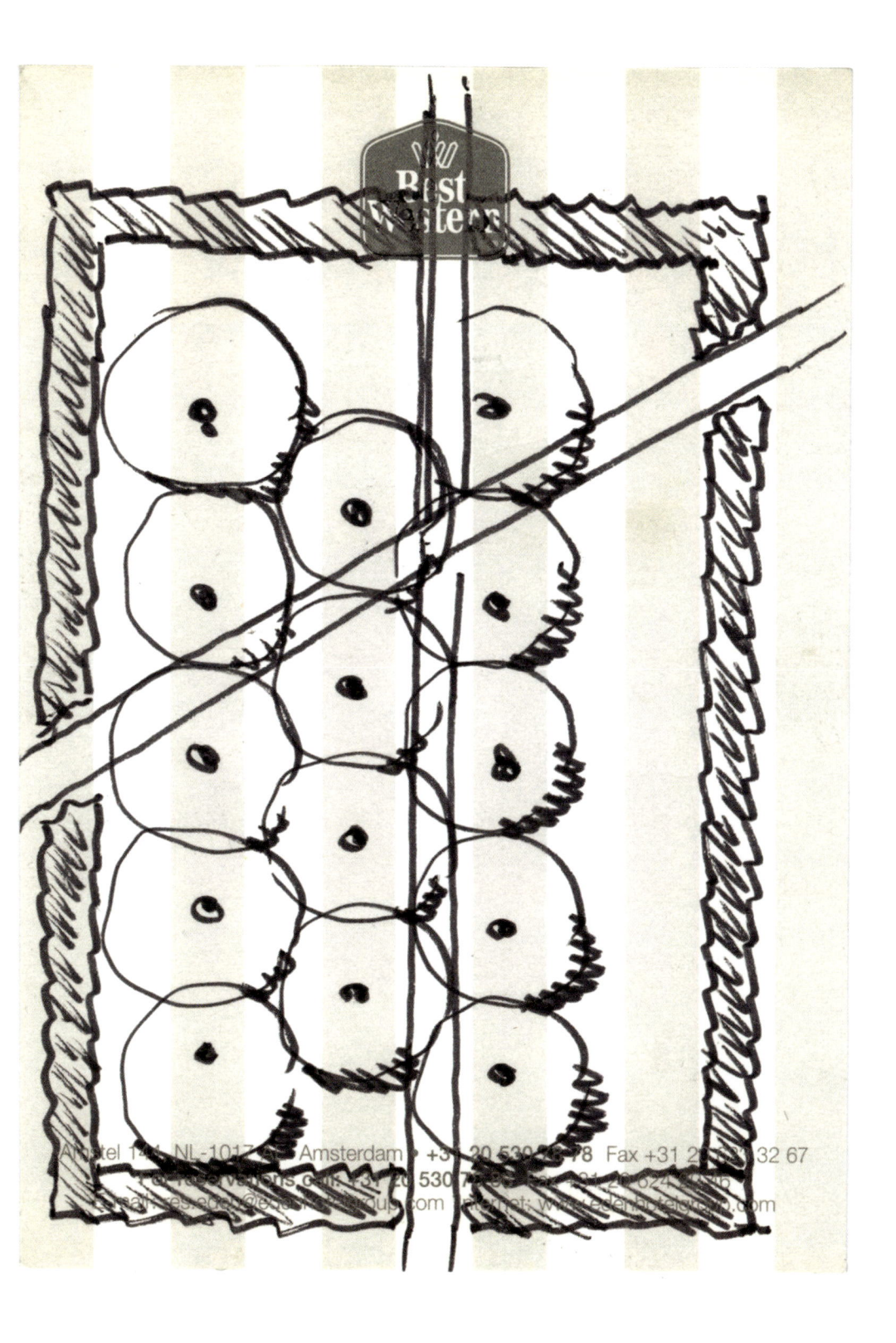

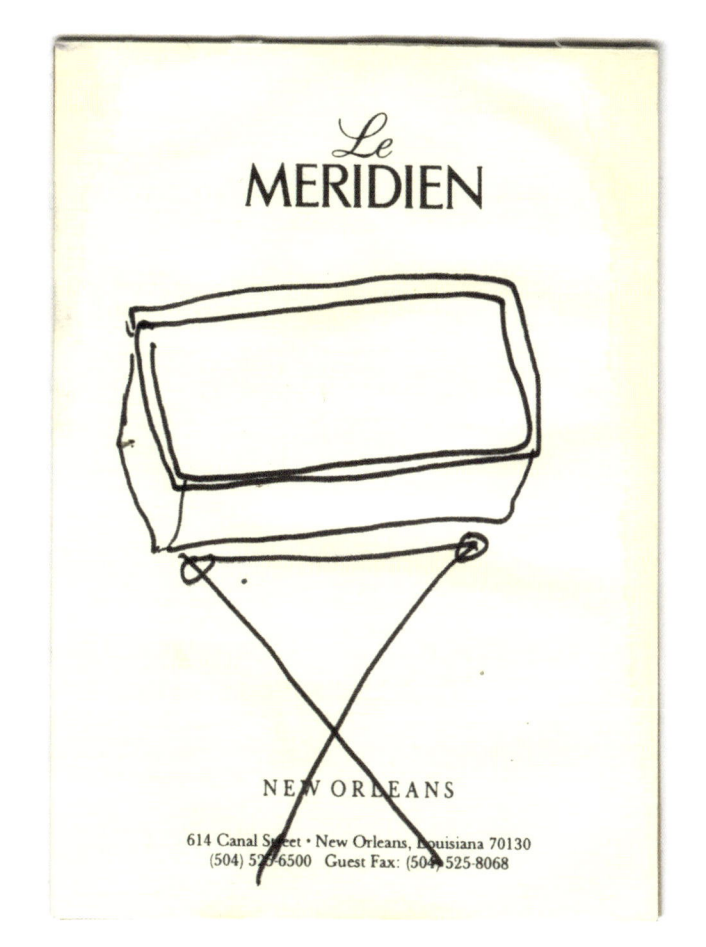

ESCARPMENT

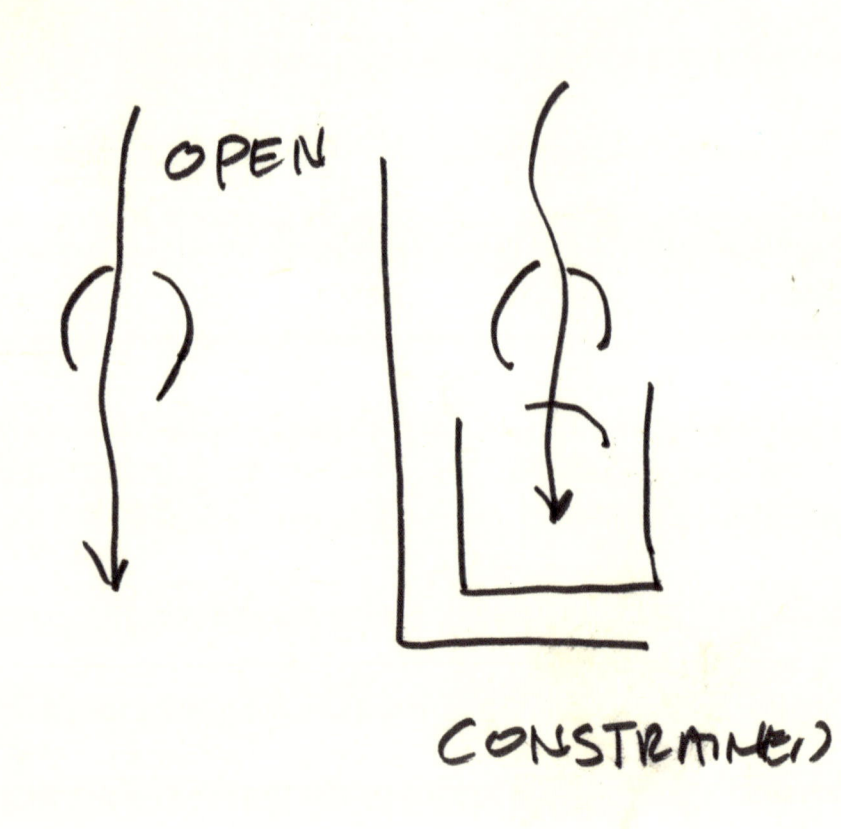

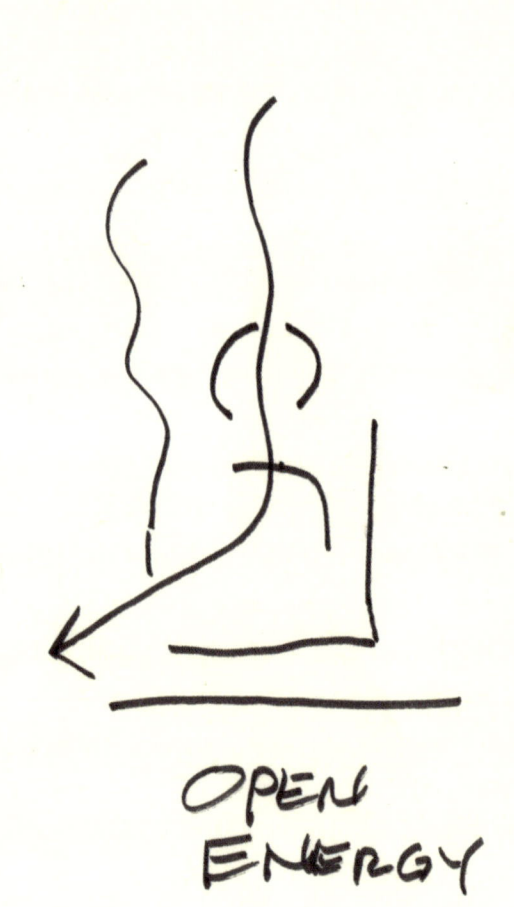

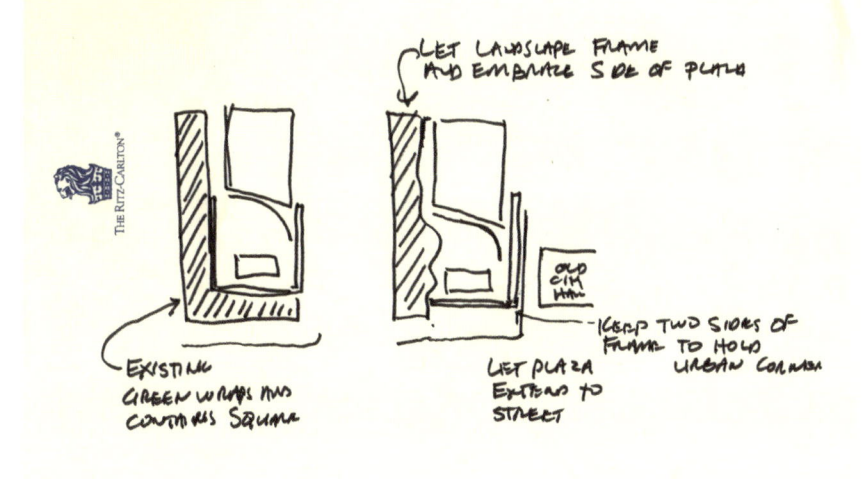

CITY HALL PLAZA,
TORONTO, CANADA
This series of diagrams was for a design competition for a City Hall plaza. One set of diagrams explores the open nature of the building and the containment of the square by an existing overhead walkway, and the notion of breaking the frame to open up the energy to the street. The other diagrams work through ideas about urban connections between the square and the context around it.

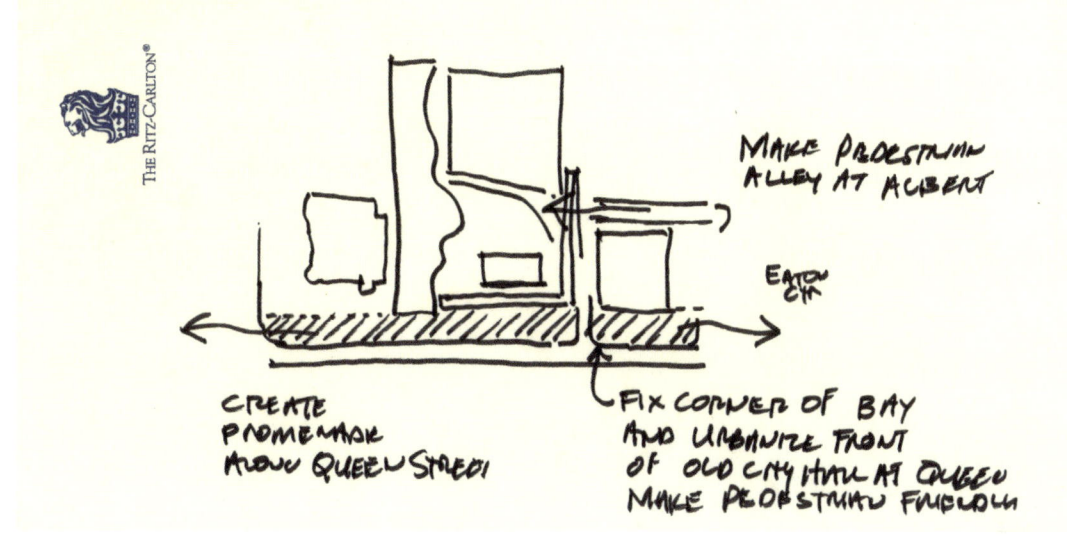

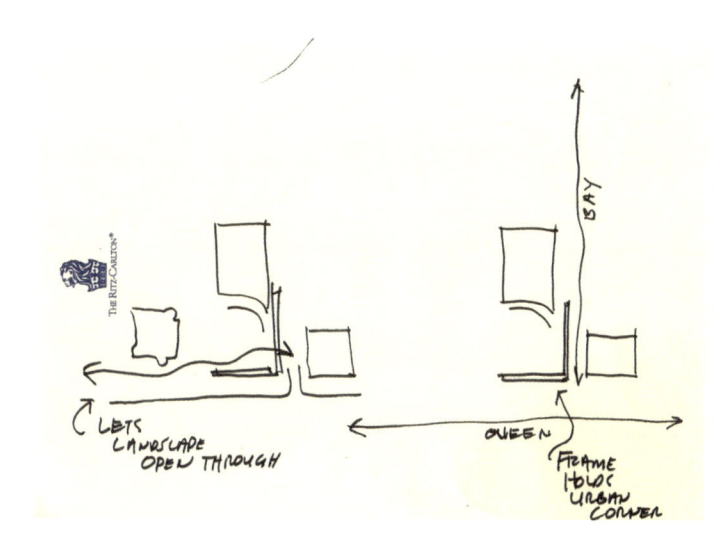

Tom Stuart-Smith

London, UK

Trained as a landscape architect, Tom Stuart-Smith is as engaged with planting as he is with space – in the English way. But it is the spatial aspect that is most clearly informed by the finely wrought drawings he produces for clients, which are often treasured by them in the future. For Stuart-Smith, drawing is part of the process of discovery of a place.

Tom Stuart-Smith writes: 'One of my first visits as an enthusiastic teenage gardener was to that shrine of Englishness: Sissinghust. Above all, it was the experience of climbing the tower that I remember. From here, everything was made clear. After being lost in the garden for hours, it was a revelation to be able to see where I had been and understand how it all interconnected. You become like an analyst of the garden, seeing how its personality is congested and intimate here, more stately and processional there. How it relates to the outside world with a guarded openness in one place; how it is dominated by order in this part and then by randomness and apparent abandon in another. Then you descend the tower and lose yourself in the complexities of the garden again.

'Drawing is for me part of the process of creating a narrative of place. It's a meditative process, but also one of commitment. I now almost always work in pencil as I feel that colour can be a distraction. The proposal seems to have a more provisional quality when sketched in pencil and, as far as my technique is concerned, says more about the structure than the content. The ability to blur some details is also a help in that it leaves a few things to the imagination – to be developed later. Over the past two years we have had regular drawing classes in the studio. Now about half of the designers in the office regularly do hand-drawings for projects. We never present computer images to clients unless they want to see different options later on in the design process.'

PRIVATE GARDEN,
LONDON, UK, 2008
Pencil drawing for a back garden, comprising an in-situ concrete terrace and a walk to the children's sandpit at the far end. The garden is planted with just four different plants, the most noticeable being the tree ferns: *Dicksonia antarctica*. This is the view from the first-floor sitting room, much as it looks today.

LAURENT-PERRIER GARDEN,
CHELSEA FLOWER SHOW,
LONDON, UK, 2008
The main drawing (right) was intended to evoke the slightly surreal, dream-like quality of the space. It is very specific as to plants, however – with *Rodgersia podophylla*, cloud-pruned hornbeam and small hostas shown in some detail. Only one person suggested the obvious: that the zinc tanks could be seen as coffins. The garden was in part inspired, in an entirely abstract way, by the third movement of Schumann's *Fantasie* (Op. 17).

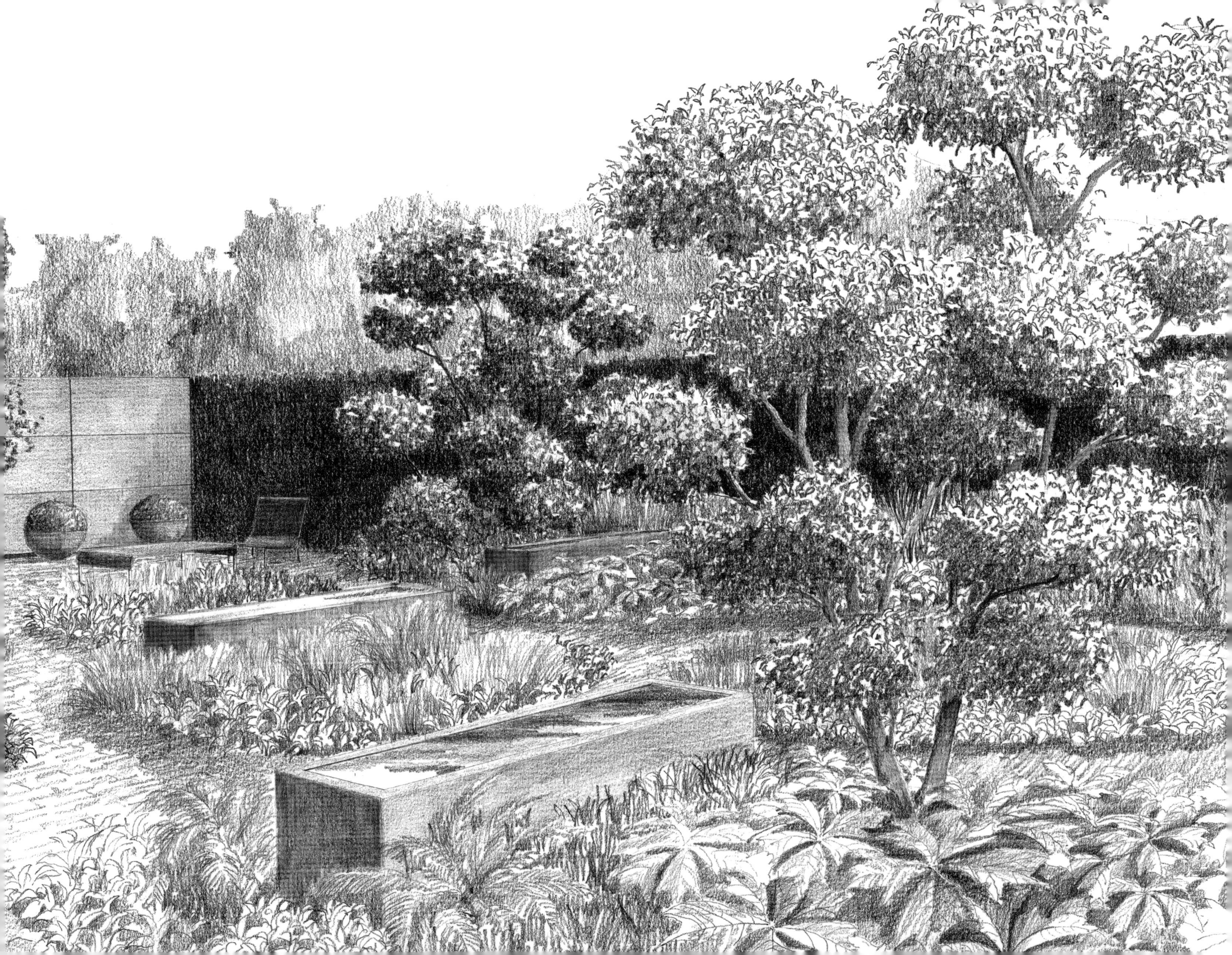

PROPOSAL FOR A GARDEN, IRELAND, 2011
A vignette of a proposed corner of a garden on the west coast of Ireland, a project with Haworth Tompkins Architects. For a more complex garden project, Stuart-Smith and his team will sometimes make many small sketches like this.

KEEPER'S HOUSE GARDEN, ROYAL ACADEMY OF ARTS, LONDON, UK, 2013
This garden, really a small terrace for a café, gets no direct sunlight, so tree ferns were ideal. It continues on the roof of a substation, which is also used as a temporary plinth for sculptures by academicians. The viewpoint is not one that can be seen, as it would be from the middle of an adjacent building, but it does demonstrate the spatial quality and potential atmosphere. Ultimately, the garden was built almost exactly as it appears in the competition drawing.

PROPOSAL FOR A GARDEN,
LONDON, UK, 2010
This proposal is actually formed of
two drawings Photoshopped together.
The first drawing originally ended
where the page gutter is, and the
second, to the left of it, was added to
show that there was another, more
natural dimension to the garden.
The planting includes cloud-pruned
hornbeam, beech hedging and clumps
of low-growing pittosporum.

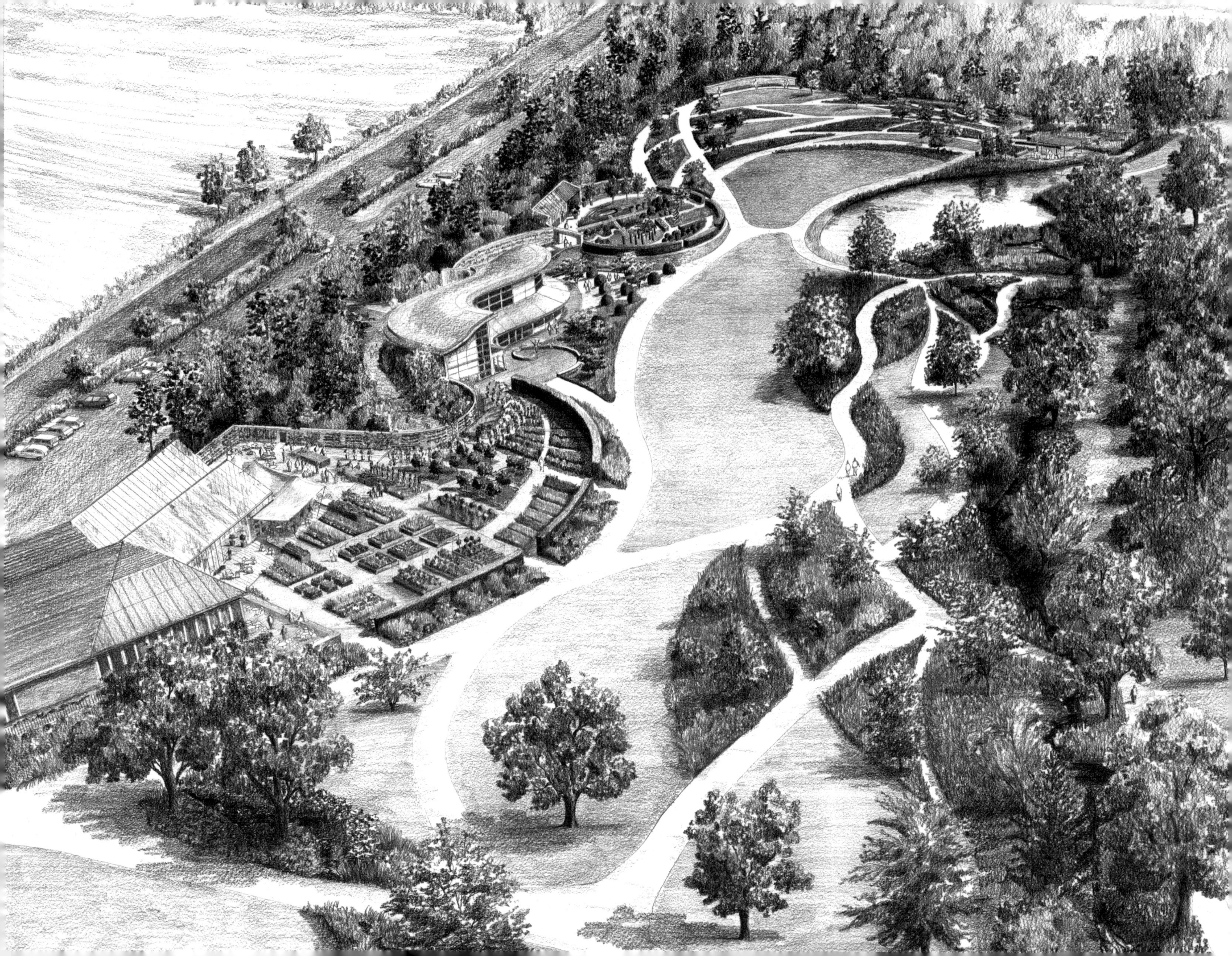

RHS GARDEN, HARLOW CARR,
YORKSHIRE, UK, 2008
The aerial view (left) of the masterplan shows how the proposal's interlocking curves pervade the whole design in a way that a ground-level view could not. While not every aspect of the proposal will be followed, the drawing acts as a statement of intent against which later initiatives can be assessed. As the site had grown in a piecemeal manner, the plan attempts to impose an overall design language, and to incorporate a wide variety of different uses and spaces.

BROUGHTON GRANGE,
OXFORDSHIRE, UK, 2001
Partly inspired by Italian models such as the Casino garden at Caprarola, in the Lazio region, this preliminary drawing (above) shows almost exactly how the garden was eventually built.

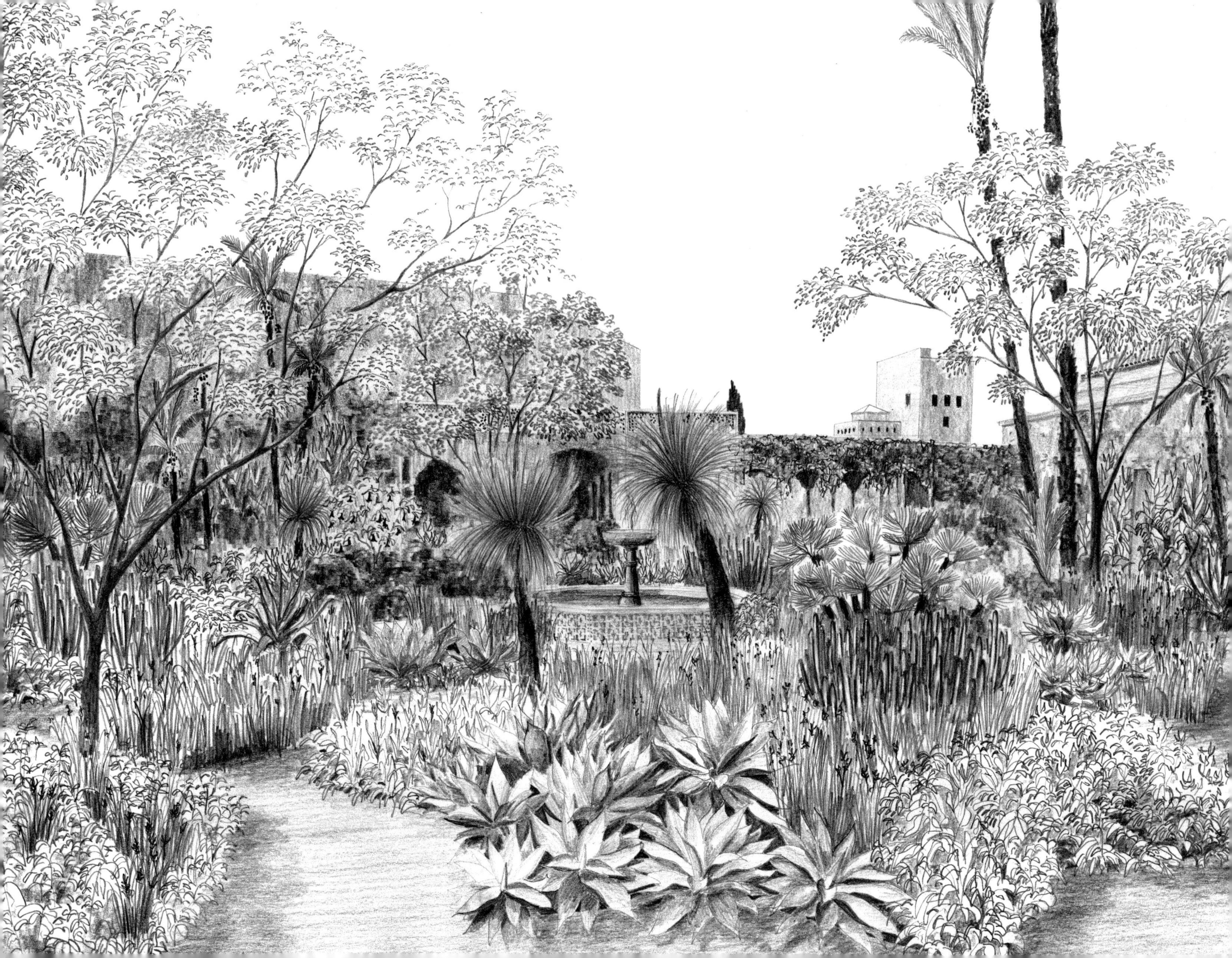

LE JARDIN SECRET,
MARRAKESH, MOROCCO, 2016

The drawing (left) is of a 'secret garden' in the middle of the medina. It is a detail of the scheme shown in the drawing below, which includes a larger garden planted in traditional Moroccan style beneath the tower. The original site was sold off at the end of the nineteenth century and disappeared under a development of more than one hundred separate dwellings. A wide range of plants from all over the world was used to recreate a garden on this site, though archaeological finds have meant that the layout has been modified.

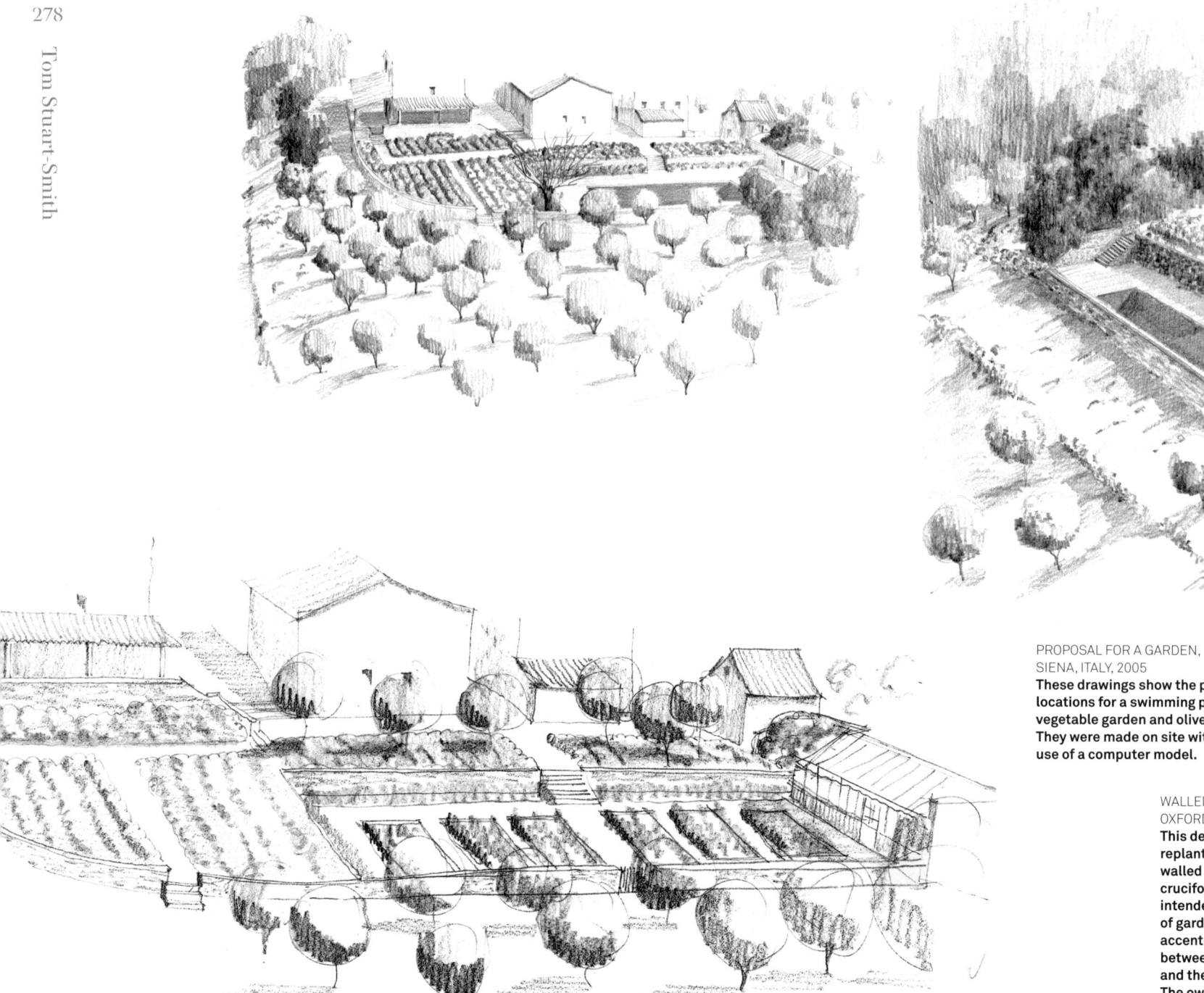

PROPOSAL FOR A GARDEN,
SIENA, ITALY, 2005
These drawings show the proposed locations for a swimming pool, vegetable garden and olive groves. They were made on site without the use of a computer model.

WALLED GARDEN, WOODPERRY,
OXFORDSHIRE, UK, 2002
This design (opposite) shows the replanting of an eighteenth-century walled garden on a traditional cruciform plan. The drawing is intended to show how the removal of garden planting beyond the wall accentuates the drama of difference between the ornamented enclosure and the wilder landscape beyond. The owner is partial to careering around the countryside on a quad bike, which explains the figure in the foreground.

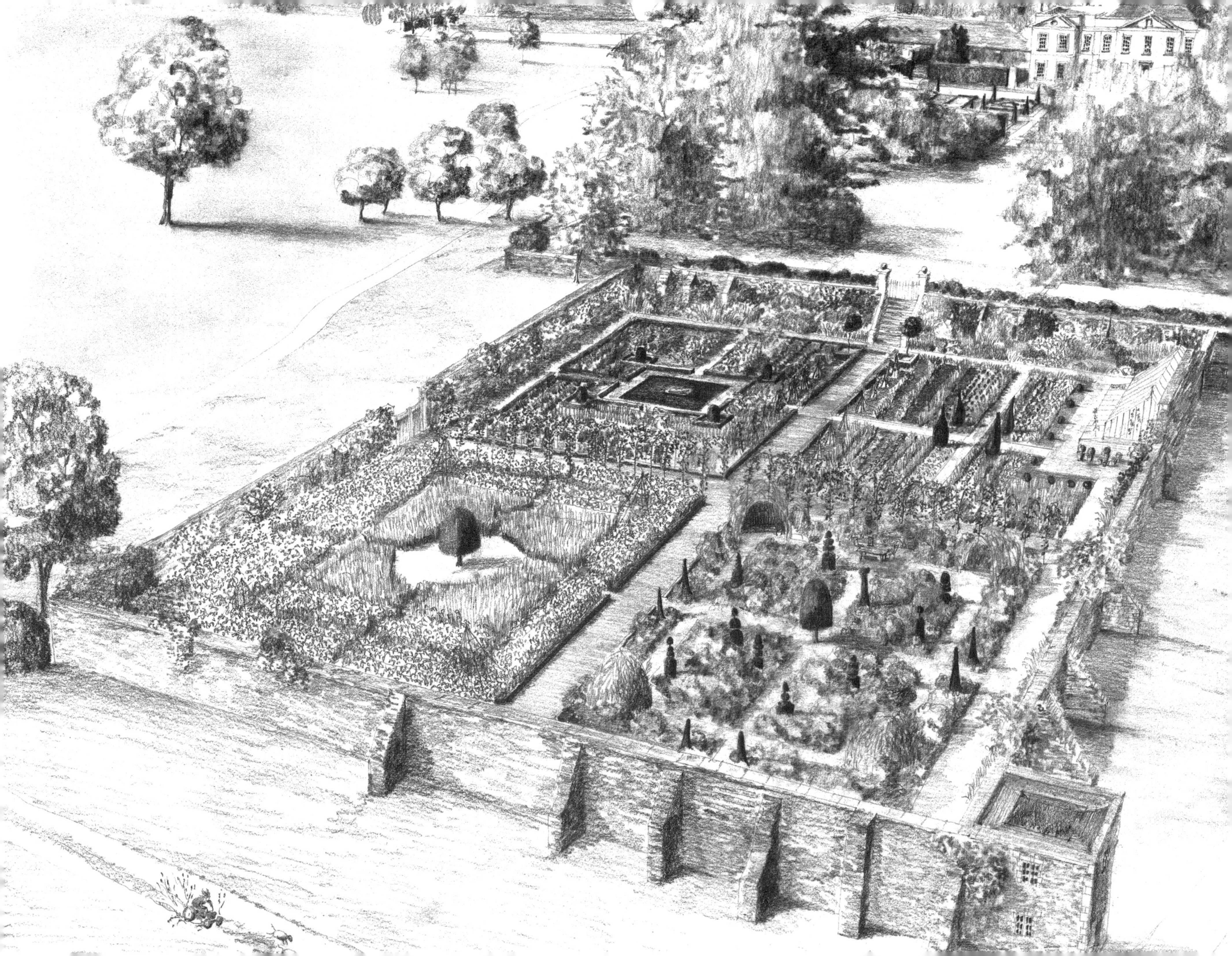

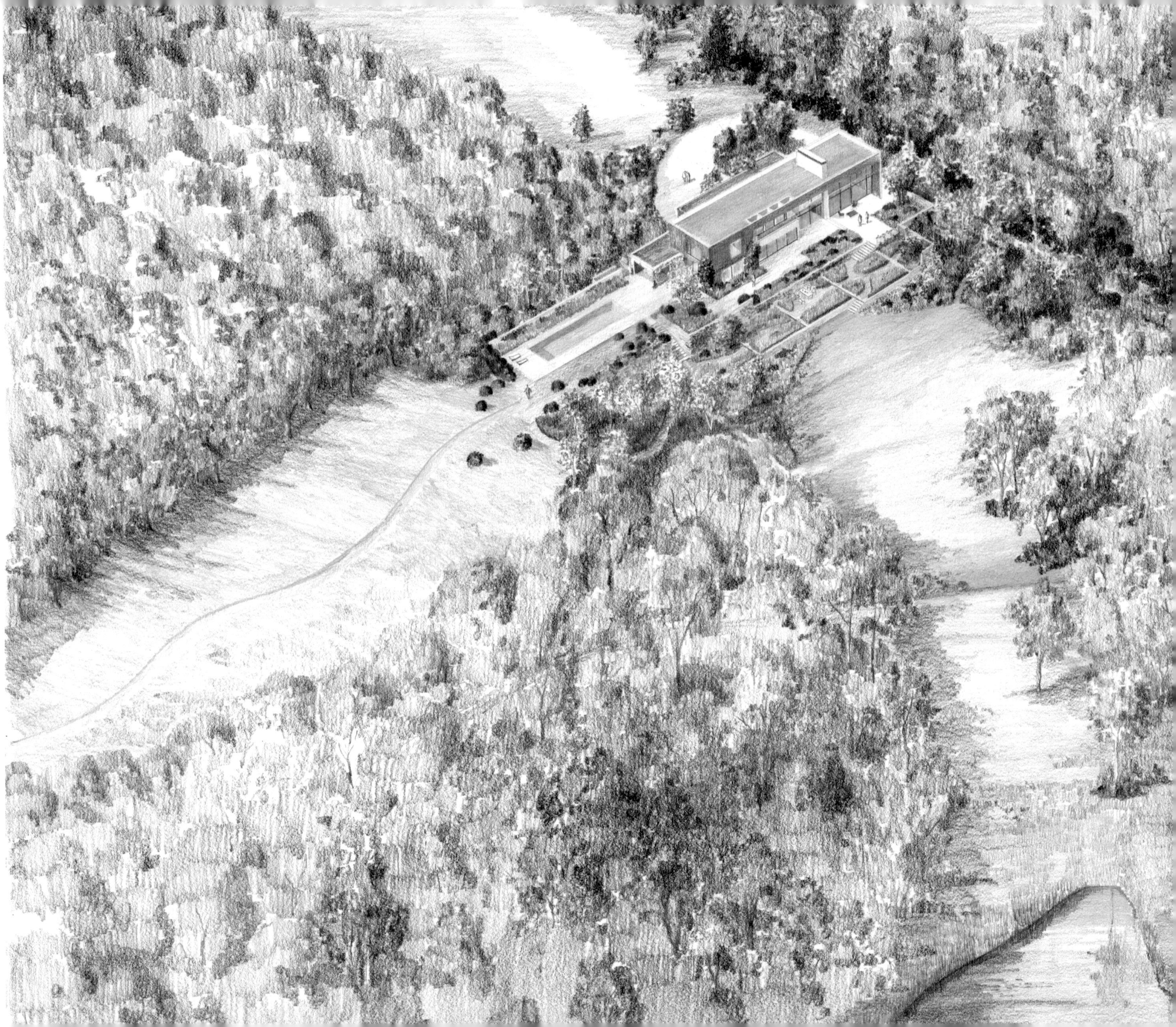

NEW HOUSE,
SURREY, UK, 2014
This drawing (left) for the setting of a house by John Pardey Architects is an attempt at demonstrating how issues of complex levels in front of a building are resolved to make a transition from the domestic to the more natural landscape. A sketch (above) shows a proposal for a new entrance drive, off an existing lane.

Taylor Cullity Lethlean
Victoria, Australia

The natural landscape of Australia has proved to be a rich seam of influence for Taylor Cullity Lethlean. The company discovered early on that hand-drawing allows for an authentic expression of an intimacy with this environment. Drawing has also proved to be a useful tool when it comes to the formulation, processing and expression of complex ideas. The late Kevin Taylor, who co-founded the company with Kate Cullity, devised a formal methodology based on drawing, which is essentially an analytical rather than an aesthetic tool.

Kate Cullity writes: 'We execute a lot of exploratory drawings quickly using trace and coloured markers, or felt pen in sketchbooks. This enables us to play with various design ideas without getting fixed on one too early. Working on trace means the markers have a watercolour-like quality, so colours can be mixed and layered easily. We also use this technique in more detail for presentation drawings, as clients and members of the public respond positively to hand-drawn images. As landscape has a fluidity of light and time, this drawing style is particularly suited to our discipline.

'Sometimes we also present our rough initial ideas, plans and sketches, if they have captured the essence or fundamentals of the design, to clients. These can be drawings that have been worked on by a number of people "in design conversation", so they have an immediacy and energy to them. Seminal to our practice has been the development of what we call "key moves": graphic diagrams that express the principles underlying the design. Each key move has an expressive title, followed by a short description. It provides clarity of intent and allows for clear communication.'

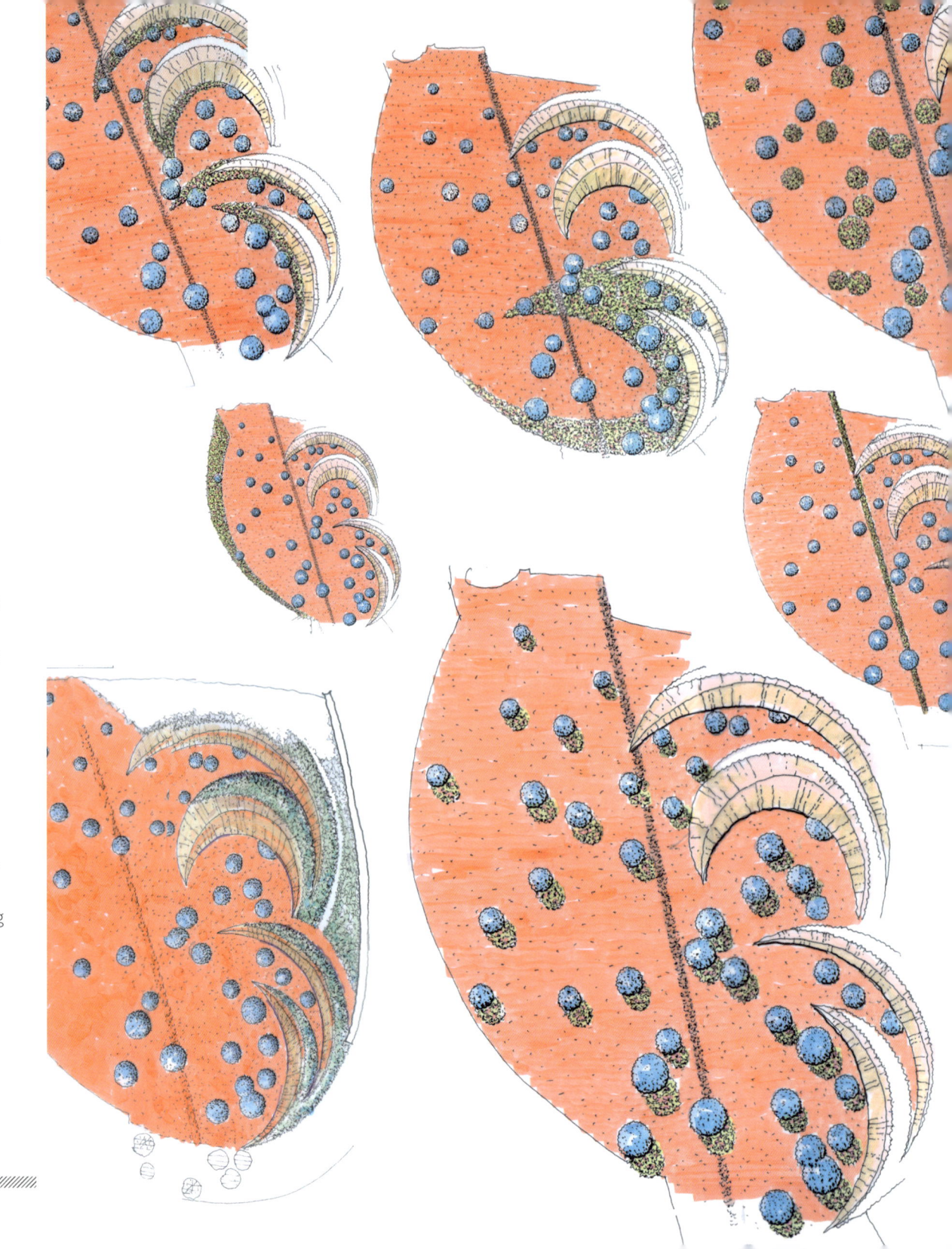

Taylor Cullity Lethlean

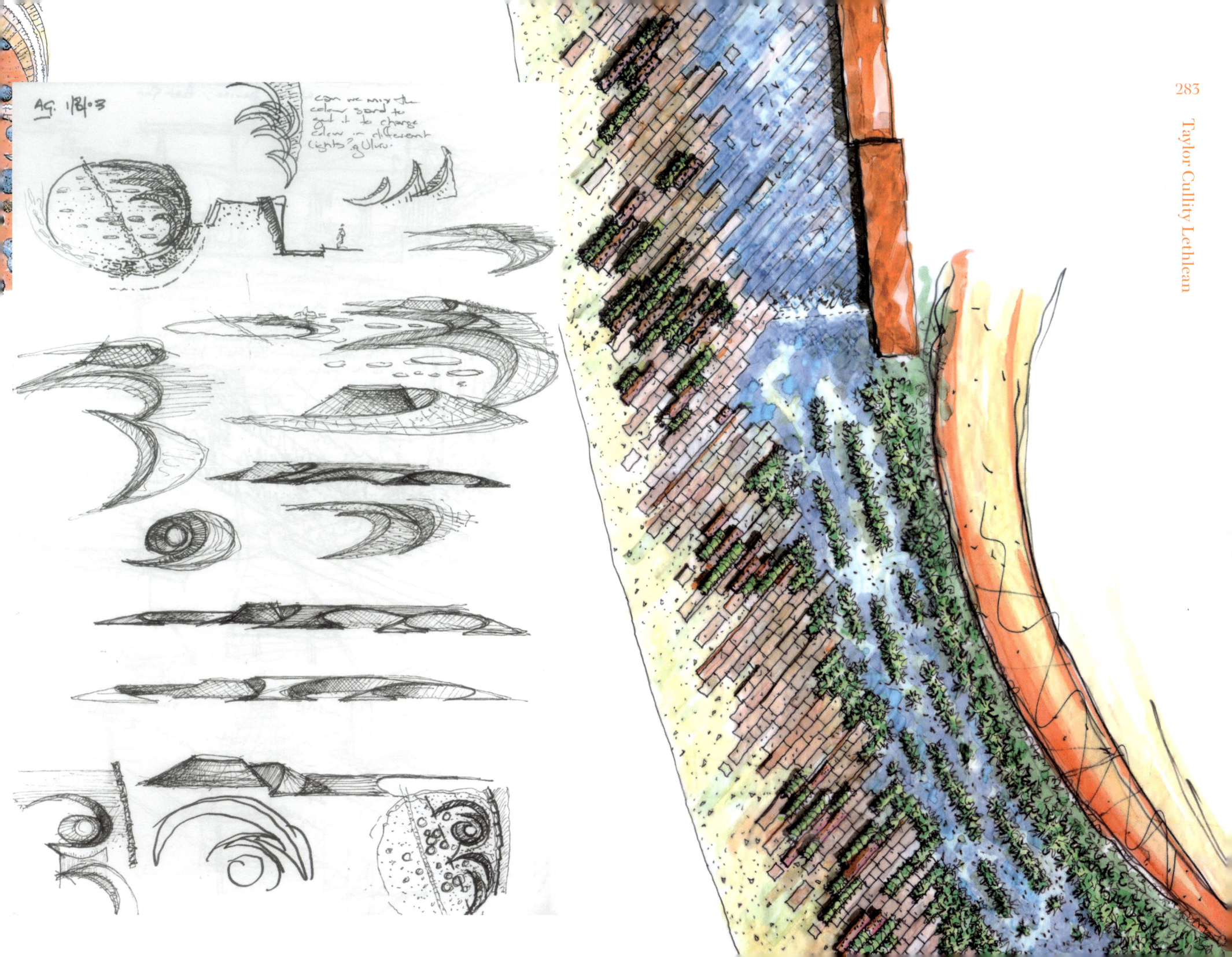

AUSTRALIAN GARDEN,
CRANBOURNE, AUSTRALIA, 2012
Sketches of a dry creek bed, an element of the garden created to explore planting compositions with planting designer Paul Thompson. The amorphic forms were initially traced from an inspiring aerial photograph of Australian dryland and desert vegetation by Richard Woldendorp in the book *Down to Earth*. These forms were later modified by means of drawing. Preparatory sketches for the Sand Garden and the Rockpool Waterway in the centre of the complex (previous pages).

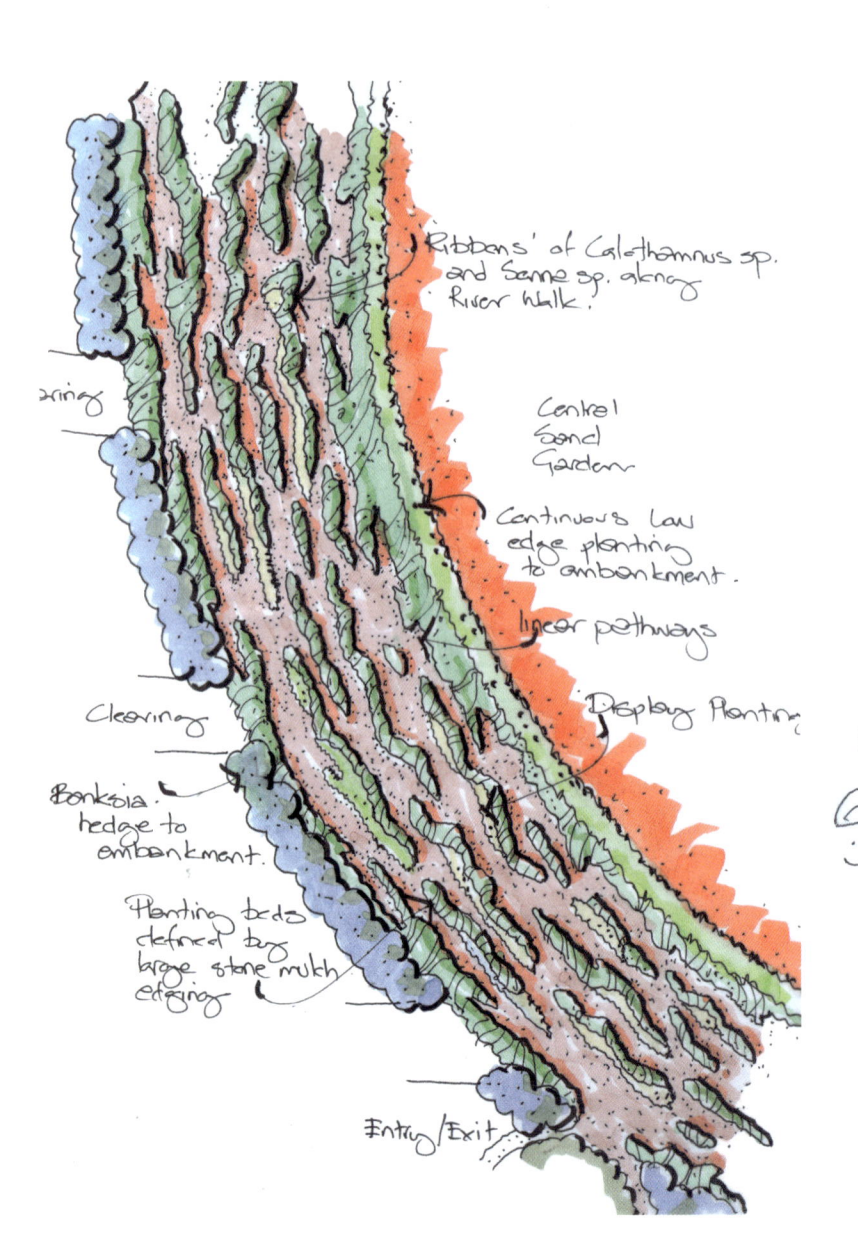

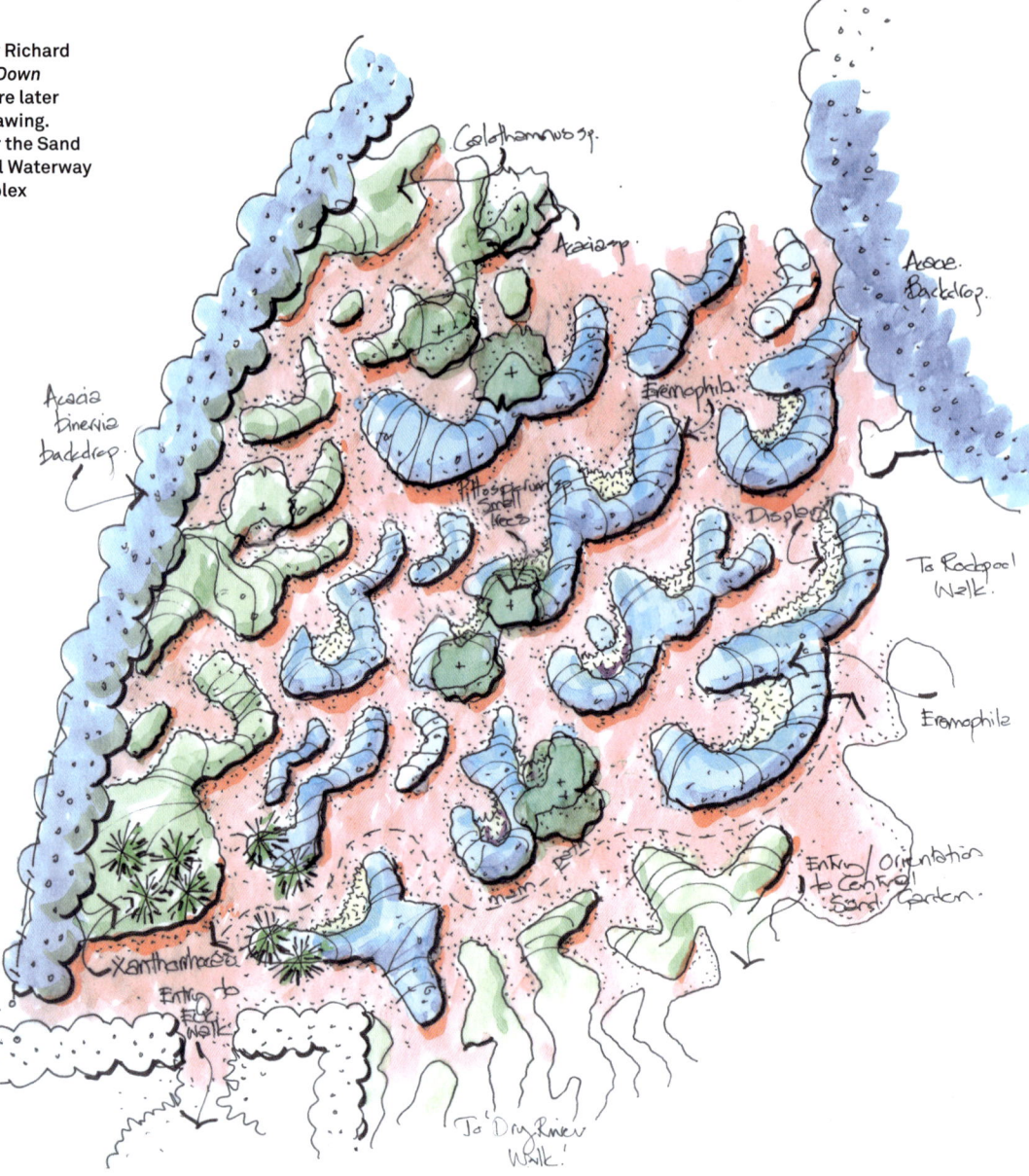

FOREST GALLERY,
MELBOURNE, AUSTRALIA, 2000
Felt-pen and coloured-pencil presentation drawings, intended to convey the potential immersive experience of the Forest Gallery, an exhibit of flora and fauna at the Melbourne Museum. These drawings are deliberately detailed both in the pen line-work and in the layering effect of the coloured pencils.

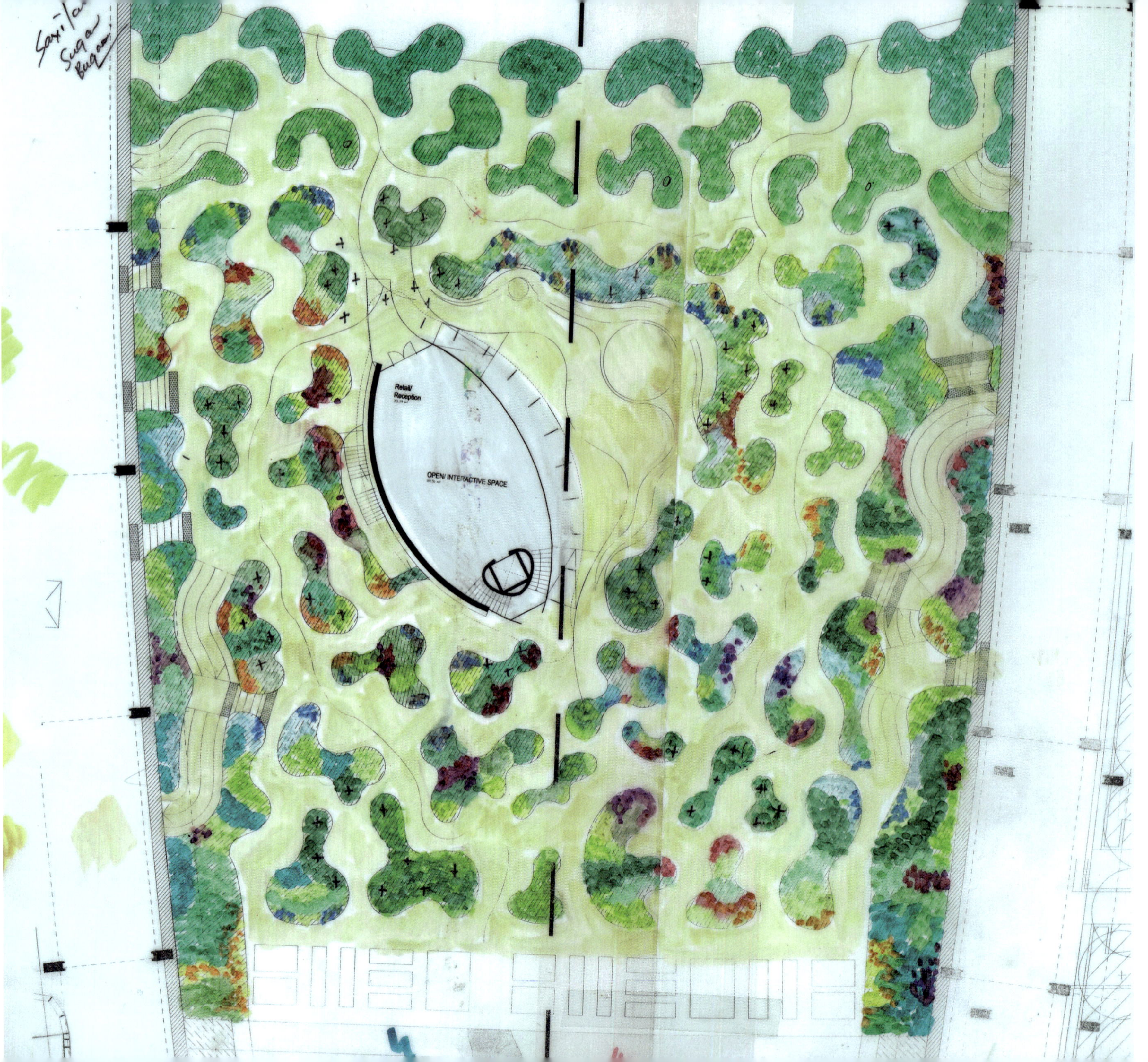
Retail/
Reception
OPEN/ INTERACTIVE SPACE

Taylor Cullity Lethlean

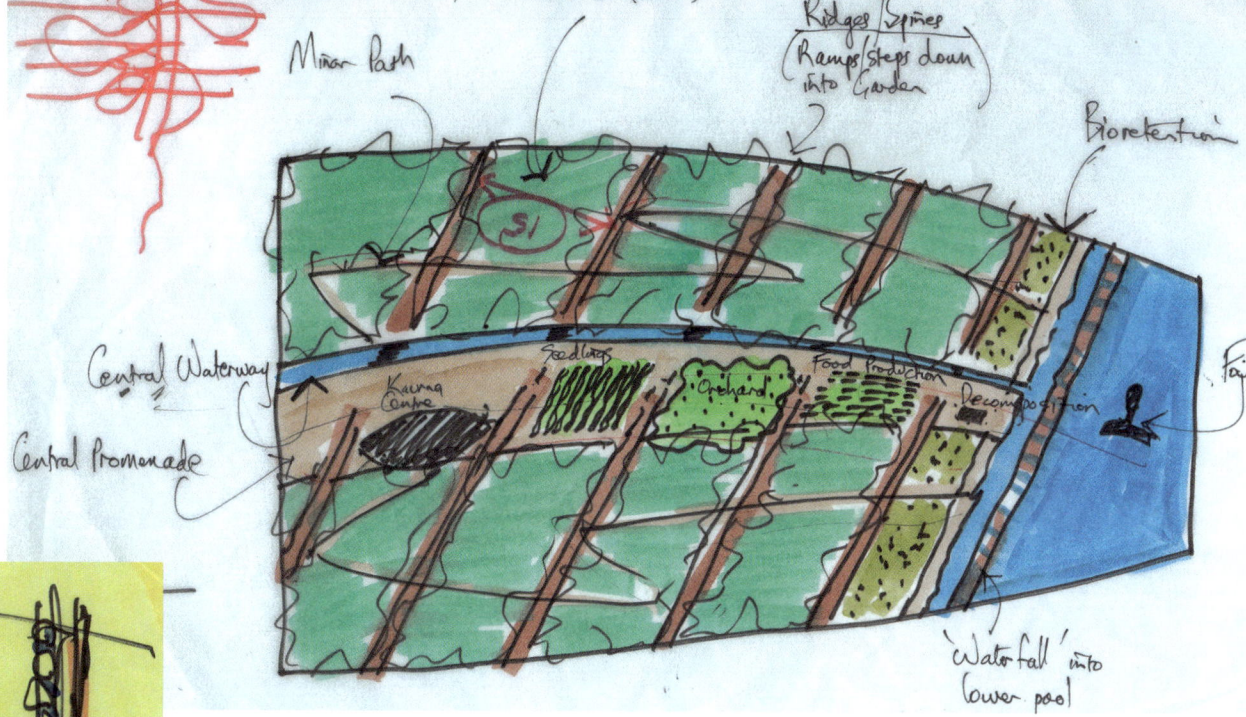

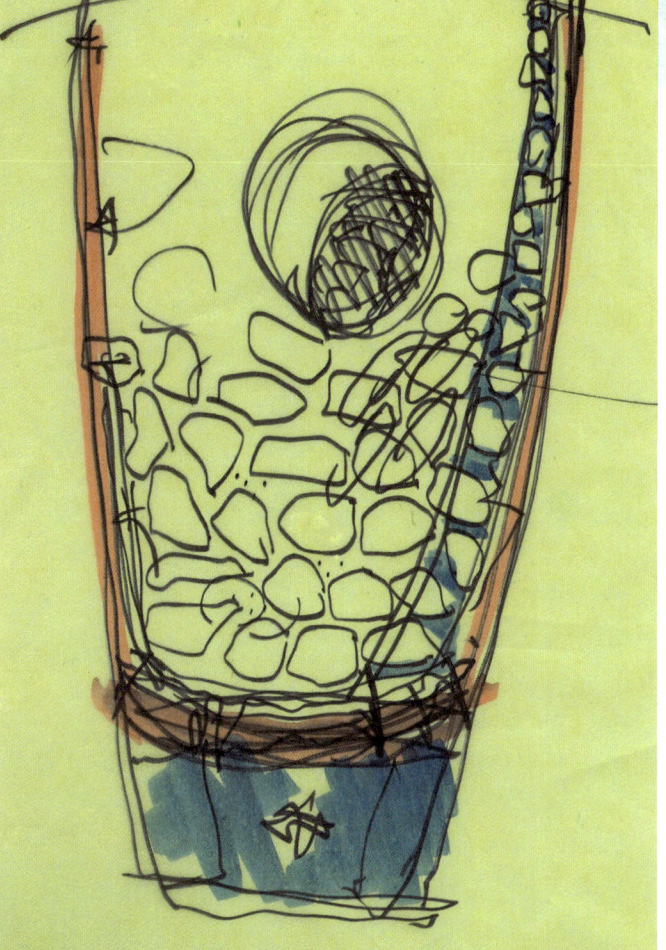

VICTORIA SQUARE,
ADELAIDE, AUSTRALIA, 2010
An early drawing (opposite), exploring potential planting textures, colours and groupings in the Mosaic Garden. The sketches and drawings on this page were made during a number of design sessions with the aim of exploring ideas for the square.

NORTH TERRACE,
ADELAIDE, AUSTRALIA, 2010
Exploratory drawings for the redevelopment of North Terrace (right and below). The drawing below, made during a collaborative design session with architect Peter Elliott, 'cracked the code' for the layout of the terrace.

VICTORIA SQUARE,
ADELAIDE, AUSTRALIA, 2010
Exploratory drawings for the redesign of Victoria Square (bottom and opposite). The diagrams are 'key moves' that express the physical manifestations, or moves, embodying the design concept. In this method, each series of drawings is given an expressive title.

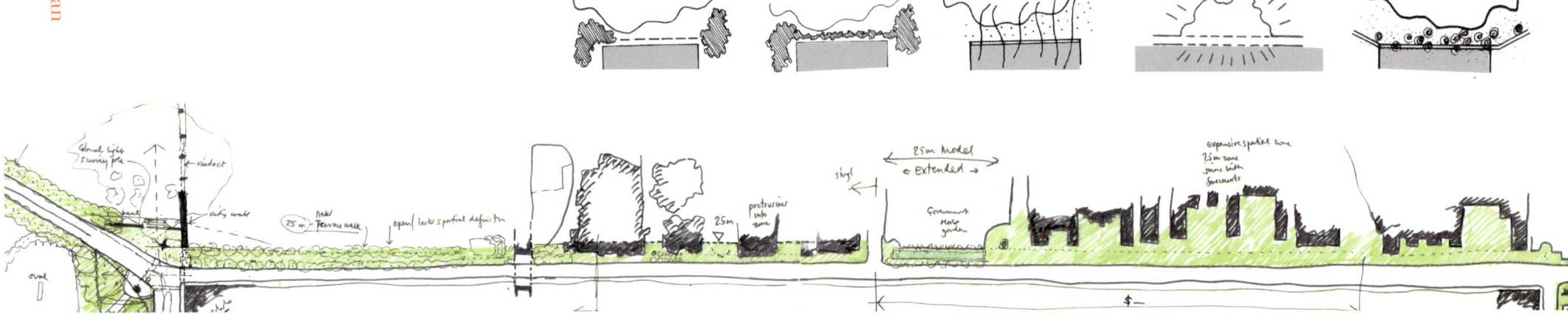

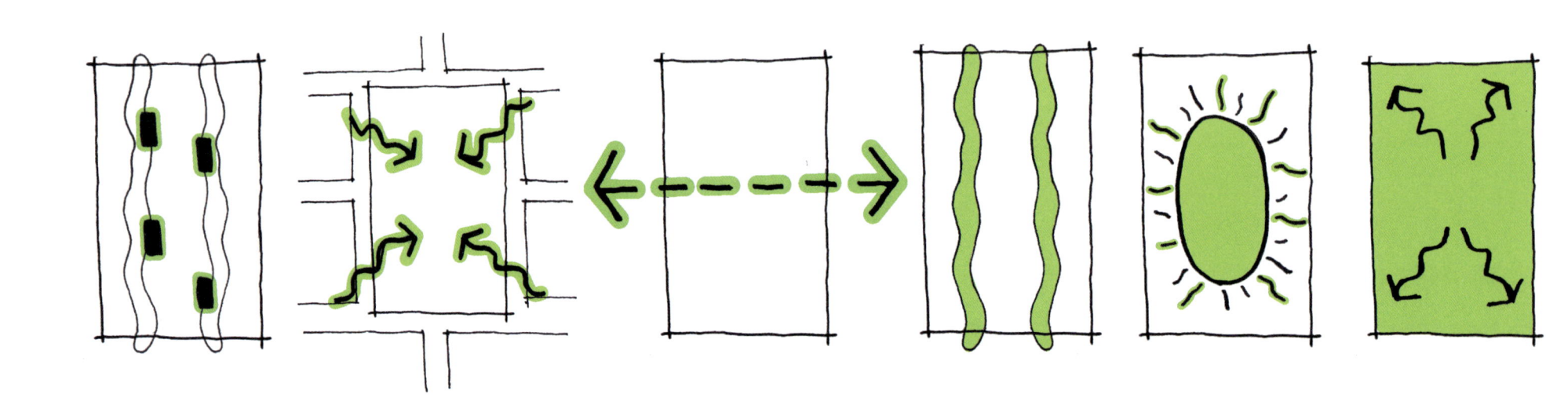

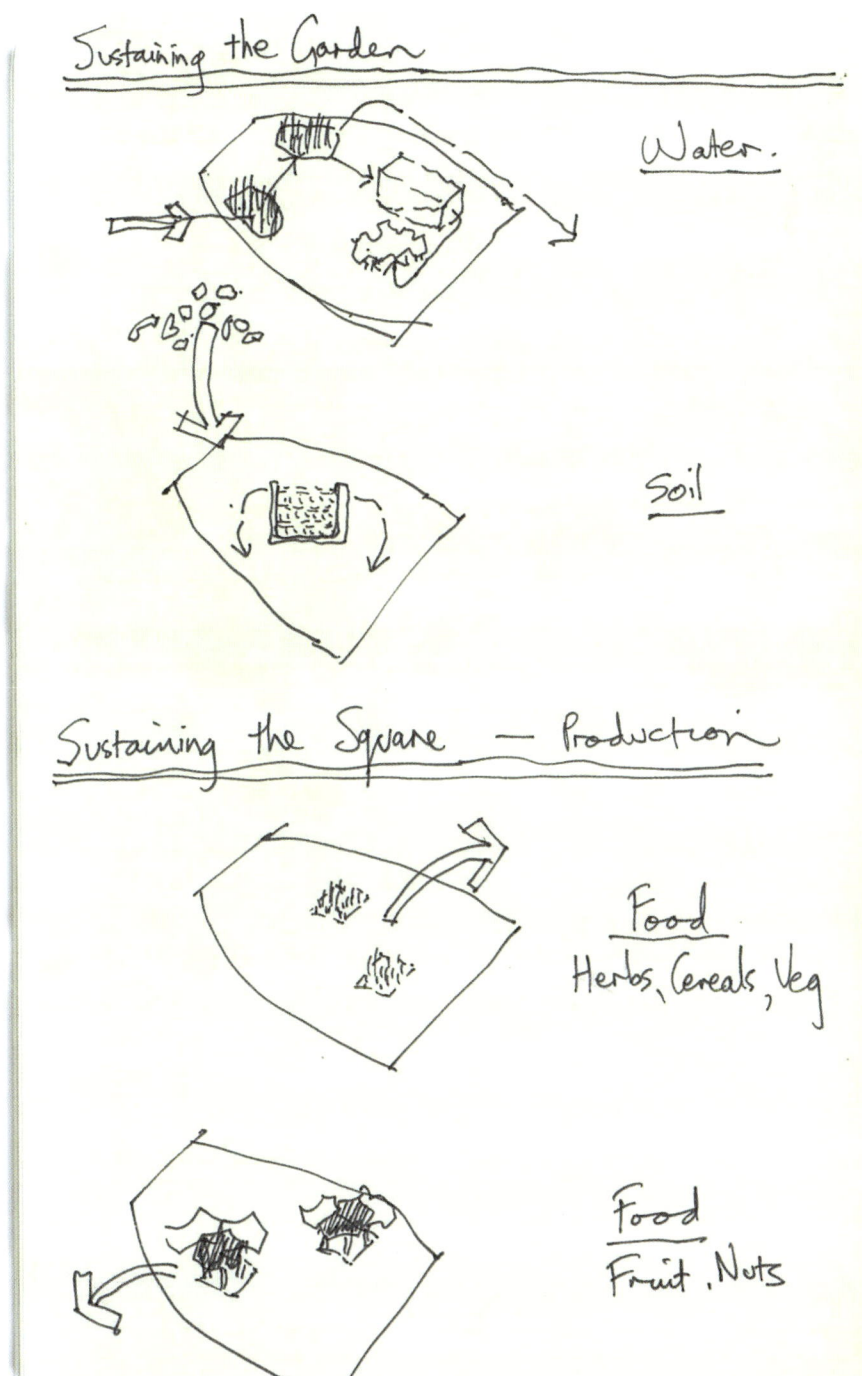

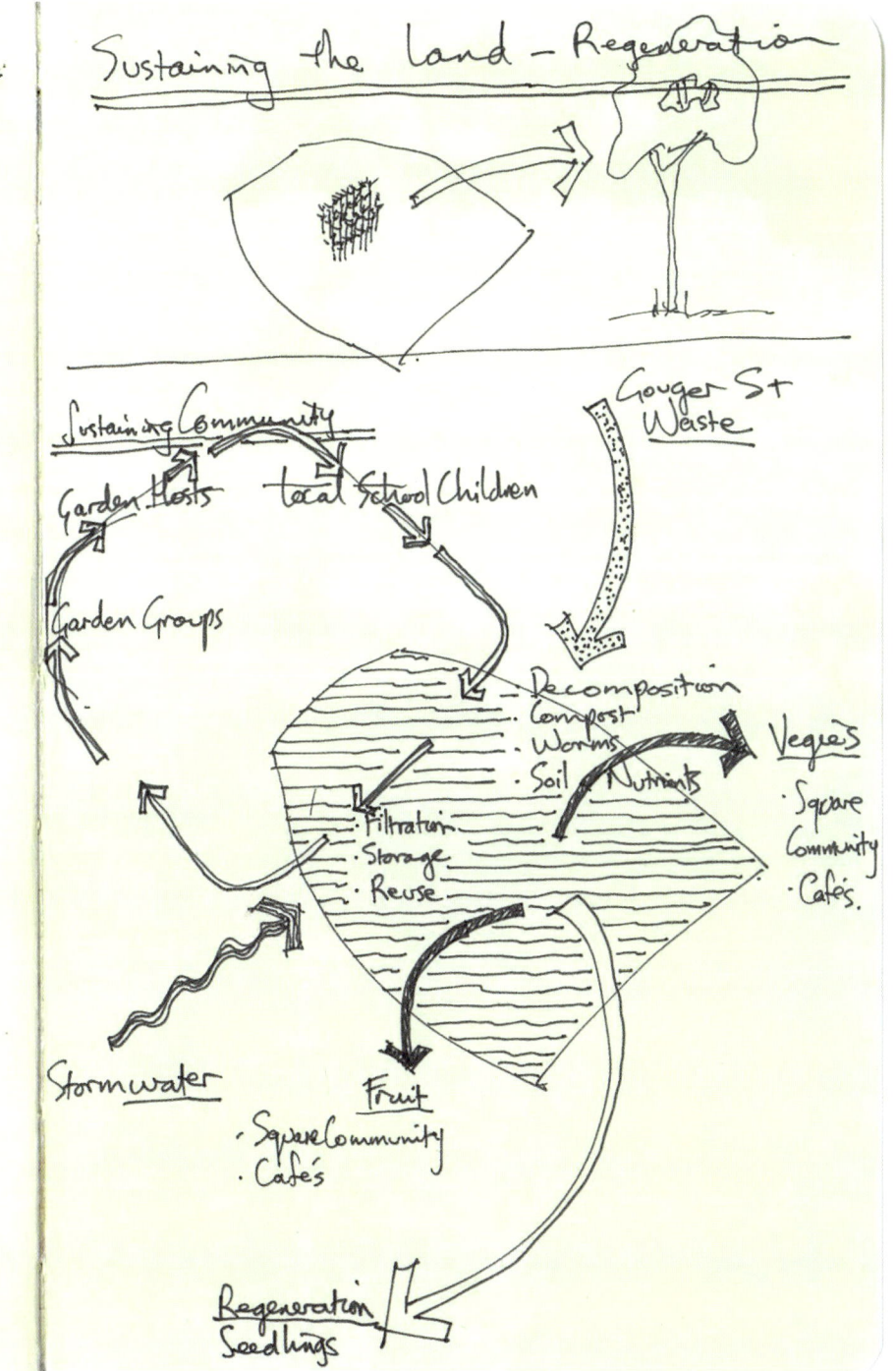

Sustaining the Garden

Water

Soil

Sustaining the Square — Production

Food
Herbs, Cereals, Veg

Food
Fruit, Nuts

Sustaining the Land — Regeneration

Sustaining Community
- Garden Hosts
- Local School Children
- Garden Groups

Gouger St Waste

- Decomposition
- Compost
- Worms
- Soil Nutrients

Filtration
Storage
Reuse

Veggies
- Square Community
- Cafés

Stormwater

Fruit
- Square Community
- Cafés

Regeneration
Seedlings

Mario Terzic
Vienna, Austria

Drawing has always been at the heart of Mario Terzic's practice. He began his academic career in 1991 as a professor of drawing and graphic art in Vienna, before going on to found an influential conceptual school of landscape design, a thriving hub of creativity that was unfortunately disbanded by the university on his retirement in 2013. For Terzic, the drawn 'life' of a project can be as important as its existence 'in reality': the many publications he has produced over the past thirty years are art objects in their own right, sited at the intersection between landscape and graphic art. In his hands, the practice of drawing becomes an exuberant exploratory tool capable of producing ideas that are novel, amusing and profound in equal measure.

Mario Terzic writes: 'Drawing is very close to gardening: tracking the core idea, intense activity, taking breaks, happiness or desperation, getting up and sitting down again, and so on. Like music, drawing is a universal language. I enjoy "speaking drawing". It is the easiest way to mediate my landscape visions.

'To realize the first steps of my concept for a piece of land between sky and earth, I need to make notes, some lines, sketches, studies. Next, I will build a series of pictures. Coloured pencils are the tools I use for tilling the land of tomorrow. The drawings document my attempts to get closer to garden reality; they are fields of development for condensing ideas and are intended to seduce both mind and eye.

'Today, I am confronted with some of my landscape design sketches and am asked to provide statements about drawing, the process, why and how to use the pencil? The more I look at the selection, the more I feel unable to write. The drawings themselves best transmit any message I have.'

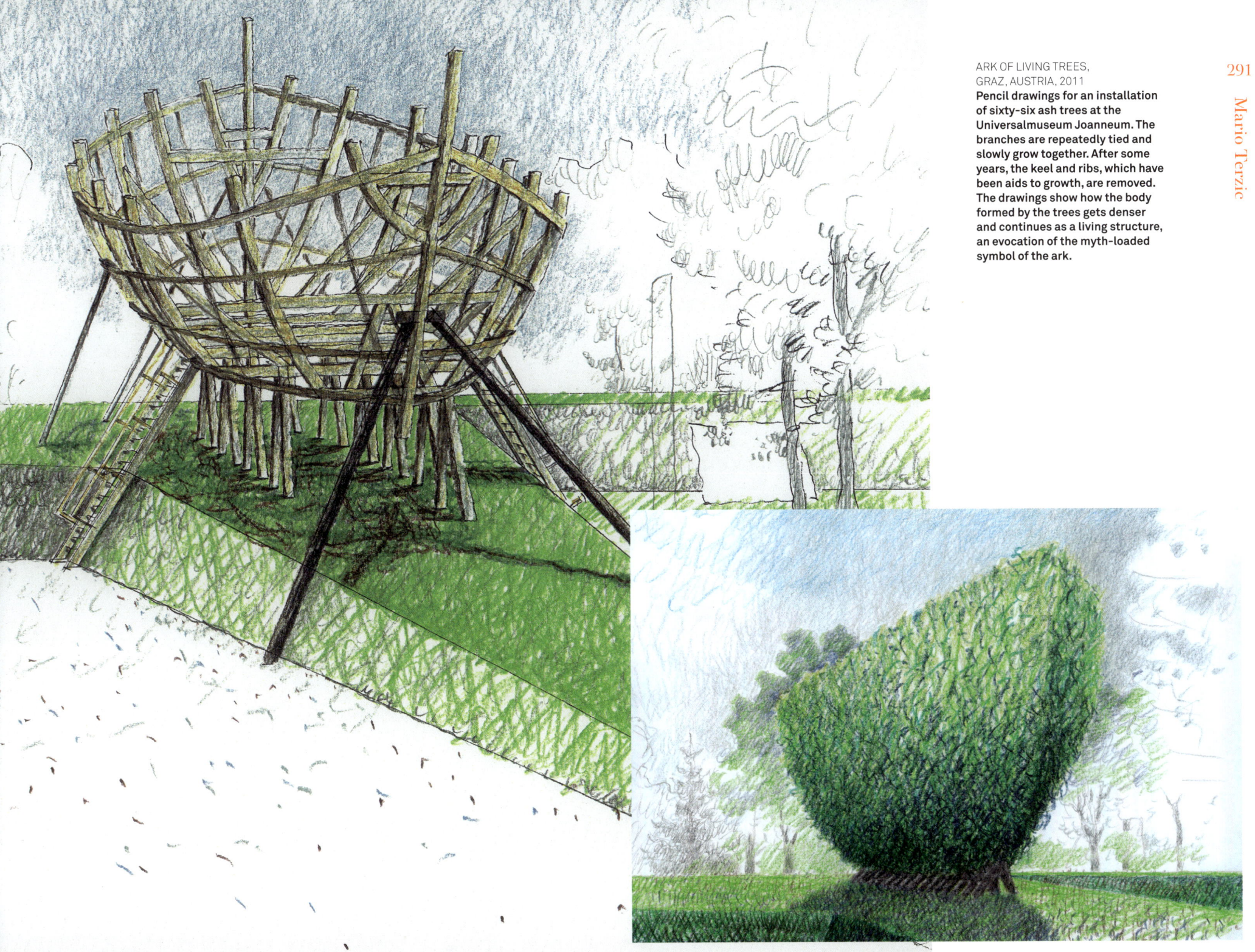

ARK OF LIVING TREES,
GRAZ, AUSTRIA, 2011
Pencil drawings for an installation of sixty-six ash trees at the Universalmuseum Joanneum. The branches are repeatedly tied and slowly grow together. After some years, the keel and ribs, which have been aids to growth, are removed. The drawings show how the body formed by the trees gets denser and continues as a living structure, an evocation of the myth-loaded symbol of the ark.

291

Mario Terzic

GARDEN OF BRITISH WORTHIES, OSTERLEY PARK, LONDON, UK, 2002
Pencil drawing (above) for an installation to show the development of English landscape art. The title of the piece refers to a celebrated garden feature at Stowe.

GRAZ REININGHAUS, GRAZ, AUSTRIA, 2008
Concept drawing in pencil, coloured pencil and marker-pen for a proposed green-space development (left), designed in collaboration with Raoul Bukor. The arena was to have a diameter of 150m (492 ft), and the surrounding ring park a diameter of 350m (1,148 ft).

LUST AU,
LINZ, AUSTRIA, 2006–7
Concept sketch in pencil on a photocopied image. The project consisted of circular fields that stand out from the dark background of the forest in various shades of colour, depending on the season. The fields should give an idea of the bucolic landscape that lies behind the wooded Pfenningberg.

ARKADIEN
BRUNNENFEST

ARCADIA, GENEVA, SWITZERLAND, AND VIENNA, AUSTRIA, 1979–81
The drawings shown here were part of a project intended to re-envision and revitalize – for about two weeks – the 'historic monuments' that are protected Baroque gardens. Study in coloured pencil and watercolour (left) of Fountain Festivity, a kind of party in the waters beneath Antoine Bourdelle's sculpture *Faun and Goat*, at Creux-de-Genthod, Geneva. Study in coloured pencil and watercolour (below) of the Revitalized Baroque Bed at the Belvedere Garden, Vienna.

THE LONG VIEW,
LONDON, UK 2002
A study in marker pen and coloured pencil (left) for a project held at Osterley Park, in West London.

LUST AU,
LINZ, AUSTRIA, 2006–7
Drawings in marker pen and coloured pencil (below and opposite). The intention was to rediscover the garden potential of an industrial area at a motorway exit.

Mario Terzic

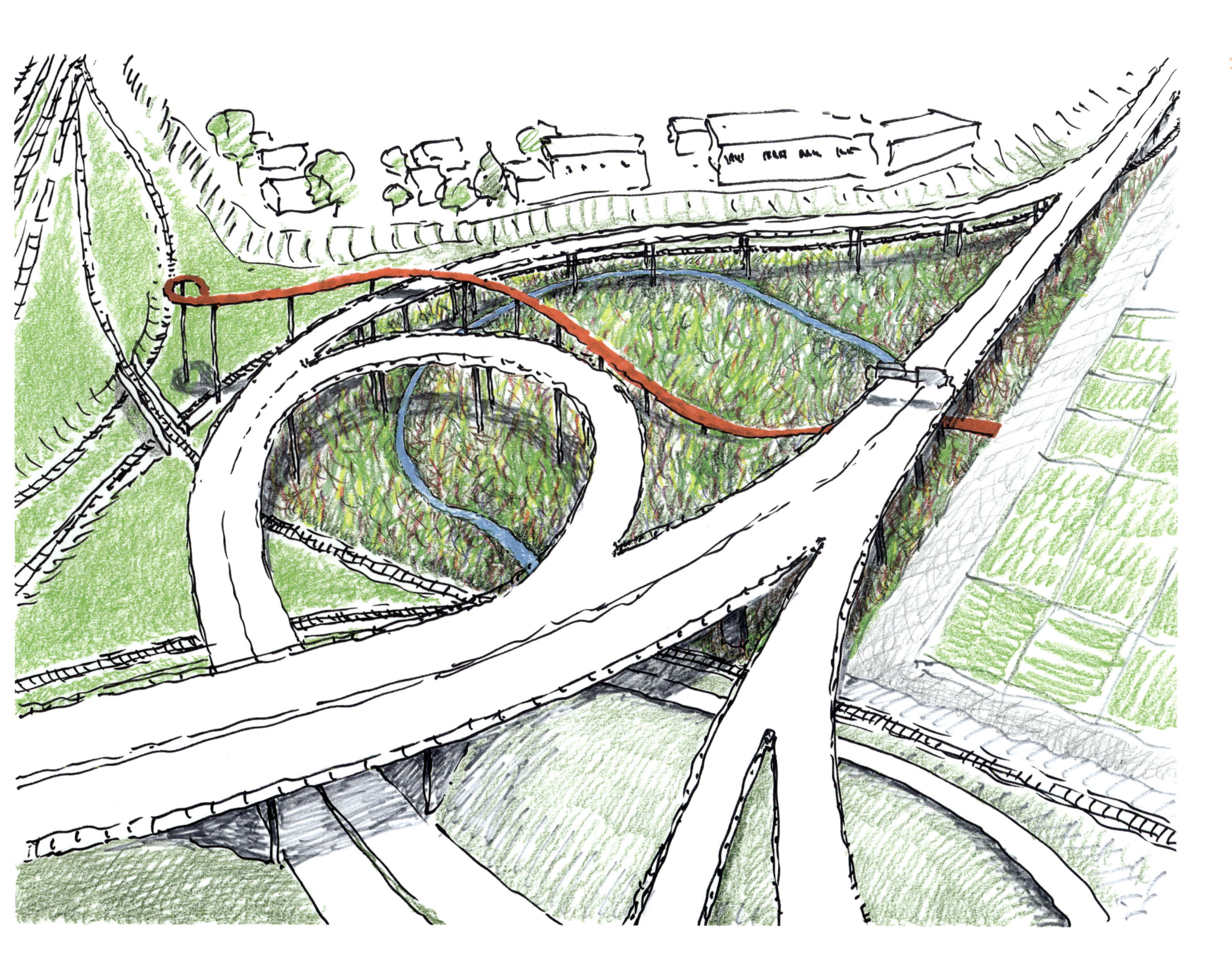

Cleve West
Surrey, UK

Cleve West has always aimed for a more intense artistic experience in his work than many of his contemporaries, who practice a blander, more scaled-down version of the polite precepts of mid-twentieth-century Modernism. He has a fondness for bold sculptural moves, realizing that the power of the work resides in the form and not the detail of the piece. The strong shapes illustrated in the pencil drawings on these pages make one wonder whether West is not, after all, essentially a sculptor of space, rather than a designer of gardens.

Cleve West writes: 'Hand-drawing can improve the way you see and relate to things. The concentration helps you focus on what is around you in a way that taking random snaps with a camera will not. Drawing helps you connect with the space in a more intimate way, so I always try to sketch in the early stages of a design. I usually work in black and white (pencil, pen, sometimes charcoal), but occasionally I use colour to emphasize a detail – water, for example. Sometimes I use plasticine to make models or maquettes for topiary or sculpture.

'My sketchbooks are very fragmented and devoid of any chronology; they contain a mix of random notes, reminders, ideas, compositions, decorative details, topiary forms and idle doodles. Sketches on thin trace paper encourage you to put down more ideas than you would if drawing on good-quality paper. Much is thrown away.

'Freehand drawing requires a lot of concentration, but then you loosen up, often drawing the subject again, but in a more relaxed fashion. Obviously computers have their uses, but there is definitely a feeling of freedom and intuitive expression when working with a pencil that you cannot attain with computer-aided design.'

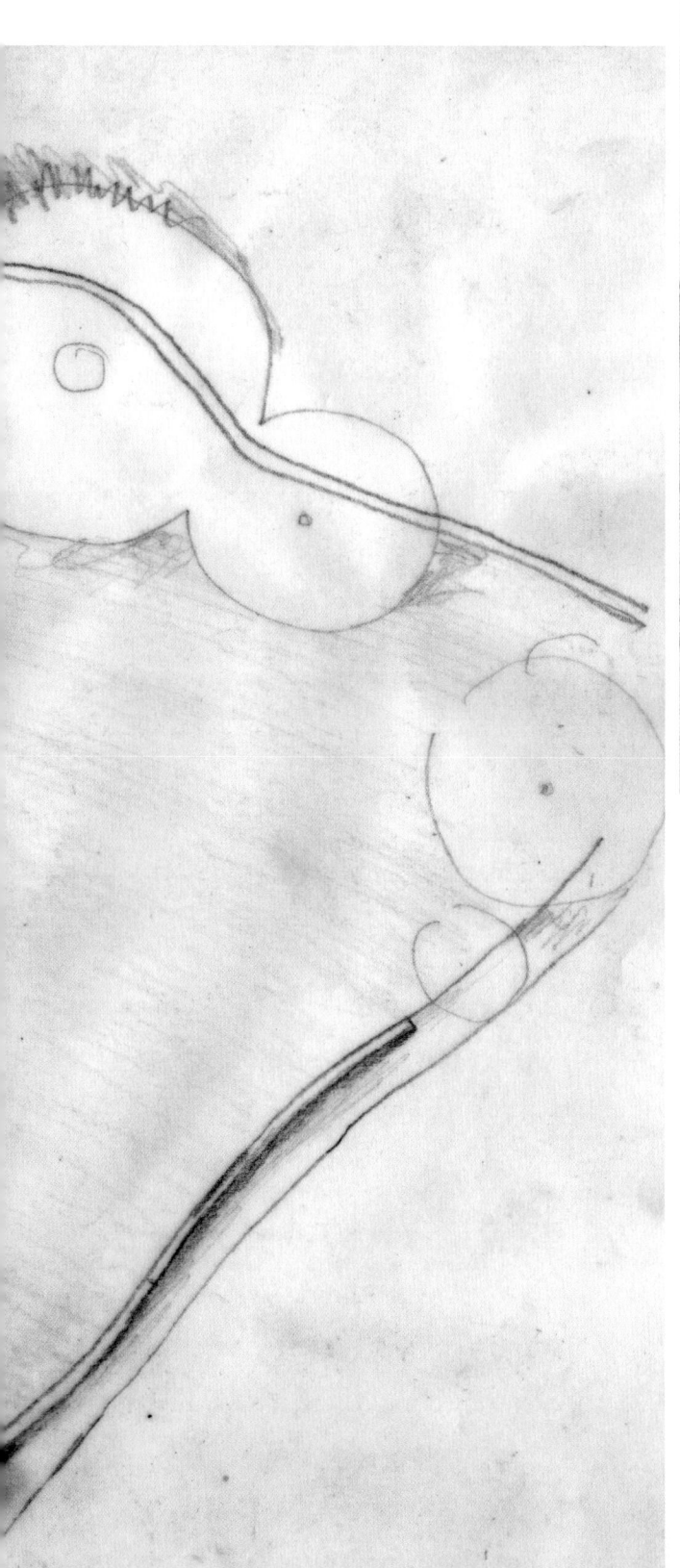

GARDEN FOR A PRIVATE RESIDENCE, GLOUCESTERSHIRE, UK, 2013

Sketch proposal (left) for a lawn space at a garden in the Cotswolds. The idea was to exploit the views, while taking advantage of water flowing through the garden. The lawn is terraced with a retaining wall forming a low ha-ha. A water rill follows the crescent shape of the wall, but cannot be seen from the house, so as to preserve the view. A couple of quick sketches (above and right), showing two treatments for a bed close to the house. Topiary forms are wonderful accent points in the garden – some of the best shapes are achieved by an intuitive response to the way a shrub responds to its given position, but it's good to explore different shapes that offer a variety of moods.

300

Cleve West

GARDEN FOR A PRIVATE RESIDENCE,
GLOUCESTERSHIRE, UK, 2013

Two rough plant sketches – *Daucus carota*, or Queen Anne's Lace (opposite, above left), and *Inula magnifica* (opposite, below left) – and a sketch plan of the same project (opposite, right). The idea for this part of the garden was to acknowledge the skewed geometry of the medieval property by creating a slightly distorted diagonal grid, which is then populated by topiary forms. It imparts a sense of belonging and adds a contemporary note. This came about from initial doodles on site, and could easily have been missed if hand-drawing had not been employed. Formal topiary forms in the diagonal grid (right) and a suggestion for a fountain in the courtyard area (below).

302

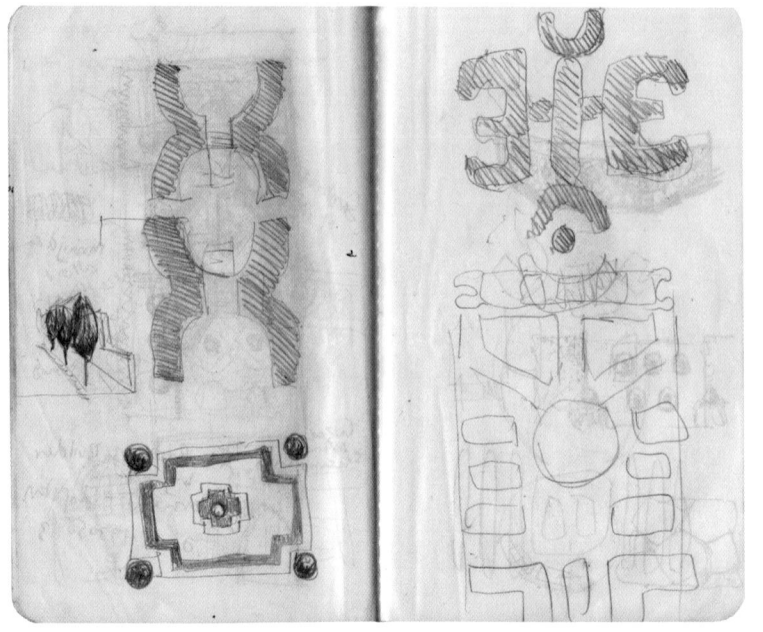

Cleve West

MAGGIES

KATE
SARAH

VARIOUS SKETCHES,
2013
Ideas for a wall feature (far left and below), which took on a life of their own when grouped together as abstract doodles. Sketches made during a visit to the British Museum (left) could later be used to inspire a pattern for a formal garden.

BREWIN DOLPHIN GARDEN,
CHELSEA FLOWER SHOW,
LONDON, UK, 2012
A collection of doodles (opposite) that came about while working on plans for the Brewin Dolphin Garden for Chelsea. West notes that he became 'a little obsessed' with the shape of a proposed stone feature, and sketched these abstract compositions.

Cleve West

WHITE
ON
WHITE
PLASTER

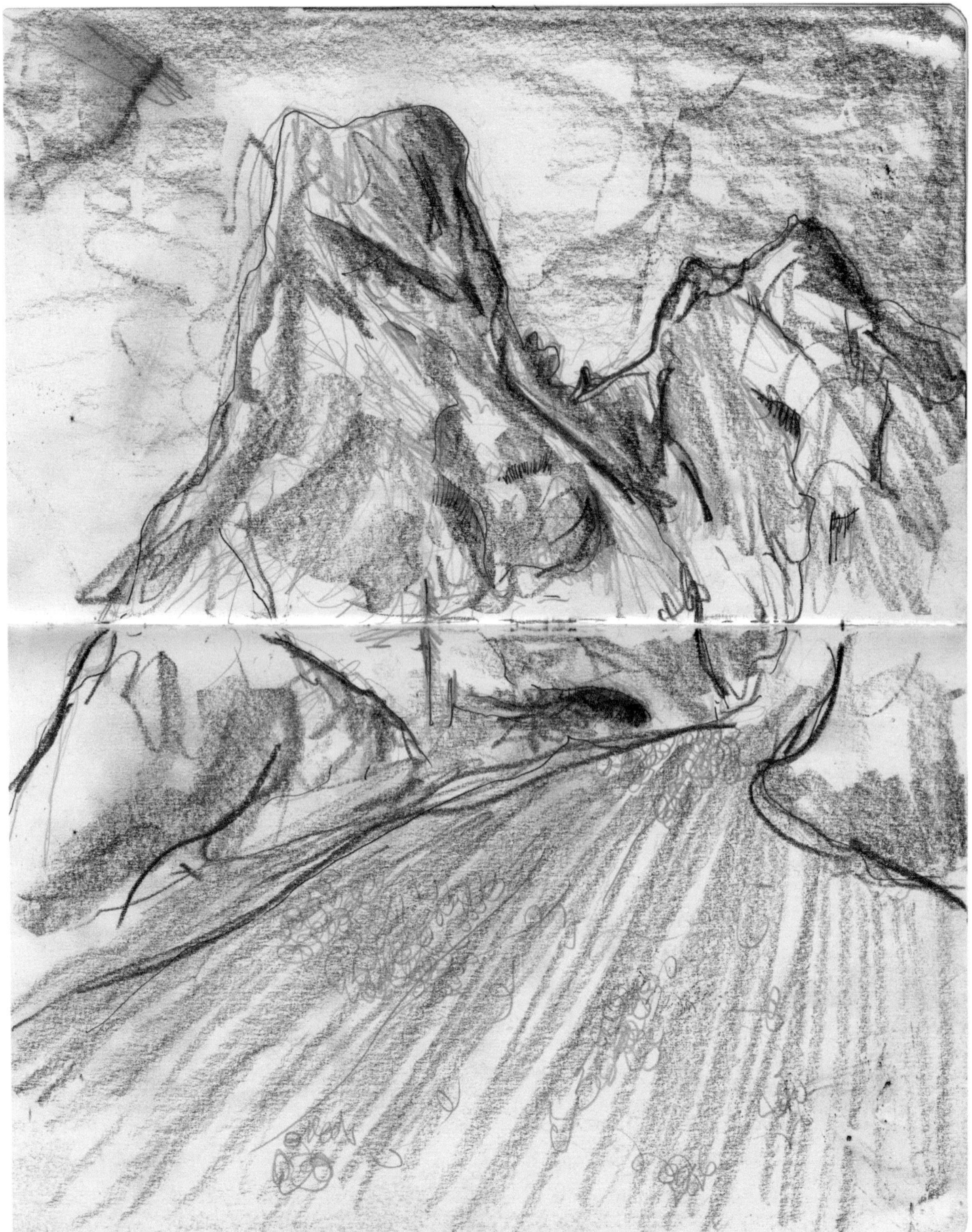

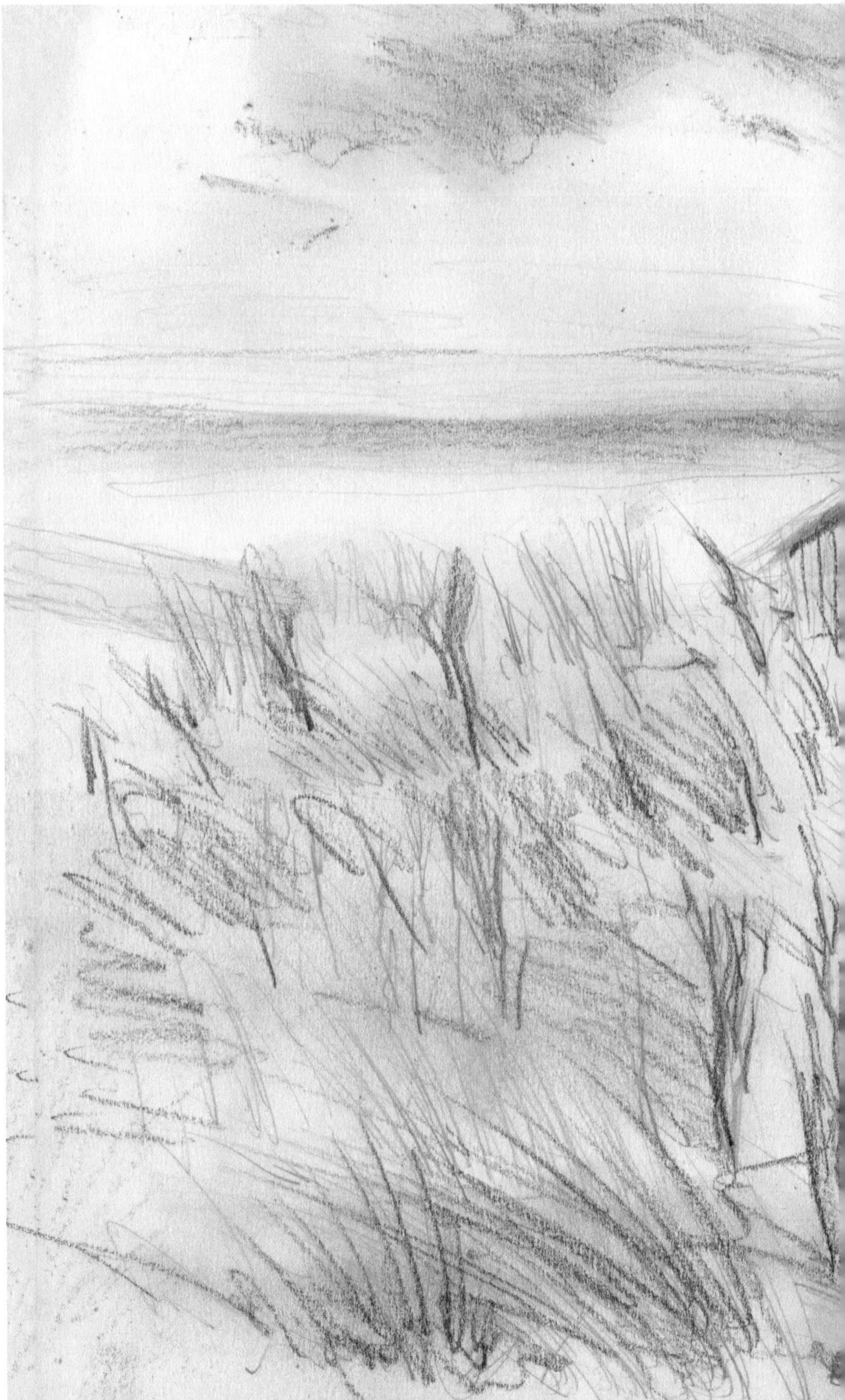

Cleve West

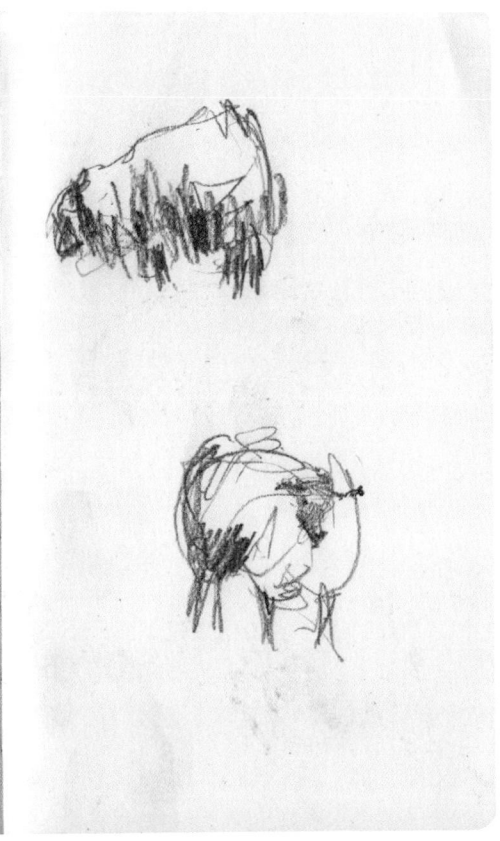

**VARIOUS SKETCHES,
ICELAND, 2012**
Sketches of outbuildings and landscape made while on holiday in Iceland, in preparation for a painting that West has 'still not got around to completing'.

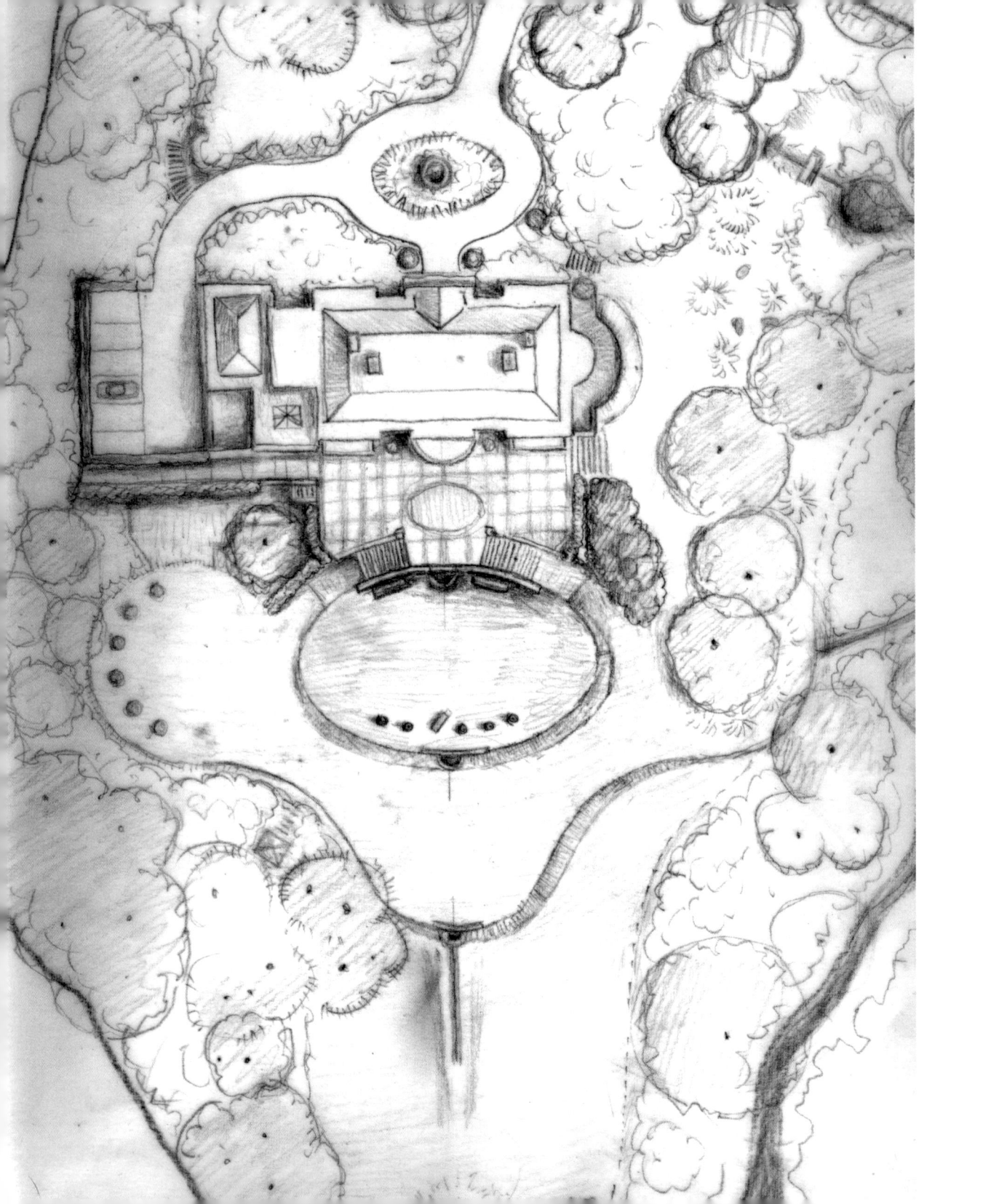

DESIGN FOR A GARDEN,
SURREY, UK, 2013
Sketch proposal for a property in Wentworth, Surrey (left).

M&G PARADISE GARDEN,
CHELSEA FLOWER SHOW,
LONDON, UK, 2014
A tortoise theme emerged during the design of this garden. When trying to come up with something novel to decorate a fountain for a sunken courtyard, West realized that knapped flint, chosen for the elliptical inlays, resembled tortoise shells, so decided that it made sense to use tortoise heads as gargoyles. Doodles of tortoise heads and shells began to appear (opposite, above), along with topiary forms (opposite, below). An early idea for a fountain (below).

17500
11-530

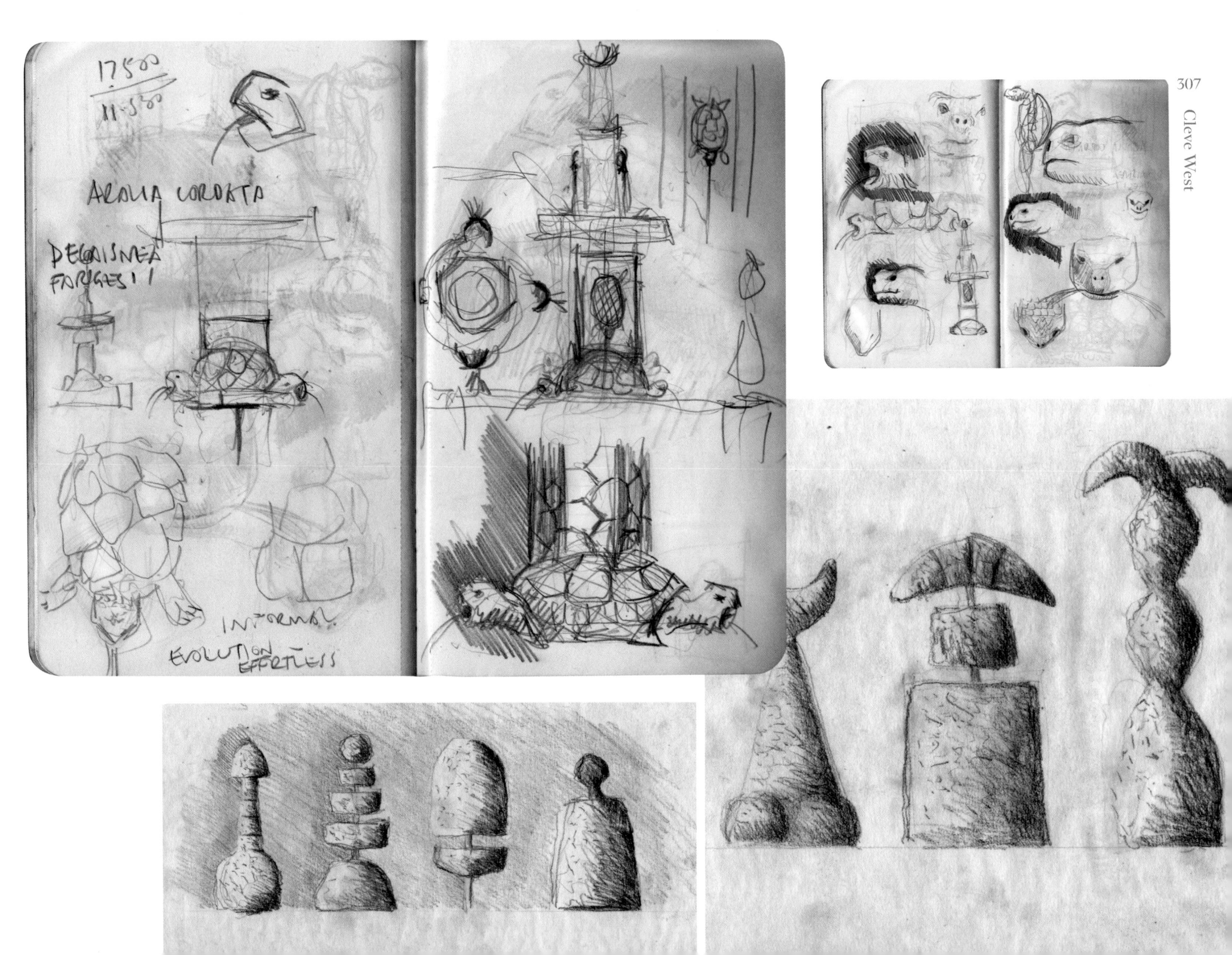

AROLIA CORDATA

DECAISNEA
FORGESII

INFORMAL
EVOLUTION
EFFORTLESS

Cleve West

Cleve West

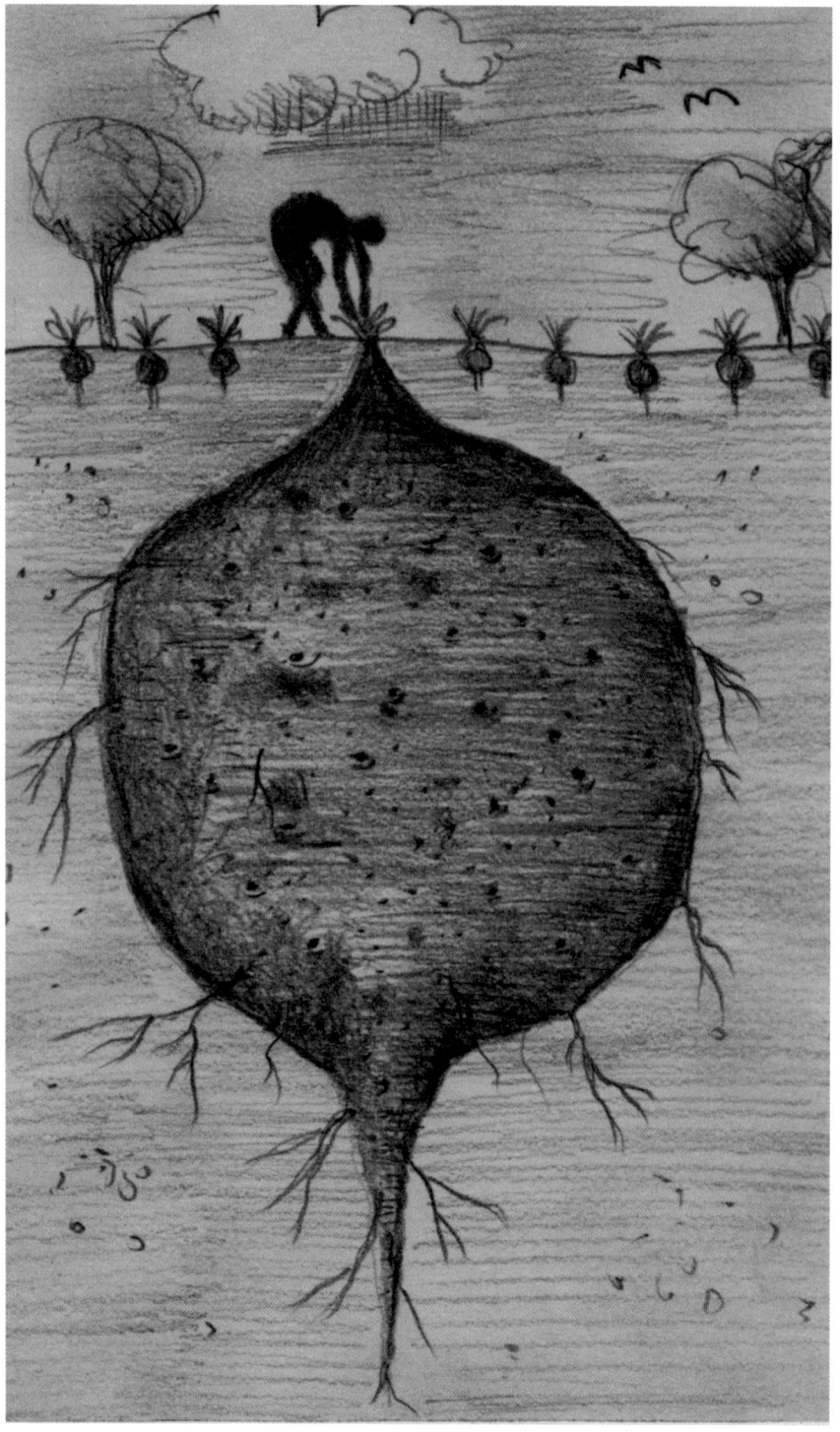

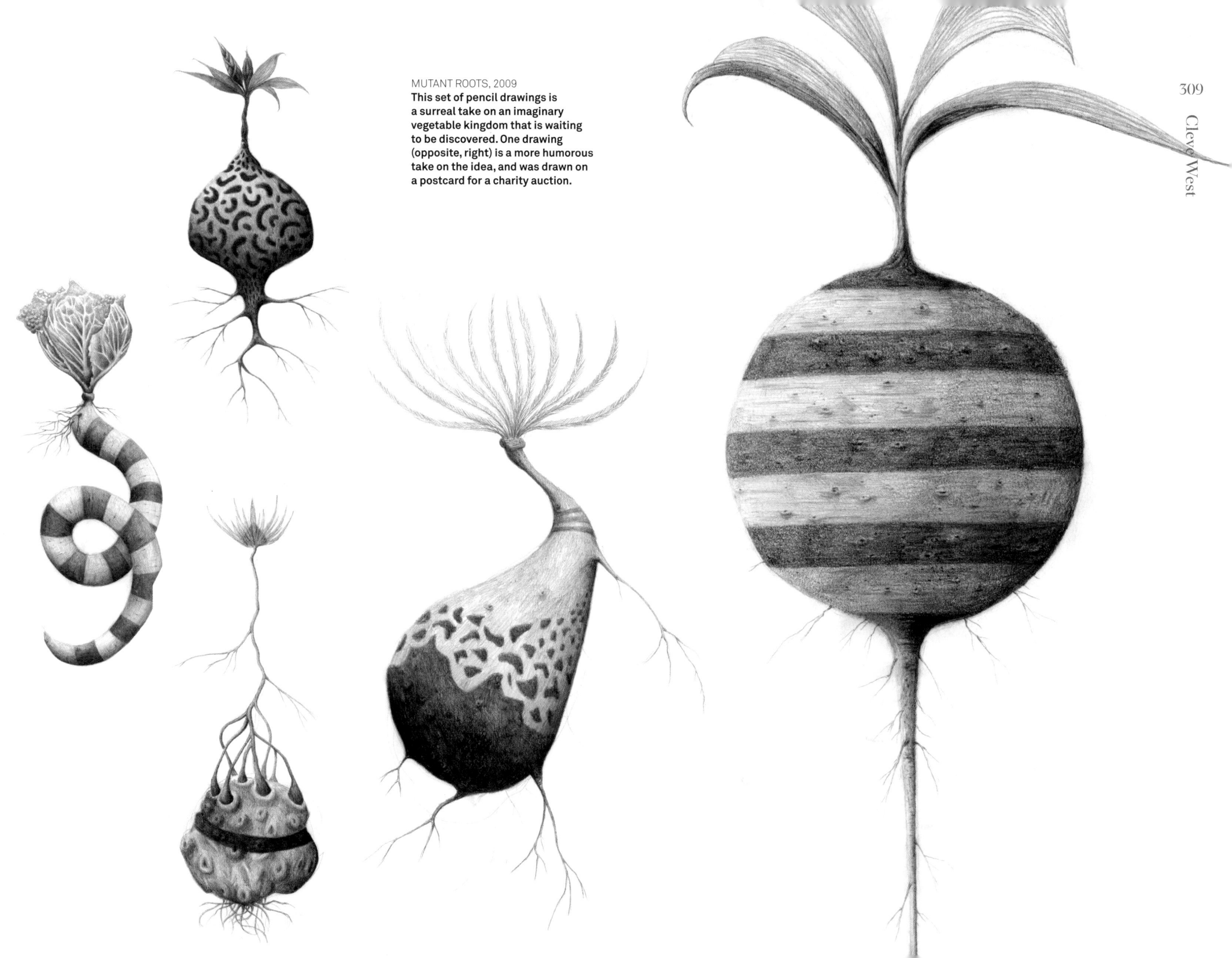

MUTANT ROOTS, 2009
This set of pencil drawings is a surreal take on an imaginary vegetable kingdom that is waiting to be discovered. One drawing (opposite, right) is a more humorous take on the idea, and was drawn on a postcard for a charity auction.

MAGGIE'S CENTRE,
CARDIFF, UK, 2013

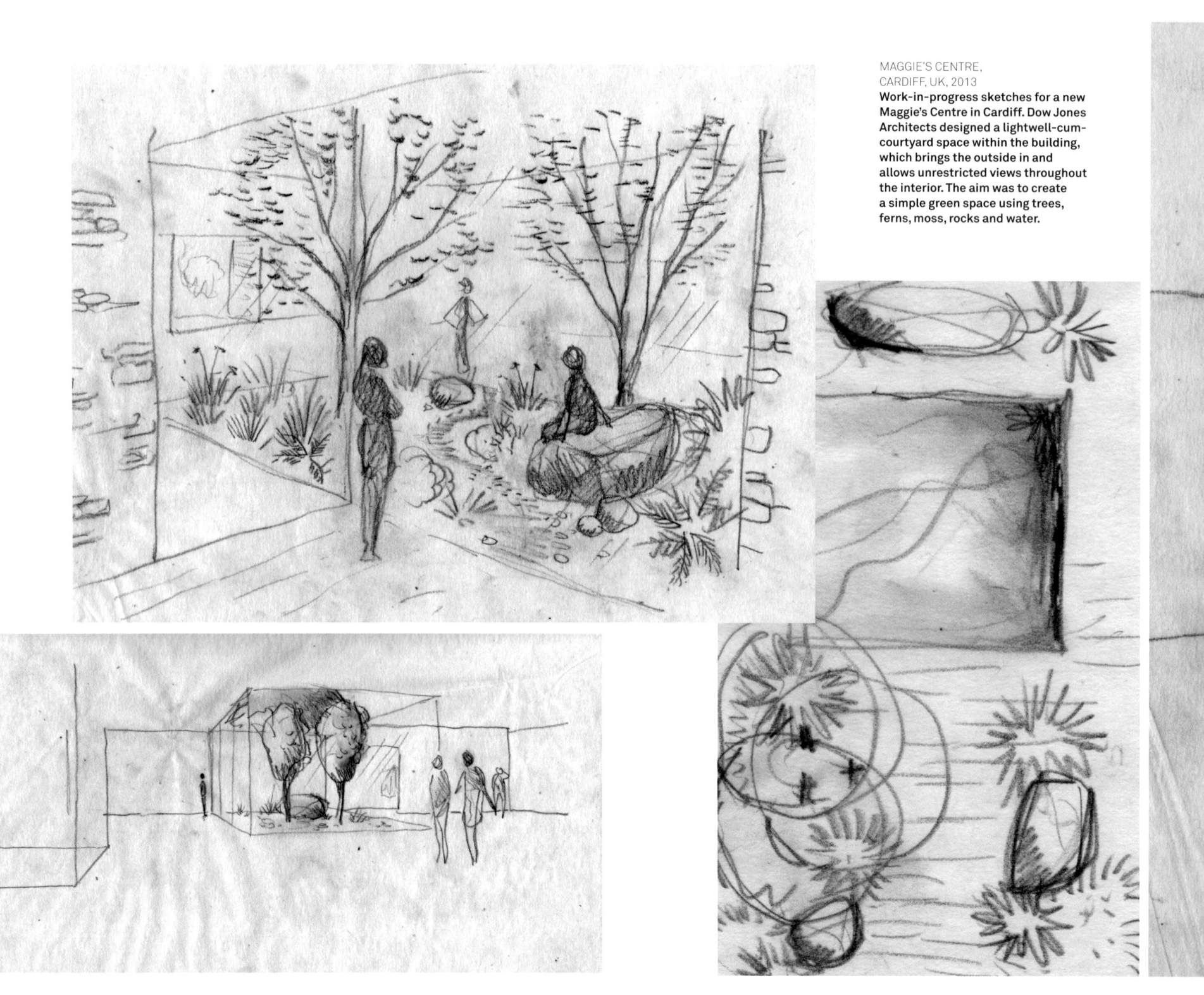

Work-in-progress sketches for a new Maggie's Centre in Cardiff. Dow Jones Architects designed a lightwell-cum-courtyard space within the building, which brings the outside in and allows unrestricted views throughout the interior. The aim was to create a simple green space using trees, ferns, moss, rocks and water.

Cleve West

ZUS

Rotterdam, Netherlands

For this firm, the political and cultural ramifications of design are as important as aesthetics and utility. In common with many other companies, ZUS (which stands for Zones Urbaines Sensibles) uses hand-drawings to convey the potential atmosphere of a proposed design – but diagrammatic sketches can also be used to convey powerful political messages, as well as major moves in landscape design.

ZUS state: 'Our sketches mostly take a diagrammatic form and immediately focus on the most important, basic aspect of the design. While certain types of computer renderings can look the same, sketches have an inherent "character" that sets them apart. Our presentation drawings are often enhanced by means of Photoshop, combining the charm of hand-drawing with the efficiency of the computer.

'Sketches also have a quality of appearing "not completely finished", and this emphasizes their role as a way of defining a guiding principle, as opposed to a fully developed design or theory. Our early diagrammatic sketches tend to stay alongside the design during the process – as a check, of sorts, on the overall direction.

'That "unfinished" quality plays an important role on another level of the design process. Large-scale "blueprint-masterplans" often do not work any more in the current economic conditions. We prefer to design flexible and adaptable frameworks that focus more on certain essential public structures, as opposed to specific building volumes.

'But we still need and want to make drawings. AutoCAD drawings inevitably generate the aura of a fixed masterplan that can be built immediately, even when you only want to communicate a suggestion or a possible outcome of a design process. By using sketches, it is much easier to convey the idea of one or more possible futures instead of a fixed one.'

SCHIPHOLSTAD: 6TH AVENUE, AMSTERDAM, NETHERLANDS, 2008
Collaged impressions of a radical proposal to transform Schiphol airport into 'Schipholstad', a diverse public domain that can handle new habitation based on consumption, leisure and entertainment. A major interpolation is a glass-covered passageway, emphasizing the split between air and land. The collages were created using hand-sketches, line drawings and stock images, combined in Photoshop. The aim was to generate the atmosphere of the design, not its specific detailing.

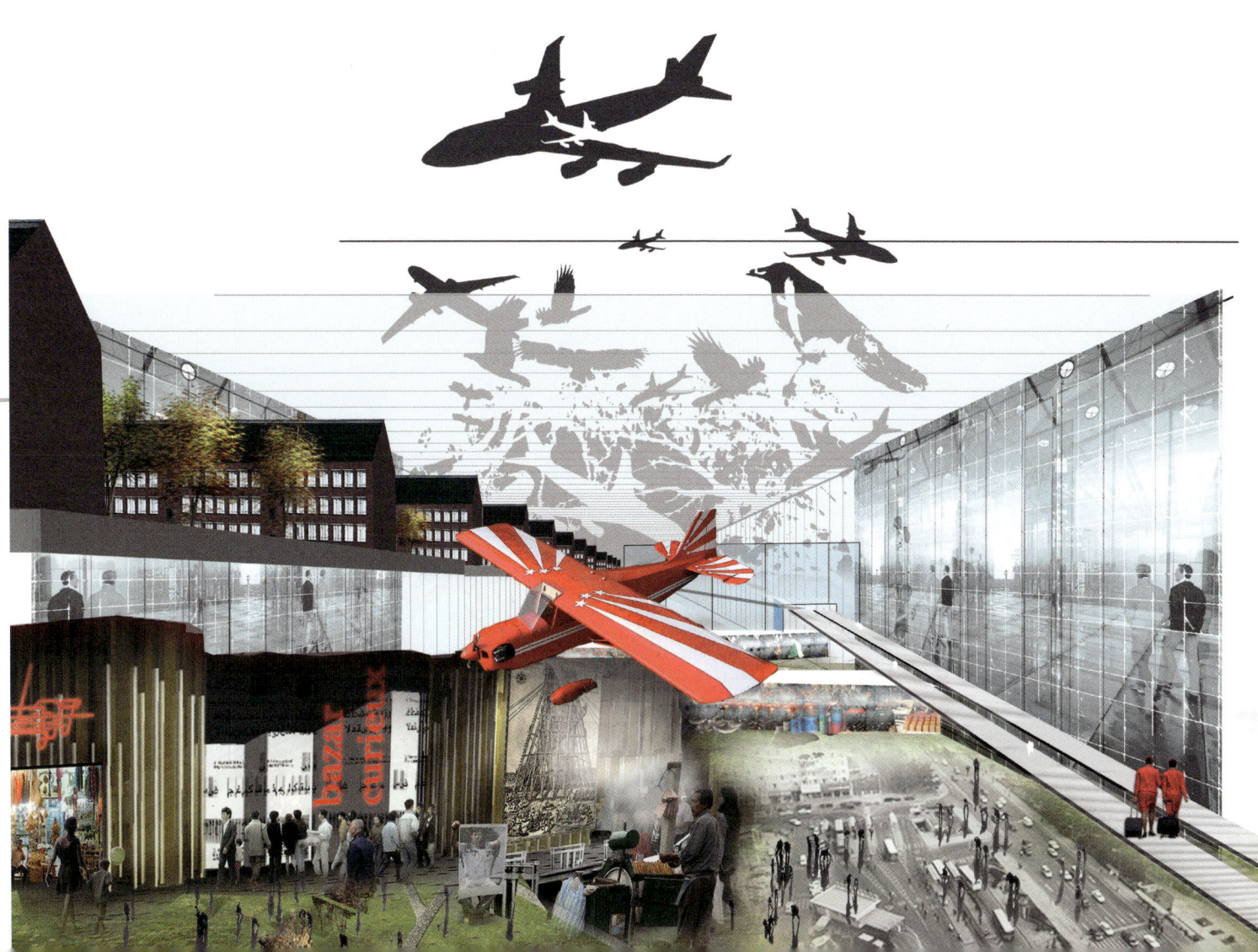

ALMERE DUIN,
NETHERLANDS, 2011
For its coastal development, the city of Almere envisioned a boulevard with high-rise luxury apartments to allow residents to enjoy the views across the water (left). The competition submission proposed a structure of three 'dunes' (below left), stretching out along the waterfront and creating a more interesting fringe between dunes and woodland. These rough hand-sketches were made at the beginning of the design process to illustrate the basic premise of the plan. It proved a good way to explain the project to the client and has remained useful, even now that the project is under way.

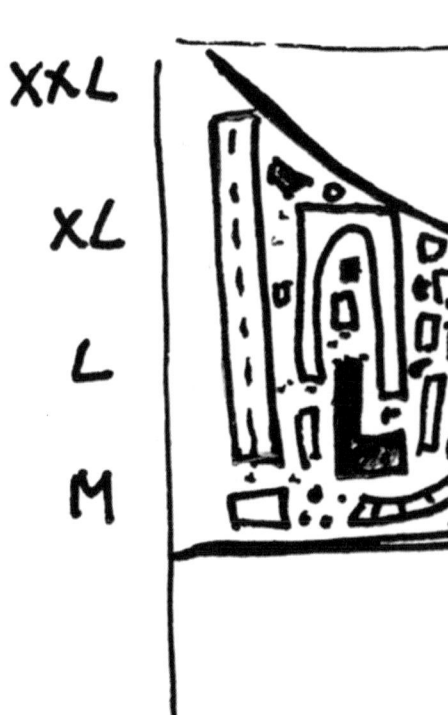

HYPERMARCHÉ

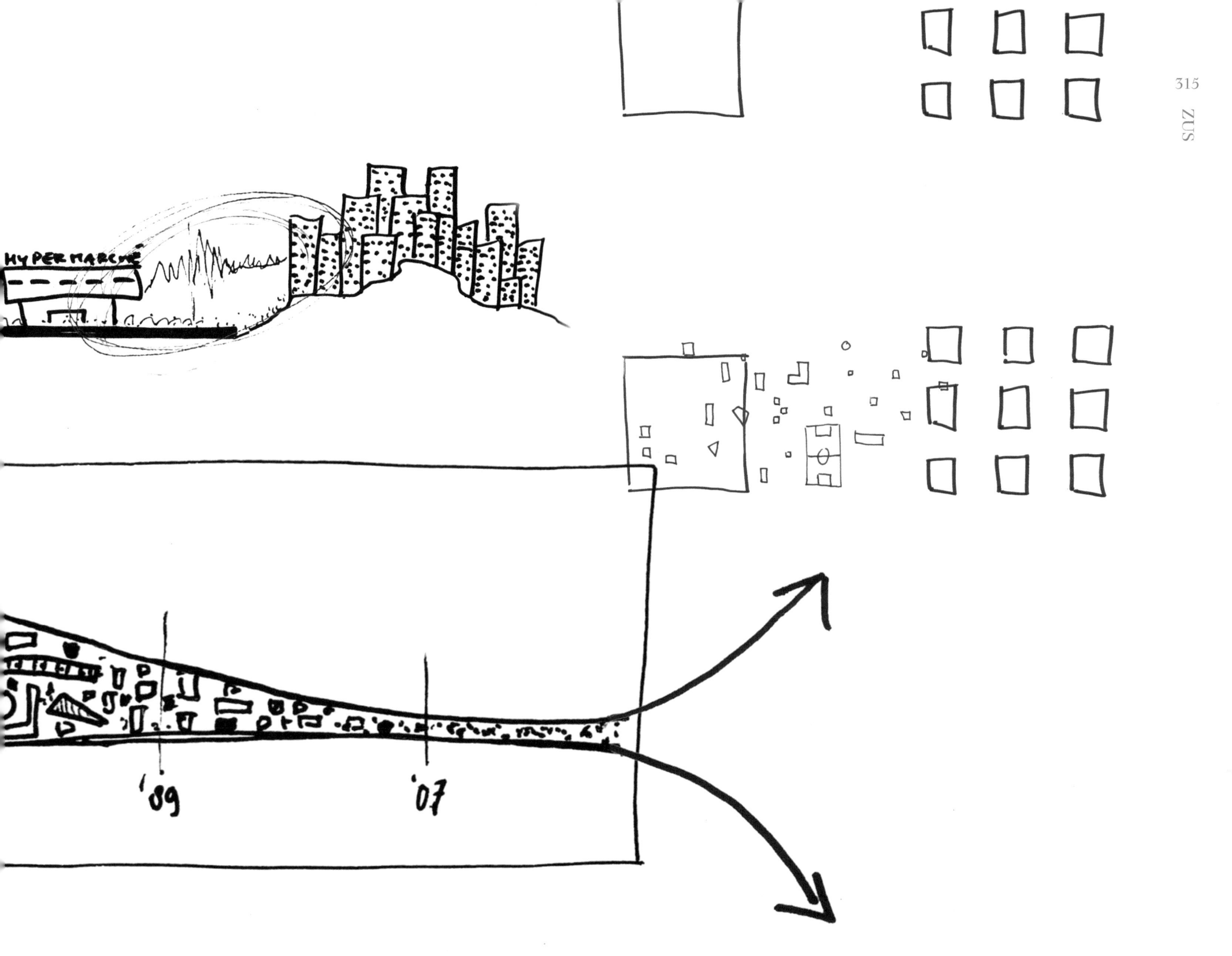

'89   '07

Directory

Atelier Dreiseitl (pp. 8–13)
Nussdorfer Straße 9,
88662 Überlingen, Germany
dreiseitl.com

Balmori (pp. 14–19)
584 Broadway, Suite 1201,
New York, New York 10012 USA
balmori.com

I & J Bannerman (pp. 20–5)
Trematon Castle, Saltash,
Cornwall PL12 4QW, UK
bannermandesign.com

BCA Landscape (pp. 26–33)
19 Old Hall Street, Liverpool L3 9JQ, UK
Studio I, Rochelle School,
Arnold Circus, London E2 7ES, UK
bcalandscape.co.uk

Prabhakar B. Bhagwat (pp. 34–45)
Unit 424, Prabhadevi Industrial Estate,
Swatantrya Veer Savarkar Marg,
Prabhadevi, Mumbai 25, India
landscapeindia.net

Cao | Perrot (pp. 46–53)
Los Angeles, California, USA, and Paris, France
caoperrotstudio.com

Fernando Caruncho (pp. 54–7)
C/Narcea, 17, 28707 Madrid, Spain
fernandocaruncho.com

Claude Cormier (pp. 58–63)
1223, rue des Carrières, Studio A,
Montreal, Quebec H2S 2B1, Canada
claudecormier.com

Paul de Kort (pp. 64–9)
Dampkring 1, 3454 RD De Meern, Netherlands
pauldekort.nl

Doxiadis+ (pp. 70–5)
6 Apollonos Street, 10557 Athens, Greece
doxiadisplus.com

Estudio OCA (pp. 76–85)
Passeig del Born 27, 3º1ª,
08003 Barcelona, Spain
65 Soi Chaloemphrakiate R. 9 - Soi 8,
Nongborn, Pravet, Bangkok 10250, Thailand
estudiooca.com

Monika Gora (pp. 86–91)
Vilebovägen 4a, 21763 Malmö, Sweden
gora.se

GreenInc (pp. 92–103)
83 6th Street, Randburg, 2193, South Africa
greeninc.co.za

Gross Max (pp. 104–9)
6 Waterloo Place, Edinburgh EH1 3EG, UK
grossmax.com

Gustafson Porter (pp. 110–21)
1 Cobham Mews, London NW1 9SB, UK
gustafson-porter.com

Hassell (pp. 122–5)
61 Little Collins Street,
Melbourne, Victoria 3000, Australia
hassellstudio.com

Hocker Design (pp. 126–33)
918 Dragon Street, Dallas, Texas 75207, USA
hockerdesign.com

Edward Hutchison (pp. 134–45)
8 Cleaver Square, London SE11 4DW, UK
edwardhutchison.com

Raymond Jungles (pp. 146–57)
242 SW 5th Street, Miami, Florida 33130, USA
raymondjungles.com

Mikyoung Kim (pp. 158–67)
119 Braintree Street, Suite 103,
Boston, Massachusetts 02134, USA
myk-d.com

Cristina Le Mehauté (pp. 168–73)
Tronador 3430, Buenos Aires, Argentina
cristinalemehaute.com.ar

Ken McCown (pp. 174–83)
University of Nevada, Las Vegas,
UNLV Downtown Design Center,
401 S. 4th Street, Suite 155,
Las Vegas, Nevada 89101, USA
unlvddc.org

Helle Nebelong (pp. 184–93)
Copenhagen, Denmark
sansehaver.dk

Piet Oudolf (pp. 194–205)
Broekstraat 17,
6999 DE Hummelo, Netherlands
oudolf.com

Péna & Peña (pp. 206–15)
15, rue Jean Fautrier, 75013 Paris, France
penapaysages.com

Pola (pp. 216–21)
via F. Redi, 8, 20129 Milan, Italy
109 Alley, Truong Chin Street,
Thanh Xuan District, Hanoi, Vietnam
polarch.eu

Patrizia Pozzi (pp. 222–9)
via Paolo Frisi, 3, 20129 Milan, Italy
patriziapozzi.it

Sarah Price (pp. 230–9)
4 The Chain, 90 Chapel Road,
Abergavenny, Monmouthshire, NP7 7BN, UK
sarahpricelandscapes.com

Proap (pp. 240–7)
Rua Dom Luis I, 19-6°,
1200-149 Lisbon, Portugal
Via Zenson di Piave, 2a, 31100 Treviso, Italy
Rua Salvador Allende, 11–13, Luanda, Angola
proap.pt

Daniel Roehr (pp. 248–57)
University of British Columbia, School of
Architecture and Landscape Architecture
402–6333 Memorial Road, Vancouver,
British Columbia V6T 1Z2, Canada
sala.ubc.ca

SLA (pp. 258–63)
Njalsgade 17B, Pakhus 2, 3.sal,
Copenhagen 2300, Denmark
Sørkedalsveien 6, Pb 7057 Majorstuen,
Oslo 0306, Norway
sla.dk

Ken Smith (pp. 264–7)
450 West 31st Street, 5th floor,
New York, New York 10001, USA
kensmithworkshop.com

Tom Stuart-Smith (pp. 268–81)
90–93 Cowcross Street, London EC1M 6BF, UK
tomstuartsmith.co.uk

Taylor Cullity Lethlean (pp. 282–9)
385 Drummond Street,
Carlton, Victoria 3053, Australia
109 Grote Street,
Adelaide, South Australia 5000, Australia
tcl.net.au

Mario Terzic (pp. 290–7)
Bäckerstraße 14, 1010 Vienna, Austria
marioterzic.com

Cleve West (pp. 298–311)
Navigator House, 60 High Street,
Hampton Wick, Surrey KT1 4DB, UK
clevewest.com

ZUS (pp. 312–15)
Schieblock, Schiekade 189, Unit 303,
3013 BR Rotterdam, Netherlands
zus.cc

left: Edward Hutchison, Eden Project,
Cornwall, UK
on p. 319: Péna & Peña, various sketches
on p. 320: Tom Stuart-Smith, Laurent-Perrier
Garden, Chelsea Flower Show, London, UK,
2008

Photo credits

All illustrations are provided courtesy of the designer or studio, unless otherwise noted below:

14 collage of printed digital renderings by Mark Thomann; **15** digital rendering by Matt Choot; **16** (left) digital rendering by Isabell Desfoux, (right) digital rendering by Alix Cohen; **17** (left) digital rendering by Conor O'Brien, (opposite, above) collage and ink drawing by Diana Balmori, (opposite, below) digital rendering by Eline Steyaert; **18** (left and above right) digital rendering by Sara Arteaga, (below right) paper model by Reva Meeks; **19** digital rendering by Monica Hernandez; **46–53** Xavier Perrot / Cao | Perrot; **70–5** Doxiadis+, Thomas Doxiadis, Terpsi Kremali, Marina Antsaklis; **84–5** drawings created with Bryan Cantwell and Ignacio Ortinez; **110–11, 112** (right), **113** concept sketches by Kathryn Gustafson; **112** (left) plant-form studies by Sibylla Hartel; **126–33** all sketches submitted by David Hocker, ASLA, and sole property of Hocker Design Group, Inc.; **146–57** © Raymond Jungles, Inc.; **154** (left) drawing by Mauricio Del Valle; **192** sketch hand-coloured by Tim Ebikon Henningsen; **216–21** Pola (Jörg Michel with Juan Saez Martinez de la Pedraja); **272** (below), **281** drawings by Jem Hanbury; **277–8** (left) drawing by Andy Hamilton; **278** (right) drawing by Tom Stuart-Smith; **282–3** drawings by Perry Lethlean; **286** drawing by Kate Cullity; **287** sketches and drawings by Kevin Taylor, Kate Cullity and Perry Lethlean; **288, 289** sketches by Kevin Taylor

Acknowledgments

The author would like to thank all of the designers and design companies involved for their help and co-operation in the preparation of this book. Thanks also to Lucas Dietrich who commissioned the book for Thames & Hudson, to Elain McAlpine who edited it and saw it through production, and to Myfanwy Vernon-Hunt for the design.

Vendredi

les tores
l'archipel arborecent

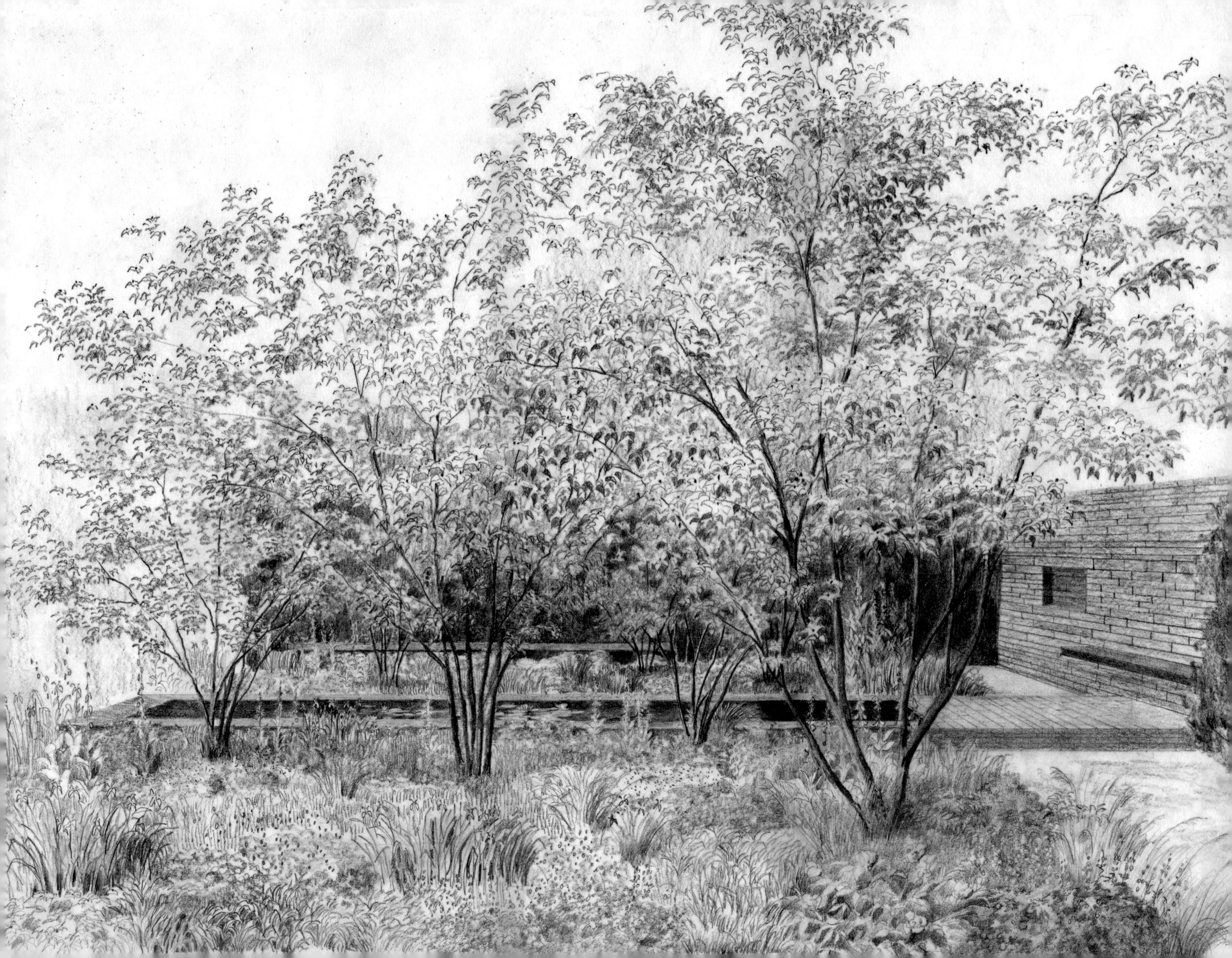